*Collaborative Teams for Students
with Severe Disabilities*

Collaborative Teams for Students with Severe Disabilities

Integrating Therapy and Educational Services

by

Beverly Rainforth, Ph.D., P.T.
School of Education and Human Development
State University of New York at Binghamton

Jennifer York, Ph.D., P.T.
Department of Educational Psychology and
Institute on Community Integration
University of Minnesota

and

Cathy Macdonald, M.A., C.C.C./S.L.P.
Institute on Community Integration
University of Minnesota

with contributions by

Christine Salisbury, Ph.D.
School of Education and Human Development
State University of New York at Binghamton

and

Winnie Dunn, Ph.D., O.T.R.
Department of Occupational Therapy
University of Kansas Medical Center

·P·A·U·L·H·
BROOKES
PUBLISHING C?

Baltimore • London • Toronto • Sydney

Paul H. Brookes Publishing Co.
P.O. Box 10624
Baltimore, Maryland 21285-0624

Typeset by Brushwood Graphics, Inc., Baltimore, Maryland.
Manufactured in the United States of America by
The Maple Press Company, York, Pennsylvania.

Library of Congress Cataloging-in-Publication Data

Rainforth, Beverly, 1949–
    Collaborative teams for students with severe disabilities :
integrating therapy and educational services / Beverly Rainforth,
Jennifer York, Cathy Macdonald ; with contributions by Christine
Salisbury and Winnie Dunn.
       p.   cm.
    Includes bibliographical references and index.
    ISBN 1-55766-088-3
    1. Handicapped children—Education—United States. 2. Handicapped
children—Rehabilitation—United States. 3. Teaching teams—United
States. I. York, Jennifer. II. Macdonald, Cathy. III. Title.
LC4031.R35 1992
371.9—dc20
                                        91-45963
                                            CIP

Contents

Contributors

Winnie Dunn, Ph.D., O.T.R.
Associate Professor
Department of Occupational Therapy
University of Kansas Medical Center
Fourth Floor, Hinch Hall
39th Street & Rainbow Boulevard
Kansas City, KS 66103

Cathy Macdonald, M.A., C.C.C./S.L.P.
Education Specialist
Institute on Community Integration
University of Minnesota
101 Pattee Hall
150 Pillsbury Drive SE
Minneapolis, MN 55455

Beverly Rainforth, Ph.D., P.T.
Assistant Professor of Special Education
School of Education and Human Development
State University of New York at Binghamton
P.O. Box 6000
Binghamton, NY 13901

Christine Salisbury, Ph.D.
Associate Professor of Special Education
School of Education and Human Development
State University of New York at Binghamton
P.O. Box 6000
Binghamton, NY 13901

Jennifer York, Ph.D., P.T.
Assistant Professor of Educational Psychology
Coordinator of Preservice Interdisciplinary
   Training
Institute on Community Integration
University of Minnesota
101 Pattee Hall
150 Pillsbury Drive SE
Minneapolis, MN 55455

Preface

THE THOUGHT OF WRITING A BOOK ABOUT TEAMWORK SEEMED GOOD, RIGHT, AND RELATIVELY SIMPLE several years ago. For a long time Jen and Bev called it "the transdisciplinary cookbook," reflecting our half-joking, half-serious thinking that there were recipes that people could follow to create an effective team. When we finally began the arduous process of putting our thoughts and experiences into writing, we entered new realms of thought and understanding about the processes of collaboration and about ourselves as team members. In the new context of book writing, we continually relearned what we already knew about collaboration in educational settings. First, Jen and Bev realized that two people with similar education and experience did not have sufficient breadth to write a book with a transdisciplinary perspective. So Cathy, Chris Salisbury, and Winnie Dunn were asked to assist with the task. At the end of the process, we knew that Chris and Winnie were valued consultants without whom the team could not have achieved its goal. We also knew that Bev, Jen, and Cathy were the core team; we had made a long-term commitment, and therefore, we felt great pride in small triumphs and deep frustration with ongoing struggles, just as do the core members of educational teams. We rediscovered that achieving a shared goal required us to communicate with one another frequently, honestly, and respectfully. Our interdependence required each of us to fulfill our commitments; it also required us to be patient and trusting when any of us needed to pull back from this commitment and attend to other needs. We reaffirmed that working together is a way of belonging, and belonging is an important ingredient in fulfilled lives. We rediscovered that relationships of this kind are likely to become personal as well as professional; the process of writing this book kindled friendships that we will value throughout our lives. And we continually reaffirmed that work is more fun when working together as a team, particularly when team members like one another.

We knew that each of us brought unique professional expertise to the book; we also discovered the personal talents that each person brought. We learned to maximize our talents and expertise, and to laugh about our quirks (we discovered many). We rediscovered that working collaboratively is more difficult and slow than working independently, but that the products of collaboration far surpass anything we could produce independently. Our collaboration both enabled and encouraged us to reassess our direction and methods, and we frequently corrected our course, continually striving for improvement, always involved in the process of growing. Even as we write this Preface, our thinking is changing; now we look back at Chapter 1 and we want to revise it. Unlike education of children and adults with severe disabilities, which is a lifelong process, writing a book is necessarily a finite process (or so our publisher has frequently reminded us). And so, complete with imperfections, we move this book forward to you. Surround yourself with colleagues who share your commitment. Use this book, *not* as a cookbook, but as a guide. The resulting process and outcomes will be uniquely yours. Learn from others, share your own discoveries, and continue in your process of growing.

Acknowledgments

WHEN THINKING ABOUT WHOM TO ACKNOWLEDGE IN A BOOK ON COLLABORATION, WE FACED THE challenge of identifying and recognizing all the people who have helped us learn about collaboration. Quickly we realized that such a list could run several pages and undoubtedly would still omit people who have influenced us in significant ways. Therefore, we apologize at the outset for not attempting to name each individual; we hope our collective statements of recognition reach all for whom they are intended.

We are especially thankful to our families and friends who supported and encouraged us throughout the long process of writing this book and through the years of experiential learning that preceded our writing.

We also wish to thank the many friends and colleagues who have helped shape our thinking about both personal and professional aspects of collaboration. Dorothy Hutchison, Pip Campbell, Mike Giangreco, Lou Brown, and Bob York are among those who deserve special recognition for sharing their wisdom and for challenging us to expand our thoughts. Working on and working closely with teams in Connecticut, Illinois, Minnesota, New York, Wisconsin, and elsewhere offered us wonderful experiences and the foundations for many of the practices described in this book. We thank the members of those teams who helped us develop as team members and who generously shared their ideas and materials.

Others who have given generously of their time and energy to produce this book include Diann Ackard, Institute on Community Integration at the University of Minnesota, who prepared our figures and tables; Kay Almer, Institute on Community Integration at the University of Minnesota, who assisted with word processing and mailing; Patricia Burke, Graduate Assistant at the State University of New York at Binghamton, who assisted with proofreading chapters and reference lists; and Mary Palombaro, Coordinator of the Collaborative Education Project at the State University of New York at Binghamton, who provided feedback on chapter content. We greatly appreciate your contributions.

Finally, we thank the staff of Paul H. Brookes Publishing Company who have worked with us on this venture. We appreciate the efforts of Roslyn Udris and other members of the editorial staff who put the book into production. We are especially grateful to Vince Ercolano, who supported and encouraged us throughout this long process, despite many delays on our part.

To those people who have the courage to embark on a collaborative process to improve education and life outcomes for students with severe disabilities

Collaborative Teams for Students with Severe Disabilities

1

Introduction

EDUCATIONAL TEAMS SERVING STUDENTS with severe disabilities are entering an exciting and challenging era. People with disabilities are becoming integrated into our society to an ever-increasing extent. Large medically oriented residential facilities are being replaced by a range of community living options, which include community supports that enable families to care for their children with disabilities at home. As they continue to live with their families, children with disabilities are being recognized as participating members of their communities, who go on family social outings, run errands to stores and other businesses, eat in restaurants, visit museums and libraries, attend church—in short, take part in the same community activities as children without disabilities. Young adults with severe disabilities are learning to perform real work in community businesses through supported work efforts, enabling them to become contributing members of society and enhancing their dignity, confidence, and self-esteem. Much of this increase in community participation is due to the guarantee of a free appropriate public education for all chil-

dren with disabilities, which affords significant support to families and provides students with instruction referenced to community participation. Having seen the successes and benefits of community participation for children and youths with even the most severe disabilities, parents and advocates recently have started seeking an even greater level of community presence: education of children with disabilities in the same school they would attend if not disabled. As a result, more children attend their neighborhood schools (even taking regular classes), ride the same buses as siblings and neighbors, participate in the same after-school activities, and take part in the same graduation ceremonies as students who are not identified as disabled.

Educational team members now have opportunities to play significant roles in assisting children and youths with severe disabilities to achieve fulfilling, integrated lives. As students with disabilities become more integrated, educational teams recognize that they must adopt more integrated approaches to service provision. As a result, teachers and therapists are more

Portions of this chapter are adapted from York, J., Rainforth, B., & Wiemann, G. (1988). An integrated approach to therapy for school aged learners with developmental disabilities. *Totline, 14*(3), 36–40.

likely to analyze student needs in actual home, school, and community environments. Team members are developing creative strategies to apply their expertise in "real-world" situations, to increase participation and contributions by students with severe disabilities. Teachers and therapists are actively pursuing collaboration with one another, both because students can achieve greater outcomes and because staff experience professional growth and satisfaction. For the same reasons, the professionals who compose the educational team are recognizing the importance of collaborating with family and friends of the student with disabilities, who know the student best.

The primary responsibility of physical, occupational, and speech-language therapists in public education is to work collaboratively with other team members to assist students with disabilities to benefit from their educational programs. This means therapists must be knowledgeable about the actual challenges experienced by students in their educational programs, and teachers and therapists together must provide support to students with severe disabilities in typical school, classroom, home, recreation, work, and community environments. This certainly presents challenges to teachers and therapists, but working as members of a collaborative team also presents many advantages and new opportunities. Team members can assess student performance in actual daily routines, allowing more accurate determinations of service needs and priorities. Team members have access to professionals with complementary areas of expertise, enabling the entire team to recognize the complex needs of students with severe disabilities and to design more comprehensive and effective interventions. Team members can evaluate effectiveness of their in-

terventions in direct relation to students' abilities to respond to demands of real-world environments and activities. When there are questions about the feasibility or effectiveness of interventions, team members share responsibility for problem solving and decision making, which produces more creative solutions and strategies. Working with students with severe disabilities in their daily routines allows teachers and therapists to teach, learn from, and engage in mutual support with others who support the students, including parents, siblings, classmates, paraprofessionals, general educators, and librarians. As teachers and therapists become more actively involved in these activities, they find that they value and are valued by other team members to an increasing extent.

In recent years, parents and professionals have largely redefined what constitutes an appropriate education for students with severe disabilities. Many of these changes, including adoption of a collaborative, rather than individualistic, approach to service provision, have caused team members to struggle with redefining roles, relationships, and responsibilities. When organizations adopt innovations in service provision, these types of struggles are characteristic and staff need a variety of supports to succeed in working through changes. Unfortunately, frustrated professionals sometimes conclude that their goal is more idealistic than realistic, and give up on adoption.

This book is written for parents of children with severe disabilities and for professionals who provide services to these students, to address issues that many team members encounter as they work to collaborate with one another. The book outlines principles, practices, and procedures for providing related services as integral components of special education programs for students with severe disabilities. The strategies presented here have been used by educational teams in various parts of the country, and the authors are indebted to the many people whose day-to-day experiences contributed to the evolution of this information.

DEFINITIONS OF CORE TERMINOLOGY

A cardinal rule for effective teamwork is to communicate clearly. We have attempted to follow this rule by avoiding jargon and defining concepts as we introduce them. Two terms that hold different meanings for readers from different backgrounds are "severe disabilities" and "related services." Since these terms define the scope of the book, it is appropriate to start by specifying how we use them.

Students with "severe disabilities" are a heterogeneous group, who have also been called "severely handicapped." Brown et al. (1983) offered a definition that is useful in depicting the breadth of this population:

> The label "severely handicapped" refers to approximately the lowest functioning 1% of the school-age population. This 1% range includes students who also have been ascribed such labels as moderately/severely/profoundly retarded, trainable level retarded (TMR), physically handicapped, multiply handicapped, deaf/blind, psychotic, and autistic. Certainly a student can be ascribed one or more of these labels and still not be referred to as severely handicapped for purposes here, as she or he may not be currently functioning intellectually within 1% of a particular age. (p. 71)

The U.S. Office of Education, Bureau of Education for the Handicapped (1974) (now the Department of Education, Office of Special Education and Rehabilitative Services) defined this population, in part, by the services they need:

> A severely handicapped child is one who, because of the intensity of physical, mental, or emotional problems, or a combination of such problems, needs educational, social, psychological, and medical services beyond those which have been offered by traditional regular and special educational programs, in order to maximize his full potential for useful and meaningful participation in society and for self-fulfillment. (45 CFR 121.2)

The term "disability" is preferable to "handicap" because it is more consistent with recognition that people with disabilities also have abilities and make contributions. "Handicap" connotes a more debilitating view of a person who has inferior status and is incapable of participating in normal life activities. While "disabilities" certainly exist, there is increasing recognition that individuals with disabilities have both the desire and the capacity to participate in normal life activities, possibly using alternative strategies or forms of participation. An important implication of this belief in abilities and contributions is that educational team members assume responsibility for discovering and using strategies that maximize student participation. The practices described in this book are intended to promote operationalization of that philosophy.

Given that the majority of the authors' work has been with children and adolescents with severe disabilities, the focus of this book is on that population. The same principles and strategies also have many direct applications to early intervention and adult services. As we work more within general education settings and with more diverse student populations, we are learning that students with milder disabilities can also benefit from an ecological perspective and from the collaborative efforts of an educational team. Although trying to discuss students of all ages and abilities would expand the focus of this book beyond a manageable level, we urge readers to adapt the strategies presented here to meet the needs of the individuals whom they support.

The principles and strategies presented in this book apply to team members from a variety of backgrounds and disciplines. The U.S. Department of Education (1990) stated that:

> The term "related services" means transportation, and such developmental, corrective, and other supportive services (including speech pathology and audiology, psychological services, physical and occupational therapy, recreation, including therapeutic recreation and social work services, and medical and counseling services. including rehabilitation counseling, except that such medical services shall be for diagnostic and evaluation purposes only) as may be required to assist (a) child with a disability to benefit from special education, and includes the early identification and assessment of disabling conditions in children. (Individuals with Disabilities Education Act of 1990, Sec. 1401(a)(17))

This book focuses on the related services of occupational, physical, and speech-language therapy. While therapy services are required by the majority of students with severe disabilities, and have an impact on large portions of many students' educational programs, occupational, physical, and speech-language therapy are frequently provided as though they were intended to be separate from and parallel to other parts of the educational program. When parents, teachers, and therapists collaborate to integrate these related services with education, the resulting program is more comprehensive and better coordinated. As detailed later in this book, preliminary research indicates that team members are more satisfied and students realize greater benefits when occupational, physical, and speech-language therapists collaborate with other members of the edu-

cational team to provide integrated related services.

ADOPTING THE COLLABORATIVE APPROACH

Some readers might think the promise of benefits to both students and team members would be sufficient to motivate teams to pioneer their way to a collaborative team approach. Unfortunately, this expectation is not supported by the research on systems change in education. Through extensive study of the adoption of innovations in educational programs, Hord, Rutherford, Huling-Austin, and Hall (1987) concluded that each individual reacts differently to change and needs support and training that respond to individual concerns about the innovation and change process. Hord et al. (1987) found that educators moved through several stages of concern, which fall into three categories:

Self-concerns, reflecting the desire for more information about what the innovation is, what type of support is available, and what personal risks are involved if the innovation is to be adopted;
Task concerns, reflecting the need for more information about how to use the innovation, and frustration with the effects of using the innovation inefficiently; and
Impact concerns, reflecting desires to determine the benefits of the innovation and to identify strategies that would improve use.

Movement through these stages of concern typically occurs in a developmental fashion, although the intensity of each stage and the rate of movement through stages vary considerably among individuals. Educational team members who are contemplating or currently working to adopt a collaborative team approach can probably identify with one or more of these concerns. In an effort to facilitate change, we have attempted to address these areas of concern throughout this book.

The book is organized into three major sections. The first section, composed of Chapters 2 and 3, presents the philosophical, legal, and programmatic foundations for a collaborative teamwork model for provision of education and integrated related services. The second section, composed of Chapters 4, 5, 6, and 7, describes how occupational, physical, and speech/language services can become integral aspects of curriculum, assessment, individualized education programs, and instruction. This section focuses on students and their programs. The third section of the book addresses supports for implementation. Chapter 8 describes strategies staff use to organize their time and to collaborate effectively in educational contexts. The final chapter of the book, Chapter 9, discusses issues and future directions in the development and provision of integrated related services.

Educational team members are encouraged to use this book as a guide and support as they adopt a collaborative approach to providing educational services for students with severe disabilities. Although teams and their students will benefit from the practices described herein, team members are reminded that concerted effort is required for initial adoption, and considerable practice is required before new strategies feel comfortable and efficient. Furthermore, the "best practices" described here continue to evolve as teams seek improvements over what they did yesterday. Finally, this book is about fluid and spiraling processes, which, in efforts to address "task concerns" effectively, have been translated into a rather linear set of procedures; therefore, teams are encouraged to re-examine the bases for their actions frequently. Rather than adopt a rigid set of procedures, readers are encouraged to approach adoption of a collaborative team approach as a process that continues to evolve just as the knowledge, abilities, goals, and needs of students and their teams evolve. This evolution is driven and guided by maintaining a focus on the desired outcomes of collaboration: student membership and participation in home and community life.

REFERENCES

Brown, L., Nisbet, J., Ford, A., Sweet, M., Shiraga, B., York, J., & Loomis, R. (1983). The critical need for nonschool instruction in educational programs for severely handicapped students. *Journal of The Association for the Severely Handicapped. 8*(3), 71-77.

Individuals with Disabilities Education Act of 1990, 20 U.S.C. 1401(a)(17).

Hord, S.M., Rutherford, W.L., Huling-Austin, L., & Hall, G.E. (1987). *Taking charge of change*. Alexandria, VA: Association for Supervision and Curriculum Development.

U.S. Office of Education, Bureau of Education for the Handicapped (1974). 45 C.F.R. 121.2.

I

Philosophical, Legal, and Programmatic Foundations

T HE IDEA THAT COLLABORATIVE TEAMWORK COULD IMPROVE SERVICES FOR PEOPLE WITH disabilities is hardly new (see, e.g., Whitehouse, 1951), yet many professionals remain reluctant to work in a collaborative manner. One challenge facing members of educational teams is that each representative of the component disciplines traditionally has been prepared and encouraged to serve as an autonomous professional. When collaboration has been modeled, practiced, or rewarded for these individuals, it has usually been with members of their own discipline. As a result, professionals often react to the concept of collaboration as if it reflects less loyalty to or even betrayal of their discipline (Houston, 1980). Although personnel preparation programs and professional organizations are now promoting thinking and experiences that support cooperative efforts among disciplines, many practicing professionals have not had the benefit of this education.

The first section of this book provides a rationale for collaborative teamwork by reviewing current thought from the fields of education, rehabilitation, public policy, and law. This section also provides team members from diverse backgrounds with a common foundation about "best practices" in educating students with severe disabilities, a foundation that will support and facilitate their efforts toward collaborative teamwork.

REFERENCES

Houston, R.W. (1980). Collaboration—see "treason." In G.E. Hall, S.M. Hord, & G. Brown (Eds.), *Exploring issues in teacher education: Questions for future research* (pp. 331–348). Austin: The University of Texas at Austin, Research and Development Center for Teacher Education.

Whitehouse, F.A. (1951). Teamwork: An approach to a higher professional level. *Exceptional Children, 18*(1), 75-82.

2

Foundations of Collaborative Teamwork

S TUDENTS WITH SEVERE DISABILITIES ARE entitled to related educational services under the provisions of Public Law 101-476 (the Education of the Handicapped Act Amendments of 1990, which changed the name of the Education for All Handicapped Children Act of 1975, Public Law 94-142, to the Individuals with Disabilities Education Act [IDEA]) and Public Law 99-457 (the Education of the Handicapped Act Amendments of 1986). As a result, it has become relatively commonplace over the last 15 years to include physical therapists, occupational therapists, and speech-language therapists on educational teams in the public schools. The educational domain has become a common arena of practice for professionals who, historically, were associated with medical models of service provision. Increasingly, therapists and other related services personnel are providing services in ways that complement the movement to integrate students with severe disabilities into their local public schools and into general education environments with special education support (Thousand et al., 1986; Williams, Fox, Thousand, & Fox,

1990). This evolution of service provision is reflected in the Position Statement on the Provision of Related Services of The Association for Persons with Severe Handicaps (TASH), which asserts that the role of related services personnel is to collaborate with each other and with teachers and families in the design and implementation of programs that support the participation of individuals with severe disabilities in typical family, school, and community life (Association for Persons with Severe Handicaps, 1986) (see Table 2.1). Other national organizations also have promoted an integrated model of therapy that supports educational programming in the public schools (American Occupational Therapy Association, 1989; American Physical Therapy Association, 1990; American Speech-Language-Hearing Association, 1991).

Educators and therapists generally recognize the benefits of collaboration, but mere recognition does not result in collaborative practices. The professionals who comprise educational teams have been prepared in different approaches to service provision, with teachers trained in an edu-

Table 2.1 TASH position statement on the provision of related services to persons with severe handicaps [a]

The Association for Persons with Severe Handicaps (TASH) is an international organization whose primary purpose is to advocate for and support exemplary models of service delivery for persons with severe handicaps.

Many persons with severe handicaps have complex and challenging needs. The expertise of related services professionals, such as physical therapists, occupational therapists, and speech and language pathologists is frequently required.

TASH believes that related services personnel have expertise and can contribute in the process of integrating persons with severe handicaps into typical home community life. A high degree of collaboration and sharing of information and skills must occur among families, direct services providers, and related services personnel.

The provision of integrated services requires that related services personnel:
1. Establish priorities with parents/advocates and other team members.
2. Observe and assess persons with handicaps in natural settings.
3. Collaborate with family and team members to provide intervention strategies and adaptations that optimize participation in natural settings.
4. Teach specific and individualized procedures to enhance functional positioning, movement, and communication abilities in natural settings.
5. Evaluate the effectiveness of intervention procedures based on performance outcomes in natural settings.

[a] From The Association for Persons with Severe Handicaps (1986, November).

cational model and therapists trained in a medical model. There are philosophical, theoretical, and practical differences between these models (see Ottenbacher, 1982) that serve as challenges to collaboration among professionals from educational and medical disciplines. Although professional preservice training sometimes includes didactic information about teamwork, few preservice training programs provide instruction or experiences that prepare graduates for truly collaborative models of service provision (Aksamit & Alcorn, 1988; Rainforth, 1985; Sapon-Shevin, 1988; Stainback & Stainback, 1987; York, Rainforth, & Dunn, 1990). Furthermore, few professional training programs have an interdisciplinary or transdisciplinary theme; rather, they perpetuate unidisciplinary thinking. Assessment, program planning, and service provision are approached in isolation from a single-discipline perspective. Therefore, it is not surprising that the challenges of collaboration often exceed the desire or ability of profes-

sionals from various disciplines to work together effectively.

Team members may communicate with one another about a child at annual and periodic review meetings, but rarely do they collaborate in ways that apply directly to the student's participation in family, school, and community life. Herein lies a problematic paradox in the design of educational programs for students with long-term, intensive, and multiple disabilities. When professionals abdicate responsibility for the synthesis, application, and generalization of fragmented, sometimes conflicting, program components, they inadvertently shift the responsibility of synthesis onto the very people who require their assistance to meet daily challenges: students with severe disabilities and their families. Traditional isolated and fragmented approaches to service provision have been problematic for students, their families, and service providers. The traditional approaches seem to be maintained more by default than by active choice because professionals have not had opportunities to learn alternatives.

This chapter establishes the foundations of a collaborative teamwork approach for integrating related services into educational programs for students with severe disabilities. Specifically, the chapter offers: 1) a definition of collaborative teamwork, 2) a rationale for collaborative teamwork, 3) an overview of team member roles and responsibilities, and 4) unifying assumptions of collaborative teamwork in educational programs for students with severe disabilities. This information provides the overarching framework for the remainder of the book. Chapter 8 presents strategies for establishing collaborative teamwork practices that support an integrated program design.

COLLABORATIVE TEAMWORK DEFINED

According to *Webster's Ninth New Collegiate Dictionary* (1987), "collaborate" is from the Latin derivatives *com* and *laborare*, which mean to "labor together." Other definitions from this source include "to work jointly with others," and "to co-operate with." "Teamwork" is defined as "work done by several associates with each doing a part but all subordinating personal prominence to the efficiency of the whole" (*Webster's*, 1987). In the education literature, "collaboration" has been defined as a process of problem solving by team members, each of whom contributes his or her knowledge and skills and is viewed as having equal status (Sileo, Rude, & Luckner, 1988; Vandercook & York, 1990; Zins, Curtis, Graden, & Ponti, 1988). A specific application of collaboration, called "collaborative consultation," is defined as "an interactive process that enables people with diverse expertise to generate creative solutions to mutually defined problems" (Idol, Paolucci-Whitcomb, & Nevin, 1986, p. 1). Put together, the essence of *collaborative teamwork* is *work accomplished jointly by a group of people in a spirit of willingness and mutual reward.*

Specific to educational teams for students with severe disabilities, a high degree of collaboration has been considered the hallmark of the *transdisciplinary* and *integrated therapy* approaches to educational teamwork (e.g., Albano, Cox, York, & York, 1981; Giangreco, York, & Rainforth, 1989; Hart, 1977; Nietupski, Scheutz, & Ockwood, 1980; Orelove & Sobsey, 1987; Peterson, 1980; Sternat, Messina, Nietupski, Lyon, & Brown, 1977; York, Rainforth, & Giangreco, 1990). In this book, collaborative teamwork is conceptualized as embracing both the transdisciplinary and integrated therapy approaches to educational teamwork for students with severe disabilities. While these two approaches have evolved in a complementary manner, there are several distinctions that are clarified below.

Transdisciplinary Teamwork

Historically, early intervention services and habilitation services for infants, children, and adults with disabilities have been deeply rooted in a medical orientation in which individuals with disabilities are perceived as sick or able to be "fixed" (see Lane, 1976). This history, paired with the preparation of many team members as health or allied health professionals, has sustained the predominance of the medical model in special education programs. A medical orientation is reflected in the practice of individual disciplines focusing on fragmented aspects of performance (e.g., gross motor, fine motor, vision, health, language) and taking children for "treatment" with the assumption that the

treatment, even though episodic and fragmented, eventually will yield improved
isolated performance that will generalize
in meaningful ways to everyday life. In a
medical model, if isolated performance is
not achieved, children are judged "unable
to benefit" and treatment is discontinued.
Prior to the legal mandate for related services, therapy for children with severe disabilities frequently was discontinued, not
because these children were incapable of
further achievement but because services
that were episodic and isolated did not tap
the child's potential. This situation improved somewhat when the transdisciplinary model was introduced. Paramount to
the transdisciplinary approach is an understanding that the multiple needs of
children are interrelated. The medical
model is better suited to treatment of people with acute illness and isolated injuries
than to long-term education of children
with significant learning difficulties.

Transdisciplinary teamwork models
emerged in recognition of the fact that children do not perform isolated skills irre-
spective of function and environmental
demands. That is, to function in any daily
environment, activity, or routine requires
efficient sensorimotor *and* cognitive *and*
communication performance. To attempt
to elicit communication without regard for
motoric influence, for example, will impede optimal performance. Understanding the varied influences on function and
the ability to integrate this understanding
into instruction requires cross-disciplinary
sharing of information and skills. Herein
lies a defining characteristic of transdisciplinary team functioning: *role release.*
Role release is a process of transferring information and skills traditionally associated with one discipline to team members
of other disciplines (Lyon & Lyon, 1980;
Patterson et al., 1976).

The role release construct as defined by
Lyon and Lyon (1980) involves just three
levels: 1) *sharing general information*
about basic concepts, approaches, and
practices; 2) *sharing informational skills,*
which includes more detailed information
about specific practices or methods; and
3) *sharing performance competencies,*
which involves actually teaching specific
interventions or methods to other team
members. The nature and degree of information that must be shared among team
members are related directly to individual
student needs in educational activities.
For example, all team members may be appropriate recipients of general information
about the sensorimotor or communication
abilities of a student with severe disabilities. Selected team members may need to
learn specific intervention methods that
facilitate and improve sensorimotor and
communication skills of students. Team
members collaborate in determining the
nature and scope of role release to ensure
that the persons who implement interventions have the necessary information,
skills, and support to do so effectively. Patterson et al. (1976) emphasized the importance of ongoing involvement and accountability, which are never abandoned,
throughout all stages of role release.

The transdisciplinary approach originally was conceived as a framework for
professionals to share important information and skills with primary caregivers, including parents of infants with complex
disabilities and aides in residential in-
stitutions (Hutchison, 1978). This enabled
primary caregivers to develop greater consistency in meeting the integrated needs of
children by developing competence in addressing motor, communication, health,
and other needs. This approach also decreased the sometimes large number of different service providers with whom the in-

dividual with disabilities, or his or her family, had to interact on an intensive basis. The transdisciplinary concept had a revolutionary and positive effect on services for people with disabilities since it initiated the sharing of skills that previously had been considered the exclusive domain of individual disciplines. Parents, educators, occupational therapists, physical therapists, speech-language therapists, psychologists, nurses, and others began implementing role release to design more integrated programs for children with disabilities. These transdisciplinary services involved a much greater degree of collaboration than traditional models that employed unidisciplinary, multidisciplinary, and occasionally interdisciplinary practices (see Table 2.2).

Although the transdisciplinary teamwork model resulted in many positive changes in service provision and collaboration, an important element was missing in its conceptualization. The transdisciplinary approach addressed *who* provides services and how multiple needs can be addressed by virtually any team member given training and ongoing support, but the context of service provision (i.e., *where and in what circumstances* services should be provided) was not a key element of the approach. As a result, parents, teachers, and health and residential service providers often became pseudo-therapists by implementing methods associated with various disciplines; however, a major struggle continued when sensorimotor, communication, or other skills were taught in contexts that were not particularly interesting or relevant for the child. Many professionals who initially were excited by the potential of the transdisciplinary approach became disillusioned in its application when context was not featured. Almost simultaneously, however, an approach that addressed the context for ther-

Table 2.2 Evolution of the transdisciplinary model

Model	Objective
Unidisciplinary	Developing competency in one's own field
Intradisciplinary	Believing that the effort you and others make in your field can make contributions to individuals with disabilities
Multidisciplinary	Recognizing the important contributions of other disciplines to individuals with disabilities. Enunciating a philosophy that comprehensive services based on individual needs must be made available to all individuals with disabilities
Interdisciplinary	Working with other disciplines in the development of jointly planned programs for individuals with disabilities
Transdisciplinary	Committing oneself to teaching, learning, and working with others across traditional disciplinary boundaries to better serve individuals with disabilities

Adapted from Patterson, E. G., D'Wolff, N., Hutchison, P., Lowry, M., Schilling, M., & Siepp, J. (1976). *Staff development handbook: A resource for the transdisciplinary process*. New York: United Cerebral Palsy Association, Inc.

apy services was evolving in many educational programs. This approach is referred to as *integrated therapy.*

Integrated Therapy *in functional, meaningful context*

The integrated therapy approach (Albano et al., 1981; Giangreco et al., 1989; Rainforth & York, 1987; Sternat et al., 1977) evolved to emphasize providing services within functional contexts, and thus has become an important complement to transdisciplinary service provision. In an integrated therapy approach, a student who is developing mobility skills, for example, receives instruction during the times of the day when he or she needs to make transitions, such as when moving between activities in the classroom or when traveling to and from the bus or cafeteria. Mobility instruction might be provided by the physical therapist or by other members of the student's educational team who have been trained and supported by the physical therapist.[1] Regardless of who provides the instruction, the intervention methods are programmatically integrated. That is, they are used in the contexts in which students need to demonstrate motor, communication, and other skills so that participation in everyday life is enhanced.

There are several benefits to providing services in these real-life situations. First, the team takes responsibility for identifying relevant contexts in which students might use emerging skills and then designs interventions to elicit desired performance, rather than leaving generalization to relevant contexts to chance. Second,

therapy services do not have to compete with the important formative aspects of typical schooling experiences because routine school activities are recognized as rich with social, cognitive, communication, and motor learning opportunities. Students do not have to be removed for the educational context. Third, by integrating therapy services into everyday contexts, children learn to respond to the natural cues and contingencies that exist in most home, school, and community environments. The net effect is that children acquire new motor and communication skills in more meaningful situations, which are also more likely to support and encourage continued use.

Many agree that it makes sense to provide direct instruction in real-life situations, but some would argue that only therapists should provide the direct instruction (therapy) for motor and communication skill acquisition in those situations. Two major problems arise when integrated therapy provided only by the therapist is the exclusive approach to service provision. First, it presumes that a therapist will always be available to teach a student during natural learning opportunities, and that no other students will need intervention during those time periods and activities. For example, if the speech-language therapist is scheduled on a daily basis to facilitate communication during the transition to first period class, that therapist cannot be in any other situation with any other students during that time. Second, such an approach is based

---

[1]State laws governing the practice of physical therapy, occupational therapy, or speech therapy often specify that physical therapy services, for example, can only be provided by a physical therapist or designated paraprofessional. Therefore, when adhering to a transdisciplinary and integrated approach to "therapy," it is appropriate to say that a teacher (or other "nontherapist") is teaching motor skills, or reinforcing the physical therapy program, but inaccurate to communicate that a teacher is providing physical therapy services. By definition, only the activities performed directly by the physical therapist are considered physical therapy.

on the inaccurate presumption that students have circumscribed disabilities and needs that can be addressed in isolation from one another—for example, that the speech-language therapist can facilitate communication without regard to interfering sensorimotor factors. As will be discussed in Chapter 4, it is most effective to provide instruction in clusters of motor, communication, social, and cognitive skills in the context of everyday activities. To do so requires team members with expertise in these areas to pool their knowledge to design comprehensive instructional methods. In other words, providing effective integrated therapy services almost always requires the role release that typifies the transdisciplinary team approach.

Collaborative Teamwork

To realize the benefits of the knowledge and skills of numerous disciplines throughout the educational program, we advocate a combination of transdisciplinary and integrated therapy approaches to service provision. For this book we have chosen the term "collaborative teamwork" to reflect the essential components of both integrated therapy and transdisciplinary approaches to service provision. "Integrated therapy" refers to the services that provide students with severe disabilities frequent opportunities to learn functional motor, communication, and other skills as part of natural routines in integrated school and community environments (Stornat et al., 1977). "Transdisciplinary" refers to the sharing of information and skills among team members across traditional discipline domains (Hutchison, 1978; Patterson et al., 1976). This enables the team to implement an integrated therapy approach to service provision. We view transdisciplinary services and integrated therapy as es-

sential and complementary components of an educational program design for students with severe disabilities. We also view these approaches as highly flexible and incorporating both direct and indirect services from therapists. Defining characteristics of a collaborative team approach that combines integrated therapy and transdisciplinary services are presented in Table 2.3.

Team members who are not therapists are likely to provide the majority of motor and communication instruction on a daily basis. Therapists, however, must maintain direct, "hands-on" involvement with students on a regular basis. The American Physical Therapy Association (1990), for example, specifies that:

> when therapists provide specific child/procedure consultation, direct service in the educational environments is required:
> - To evaluate the child's initial abilities and needs;
> - To determine appropriate intervention procedures;
> - To train other team members to use the procedures;
> - To confirm that others use the procedures properly;
> - To confirm that procedures are promoting the desired outcome for the child;
> - To revise procedures when the child achieves objectives or is not making satisfactory progress; and
> - To provide ongoing supervision (including retraining) to team members who use the procedures. (p. 3.8)

An essential component of an integrated model of programming, therefore, is a structure that provides opportunities for therapists to remain involved directly with students. The major differences between the integrated model and traditional service provision models are where, how frequently, and in what capacities or roles the therapists have that direct involvement.

Table 2.3 Defining characteristics of collaborative teamwork

1. Equal participation in the collaborative teamwork process by family members and the educational service providers on the educational team

2. Equal participation by all disciplines determined to be necessary for students to achieve their individualized educational goals

3. Consensus decision making about priority educational goals and objectives related to all areas of student functioning at school, at home, and in the community

4. Consensus decision making about the type and amount of support required from related services personnel

5. Attention to motor, communication, and other embedded skills and needs throughout the educational program and in direct relevance to accomplishing priority educational goals

6. Infusion of knowledge and skills from different disciplines into the design of educational methods and interventions

7. Role release to enable team members who are involved most directly and frequently with students to develop the confidence and competence necessary to facilitate active learning and effective participation in the educational program

8. Collaborative problem solving and shared responsibility for student learning across all aspects of the educational program

Therapists' roles shift to spending more time observing and analyzing student abilities in educational activities and more time collaborating with classroom staff to integrate instructional methods.

There are many ways to implement collaborative teamwork services in educational programs. Since teachers, paraprofessionals, and parents are the most likely individuals to accompany and support students with severe disabilities during natural learning opportunities at home, at school, and in the community, they are logical implementers of ongoing instruction to promote improved motor and communication skills. Perhaps the most frequent strategy, therefore, involves teachers and teacher aides learning to incorporate methods traditionally associated with physical, occupational, and speech-language therapy throughout daily educational activities. Many parents, special education teachers, and paraprofessional aides have developed competence in implementing methods traditionally associated with the practices of physical and occupational therapy and speech-language pathology (Albano, 1983; Inge & Snell, 1985; McCollum & Stayton, 1985).

Another strategy is team teaching, such as a teacher and a speech therapist conducting reading class together, or a physical therapist and a physical education teacher teaching a physical education unit together. A variety of team teaching and other adult collaboration strategies have evolved recently in an effort to combine expertise so that students with diverse needs' can remain in general education and other integrated environments (Stainback & Stainback, 1992). All collaborative teamwork approaches require team members to engage in joint planning and role release. The exact way in which team members collaborate to design and implement effective educational plans, including related services, will vary according to local resources, logistical considerations, local school district program design, and particular experience and expertise of team members.

A third strategy is to recruit support from classmates and friends of students with disabilities who are available to provide support throughout daily school activities. Many are interested and extremely competent in assisting their classmates and friends with disabilities to meet the motor and communication needs of daily life at school (Perske, 1988). Although we do not advocate delegating professional responsibilities to students, we recognize their important contributions and encourage their participation in the educational process. Fostering positive interdependence and a sense of community among students during their public schooling is emerging as a critical component in the bigger arena of educational reform as well. Scheduling and logistics that support a more integrated approach to service provision are addressed in detail in Chapter 8.

RATIONALE FOR COLLABORATIVE TEAMWORK

Goal of Collaborative Teamwork

The collective work, or goal, of individuals comprising a collaborative educational team is to design and implement programs in which individual students achieve their educational goals. Broadly stated, the goals of each student's education are presence, participation, achievement, contribution, and satisfaction in home and community life (National Center for Educational Outcomes, 1991). Such goals or outcomes of education are found in the statutes, regulations, mission statements, and goals of increasing numbers of state and local education agencies. For example, the legislatively declared purpose of public education in Minnesota is as follows:

> In accordance with the responsibility vested in the legislature in the Minnesota Constitution, Article XIII, Section 1, the legislature declares that the purpose of public education in Minnesota is to help all individuals acquire knowledge, skills, and positive attitudes towards self and others that will enable them to solve problems, think creatively, continue learning, and develop maximal potential for leading productive, fulfilling lives in a complex and changing society. (Minn Stat §120.011)

Minnesota statutes also state that:

> The Individualized Education Plan for each child with disabilities shall address the student's needs to develop skills to live and work as independently as possible in the community. (Minn Stat §120.17, 1985, Subd. 3a)

Readers are encouraged to obtain the mission statements of their respective state and local education agencies. Reviewing the mission statements or other documents expressing desired educational outcomes helps to clarify the purpose of collaborative educational teams whose responsibility it is to maximize the educational outcomes for each student. Clarity regarding outcomes serves as the basis for designing and redesigning educational service delivery systems.

There are numerous sources of support for the assertion that collaborative teamwork is an essential component of the program design for educating students with severe and multiple disabilities (Table 2.4). First, the learning and performance characteristics of this heterogeneous population of students make collaboration essential (L. Brown et al., 1979; Falvey, 1989;

Ford et al., 1989). Second, collaboration results in more effective problem-solving and greater support among team members (Johnson & Johnson, 1989). Third, collaboration among team members is identified by many practicing educators as necessary for implementing the best curricular and instructional practices for students with severe disabilities (Idol et al., 1986; Institute on Community Integration, 1991; Powell et al., 1985; Williams et al., 1990). Fourth, legal mandates and precedents support a collaborative teamwork model. Finally, recent versions of professional guidelines for the practice of therapy in educational environments support a model of collaboration among team members and the provision of educationally relevant therapy services (American Occupational Therapy Association, 1989; American Physical Therapy Association, 1990; American Speech-Language-Hearing Association, 1991). Student learning characteristics, benefits of collaborative teamwork, and best educational practices provide the programmatic bases for the emergence of the legal mandates and professional practice guidelines. Each of these sources of support for collaboration is discussed separately below.

Characteristics of Students with Severe Disabilities

The "developmental principle" asserts that all people are capable of learning, without regard to age, abilities, or extent of disabilities (Perske, 1981). In designing educational programs for students with severe disabilities, educational team members assume that all children are capable of learning because it is impossible to prove, and irresponsible to assume, otherwise (Baer, 1981). To assume that some students are not capable of learning increases the probability that these individuals will not be provided with opportunities to learn. It is the responsibility of educational teams to design programs that address the learning abilities and needs of all students. In designing effective educational programs, it is important to consider the implications of learning characteristics, including individual assets, capacities, and difficulties.

All students have characteristics that are strengths in the learning process. Team members identify general and specific assets or strengths, such as perseverance, pleasantness, and good eye-hand coordination, which can be useful in designing the educational program and intervention methods. Team members address learning challenges of individual students by considering the impact of those challenges on educational performance. When compared with individuals who do not have identified disabilities, most students with severe disabilities experience greater difficulty with skill acquisition, retention, generalization, and synthesis (L. Brown, Nietupski, & Hamre-Nietupski, 1976; Peterson, 1980). These learning difficulties and their implications are described in greater detail below. The team designs and implements curricular and instructional strategies that capitalize on student strengths while addressing and minimizing the effects of learning challenges.

Skill Acquisition   First, children having severe disabilities typically learn certain skills more slowly and, therefore, are likely to acquire fewer skills than their peers without labels. Both the quantity and the quality of their performance frequently differ from that of children without identified disabilities. A child with severe cerebral palsy, for example, will learn motor skills more slowly and will demonstrate less efficient movement patterns than children without cerebral palsy. Movement quantity and quality usually

Table 2.4 Major reasons for a collaborative teamwork model of service provision for students with severe disabilities

Learning characteristics of students with severe disabilities

Benefits of collaboration

Best educational practices

Legal mandates and precedents

Guidelines for professional therapy practice

can improve to some extent, but many children will continue to have motor skill difficulties even as adults. A child with autism and mental retardation would be expected to learn language more slowly than peers without labels and to continue to have communication challenges even as an adult. Because children and adults with severe disabilities acquire fewer skills over a lifetime than do peers without identified disabilities, educational teams must focus instruction on each student's most crucial needs, maximizing assets and strengths while minimizing and accommodating for challenges. In doing so, teams also must make the most of the natural learning opportunities that arise throughout each day's activities.

Retention Another learning characteristic of students with severe disabilities is that they tend to forget skills they do not practice. Horner, Williams, and Knobbe (1985) found that the greatest single predictor of whether students would retain skills they had mastered was whether or not they continued to practice the skills. Even children and adults without apparent disabilities have difficulty remembering the Pythagorean theorem or Hamlet's soliloquy given the infrequent demands for these skills in daily life. Frequent practice, which increases the probability of skill retention, is most likely to occur

when students perceive skill performance to be purposeful (Steinbeck, 1986), and when skills are natural components of their daily routines (F. Brown, Evans, Weed, & Owen, 1987; Holvoet, Guess, Mulligan, & Brown, 1980). Educational teams must select for instruction skills that students have a high probability of using frequently in current and future school, home, and community environments.

Generalization A third learning characteristic of students with severe disabilities is difficulty generalizing skills from one situation to another. Some children, for example, have large repertoires of skills at home that they never demonstrate at school, and vice versa. Even at school, a student who reliably points to communication symbols in a speech therapy room may not point to the same symbols when he or she has information to share in the classroom or cafeteria. In many situations, lack of generalization results from poor instructional design. There is considerable evidence that generalization is thwarted for students with severe disabilities when skills are taught in isolated, controlled environments (Haring, 1988). Teaching functional motor and communication skills in many naturally occurring daily routines increases the likelihood of generalization to new situations (Stokes & Baer, 1977). Furthermore, research indicates that skills can be taught just as effectively through distributed practice within daily routines as through the traditional approach of predominantly massed practice (Mulligan, Lacy, & Guess, 1982). Although some teachers and therapists argue that their students are "bright enough" to generalize and therefore can benefit from isolated training activities, generalized outcomes are rarely assessed or validated. (The authors have observed that even very bright adults sometimes have difficulty generalizing from the college classroom to their day-to-day activities in the public schools.) Therefore, the implication for therapists and other team members in educational settings is, once again, to direct most of their effort toward student acquisition and performance of skills in naturally occurring environments and functional routines and activities.

Synthesis A fourth learning characteristic of students with severe disabilities is difficulty synthesizing skills learned separately. For example, a child may learn to maintain upright postures in physical therapy, gaze at preferences in speech-language therapy, and bite and chew in occupational therapy. During an actual mealtime, however, the child may experience extreme difficulty sequencing or combining these skills for meaningful use. To ensure skill synthesis in naturally occurring daily routines, educational team members need to analyze each student's daily activities, identify the skill clusters that are most important to teach, and integrate relevant knowledge and methods from each discipline to design effective instructional procedures. Although teachers and therapists initially find this process of integrating diverse intervention methods challenging, failure to do so places the responsibility for skill synthesis on the students. If the educational team members have difficulty

with synthesis, is it realistic to expect students with significant learning challenges to synthesize skills on their own?

Multiple Challenges One final characteristic of many students with severe disabilities is the multiplicity of their challenges. Many students not only have intellectual challenges but have needs related to medical, health, orthopedic, sensory, and affective conditions as well. Given the varied knowledge and skills required to meet multiple and complex needs, a very high degree of service coordination is necessary. For an individual student, the team may include/consist of professionals from many disciplines and often from many agencies (e.g., education, human services). A collaborative and integrated approach to service provision is necessary both to manage the number of professionals with whom students with disabilities and their families must interact routinely, and to increase the coordination and consistency across disciplines and agencies. Bricker (1976) recommended that the teacher assume the role of *educational synthesizer,* to integrate input from other members of the educational team and to serve as the primary contact person for the family. As more students with severe and multiple disabilities are integrated into general education environments, the most effective way to coordinate services will need to be determined on an individual basis given local resources and circumstances. Any team member, including the parent, could serve as program coordinator, team leader, or case manager.

The learning challenges of students with disabilities, which are compounded when these students have multiple and complex needs, require carefully designed and implemented educational programs and extraordinary coordination of service provision. Team members, therefore, must spend time together on a regular basis to collaborate in the design and implementation of educational services.

Benefits of Collaboration

There are two primary benefits of collaboration among members of the educational team. First, there are the benefits realized because of the diverse perspectives, skills, and knowledge available from the variety of disciplines represented on the educational team. This creates a tremendous resource for problem solving and support. A second benefit of collaboration is derived from the group interaction if structured for cooperative, as opposed to individualistic or competitive, interactions (Johnson & Johnson, 1989).

Each team member brings a unique perspective about an individual student's strengths and challenges. For example, parents have the greatest information about the student's daily life outside of school; teachers are most knowledgeable about requirements and opportunities in the classroom and about curricular and instructional adaptations; physical and occupational therapists bring to the team their knowledge of sensorimotor functioning; and speech-language therapists contribute strategies for alternative and augmentative communication, including use of language for social interactions. Because of the diversity of the team composition, a wide array of information is brought to bear on common problems and provides the basis for a relevant and effective curricular and instructional design.

Several authors provide examples from practice of both the disciplinary diversity and the benefits of collaboration available through collaborative teamwork. Albano and colleagues (1981) reported that collaboration among disciplines for students with severe disabilities can serve to "unite the highly specialized and fragmented array of professional services with the information and concerns of the family" (p. 23). They went on to report that integrating the knowledge, skills, and services of individual team members can result in reduced duplication of services, more consistent attention to areas of student need throughout the school day, more relevant application of the knowledge and skills of individual disciplines to educational difficulties experienced by students, and ongoing professional growth and development by learning from professionals with differing knowledge and skills. These assertions were subsequently verified in a comprehensive case study for a program that implemented a collaborative teamwork approach to service provision (Albano, 1983). McCormick, Cooper, and Goldman (1979) found that integrating therapy methods in functional daily activities (e.g., dressing, using the rest room) increased the amount of instructional time for students with severe and multiple disabilities, primarily by decreasing the time spent in transport and by replacing passive caregiving with active instruction in daily living activities. Furthermore, they found that efficiency was particularly increased for teachers because they typically assumed primary responsibility for routine caregiving needs. Campbell, McInerney, and Cooper (1984) and Giangreco (1986) found that by integrating therapy methods in functional activities, skill acquisition increased for individual students.

A second major benefit of collaboration is realized for the group members themselves. Collaborative efforts to achieve mutual goals promote caring and committed relationships and skills critical for psychological health, including developing social competencies, helping others achieve, coping with failure, controlling anxiety, managing conflict, confiding feelings, and expressing needs (Johnson & Johnson, 1989). Positive interdependence among team members can develop such that they recognize the need for and seek out the perspective of other team members when a problem needs to be solved. Group problem solving, specifically, has numerous advantages over individual approaches: group membership stimulates greater interest in the problem, collective contributions bring more information to bear on the problem, individual contributions have a summative effect, and a group has a greater capacity to recognize and reject poorly conceived solutions (Kruger, 1988). Brandt (1988) asserted that adults and children have basic needs for belonging, support, and power. Being a member of a collaborative educational team enhances one's sense of belonging. Support is realized when fellow team members listen and acknowledge contributions. Power, in a very positive sense, is felt when team members not only acknowledge contributions but value and incorporate contributions into problem resolution. Learning teams (Glasser, 1986) and cooperative teams (Johnson & Johnson, 1987a, 1987b; Johnson, Johnson, & Maruyama, 1983; Slavin, Madden, & Leavey, 1984) have been advocated to realize the benefits of group process and collaborative teamwork.

For most teams, adopting a collaborative mode of interaction, as opposed to individualistic or competitive modes, requires change in existing organizational structures, as well as in existing job roles and responsibilities. Many of the existing structures in educational programs foster individualistic efforts, such as teachers teaching alone behind closed doors, therapists conducting back-to-back therapy sessions in separate rooms throughout the entire school day, lack of regularly scheduled team meetings, lack of training to develop collaboration skills (e.g., problem solving, conflict resolution, decision making), and individualized education programs (IEPs) organized to require separate reports and objectives from each discipline. In general, schools are not structured to support collaboration among service providers. Educators and therapists primarily work in isolation and do not realize the support available when ownership and responsibility for student learning is shared.

Best Educational Practices for Students with Severe Disabilities

More than a decade ago, L. Brown and colleagues (1976) presented the *criterion of ultimate functioning* as a standard against which to evaluate educational program components for students with severe disabilities. They asserted that the goal of an education for students with severe disabilities is preparation for participation in regular community life, but that the practices in the education of students with severe disabilities were not consistent with this goal. In their article, they posed a series of questions to be addressed prior to initiating instruction on any skill or activity. These questions, and the related criteria, remain relevant today:

- Why should the student engage in the activity?
- Is this activity necessary to prepare the student to ultimately function in complex, heterogeneous community settings?
- Could the student function as an adult just as well if he/she did not acquire the skill?
- Is there a different activity that would allow the student to approximate realization of the criterion of ultimate functioning more quickly or efficiently?
- Will the activity impede, restrict, or reduce the probability that the student will ultimately function in community settings?

- Are the skills, materials, tasks, and criteria similar to those encountered in real life? (p. 6)

Consider the following applications of these criteria to the provision of educationally related services.

David is a 6-year-old boy who loves to move and is fascinated with mobile toys that have wheels. He also happens to have severe developmental delays. Because he tends to "bunny hop," the physical therapist has designed a program to teach David to creep reciprocally. Recently, David started pulling to stand spontaneously. The physical therapist instructed David's parents and teacher to discourage this, since David does not yet have the foundation of reciprocal movement needed to rise from the floor to stand and to walk. After much discussion, the team agreed that discouraging David from spontaneously rising to stand could actually impede his already slow progress toward walking. Instead, they decided to shape David's spontaneous movement. During designated transition times throughout the school day, when David had opportunities to initiate pulling to stand and lowering to kneel, team members trained by the physical therapist would facilitate David's movement to emphasize quality reciprocal movement patterns and weight shifting. They also decided to facilitate reciprocal creeping when David was playing on the floor, and to teach him to ride a tricycle. Although the team could only theorize that tricycle riding might help promote acquisition of some reciprocal movement skills needed for walking, they agreed that, at a minimum, riding a tricycle would provide David another option for playing with his friends, and thus met several of the criteria of ultimate functioning.

Melanie is a young woman who enjoys hanging out at the mall with her girlfriends, especially when she has money to buy accessories. She has developed an increased interest in work since she has learned that, through working, she can earn money. Melanie is labeled as severely disabled and has difficulty with eye-hand coordination and motor planning. In an attempt to address Melanie's perceptual-motor needs, the occupational therapist taught Melanie to put graduated pegs in a board and rings on a cone. When the team reviewed Melanie's performance, they found that she did learn the pegs and rings tasks, but the skills had not translated to improved performance related to the priority educational goals identified by Melanie's parents, teacher, and occupational therapist. These goals were working at the neighborhood grocery store, going out to the mall with friends, and engaging in independent leisure activities in and around her home. To address the lack of generalization, the occupational therapist first identified the perceptual-motor demands of the priority goal activities in the grocery store, in the mall, and at home. For example, at work, Melanie had to stock various items on shelves and hooks; at the mall, she and her friends browse through clothing and accessories and play video games; and at home, Melanie preferred yarn and needlework craft activities and using a Walkman-type cassette player. With the perceptual-motor demands of priority goal activities identified, the occupational therapist and other members of the team devised strategies to teach the requisite skills as part of the instruction provided in the neighborhood grocery store, mall, and other relevant designated community environments.

Frank is an outgoing middle school student. Although he is challenged by severe physical disabilities, he displays extraordinary charm, making him a favorite of friends and family alike. When identifying learning opportunities in his seventh grade science class, the team considered teaching grasp and manipulation skills required to engage in various lab activities. Upon further consideration, however, the team realized that direct instruction to increase fine motor skill efficiency had not proven effective for functional participation during the past 10 years. Therefore, they decided that a more functional option was to teach Frank to identify the materials needed for the lab sessions and to request the assistance of classmates in gathering the materials. The team reasoned that: 1) it was likely that Frank would always require assistance in tasks requiring fine motor skills; and 2) as an adult, Frank was likely to have personal care attendants with whom he would need to communicate his needs and desires. Teaching Frank to identify needed materials and to direct others to provide assistance are self-determination skills that serve as a foundation for participation and control in his home and integrated community life.

The criterion of ultimate functioning construct highlighted the need to shift away from strictly developmental and prerequisite curricular paradigms to determine practices that maximize adaptive functioning in regular home and community environments. During the past 2 decades, discussion of considered best practices has dominated special education literature (see Browder, 1991; Brown & Lehr, 1989; Falvey, 1989; Gaylord-Ross, 1989; Horner, Meyer, & Fredericks, 1986; Orelove & Sobsey, 1991; Sailor et al., 1989; Sailor & Guess, 1983; Sailor, Wilcox, & Brown, 1980; Snell, 1987; Sontag, Smith, & Certo, 1977; Thomas, 1976; Wilcox & Bellamy, 1982). Researchers have identified, defined, and validated nine "best practices" in education of students with severe

disabilities (Williams et al., 1990): age-appropriate placement in local public schools, integrated provision of services, social integration, transition planning, community-based training, functional curricular expectations, systematic data-based instruction, home-school partnership, and systematic program evaluation. These practices are defined in Table 2.5 and referenced in subsequent chapters of this book. Collaborative teamwork is clearly identified as an essential element in several of these practices and is necessary to fully implement the complement of best practices for educating students with severe disabilities.

As best educational practices have evolved to support the education of children with disabilities in the full range of typical activities in local public schools, the models of educational and related service provision have necessarily changed. Teachers and therapists now recognize that they cannot ensure educational relevance through isolated, pull-out assessments and services. To promote educational relevance, related services personnel must observe and work with the students in the context of educational programs in order to: 1) identify functional, educationally relevant challenges that could be addressed through the provision of related educational services; and 2) determine interventions that could be both effective and appropriate in the context of educational activities. It is exceedingly difficult, if not impossible, for related services personnel to contribute in a meaningful way to the design and implementation of an effective educational program without first-hand knowledge of the student's performance in educational environments and activities. A collaborative teamwork approach that provides the structure and opportunity for therapists to provide services

Table 2.5 Best educational practices for students with severe disabilities

1. Age-appropriate placement in local public schools
The placement of choice for all students (with and without handicaps) should be within chronologically age-appropriate regular classrooms in the student's local public schools.

2. Integrated delivery of services
IEPs and instructional programs should indicate the integration of instruction on education and related service goals into everyday school, home, and community activities. Related service providers should offer consultation and assistance to special and regular educators, parents, and others on developing, implementing, and integrating instruction on related service goals.

3. Social integration
Students with handicaps should have access to the same environments as non-handicapped peers of similar chronological age. Primary goals of social integration should be to increase the number of integrated community and school environments and to improve the quality of interactions in those environments.

4. Transition planning
Transition planning should occur well in advance of major moves (e.g., early education/special education to elementary school, elementary to high school, high school to adult services). Transition objectives should be included in IEPs and reflect the input of significant parties affected by the transition.

5. Community-based training
Students should have the opportunity to acquire and demonstrate specific skills within appropriate community settings. Conditions and criteria of IEP goals and objectives should include performance in natural environments.

6. Curricular expectations
There should be curricula or curriculum guidelines which progress from no skills to adult functioning in all areas of integrated community life. There should be a system for longitudinal monitoring of student progress.

7. Systematic data-based instruction
There should be written schedules of daily activities, clearly defined objectives, reliably implemented instructional programs, and systematic data collection and analysis. Instructional decisions should be based upon documentation of students' progress.

8. Home-school partnership
Parents should have ongoing opportunities to participate in the development of their child's IEP and the delivery of educational and related services. There should be a clearly delineated system for regularly communicating with parents and providing parents with information. Parental concerns should be reflected in IEP goals and objectives.

9. Systematic program evaluation
Educational and related services should be evaluated on a regular basis. Evaluations should actively involve the entire program staff and provide administrators and staff with information regarding the achievements of program goals; student progress; discrepancies needing remediation; directions for future programs change; and program impact upon students, their families, and the community.

From Williams, W., Fox, T. J., Thousand, J., & Fox, W. (1990). Level of acceptance and implementation of best practices in the education of students with severe handicaps in Vermont. *Education and Training in Mental Retardation, 25* (2), 120-131; reprinted by permission.

(direct and indirect) in integrated educational environments and activities is a complementary model of service provision for implementing best educational practices designed to achieve integrated life outcomes (Giangreco et al., 1989).

Legal Mandates and Precedents

Further support for collaborative teamwork is found in various legal mandates and precedents. Strong advocacy from parents and professionals resulted in the passage of Public Law 94-142 (the Education for All Handicapped Children Act [EHA] of 1975, now entitled the Individuals with Disabilities Education Act [IDEA]). This major Federal legislation guarantees *special education* and *related services* in *least restrictive environments* to children ages 6 to 21 with handicapping conditions; Public Law 99-457 (the EHA Amendments of 1986) extends these guarantees to preschool children, ages 3 through 5. These mandates provide both legal and programmatic bases for the design of special education and related services, as specified in the federal definitions that follow.

Related services are defined as:

> transportation and such developmental, corrective, and other supportive services (including speech pathology and audiology, psychological services, physical and occupational therapy, recreation, and medical and counseling services, except that such medical services shall be for diagnostic and evaluation purposes only) as may be required to assist a handicapped child to benefit from special education, and includes the early identification and assessment of handicapping conditions in children. (20 U.S.C. §1401[17], 1975)

The phrase *as may be required to assist a handicapped child to benefit from special education* suggests that the related services of physical and occupational therapy and speech/language pathology must both

relate directly to the child's educational program and be provided in such a way that the child receives a greater benefit from the educational program than if related services were not provided. As noted previously in this chapter, both educational relevance and student benefit are addressed when therapists integrate their knowledge and skills into instruction provided in the context of routine daily activities that comprise the student's educational program, whether at school, in the community, or at home.

Special education is defined as "specially designed instruction, at no cost to the parent, to meet the unique needs of a handicapped child" (20 U.S.C. §1401[16], 1975). Traditionally, special education and related services have been associated with or even defined in terms of special places where children with handicaps go to receive services. For example, in many school districts children can only receive special education and related services by going to special education classes, therapy rooms, and even separate schools. As students with disabilities are included more fully in neighborhood schools and general education classes, special education is increasingly conceptualized as a service and support rather than a program or place (Taylor, 1988). As a component of special education, therefore, related services also are viewed as services and supports provided in the context of the educational program. Both special education and related services can be implemented in a variety of places, including general education classes and off campus in integrated community settings.

Another implication derived from the definition of special education is that instruction, if designed specifically to meet a student's unique educational needs, would reflect an integration of effective intervention methods from all disciplines supporting the student. Rather than using fragmented and sometimes conflicting intervention methods, teachers, therapists, family members, and others on the team design and implement instructional procedures that integrate methods across disciplines into a more comprehensive, balanced, and consistent set of methods. For example, an essential component of instructional programs for many students with physical challenges is infusion of interventions to ensure achievement of an effective body position for optimal participation.

With reference to *least restrictive environment*, the Education for All Handicapped Children Act requires assurances that:

> to the maximum extent appropriate, handicapped children . . . are educated with children who are not handicapped, and that special classes, separate schooling, or other removal of handicapped children from the regular education environment, occurs only when the nature or severity of the handicap is such that education in regular classes with supplementary aids and services cannot be achieved satisfactorily. (20 U.S.C. §1412[5], 1975)

Despite the expressed preference for providing services and supports in general education environments, professionals routinely assume that certain students cannot be educated in general education settings and that certain services cannot be provided in general education settings. Most disconcerting is that teams draw this conclusion without first making a sincere effort to design and implement interventions (i.e., supplementary aids and services) that could meet individual student needs in general education settings. In part, this stems from an assumption that if a child cannot meet the same core or subject area curricular competencies as gen-

eral education classmates, he or she should be removed to receive alternative curricula, instruction, and services.

Taylor (1988) articulated some of the confusion or "pitfalls" that exist in interpreting the least restrictive environment (LRE) mandate. His LRE pitfalls have direct application to the misconception that special education and related services are places that children go to receive services and are services that are mutually exclusive of general education. Most relevant to our discussion here are five of Taylor's (1988, pp. 45–48) seven "pitfalls":

1. *The LRE principle legitimizes restrictive environments. As long as a continuum exists, every point on the continuum is legitimized and therefore can be used in practice.*
2. *The LRE principle confuses segregation and integration on the one hand with intensity of services on the other. In other words, in order to get intensive services (or any services at all), one must be in a more restrictive (less integrated) environment.*
3. *The LRE principle is based on a "readiness model." This assumes that individuals get ready for less restrictive environments by learning appropriate behavior in a more restricted environment.*
6. *The LRE principle implies that people must move as they develop and change.* Following from the previous pitfall, once new skills are learned, individuals must move.
7. *The LRE principle directs attention to physical settings rather than to the services and supports people need to be integrated into the community.*

Increasingly, the concept of "ordinary environments . . . extraordinary supports" is advocated as the basis of service design.

In other words, all students with disabilities or handicaps can participate in and benefit from the same educational environments as students without labels, but to do so may require more support than typically provided to students without labels.

The related services mandate of Public Law 94-142 has been one of the most litigated aspects of the legislation, largely because of questions concerning the parameters of educational relevance (Osborne, 1984). Giangreco (1989) presented a chronology of the major legislation and litigation affecting the provision of related services (Table 2.6). Central to the outcome in each case was deference to services that allow both access to and participation in an educational program in the most integrated settings deemed reasonable. One additional case not included in Giangreco's synopsis, *Roncker v. Walter* (1983), established the "standard of portability," a precedent with significant impact on the provision of related services. In the Roncker case, the court ruled that the availability of special services only in segregated settings did not justify excluding a child from integrated settings. The decision explicitly identified related services, special equipment, and specially designed (i.e., accessible) environments as provisions that could be, and would be, arranged in integrated environments.

In schools throughout the country, an increasing number of parents of children with disabilities, including children labeled as profoundly and multiply disabled, have requested that their children be educated exclusively in general education and other integrated settings, with no "pull-out" services. Since most related services personnel were trained to provide direct services in segregated settings, it is challenging (if not frightening) to shift to other models of service provision (e.g., to

integrate physical therapy services for a child with severe disabilities into a regular fourth grade class). Similarly, as children with disabilities become more fully included in general education, the role of special education teachers is beginning to shift to a more indirect model of service provision also (Stainback, Stainback, & Harris, 1989; Thousand, Nevin-Parta, & Fox, 1987). Increasingly, therapists and special educators will be required to shift from a model of providing service and support in self-contained environments to collaborating with general educators and community members in integrated environments.

Guidelines for Therapy Practice in Educational Environments

Recent publications by the American Physical Therapy Association (1990), the American Occupational Therapy Association (1989), the American Speech-Language-Hearing Association (1991), and the Neurodevelopmental Treatment Association (DeMauro, 1988) reflect the unique nature of therapy practice in educational settings that is due, at least in part, to the special education mandates that guide the provision of related services. Contained within professional policies and guidelines are statements that endorse alternatives to the traditional models of therapy service provision (Table 2.7).

As discussed previously, *educationally relevant services* are provided in a way that ensures direct application of team member knowledge and skills to students' educational programs. Earlier in this chapter, routine activities and environmental demands were identified as the natural and functional contexts in which to teach motor and communication skills (discussed in greater detail in Chapter 4). The need for a particular related service is de-

Table 2.6 Chronology and synopsis of major related services legislation and litigation

√ *PARC v. Pennsylvania* (1972)

Established the legal right of students with severe handicaps to receive public education.

√ *Education for All Handicapped Children Act* (1975)

In addition to ensuring a free, appropriate, public education for all students with handicapping conditions, this legislation established that students have a right to receive related services that "...may be required to assist a handicapped child to benefit from special education." Related services are developmental, corrective, or other supportive services including, but not limited to, speech pathology, audiology, psychological services, physical therapy, occupational therapy, counseling, and medical services. Medical services shall be for diagnostic and evaluation purposes only. The Code of Federal Regulations (1987) Section 300.13 extended this list to include school health services, social work services in schools, and parent counseling and training.

Espino v. Besteiro (1981)

School was ordered to provide an air conditioned classroom as a related service for a 7-year-old child who could not regulate his own body temperature. The school had previously agreed to provide an air conditioned cubicle to be placed in a classroom that was not air conditioned, but the court ruled that the cubicle restricted the student's interactions with peers.

Hymes v. Harnett Board of Education (1981)

Court ruled that the school must provide mangement of a student's tracheostomy tube during the school day to allow access to school-based education. The school's plan to provide homebound instruction because of the tracheostomy was deemed unduly restrictive.

√ *Tokarick v. Forest Hills School District* (1981)

School was ordered to provide clean intermittent catheterization (CIC) as a related service because the "...absence of such a service would prevent the child from participating in the regular school program."

√ *Board of Education of the Hendrick Hudson Central School Board v. Rowley* (1982)

In this Supreme Court decision, a sign-language interpreter was denied as a related service to a student with a hearing impairment because the Court ruled that she was, and had been, benefiting from instruction. Justice Renquist ruled that, "Free appropriate public education is satisfied when state provides personalized instruction with sufficient support services to permit the handicapped child to benefit educationally from instruction" (p. 3034) and that the requirement of free appropriate public education does not require the state to maximize the potential of each child.

Stacy G. v. Pasadena Independent School District (1982)

In this case regarding a student with severe retardation and behavioral problems, the court ruled that related services must be provided in the form of parent training in behavioral management techniques and counseling to the parents to help relieve emotional stress.

PARC V. Pennsylvania Consent Decree of Enforcement Petition in Fialkowski v. School District of Philadelphia (1982)

In anticipation of the outcome of court proceedings, the Philadelphia City School District settled out of court with plaintiffs in 1982. The agreement bound the school district to provide extensive retraining and

(continued)

Table 2.6 *(continued)*

instructional support to staff in classrooms for students with severe handicaps. In part, this agreement called for the provision of transdisciplinary services including: a) "For students receiving related services, collaboration between the teacher and specialist for planning and evaluating programs," and b) "For students with therapeutic goals, techniques are carried over into educational activities with input from the therapist."

Birmingham & Lamphere School Districts v. Superintendent (1982)

Court ruled that a local hearing officer did have the right to order the school district to provide related services in the form of summer enrichment activities that were essentially noninstructional in nature.

Department of Education, State of Hawaii v. Katherine D. (1983)

In this case regarding a student with cystic fibrosis and tracheomalacia, the court ruled that the school recommendation for homebound instruction did not meet the requirement of a free appropriate public education. The court ordered placement in regular public school with staff being trained in management of the student's tracheostomy tube (dispense medication, suction lungs, reinsert tube if dislodged). The court tempered its position by saying the schools were required to make accommodations "within reason" and that budgetary constraints and realistic resources are considered by the court.

Hurry v. Jones (1983)

The court ruled that the school must provide transportation as a related service for a student with mental and physical handicaps. This transportation was inclusive from the child's home to the school bus and from the bus to the classroom.

Rettig v. Kent City (1983)

In part, this decision ordered a school to provide related services in the form of one hour per week of extracurricular activities to a 10-year-old student with severe handicaps. This decision was based in part on the Code of Federal Regulations Section 300.306 (Nonacademic Services) "Each public agency shall take steps to provide nonacademic and extracurricular activities in such a manner as is necessary to afford handicapped children an equal opportunity for participation in those services and activities" and that "...they be exposed on an equal basis as nonhandicapped children."

√ Irving Independent School District v. Tatro (1984)

This Supreme Court ruling designated clean intermittent catheterization as a related service. It distinguished it as a support school health service, not a medical service. The Court explained that provision of such a service did not place an undue burden or expense on the school district.

Detsel v. Sullivan (1990)

This case began with a local hearing officer determining that constant in-school nursing care was a related service for a child with a life threatening lung condition who requires 24-hour day nursing services. The decision was overruled by the State Commissioner of Education whose decision was upheld through the courts. The Supreme Court refused to hear the case. While nursing has been considered a "school health service" and appropriately provided as a related service, the courts ruled that the constancy and nature of this service qualified it as "medical" and thus excluded it as a related service because it was beyond the competence of the school nurse. The service also was denied because it placed an undue financial burden on the school district. The family then sued Medicaid for payment of nursing services. The United States Court of Appeals (second circuit) determined that Medicaid would pay for nursing services while the student was attending public school.

(continued)

Table 2.6 *(continued)*

✓ *Individuals with Disabilities Education Act (IDEA, PL 101-476)* (1990)

This amendment to the Education for All Handicapped Children Act of 1975 (PL 94-142) adds rehabilitation counseling and recreation, including therapeutic recreation and social work services, to the federal
definition of related services. *added transition, rehab counsel, s*

From Giangreco, M. F. (1989). *Making related service decisions for students with severe handicaps
in public schools: Roles, criteria, and authority. Dissertation Abstracts International, 50,* 1624A. (University Microfilms No. 89-19, 561); reprinted by permission.

termined by the need for knowledge and
skills from that discipline to improve
student participation in the educational
program.

Considerations for Determining Educational Relevance of Related Services

In considering the learning characteristics
of students with severe disabilities, legal
mandates of special education, and best
educational practices, it seems important
to pose a framework for determining
whether physical and occupational therapy and speech-language pathology services are educationally relevant and therefore appropriately provided to individual
students. Table 2.8 presents a checklist of
practices that are likely to indicate the educational relevance of related services provided to students with severe disabilities
in educational settings. Therapists and
other related services personnel can engage in these practices only if they work
as members of collaborative educational
teams and are knowledgeable about the
contextually relevant educational demands
and opportunities for each student.

COLLABORATIVE TEAM MEMBERS AND THEIR ROLES

With the outcomes, characteristics, and
reasons for collaborative teamwork articulated, it is appropriate to discuss the individuals who comprise the collaborative
team and their respective roles and responsibilities.

Defining Who Is on the Collaborative Team

Participation on a collaborative educational team can and should vary depending upon current educational priorities for
individual students. First, there are usually team members who are involved very
directly in the design and implementation
of the day-to-day educational program. We
refer to these team members as the *core
team.* For many students with severe disabilities, the core team consists of the student, family members, teachers (special
and general educators), a communication
specialist (speech-language therapist with
expertise in augmentative and alternative
communication), a physical and/or occupational therapist, and a paraprofessional or teaching associate who provides instructional and management support to
the student and class (Giangreco & Eichinger, 1990; Orelove & Sobsey, 1987). When
students have extensive sensory or medical needs, a vision or hearing specialist
and a nurse may be members of the core
team. In addition, some school districts
have case managers or social workers who
assist with coordination of services. In
such situations, these individuals also
would be logical members of the core
team.

Table 2.7 Excerpts from professional policies and guidelines on the provision of related services

Source	Major Provisions in Support of Collaborative Teamwork
American Physical Therapy Association (1990). *Physical therapy practice in educational environments.*	Physical therapy traditionally has been considered something that occurs in a specially equipped and private room during a scheduled block of time. The LRE requirement means that physical therapists need to: a) emphasize intervention strategies rather than places and b) make every effort to identify strategies that team members can use in the course of the child's daily routines, when postural control, mobility, and sensory processing are really required. When related services focus first on the natural opportunities for children to develop and practice motor competence in routine activities in integrated environments, there is greater assurance that the related services will fulfill their mandated purpose: "to assist a handicapped child to benefit from special education."
American Occupational Therapy Association (1989). *Guidelines for occupational therapy services.*	Intervention refers to all activities performed by occupational therapy personnel to carry out IEP. In the educational setting, intervention includes direct therapy, monitoring, and several types of consultation. "Occupational therapy treatment refers to the use of specific activities or methods to develop, improve, and/or restore the performance of necessary functions; compensate for dysfunction; and/or minimize debilitation." The intervention must be planned and provided within the child's least restrictive environment.
American Speech-Language-Hearing Association (1991). *A model for collaborative service delivery for students with language learning disorders.*	The collaborative service delivery model affords the speech-language pathologist the opportunity to: a) observe and assess how the student functions communicatively and socially in the regular classroom, b) describe the student's communicative strengths and weaknesses in varied educational contexts, and c) identify which curricular demands enhance or interfere with the student's ability to function communicatively, linguistically, and socially.

Second, there are individuals who serve as team members on a more itinerant basis—that is, their roles do not support as intensively or directly the day-to-day educational program. We refer to individuals with this level of involvement as the *support team.* For students who have no functional sensorimotor limitations or for whom motoric difficulties are deemed a very low priority in the educational program, physical and occupational therapists may be support rather than core team members. Frequently, vision specialists, audiologists, psychologists, social work-

ers, nurses, dietitians, and orientation and mobility specialists serve as support team members and are called in to consult as needed (Orelove & Sobsey, 1991).

Distinguishing between core and support team members is helpful from a practical standpoint. Coordination efficiency declines as the number of team members increases. Members of the core team need frequent access to each other for problem solving, decision making, and support. Assuring this access is foremost in scheduling. Members of both the core and the support team need flexible schedules to allow

Table 2.8 Checklist for discussion of educational relevance of related services provided to students with severe disabilities in educational settings

✓	The need for collaboration with related services personnel is determined by that person's potential contribution to student achievement of priority educational goals.
✓	Related services personnel assess student capabilities in the context of the educational program, including the typical school, home, and community environments, routines, and activities determined to be priorities for each student.
✓	Related services personnel work directly with students within the context of the educational program.
✓	Related services personnel work with teachers and other team members to identify motor and communication priorities within the educational program.
✓	Objectives related to improving motor and communication abilities are embedded throughout the IEP, as opposed to being separate components.
✓	Related services personnel and teachers work together to design instructional methods for teaching students to participate to a greater degree and with more success in the educational program.
✓	Therapists teach others to use the instructional methods they have found effective in facilitating improved motor, communication, or other competencies.
✓	Related services personnel work on an ongoing basis with students and other team members to evaluate student progress in educational activities.

for consultation and formal involvement in team meetings when their expertise and other contributions are deemed necessary. For support team members, we suggest involvement at least annually with contributions directed to priority educational goals.

As students' priorities change, the degree and nature of individual team member participation should change accordingly. For example, the team of a student who is transitioning from a self-contained early childhood special education program to an integrated, regular kindergarten might decide that the highest priority for that student during the first month of school will be successful inclusion into the social culture of the kindergarten class. The speech-language therapist, therefore, initially might be intensively involved in the kindergarten classroom to serve the following functions: modeling effective communication strategies, teaching classmates to use the student's augmentative communication system, determining social opportunities and demands requiring instructional emphasis, facilitating interactions with classmates, supporting the classroom teacher with strategies for student participation, and assessing the effectiveness of communication interventions. The therapist might be involved almost daily for the first 2 weeks of school and then reduce his or her time to provide weekly in-classroom consultation and support. During the initial transition time to kindergarten, other support personnel (e.g., physical therapist) might not be involved in an effort to minimize the number of people present in and imposing demands on the regular kindergarten.

Team Member Roles and Responsibilities

Generic Team Member Roles There are roles and responsibilities of a generic nature that are shared by all team members. These common roles and responsibilities include: 1) participating in team decisions about educational priorities and interventions for each student; 2) contributing to problem-solving efforts across all aspects of a student's educational program; 3) sharing discipline-specific knowledge and skills to promote student participation in the educational program and staff understanding of student capabilities; 4) supporting the contributions and efforts of fellow team members; and 5) continuing to grow and learn about practices that support the participation and contribution of individuals with severe disabilities in regular family, school, and community life.

Discipline-Specific Roles In addition to the general roles and responsibilities shared by all team members, there are specific contributions in terms of knowledge and skill areas associated with different disciplines. There is, however, overlap of knowledge and skills among disciplines given the specific training, experience, and interests of each individual professional. Furthermore, while each discipline claims a core set of skills, two people with the same discipline credentials do not necessarily have the same skills. Table 2.9 presents areas of expertise often associated with specific disciplines (Campbell & Banevich, 1986). In determining the need for specific support personnel, educational teams first must identify student needs or challenges and then determine which specific team members (regardless of discipline label) can contribute the necessary knowledge and skills (see Chapter 8).

Related Services Personnel Roles In addition to generic team member roles and discipline specific contributions, there are common roles among related services personnel. Giangreco (1990) identified 10 roles of related services personnel from a review of professional literature. Through ratings from 312 parents, special educators, and therapists, he then established the perceived relative importance of each role in the processes of assessing, planning, implementing, and evaluating programs for students with severe disabilities in public schools. Although there were some variations among the perceptions of the parents, educators, and therapists, he found general agreement as to the importance of the 10 roles.

Giangreco (1990) classified the two roles ranked most important as "outcome roles" because they "focus on the outcomes of educational and related services efforts [as affecting student] participation" (p. 138):

1. Developing adaptations and/or equipment to encourage functional participation
2. Facilitation of functional skills and activities

The next most important roles were classified as "enabling roles" because therapists engage in them "to assist students to attain the outcomes mentioned in the highest level" (p. 138):

3. Reciprocal consultation with colleagues
4. Removing or modifying barriers to participation
5. Preventing regression, deformity, and/or pain
6. Being a resource and support to families

The four roles ranked as least important were classified as "discretionary roles" because therapists engaged in them as indi-

Table 2.9 Areas of expertise of team members

Discipline	Areas of Expertise

Occupational Therapy	Sensory factors related to posture and movement
	Muscle tone
	Range of motion
	Posture / postural alignment
	Functional use of movement
	    1. Self-care
	    2. Recreation / leisure
	    3. Work
	Adaptive positioning equipment
	Adaptive devices for learning
	Materials and task adaptation
	Splinting

Physical Therapy	Sensory factors related to posture and movement
	Muscle tone
	Range of motion
	Muscle strength
	Joint mobility
	Endurance
	Flexibility
	Posture / postural alignment
	Balance and automatic movement
	Functional use of movement
	    1. Mobility (e.g., walking)
	    2. Recreation / leisure
	Adaptive positioning equipment
	Lower limb bracing / splinting / inhibitive casting
	Task adaptation

Speech - Language Therapy	Neuromotor factors related to oral musculature and respiration/phonation
	Hearing (screening)
	Functional use of movement
	    1. Communication
	    2. Social
	    3. Self-care (prespeech and feeding)
	Cognition
	Communication devices
	Communicative / social interactions

Education	Sensory factors related to learning and performance
	    (Instructional methods for students with visual, auditory,
	      or multisensory impairment)
	Functional use of movement
	    1. Environmental problem solving
	    2. Social
	    3. Communication
	    4. Self-care
	    5. Recreation / leisure
	    6. Work

Audiology	Hearing (and aural rehabilitation) Hearing aids

(continued)

Table 2.9 *(continued)*

Vision	Vision (and training procedures to enhance vision) Vision prostheses
Parent	Functional use of movement 1. Communication 2. Social 3. Recreation / leisure 4. Self-care Determining motivators

Adapted from Campbell, P., & Banevich, C. (1986). *The integrated programming team: An approach for coordinating multiple discipline professionals in programs for students with severe and multiple handicaps.* Akron, OH: Children's Hospital Family Child Learning Center, Integrated Services Project; reprinted by permission.

vidual circumstances made them appropriate and necessary:

7. Remediation/restoration of identified deficits

8. Promoting normal developmental sequences

9. Serving as an advocate for the student

10. Being a liaison between the medical community and the school team

These rankings suggest that members of the educational teams for students with severe disabilities in Giangreco's sample recognized the major tenet of service provision outlined earlier in this chapter—that related services personnel on educational teams function to support the educational program. In contrast with the ranked priorities, however, the therapists in the Giangreco (1990) study reported that they continued to invest most of their professional energies in discretionary roles, which are their lowest priorities. These findings suggest that priorities and practices do not necessarily match, and that merely identifying priorities does not ensure that they actually receive priority attention. Changing old models of service provision requires substantial professional and organizational change, which takes time, commitment, and long-term systematic efforts.

ASSUMPTIONS OF COLLABORATIVE TEAMWORK FOR STUDENTS WITH SEVERE DISABILITIES

This chapter has provided foundational information that supports a collaborative teamwork approach to integrating related services in educational programs for students with severe disabilities. The day-to-day actions of individual team members are shaped by a combination of foundational knowledge and personal values. Effective teams explore the knowledge and values of their members, and work to articulate a set of beliefs that all members can support. It is these shared beliefs, then, that largely determine the nature and scope of the collaborative teamwork employed in the design and implementation of education, including the provision of related services. When teams experience conflict, it is often because they have not established this foundation and each individual team member operates from a different set of beliefs and assumptions.

Table 2.10 Assumptions of a collaborative teamwork approach to education and related services for students with severe disabilities

1. All students can learn given the opportunity and appropriate support.

2. The desired educational outcomes for all students are participation in, contribution to, and enjoyment of family, school, and community life, now and in the future.

3. All students, regardless of abilities, interests, and needs, must grow up and learn together in the same school and community environments in order to achieve desired educational outcomes.

4. It is the explicit responsibility of the collaborative educational team to assist students in achieving desired educational outcomes.

5. The collaborative team is comprised of the student, significant family members, friends, and the education and related services personnel required to assist students in achieving desired educational outcomes.

6. Positive social interdependence among team members must be structured to realize the benefits of collaborative teamwork.

7. Discipline-referenced knowledge and skills are shared among team members so that relevant expertise is available to students in all aspects of their educational program.

8. An ecological curricular design is required to assist students in achieving desired educational outcomes.

9. An Individualized Education Program (IEP) is developed jointly by the collaborative educational team and reflects an integrated approach to service, design, and provision.

10. Collaborative teamwork strategies must remain flexible in order to meet changing needs of students and families.

Tables 2.3 and 2.8, presented earlier in this chapter, contain principles about collaborative teamwork and educational relevance of services. These constitute important assumptions about these aspects of service provision. Table 2.10 presents a third set of assumptions for the design and provision of education and related services for students with severe disabilities. These assumptions are shared by the authors and, collectively, they form the basis for the information and strategies offered in this book. Readers are encouraged to discuss these assumptions with teammates as a first step toward articulating their own shared set of assumptions about a collaborative teamwork approach for supporting the educational program of students with severe disabilities.

REFERENCES

Aksamit, D., & Alcorn, D. (1988). A preservice mainstream curriculum infusion model: Student teachers' perceptions of program effectiveness. *Teacher Education and Special Education, 11*, 52–58.

Albano, M.L. (1983). *Transdisciplinary team-*

ing in special education: A case study. Urbana: University of Illinois-Urbana/Champaign.

Albano, M., Cox, B., York, J., & York, R. (1981). Educational teams for students with severe and multiple handicaps. In R. York, W.K. Schofield, D.J. Donder, D.L. Ryndak, & B. Reguly (Eds.), *Organizing and implementing services for students with severe and multiple handicaps* (pp. 23–34). Springfield: Illinois State Board of Education.

American Occupational Therapy Association. (1989). *Guidelines for occupational therapy services in the public schools* (2nd ed.). Rockville, MD: Author.

American Physical Therapy Association. (1990). *Physical therapy practice in educational environments.* Alexandria, VA: Author.

American Speech-Language-Hearing Association, Committee on Language Learning Disorders. (1991). A model for collaborative service delivery for students with language-learning disorders in the public schools. *American Speech-Language-Hearing Association, 3*(33) (Suppl.).

Association for Persons with Severe Handicaps. (1986). *Position statement on the provision of related services.* Seattle, WA: Author.

Baer, D. (1981). A hung jury and a Scottish verdict: "Not proven." *Analysis and Intervention in Developmental Disabilities, 1*(1), 91–97.

Brandt, R. (1988). On students' needs and team learning: A conversation with William Glasser. *Educational Leadership, 45*(6), 38–45.

Bricker, D. (1976). Educational synthesizer. In M. A. Thomas (Ed.), *Hey, don't forget about me!* (pp. 84–89). Reston, VA: Council for Exceptional Children.

Browder, D.M. (1991). *Assessment of individuals with severe disabilities: An applied behavior approach to life skills assessment* (2nd ed.). Baltimore: Paul H. Brookes Publishing Co.

Brown, F. Evans, I., Weed, K., & Owen, V. (1987). Delineating functional competencies: A component model. *Journal of the Association for Persons with Severe Handicaps, 12*(2), 117–124.

Brown, F., & Lehr, D.H. (Eds.). (1989). *Persons with profound disabilities: Issues and practices.* Baltimore: Paul H. Brookes Publishing Co.

Brown, L., Branston, M.B., Hamre-Nietupski, S., Pumpian, I., Certo, N., & Gruenwald, L. (1979). A strategy for developing chronological age appropriate and functional curricular content for severely handicapped adolescents and young adults. *Journal of Special Education, 13*(1), 81–90.

Brown, L., Nietupski, J., & Hamre-Nietupski, S. (1976). The criterion of ultimate functioning. In M.A. Thomas (Ed.), *Hey, don't forget about me!* (pp. 2–15). Reston, VA: Council for Exceptional Children.

Campbell, P.H., & Banevich, C. (1986). *The integrated programming team: An approach for coordinating multiple discipline professionals in programs for students with severe and multiple handicaps.* Akron, OH: Children's Hospital Family Child Learning Center, Integrated Services Project.

Campbell, P.H., McInerney, W., & Cooper, M. (1984). Therapeutic programming for students with severe handicaps. *American Journal of Occupational Therapy, 38*(9), 594–602.

DeMauro, G. (1988, January). Member's hotline. *NDTA Newsletter,* 5.

Falvey, M.A. (1989). *Community-based curriculum: Instructional strategies for students with severe handicaps* (2nd ed.). Baltimore: Paul H. Brookes Publishing Co.

Ford, A., Schnorr, R., Meyer, L., Davern, L., Black, J., & Dempsey, P. (Eds.). (1989). *The Syracuse community-referenced curriculum guide for students with moderate and severe disabilities.* Baltimore: Paul H. Brookes Publishing Co.

Gaylord-Ross, R. (Ed.). (1989). *Integration strategies for students with handicaps.* Baltimore: Paul H. Brookes Publishing Co.

Giangreco, M. (1986). Effects of integrated therapy: A pilot study. *Journal of The Association for Persons with Severe Handicaps, 11*(3), 205–208.

Giangreco, M. (1989). Making related service decisions for students with severe handicaps in public schools: Roles, criteria, and authority. *Dissertation Abstracts International, 50,* 1624A. (University Microfilms No. DA8919516).

Giangreco, M.F. (1990). Making related service decisions for students with severe disabilities: Roles, criteria, and authority. *Journal of The Association of Persons with Severe Handicaps, 15*(1), 22–31.

Giangreco, M., & Eichinger, J. (1990). *Related*

services and the transdisciplinary approach: Parent training module. Seattle, WA: The Association for Persons with Severe Handicaps, TASH–Technical Assistance for Services to Children with Deaf-Blindness.

Giangreco, M., York, J., & Rainforth, B. (1989). Providing related services to learners with severe handicaps in educational settings: Pursuing the least restrictive option. *Pediatric Physical Therapy, 1*(2), 55–63.

Glasser, W. (1986). *Control theory in the classroom.* New York: Harper & Row.

Haring, N.G. (Ed.). (1988). *Generalization for students with severe handicaps: Strategies and solutions.* Seattle: University of Washington Press.

Hart, V. (1977). The use of many disciplines with the severely and profoundly handicapped. In E. Sontag, J. Smith, & N. Certo (Eds.), *Educational programming for the severely and profoundly handicapped* (pp. 391–396). Reston, VA: Council for Exceptional Children.

Holvoet, J., Guess, D., Mulligan, M., & Brown, F. (1980). The individualized curriculum sequencing model (II): A teaching strategy for severely handicapped students. *Journal of The Association for the Severely Handicapped, 5*(4), 337–352.

Horner, R.H., Meyer, L.H., & Fredericks, H.D.B. (Eds.). (1986). *Education of learners with severe handicaps: Exemplary service strategies.* Baltimore: Paul H. Brookes Publishing Co.

Horner, R.H., Williams, J.A., & Knobbe, C.A. (1985). The effect of "opportunity to perform" on the maintenance of skills learned by high school students with severe handicaps. *Journal of The Association for Persons with Severe Handicaps, 10*(3), 172–175.

Hutchison, D.J. (1978). The transdisciplinary approach. In J.B. Curry & K.K. Peppe (Eds.), *Mental retardation: Nursing approaches to care.* St. Louis: C.V. Mosby Co.

Idol, L., Paolucci-Whitcomb, P., & Nevin, A. (1986). *Collaborative consultation.* Rockville, MD: Aspen Publishers.

Individuals with Disabilities Education Act of 1990, 20 U.S.C. 1401(a)(17).

Inge, K., & Snell, M. (1985). Teaching positioning and handling techniques to public school personnel through inservice training. *Journal of The Association for Persons with Severe Handicaps, 10*(2), 105–110.

Institute on Community Integration, University of Minnesota. (1991). *Collaborative teamwork: Working together for full inclusion.* Minneapolis: Author.

Johnson, D.W., & Johnson, F.P. (1987a). *Joining together: Group theory and group skills* (3rd ed). Englewood Cliffs, NJ: Prentice Hall.

Johnson, D.W., & Johnson, R.T. (1987b). Research shows the benefit of adult cooperation. *Educational Leadership, 45*(3), 27–30.

Johnson, D.W., & Johnson, R.T. (1989). *Cooperation and competition: Theory and research.* Edina, MN: Interaction Book Company.

Johnson, D.W., Johnson, R.T., & Maruyama, G. (1983). Interdependence and interpersonal attraction among heterogeneous and homogeneous individuals: A theoretical formulation and a meta-analysis of the research. *Review of Educational Research, 53*, 5–54.

Kruger, L. (1988). Programmatic change strategies at the building level. In J.L. Graden, J.E. Zins, & M.J. Curtis (Eds.), *Alternative educational delivery systems: Enhancing instructional options for all students* (pp. 491–512). Washington, DC: National Association of School Psychologists.

Lane, H. (1976). *The wild boy of Aveyron.* Cambridge, MA: Harvard University Press.

Lyon, S., & Lyon, G. (1980). Team functioning and staff development: A role release approach to providing integrated educational services for severely handicapped students. *Journal of The Association for the Severely Handicapped, 5*(3), 250–263.

McCollum, J., & Stayton, V. (1985). Infant-parent interaction: Studies and intervention based on the SIAI model. *Journal of the Division for Early Childhood, 9*(2), 125–135.

McCormick, L., Cooper, M., & Goldman, R. (1979). Training teachers to maximize instructional time provided to severely and profoundly handicapped children. *AAESPH Review, 4*(3), 301–310.

Minnesota Statutes, §120.011.

Minnesota Statutes, §120.17 (1985).

Mulligan, M., Lacy, L., & Guess, D. (1982). Effects of massed, distributed, and spaced trial sequencing on severely handicapped students' performance. *Journal of The Association for the Severely Handicapped, 7*(2), 48–61.

National Center for Educational Outcomes, University of Minnesota. (1991). *Definitions, assumptions, and a preliminary conceptual*

model for a comprehensive system of outcomes indicators for children and youth with
disabilities (working draft: 1/28/91). Minneapolis. Author.

Nietupski, J., Scheutz, G., & Ockwood, L.
(1980). The delivery of communication therapy services to severely handicapped students: A plan for change. *Journal of The Association for the Severely Handicapped, 5*(1),
13–23.

Orelove, F.P., & Sobsey, D. (1987). *Educating
children with multiple disabilities.* Baltimore: Paul H. Brookes Publishing Co.

Orelove, F.P., & Sobsey, D. (1991). *Educating
children with multiple disabilities: A transdisciplinary approach* (2nd ed.). Baltimore:
Paul H. Brookes Publishing Co.

Osborne, A.G., Jr. (1984). How the courts have
interpreted the related services mandate. *Exceptional Children, 51*(3), 249–252.

Ottenbacher, K. (1982). Occupational therapy
and special education: Some issues and concerns related to Public Law 94-142. *American
Journal of Occupational Therapy, 36*(2), 81–
84.

Patterson, E.G., D'Wolff, N., Hutchison, D.,
Lowry, M., Schilling, M., & Siepp, J. (1976).
*Staff development handbook: A resource for
the transdisciplinary process.* New York:
United Cerebral Palsy Associations, Inc.

Perske, R. (1981). *Hope for the families.* Nashville, TN: Abingdon Press.

Perske, R. (1988). *Circle of friends.* Nashville,
TN: Abingdon Press.

Peterson, C. (1980). Support services. In B.
Wilcox & R. York (Eds.), *Quality education
for the severely handicapped: The federal investment* (pp. 136–163). Washington, DC:
U.S. Department of Education, Office of Special Education and Rehabilitative Services.

Powell, T.H., Rainforth, B., Hecimovic, A.,
Steere, D.E., Mayes, M.G., Zoback, M.S., &
Singer, A.L.T. (1985). *Connecticut's data-
based model.* Storrs: University of Connecticut, University Affiliated Program.

Rainforth, B. (1985). *Collaborative efforts in the
preparation of physical therapists and teachers of students with severe handicaps.* Unpublished doctoral dissertation, University
of Illinois at Urbana-Champaign.

Rainforth, B., & York, J. (1987). Integrating re-
lated services into community instruction.
*Journal of The Association for Persons with
Severe Handicaps, 12*(3), 188–198.

Roncker v. Walter, 700 F.2d 1058, *certiorari denied*, 104 S.Ct. 196, 464 U.S. 864, 78 L.Ed.2d
171. (6th Cir. 1983).

Sailor, W., Anderson, J.L., Halvorsen, A.T.,
Doering, K., Filler, J., & Goetz, L. (1989). *The
comprehensive local school: Regular education for all students with disabilities.* Baltimore: Paul H. Brookes Publishing Co.

Sailor, W., & Guess, D. (1983). *Severely handicapped students: An instructional design.*
Boston: Houghton Mifflin.

Sailor, W., Wilcox, B., & Brown, L. (Eds.).
(1980). *Methods of instruction for severely
handicapped students.* Baltimore: Paul H.
Brookes Publishing Co.

Sapon-Shevin, M. (1988). Working toward merger together: Seeing beyond the distrust and
fear. *Teacher Education and Special Education, 11,* 103–110.

Sileo, T.W., Rude, H.A., & Luckner, J.L. (1988).
Collaborative consultation: A model for transition planning for handicapped youth. *Education and Training in Mental Retardation,
23,* 333–339.

Slavin, R.E., Madden, N.A., & Leavey, M. (1984).
Effects of cooperative grouping and individualized instruction on mainstreamed students. *Exceptional Children, 50*(5), 434–443.

Snell, M.E. (Ed.). (1987). *Systematic instruction
of persons with severe handicaps* (3rd ed.).
Columbus: Charles E. Merrill.

Sontag, E., Smith, J., & Certo, N. (1977). *Educational programming for the severely and profoundly handicapped.* Reston, VA: Council
for Exceptional Children.

Stainback, S., & Stainback, W. (1987). Facilitating merger through personnel preparation.
*Teacher Education and Special Education,
10,* 185–190.

Stainback, S., & Stainback, W. (Eds.). (1992).
*Curriculum considerations in inclusive
classrooms: Facilitating learning for all students.* Baltimore: Paul H. Brookes Publishing
Co.

Stainback, S.B., Stainback, W.C., & Harris, K.C.
(1989). Support facilitation: An emerging role
for special educators. *Teacher Education and
Special Education, 12,* 148–153.

Steinbeck, T. (1986). Purposeful activity and
performance. *American Journal of Occupational Therapy, 40*(8), 529–541.

Sternat, J., Messina, R., Nietupski, J., Lyon, S., &
Brown, L. (1977). Occupational and physical
therapy services for severely handicapped

students: Toward a naturalized public school service delivery model. In E. Sontag, J. Smith, & N. Certo (Eds.), *Educational programming for the severely and profoundly handicapped* (pp. 263–287). Reston, VA: Council for Exceptional Children.

Stokes, T., & Baer, D. (1977). An implicit technology of generalization. *Journal of Applied Behavior Analysis, 10*(2), 349–367.

Taylor, S. J. (1988). Caught in the continuum: A critical analysis of the principle of the Least Restrictive Environment. *Journal of The Association for the Severely Handicapped, 13*(1), 41–53.

Thomas, M.A. (Ed.). (1976). *Hey! Don't forget about me: Educating the severely profoundly handicapped.* Reston, VA: Council for Exceptional Children.

Thousand, J., Fox, T., Reid, R., Godek, J., Williams, W., & Fox, W. (1986). *The homecoming model: Educating students who present intensive educational challenges within regular education environments.* Burlington: University of Vermont.

Thousand, J., Nevin-Parta, A., & Fox, W. (1987). Inservice training to support the education of learners with severe handicaps in their local public schools. *Teacher Education and Special Education, 10,* 4–13.

Vandercook, T., & York, J. (1990). A team approach to program development and support. In W. Stainback & S. Stainback (Eds.), *Support networks for inclusive schooling: Interdependent integrated education* (pp. 95–122). Baltimore: Paul H. Brookes Publishing Co.

Webster's ninth new collegiate dictionary.

(1987). Springfield, MA: Merriam-Webster Inc.

Wilcox, B., & Bellamy, G.T. (1982). *Design of high school programs for severely handicapped students.* Baltimore: Paul H. Brookes Publishing Co.

Williams, W., Fox, T., Thousand, J., & Fox, W. (1990). Level of acceptance and implementation of best practices in the education of students with severe handicaps in Vermont. *Education and Training in Mental Retardation, 25*(2), 120–131.

York, J., Giangreco, M.F., Vandercook, T., & Macdonald, C. (1992). Integrating support personnel in the inclusive classroom. In S. Stainback & W. Stainback (Eds.), *Curriculum considerations in inclusive classrooms: Facilitating learning for all students* (pp. 101–116). Baltimore: Paul H. Brookes Publishing Co.

York, J., Rainforth, B., & Dunn, W. (1990). Training needs of physical and occupational therapists who provide services to children and youth with severe disabilities. In S. Kaiser & C. McWorter (Eds.), *Preparing personnel to work with persons with severe disabilities* (pp. 153–180). Baltimore: Paul H. Brookes Publishing Co.

York, J., Rainforth, B., & Giangreco, M.F. (1990). Transdisciplinary teamwork and integrated therapy: Clarifying some misconceptions. *Pediatric Physical Therapy, 2*(2), 73–79.

Zins, J.E., Curtis, M.J., Graden, J.L., & Ponti, C.R. (1988). *Helping students succeed in the regular classroom.* San Francisco: Jossey-Bass.

3

Parents as Team Members
Inclusive Teams, Collaborative Outcomes
Christine Salisbury

C HILDREN WHOSE PARENTS ARE INVOLVED in their education experience more success in school than students whose parents are not as involved (Epstein, 1987; Guralnick, 1989; Powell, 1989). Given the contributions that parents can make toward their child's achievements, it is important that professionals create a variety of ways in which parents can be meaningfully included in their child's education (Shevin, 1983; Vincent, Laten, Salisbury, Brown, & Baumgart, 1980).

Under current federal laws, decision making is clearly the prevailing form of parent participation on an educational team. While the inclusion of parents on such teams is acknowledged in the educational (Turnbull & Turnbull, 1986a; Turnbull & Winton, 1984) and related services (Bazyk, 1989; Campbell, 1987; Carney, 1987; Rainforth & York, 1987; Salisbury,

McLean, & Vincent, 1990) literatures, much of what transpires during team meetings does not meaningfully include parents in the decision-making process, nor yield collaboratively derived outcomes. This point becomes critical when parents are expected to support decisions of the team. that directly affect the family as well as the child, such as recommendations for how to carry over activities into the home or what goals will be addressed first.

Over the past century a number of role changes have emerged for parents of children with disabilities. Parents have moved from being perceived as the source of their child's problems to more proactive roles as service developers, learners, teachers of their child, advocates, and educational decision makers (Summers, Behr, & Turnbull, 1989; Turnbull & Turnbull, 1986a). Unfortunately, in our zealousness to create

Preparation of this chapter was supported, in part, by grant H086D90006 from the U.S. Department of Education, Special Education Programs, to the State University of New York at Binghamton. The opinions expressed herein do not necessarily reflect the position or policy of the U.S. Department of Education, and no official endorsement should be inferred.

Christine L. Salisbury, Ph.D., Associate Professor of Special Education, School of Education and Human Development, State University of New York at Binghamton, P.O. Box 6000, Binghamton, New York 13902-6000.

more substantive roles and responsibilities for parents within the educational context, we have forgotten the primary role of these individuals—parents as family members. Parents' abilities to function effectively as integral members of a transdisciplinary team will, in large part, be mediated by a variety of other factors, principally their responsibilities to their child and family. Failure to acknowledge and address these factors in the design and development of educational programs and policies will minimize the willingness and ability of parents to participate, and hamper the development of collaborative home-school relationships.

The link between home and school is an essential one that can be optimized when professionals understand how families function and how to match programs with family needs. Dunst, Trivette, and Deal (1988) noted that the mismatch between what professionals and families see as needs can create conflict, and can result in families failing to follow professionally prescribed intervention programs. Specifically, they suggest that:

> what may be viewed as either oppositional or apathetic behavior may have less to do with contempt for professional opinion and more to do with lack of consensus regarding the nature of the presenting problem, the need for treatment (medical, educational, therapeutic), and the course of the action that should be taken. (p. 3)

It is therefore incumbent upon professionals to engage in a consensus-building process within the team and acknowledge the acceptability of differences among families, and between professional and parent agendas.

The purposes of this chapter are threefold: first, to briefly review the rationale for parent/family participation in the educational process; second, to identify factors that affect parent participation; and finally, to describe guidelines and strategies for including parents as transdisciplinary team members.

WHY SHOULD PARENTS BE INVOLVED?

Legal Basis for Participation

Public Law 94-142 stipulates that parents be afforded the opportunity to actively participate in planning for their child's educational program and that such participation be as an equal member of the individualized education program (IEP) planning team. Turnbull and Turnbull (1986a) cited a policy interpretation of IEP requirements prepared by the Office of Special Education, U.S. Department of Education. This policy statement clarifies the expectations for state and local educational agencies related to the inclusion of parents in the decision making process:

> The parents of a handicapped child are expected to be equal participants, along with school personnel, in developing, reviewing, and revising the child's IEP. This is an active role in which the parents (a) participate in the discussion about the child's need for special education and related services, and (b) join with the other participants in deciding what services the agency will provide the child. (Turnbull & Turnbull, 1986a, p. 226)

Parent participation on teams and in the educational process is a priority. Compliance with legal and legislative requirements should be the last reason we choose to include parents. Rather, the most defensible arguments are based on a commitment to a set of values, principles, and practices that compel us to include parents because it is good for children, families, and schools.

While there is a clear mandate requiring the active participation of parents in the IEP process, problems with interpretation of these regulations have hindered implementation efforts. Research on the nature of parent involvement in the IEP process since the passage of Public Law 94-142 indicates that participation has, in reality, been passive rather than active (Goldstein, Strickland, Turnbull, & Curry, 1980; Lynch & Stein, 1987; Turnbull & Turnbull, 1986a). These studies indicate that in at least half of the cases cited IEPs were completed by the staff *prior to* meeting with the parents and that parents had little knowledge of the content of the IEP document. For the parents, "participation" in these cases meant listening to professionals and approving the IEP already prepared for their review. Such practices are clearly inconsistent with the intent of the legislation.

Findings of limited participation may also be linked to the reality of who actually attends the IEP meetings and how professionals view the involvement of parents. In a study by Scanlon, Arick, and Phelps (1981), the special education teacher and the mother attended the IEP meetings 75% of the time, whereas professionals from other disciplines attended only about 30% of the time. It clearly becomes difficult to function as a "team" when attendance disparities such as this exist. Other research indicates that school staff often rank parent contributions as less important than their own (Gilliam & Coleman, 1981; Morgan & Rhode, 1983; Yoshida, Fenton, Kaufman, & Maxwell, 1978), or view the involvement of parents as an encroachment on the school's area of expertise (Allen & Hudd, 1987).

Recent federal legislation in the field of early intervention significantly broadened the scope of responsibilities for profes-

sionals working with infants and toddlers who are at risk for developmental disabilities or who evidence handicapping conditions. The Individuals with Disabilities Education Act Amendments of 1991 (Public Law 102-119) and its predecessor (Public Law 99-457) amended Public Law 94-142 to create Part H, the Program for Infants and Toddlers with Handicaps. This law requires each state to develop a state-wide system that includes provisions for addressing all required components of the law. A multidisciplinary evaluation and an individualized family service plan (IFSP) are among the required components of Part H.

Conceptually similar to the IEP, the IFSP is a central component in the implementation of Part H and, therefore, must be addressed by professionals at the direct service level. However, the focus of services under Part H is on the capacity of families to meet the needs of their infants and toddlers, making it necessary that teams become family centered, rather than solely child focused in their orientation. Walsh, Campbell, and McKenna (1988) pointed out that the IFSP, like the IEP, is based on information derived from a multidisciplinary assessment of child and family needs, and includes an assessment of family strengths and needs.

However, professionals working with infants and young children with disabilities are generally poorly prepared to develop quality IEPs and IFSPs, and few outside the field of social work and psychology have adequate preparation in working with families (Bricker & Veltman, 1990; Simeonsson & Bailey, 1990). The lack of professional preparedness jeopardizes the integrity of the program planning process and the validity of the process outcomes from the outset. The challenge facing professionals is how to acquire the skills necessary to ensure that the outcomes of planning and service design are socially, as well as educationally, valid.

Conceptual and Research Bases for Participation

Children do not exist in isolation. They function as members of interdependent systems within the family, school, and community. Within each system exist forces and supports that influence the child's behavior both within and among a variety of environments (Bronfenbrenner, 1979; Minuchin, 1974). Placing the child within an ecological context, it then becomes clear that the child's performance in school will be affected, in large part, by what transpires at home. Parents are the only ones who will be able to contribute information about the values, priorities, and supports available within the home environment. Because research indicates that parents are reliable sources of information (Beckman, 1984; Gradel, Thompson, & Sheehan, 1981), the formulation of ecologically valid and educationally functional goals is logically dependent upon the participation of parents in the planning and decision-making process.

Home and community environments represent important natural contexts where children with developmental disabilities will need to demonstrate skills acquired at school. If professionals are to adequately prepare students to successfully function in future environments (Brown, Nietupski, & Hamre-Nietupski, 1976; Salisbury & Vincent, 1990; Vincent, Salisbury, Brown, Gruenewald, & Powers, 1980), they will need to teach students in such a way that skills can be effectively generalized to settings beyond the school context. An ecologically grounded, home- and community-referenced curriculum provides information on those natural contexts that

professionals can then use to develop appropriate intervention strategies (Rainforth & Salisbury, 1988; Salisbury et al., 1990; Snell, 1987; Vincent, Salisbury, Strain, McCormick, & Tessier, 1990).

Research across the age span provides evidence of the importance of the home environment for the cognitive, emotional, and physical development of the child. The early childhood literature, in particular, reveals that the quality of the home environment, the parents' interaction styles, and the experiences provided during the early years each play a role in the development of the young child (Barnard & Kelly, 1990; Greenspan, 1990; Guralnick, 1989; Sameroff & Fiese, 1990; Silber, 1989). Research with school-age children and their families has produced similar findings. Work by Mink and colleagues (Mink, 1986; Mink, Nihara, & Meyers, 1983; Nihara, Mink, & Meyers, 1981), as well as others (Greenspan & Budd, 1986), provides additional evidence of the continuing effects of family influence on the achievements and adaptive competence of children with disabilities.

There are at least two significant trends emerging from recent empirical and conceptual work in the field of special education and related services that have implications for the parent as team member. First, while there are considerable data to support the efficacy of didactic (adult-initiated and -directed) interventions using parents as "therapists" or "teachers," there is also evidence to support the efficacy of ecologically based intervention strategies that de-emphasize the direct instruction role for parents. These data indicate that children learn well when adults capitalize on child-initiated activities. Activities selected by the child, rather than the parent, are inherently motivating to children and create opportunities in which adults can reinforce and extend important skills within natu- rally occurring routines in ways that mini- mize the role of "teacher" or "therapist" (Bazyk, 1989; Bricker & Cripe, 1989; Bricker & Veltman, 1990; Lucca & Settles, 1981; MacDonald & Gillette, 1986; Mahoney & Powell, 1988; Rainforth & Salisbury, 1988; Salisbury et al., 1990; Vincent, Salisbury, Laten, & Baumgart, 1979; Warren & Kaiser, 1986). By emphasizing the value of inci- dental teaching, it is possible to preserve the primary role of parent while helping the parents promote their child's development.

Second, ecologically based intervention programs have the potential of preserving and strengthening the positive reciprocal qualities of parent-child relationships that can otherwise be impaired when the par- ent is placed in a more directive role of "therapist" or "teacher" (Bazyk, 1989; Humphry, 1989; Seitz & Provence, 1990; Simeonsson & Bailey, 1990; Summers et al., 1989; Turnbull & Turnbull, 1986b; Tyler & Kogan, 1972). By vesting the control for the interaction with the child and encouraging parents to interact with their child "natu- rally," it is possible to minimize some of the frustrations, stress, and resentment that can occur when the parents feel pressed to "make progress" with their child (Bazyk, 1989; Turnbull & Turnbull, 1986b).

Recently, the American Occupational Therapy Association (AOTA 1989) recom- mended that parents be given the freedom to determine the extent and nature of their involvement in therapy and home activi- ties (Bazyk, 1989). Altheide and Livermore (1987) reported that the American Speech- Language-Hearing Association (ASHA) has highlighted the importance of giving con- sideration to the needs of families in the development of communication systems. According to the authors, ASHA goes fur- ther by endorsing the inclusion of families

on the interdisciplinary evaluation team. Positive parent-child relationships are viewed by these two professional organiza- tions as an important outcome of therapy with the child.

Beyond the conceptual, empirical, and legal arguments for parent inclusion lie the practical realities that parents serve as long-term advocates and supports to their son or daughter. Because team member- ship is subject to change on a frequent basis, parents provide a source of con- tinuity essential for smooth transitions during and after the school years. This continuity becomes critical during the postschool years as young adults become "integrated" into a variety of residential, vocational, and leisure environments.

Without question, parents have influ- enced the course of educational policy in this country more than any other group. While their contributions have been incor- porated and valued at both the state and federal levels, it is ironic that parent in- volvement and inclusion in local program planning remains an area of some concern.

FACTORS AFFECTING PARENT PARTICIPATION

If teams of professionals are to move be- yond compliance to commitment and the meaningful inclusion of parents as equal team members, it will be necessary for all school personnel to recognize those pol- icies and practices that function as barriers to parent inclusion. This section briefly re- views some of the key factors that parents and professionals identify as influences on the quality of home-school relationships. The factors highlighted here are drawn from collaborations between myself and colleagues (Salisbury, 1987; Salisbury & Evans, 1988; Salisbury, Vincent, & Gorrofa, 1987; Salisbury et al., 1990; Vincent et al.,

1990), as well as from studies by others in the fields of special education and related services (e.g., Altheide & Livermore, 1987; Bazyk, 1989; Carney, 1987; Cutler, 1981; Epstein, 1987; Humphry, 1989, Lynch & Stein, 1987; Turnbull & Turnbull, 1986a; Walker, 1989; Warren & Kaiser, 1986). The following examples are not intended to be exhaustive.

Communication

Difficulties often arise when parents and professionals are not able to communicate effectively, either in person or through written correspondence. The two most obvious points of difficulty relate to: 1) what is communicated and, 2) how it is communicated. Communication problems between home and school may arise because of one or more of the following factors:

(1) Communications are not in the parents' primary language (sign or non-English). Clearly, if professionals do not provide translators or bilingual services for both written and personal communications, the likelihood of parent participation will be significantly reduced. When professionals cannot ensure that parents comprehend the information presented, then parents cannot provide either informed consent or effective support to teachers or their children.

(2) Professionals use jargon. Using terms that someone does not understand functionally excludes that person from the conversation. Many excellent recommendations and thoughts become lost when they are obscured by terminology that is foreign not only to parents, but often to other members of the team as well. Using "plain English" enables everyone to be included in the conversation.

(3) Parents may have limitations. If parents have intellectual or physical lim-

itations, they may not be able to comprehend the newsletters, notes, and notices from the school and/or may not be able to respond to inquiries. This point is particularly critical as it relates to the IEP process. In order for consent to be "informed," professionals must ensure that the information in forms and notices associated with the IEP process is fully understood by the parents (Shevin, 1983; Turnbull & Turnbull, 1986b). This may require follow-up telephone calls, face-to-face reviews, and/or alternative versions/modes of imparting important information. It should be noted that many literate and well-educated parents find it difficult to understand the jargon-laden letters from school about their rights and protections in the IEP process. It is imperative that administrators demystify both the proceedings and the material to ensure what Shevin (1983) refers to as "informed participation."

(4) Professionals limit communication to administrative tasks. Research in both general and special education indicates that professionals most often communicate with parents to report academic progress, send home information, and report behavior problems. Parents of children in early intervention classes and primary grades report that professionals share positive information about their child, but the nature and frequency of this sharing, as well as the amount of parent involvement, appears to decline sharply as the child moves through the school grades (Epstein, 1987; Salisbury & Evans, 1988). Parents need to hear what their child is doing well just as much as they need to hear about the problems.

(5) Interpersonal communication skills may be ineffective. Turnbull and Turnbull (1986a) provided a cogent description of nonverbal communication skills and

their effects on parent–professional interactions. (The reader is referred to the chapter in that text for more detailed information.) Conceptually, the words professionals use are only one small piece of the communication interchange. Nonverbal actions and the paralinguistic features (tone, emphasis, timing) of what is said are equally important in communication with parents and other team members. The sum of both verbal and nonverbal elements of the message can facilitate or hinder contributions from others.

Parents may be ineffective in getting their messages across to professionals for a variety of reasons. For example, parents may be imprecise in their choice of words, making it difficult for others to grasp their message; they may be tense and angry if they perceive their contributions are not valued by others in the group; they may be demanding in their tone and/or actions if their history with professionals has taught them that such behavior was necessary to get appropriate services for their child; or they may be noncommunicative because they are intimidated by the size and composition of the team. However, it is the professionals', rather than the parents', responsibility to ensure that parents are heard empathetically and that they are afforded meaningful participation.

Perceptions, Attitudes, and Values

How team members perceive themselves and each other, the attitudes they bring to the team meeting, and their own personal and professional value systems all play an important role in interpersonal interactions. Consequently, if we attempt to foster opportunities for meaningful parent and family inclusion in the educational process, it will be important for all members of the team to be aware of how these factors affect both the process and the outcomes of the interactions. The following are some of the key "blocks" to effective interactions with parents and other family members.

Insensitivity to Differences Among Families It is important for professionals to understand how families differ and what the implications of these unique characteristics are for home-school relationships. Families differ in membership, structure, ideology, culture, beliefs/values, and resources. Recognition of these unique qualities is a necessary prerequisite to effective inclusion of parents as team members. The demographics of America's families are changing, which, in turn, can affect the involvement of parents in the school context (Vincent & Salisbury, 1988). Professionals can no longer assume that every family is headed by two parents, that English is the primary language, that school is the highest priority for families, or that the child's parents are necessarily the decision makers in the family unit. The family's cultural beliefs will similarly affect their views of education and the manner in which they choose to participate in the educational process. Additionally, it is important to recognize that families' resources are different and they will mobilize their resources to address *what they perceive* to be the most important priorities first (Dunst et al., 1988; Geismar, 1971). Parents will act to stabilize and meet the family's needs for survival before they will concern themselves with school-valued agendas (Epstein, 1987). Because the structure, resources, and functions within a family change over time, programs need to accommodate to these changes and create options that are both flexible and responsive to the changing priorities and needs of children and their families. Extensive discussion of family characteristics is beyond the scope of this chapter. The reader is referred to the works of Turnbull, Dunst, Bailey, and/or Vincent for additional information on this topic.

Parents Viewed as Adversaries Rather Than Partners   Our perceptions of others are affected by our experiences, values, and beliefs. When the values and priorities of professionals conflict with those of parents, tensions may surface and effective communication becomes difficult. When the goals of professionals do not apparently match those of parents, some professionals move to judge the parents as somehow less effective or caring. It is counterproductive to the development of a collaborative relationship to assume that, because there is a difference of opinion, parents do not have the best interests of their child at heart. The goals of collaboration are better served by trying to understand what motivates parents to respond as they do and how professionals can work effectively with parents to identify the information necessary to address mutually valued goals and priorities.

Parents Viewed as Less Observant, Perceptive, or Intelligent Than Professionals   There is a critical need to "elevate" the status of parents in the eyes of professionals. Research by Gilliam and Coleman (1981), coupled with observations of professionals in the field (i.e., clinical wisdom), highlights the fact that many administrators and practitioners do not value the input of parents in the planning process. Examples include completing the IEP prior to the meeting, failing to provide strategies so that parents can participate, making condescending or judgmental statements when parents do make contributions, and displaying an "aura" of preeminent professional knowledge. Each serves as a deterrent to parent participation in the educational process. Data from

research by Bricker and others indicate that parents are accurate assessors of their child's abilities and that their contributions can be extremely valuable in the program planning process (e.g., Bricker & Squires, 1989).

Parents' Priorities and Expectations Not Matching Those of Professionals   Priorities and expectations surface at different points in the parent-professional relationship. The personal needs of the parent, child, and/or family may displace or reduce the parents' involvement in school activities. Parents must allocate finite time and energy in ways they feel best meet individual and family needs. Parents' capacity for involvement fluctuates over time and is best addressed by the development of a flexible array of program options.

The notion of creating an array of program options for parent involvement is not new, but its importance cannot be overemphasized (MacMillan & Turnbull, 1983). Parents, not professionals, must be the ones to choose whether, how often, and in what capacity they will be involved in their child's program. The fact that the law requires that parents be afforded the opportunity to be actively involved in the decision-making process does not mean that parents must be actively involved. Ultimately, parents must make the decision about involvement. Schools and programs are responsible for ensuring that the decision is an informed one.

Parents may hold markedly different views about the nature of their involvement in the educational process. Some may wish only to receive the school newsletter, others may choose to attend occasional meetings at school, and still others may wish to serve as officers in the parent–teacher organization or as members of the school board. There is growing concern in the field of special education that parent participation is being viewed as an obligation, rather than a right (Allen & Hudd, 1987). We must remember that parents have the right to decide what is most important for them, their child, and their family. Parents may decide on minimal levels of involvement. As long as this choice is an informed one, professionals should respect whatever decision parents make. At the same time, professionals need to recognize that needs and priorities change over time and parents may elect different levels and types of involvement at different points in their child's life. Schools therefore have an obligation to promote the inclusion of parents and families on a continuing basis by offering a range of flexible involvement options throughout the school years.

How professionals and parents view their respective roles and responsibilities will directly affect the decision-making process and its outcomes for the team. Specifically, if parents see their role as primarily parents, family providers, and family "stabilizers," whereas professionals see parents as teachers or therapists of their children or more active participants in school-sponsored activities, then there is a mismatch in the respective "pictures." In such cases teams must then discuss priorities and expectations. Because decisions are needed throughout every phase of the child's education, parents can, and should, be afforded the opportunity for participation at all points throughout the educational process. Other chapters in this book describe specific opportunities and strategies for involving parents.

Finally, while parents and professionals frequently agree on the needs of children with disabilities, they may, from time to time, differ in their goals or expectations for the child. There are at least two types of disagreements I have seen emerge over

time. The first involves *conflicting timelines.* For example, parents may propose a goal that they see as attainable in the short run, one that would promote more positive interactions or reduce caregiving responsibilities (e.g., intelligible communication or independent toileting). Professionals on the team may concur that such goals are desirable, but may propose supporting them as long-term, rather than short-term, goals. The reluctance of professionals to identify these goals as short term may reflect: 1) a hesitation to commit to something they are not sure they can achieve given the limits of therapeutic or instructional intervention, 2) a different appraisal of the child's capabilities, and/or 3) a different set of instructional priorities for the child. Parents and professionals should be encouraged to share their differing perspectives and work toward consensus.

A second type of disagreement can emerge when parents place a priority on a goal that professionals see as minimally related to the child's educational program. Such disagreements arise because of *discrepant agendas.* For example, the family may express an interest in having a child with significant speech and language difficulties learn the family's native language, whereas professionals may place a priority on production of four-word utterances that incorporate proper syntax. Family-valued goals, while perhaps not immediately related to the child's assessed needs, must be given consideration in the development of the IEP/IFSP. "School-valued, school generated" goals may or may not be important to the family. When they are not, professionals should not be surprised at overt or covert lack of commitment or follow-through from families (Dunst et al., 1988). To the extent that parents are provided meaningful vehicles for input into the development of program activities (both instructional and noninstructional), there will be an increased probability that the content will be socially and educationally valid, and that implementation will be supported by family members.

Professional Constraints Professionals may experience both professional and logistical constraints that affect their ability to be effective team members. They may feel pressured to "have all the answers" when they do not. Since many children with disabilities present complex diagnostic and educational challenges for professionals, it is neither realistic nor appropriate to expect that one discipline will possess all the information necessary to assess and remediate a child's learning difficulties. In addition, to take such a myopic view can convey competitiveness, "turf protection," and/or individualistic agendas. These messages are counterproductive to a cooperative team process and implicitly constrain opportunities for collaboration with other members of the team.

Professionals may also experience time constraints. Some professionals belong to several teams, or serve on one team that has responsibility for students in many buildings. Consequently, it is difficult to be in several places at one time and relate effectively to individuals in each of those settings in which contact is episodic. Similarly, the ability to organize and manage the scheduling, service delivery, and evaluation elements across teams or sites can make teamwork itself a significant stressor for professionals. Thus, it is important for professionals to be aware that role and time constraints can affect their attitudes, perceptions, and interactions with others.

Logistical Difficulties

Parent attendance at team meetings will be affected by availability of child care and transportation, as well as scheduling of the IEP meeting. For example, if a mother cannot find or afford child care during the day and must bring small children along to a meeting, she may consider the effort too great compared to the meager amount of input she is given in the decision-making process. If, however, she knew that there would be child care provided at the school and that her input was sought and valued, she might reconsider the amount of time and effort that would be involved to get herself and her young children to the meeting. Each of these logistical factors are described in greater detail by Turnbull and Turnbull (1986a). Similarly, the extent to which fathers participate will be affected by these and other logistical factors (Vadasy, 1986).

Parent involvement is also affected by the dynamics of the team meeting—that is, how it is conducted and who is in attendance. Specifically, if the meeting is set in a formal conference room with the parents seated opposite a table of professionals, the parents will likely be intimidated and reluctant to contribute. If the process at the meeting involves a "round-robin" sharing of formal assessment results rather than an informal discussion of expectations and needed supports, the parents are also less likely to contribute actively to the discussion. This process is exacerbated by the number of professionals attending the meeting. Thus, by taking the perspective of the parents, it is easy to understand their reluctance to attend, much less contribute to, a meeting where they perceive themselves as "outnumbered" by a plethora of professionals. Finally, if the program planning meeting is one of 10 for the day, scheduled for 20 minutes each, it is likely that parents will sense that the process is *pro forma* and that their "participation" is merely required to rubber stamp the planning document. It is important that professionals realize the impact of such factors, singly or in combination, on the nature of their relationships with parents and families.

BEYOND PARTICIPATION . . . TOWARD INCLUSION AND COLLABORATION

If parents and family members are truly thought of as equals on the transdisciplinary team, then our actions toward them should be the *same* as those toward our professional colleagues. But are they? If we use the research literature on parent participation as a source of exemplars, and reflect on the way we, as professionals, typically interact with our colleagues (see Table 3.1), our differential treatment of parents as team members becomes graphically apparent. Because these examples are drawn from the literature on preschool and

school-age students, generalization to the birth to 24-month age range (IFSP team situations) may not be appropriate. For many professionals, however, this exercise helps illustrate areas in which current practices do not foster inclusive team relationships.

Programs based upon a belief of inclusion go beyond the invitation to parents for "participation" in mandated activities such as IFSP or IEP meetings. Rather, inclusive schools and teams commit themselves to the development of collaborative home-school relationships that are longitudinal in nature, allow for fluctuating and flexible interactions across the school years, and respect the unique qualities and abilities of each participant and their contributions to the team process.

Based upon the literature and constructs described in the preceding sections of this chapter, it is now possible to generate a preliminary list of promising practices to

Table 3.1 Differential interactions with colleagues and parents

With my colleagues, I . . .	With parents, I frequently . . .
Take no action without first soliciting their input.	Complete the IEP before they arrive.
Value and respect their comments.	Am skeptical of their motivations and judgmental in my perceptions.
Schedule meetings to fit their commitments.	Notify them about when and where the meeting will be held.
Communicate regularly on progress and problems.	Notify them only when there are problems.
Accept their judgments about how much they need to be involved.	Question their commitment to their child when they do not attend meetings/events.
Collaboratively identify skills and activities to be worked on at school.	Inform them of the tasks they need to follow through on at home.
Suggest activities that are important for school or the community.	Recommend they reinforce skills that are important for school.
Reach consensus when there are differing opinions.	Note their concerns, but then move on.

guide the actions of transdisciplinary teams as they move toward the development of collaborative relationships with parents and the inclusion of parents as full and equal team members. These principles appear in Table 3.2.

Program planning and policy development are greatly enhanced when professionals have a clear idea of the outcomes or goals they wish to achieve. Program quality is directly affected by the extent to which the program's beliefs, knowledge base, and actions are internally consistent and supportive of the attainment of such outcomes (Salisbury, 1991). The first section of this chapter provided a rationale for the inclusion of parents and families in the educational context (outcomes). These outcomes are summarized in Table 3.2. The second section provided a review of philosophical and conceptual literatures (beliefs), as well as research on the status of parent involvement (knowledge). This final section of this chapter offers preliminary recommendations for promising practices (actions) that are linked to the attainment of positive parent inclusion outcomes. The principles listed in Table 3.2 will be used here as a means of organizing the information on strategies for achieving optimal inclusion of parents and family members in the educational context.

Determination of Parent/Family Involvement in the Child's Educational Program

Teams need to adopt strategies and procedures for obtaining information from families about their desired involvement. Many programs and schools use checklists, while others conduct home visits or conferences. Regardless of the form or process used to gather information, it is important for educational programs to obtain at least the following information:

1. Desired frequency of contact with program/school
2. Preferred type of contact from school (written, phone, personal)
3. Preferred location of meetings, if necessary, as well as child care and transportation needs
4. Preferred type of involvement with school/program

Those programs opting for the checklist approach will find several examples in the literature (e.g., Ford et al., 1989; Snell, 1987; Turnbull & Turnbull, 1986a). Figures 3.1 and 3.2 provide examples of such checklists.

Based upon my experience, I recommend sending such inquiries home after staff have determined whether families of

Table 3.2 Principles of inclusionary practices

1. Each parent/family is given the opportunity to identify how and to what degree they wish to become involved in their child's educational program.

2. Schools develop a continuum of strategies and options for enhancing the inclusion of parents/families in the educational context.

3. Parents are treated as equal members of teams.

4. Schools support and promote the self-sufficiency and development of families through integrated and normalized resources.

What Does Your Family Consider Important About School Contacts?

Parents have different ideas about the kinds and amounts of information they want to get from school about their child. The list below contains different ways you and your child's teacher might communicate with each other. Please circle the number to the right of the phrase to show how important each type of contact is to you.

		NA	not at all					extremely	RANK	COMMENTS
1	Written notes	0	1	2	3	4	5	⑥	_3_	
2.	School newsletters	0	1	2	③	4	5	6	___	
3.	Parent/teacher conferences or individualized education program (IEP) meetings.	0	1	2	3	4	5	⑥	_2_	
4.	Open house	0	1	②	3	4	5	6	___	
5.	Informal contacts	0	1	2	3	4	⑤	6	_1_	*Phone call*
6.	Parent / Teacher Organization (PTO) meetings	0	1	2	③	4	5	6	___	
7.	Classroom observation	0	1	2	3	④	5	6	___	
8.	Other, please specify: _____	0	1	2	3	4	5	6	___	

Using the above list, place the numbers 1, 2 or 3 next to the three most important ways of communicating between your family and your child's teacher.

A. How much contact do you want to have with your child's teacher after your child begins public school?
✔Daily ___Once a week ___Once a month
___Once a semester ___Other (specify)

B. Would you prefer
___to initiate most of the contacts with your child's teacher?
___the teacher to initiate contacts with you?
✔or both?

Figure 3.1. Sample checklist on school communication (source unknown).

the children they serve have any unique needs (e.g., English not primary language; child does not live with parents; parent or guardian has limited reading ability). The information detailed in such a survey will be most useful for long-range planning when it is gathered at the start of the school year. I also recommend that the survey document be in a checklist format and limited to one page. While there are admit-

What Is Important for Your Child To Learn at School?

Parents want their child to go to a classroom where he or she will make progress. Children can make progress in different areas, and some areas may be more important than others. The list below contains different areas your child may progress in next year. Please circle the number to the right of the phrase to show how important it is for your child to progress in this area next year.

		NA	not at all					extremely	RANK
1.	Learn basic concepts such as colors, numbers, shapes, etc.	0	1	2	(3)	4	5	6	___
2.	Learn prereading and reading skills such as letters.	0	1	2	3	(4)	5	6	___
3.	Learn to use a pencil and scissors.	0	1	(2)	3	4	5	6	___
4.	Learn to listen and follow directions.	0	1	2	3	4	(5)	6	___
5.	Learn to share and play with other children.	0	1	2	3	4	5	(6)	*1*
6.	Learn to be creative.	0	1	2	(3)	4	5	6	___
7.	Learn more communication skills.	0	1	2	3	4	5	(6)	*3*
8.	Learn confidence and independence.	0	1	2	3	4	(5)	6	___
9.	Learn to work independently.	0	1	2	3	4	(5)	6	___
10.	Learn to climb, run, and jump.	0	(1)	2	3	4	5	6	___
11.	Learn self-care skills such as toileting, dressing, feeding.	0	1	2	3	4	5	(6)	*2*
12.	Learn to follow classroom rules and routines.	0	1	2	3	(4)	5	6	___

Using the above list, place the numbers 1, 2, and 3 next to the three most important areas for your child to progress in next year.

Figure 3.2.   Sample checklist on child learning (source unknown).

tedly drawbacks to forced-choice formats, I have found that open-ended questions frequently do not yield information that is specific enough for designing program options.

The wording on checklists is very important since it conveys attitudes about parents. Using a gradient from "prefer not to be involved at this time" to "would like to be directly involved" conveys a more positive array of choices to parents than does "No involvement" to "Actively involved." I also recommend that parents be encouraged to send the checklists back in their child's backpack or lunchbox as a means of increasing the rate of return.

Programs opting for conference-based information gathering will need to plan for a greater investment of time. That is, while this approach offers a more personal and richer base of information, it also requires considerably more time and energy on the part of staff. For many families, such an approach is more appealing and practical. Consequently, staff must be clear about their objectives prior to initiating contact with the family.

Each approach has advantages and disadvantages that must be balanced against the resources of the program, the needs of the child and family, and the goals toward which all participants are working. Many programs incorporate several methods of information gathering, tailoring each to the outcomes they wish to achieve. Regardless of the method selected, professionals must remain cognizant of how such strategies will affect the family and how the nature of the family will influence the validity of the survey results.

Development of Strategies and Options for Inclusion of Parents/ Families in Educational Context

It is very important that parent inclusion be defined more broadly than involvement in the IEP or IFSP meeting. Only recently have we begun to accumulate empirically based information about the scope of parents' involvement outside of the conference situation (e.g., Epstein, 1987; Salisbury & Evans, 1988). This research indicates that parents are "involved" more frequently than professionals believed in activities such as reading to their children, checking their children's homework, and discussing events at school.

However, even these "pictures" of parent involvement are traditional and more constrained than they need to be. In reality, the child's educational context encompasses home, school, and community. Such a conceptualization requires that parent, child, and family priorities and interests be explored relative to each envi-

ronment. Each environment becomes an extension of the school and a viable location for intervention with or on behalf of the child. Regardless of where instruction occurs, children emerge as the prime benefactors when parents and professionals work together during assessment, program design, teaching, and evaluation.

The quality of this partnership will rest, in large part, on the value that schools place on parent involvement. One index of such an investment is the nature and frequency of contact between parents and teachers. There is no substitute for personal contact between schools and families. Parents report a preference for more frequent, but informal, contact with professionals (Turnbull & Turnbull, 1986a). I have found that having one or two team members cultivate a relationship with parents over a period of time sends a strong message that each partner (parent and professional) cares about the child and the family. I find, for example, that "shuttle notebooks," weekly newsletters, "minute-a-day" phone calls, "good news notes," and home and class visits foster an important connectedness between home and school.

Cervone and O'Leary (1982) offered a matrix of program options. The unique feature of their model is that both the horizontal and the vertical axes reflect a gradient of opportunities for parent involvement. Each axis moves from greater to lesser degrees of personal time investment on the part of the parents. Their conceptual framework for parent involvement is presented in Figure 3.3. While some would take issue with the connotations of their gradient labels, Cervone and O'Leary's matrix is pertinent to a broader definition of school boundaries in that it also includes reference to community and home environments. As an example of involvement

	Progress Reporting	Special Events	Parent Education	Parents Teaching
Parents as Passive Participants	Good News Notes	Open House	Welcoming Committee	
	60 Second Phone Calls	Audiovisual Presentations	Parent Bulletin Board	
	Star of the Week	Potluck Supper	Information on Home & Weekend Activities	
	Newsletter	Father's/Mother's/ Sibling's Day	Information on Community Resources	
		Spring Fling	Lending Library (Book, Toy, Record)	Make and Take Workshop
		End-of-the-Year Picnic	Classroom Observations	Teachable Moments
	Call-in Times	The Gym Show	Workshops on Topics of Interest to Parents	Home Worksheets
	Parent-Teacher Conferences		A Course for Parents	Parents Teaching in the Classroom
Parents as Active Participants	Home-School Notebooks		Parent-to-Parent Meetings	Parent Objectives in the IEP
	(Parent Leaders)	(Parent Leaders)	(Parent Leaders)	(Parent Leaders)

Parents as Passive Participants	——————————————————————→	Parents as Active Participants

Figure 3.3. Parent involvement continuum. (From Cervone, B.T., & O'Leary, K. [1982]. A conceptual framework for parent involvement. *Educational Leadership, 40*[2], 48–49; reprinted by permission of the Association for Supervision and Curriculum Development. Copyright © 1982 by ASCD. All rights reserved.)

options, their model offers readers a basis for adopting or adapting the content to suit their program's unique needs.

Professionals often find that parents are more willing to become involved in school-sponsored activities when such events are family focused rather than exclusively parent centered. Specifically, di-

dactic presentations on topics of presumed or expressed interest to parents (e.g., parents' rights, behavior management, advocacy, transition planning) draw smaller, more proactive groups of parents. These activities clearly have merit and should be offered as options for parents and families. In contrast, family-focused activities such as picnics, open houses, potlucks, holiday craft workshops, and "make-and-take" toy workshops frequently draw more of a cross section of families to the school. While these latter activities are more labor intensive for staff, the effort necessary to orchestrate the event should be weighed against the potential gains for developing family connectedness to the program. As mentioned earlier, programs that offer child care and transportation often see greater levels of parent attendance.

Rainforth and Salisbury (1988) described a practical strategy for assessing each family's typical daily routine as a basis for decision making and intervention in the home. This strategy involves asking a parent(s) to chart the typical flow of family activities during the week, making particular note of what their child with special needs is doing during those times. They are then asked to identify opportunities within that schedule when they normally interact with their child. Finally, they are asked to judge the suitability of these interactions as potential teaching times. Parent-identified times are used as the basis for discussing the feasibility of embedding goals/objectives into naturally occurring family routines. Embedding home programming recommendations into existing family daily routines enables target skills to be taught or reinforced on a consistent basis with minimal inconvenience to the family. The daily routine information can also be used as a basis for parent contributions during the IEP meeting, as well as a tool for identifying appropriate times and situations into which intervention goals can be embedded.

In a similar paper, Brinckerhoff and Vincent (1986) described the application of the same "family daily routine" strategy to the IEP context as a vehicle for enhancing meaningful parent contributions. Their data indicate that parent contributions increased significantly during IEP meetings after introduction of the daily routine strategy. These papers highlight one strategy through which parents are afforded equal status as contributing team members.

Early intervention programs, particularly those serving infants and toddlers, are embracing a family-focused approach to assessment and intervention. Structured interviews described by Bailey and colleagues (1986), Dunst and coworkers (1988), and Mahoney, O'Sullivan, and Dennebaum (1990) are particularly useful for obtaining in-depth information from parents about their family. While there are conceptual differences among these approaches, each emphasizes the importance of assessing the expectations, resources, and interests of families prior to the development of child and family interventions.

If staff experience difficulties operationalizing the suggestions mentioned above, it will be important to determine whether the problems are interpersonal, systemic, and/or instructional in nature. Strategies will need to be developed for addressing "blocks" to implementation and evaluating the outcomes of their efforts. While parents can be contributors to group process and decision-making difficulties, many of the "blocks" can be addressed by altering the attitudes, beliefs, and actions of the professionals on the team. It is incumbent upon the professionals, not the parents, to assume a leadership role in promoting the inclusionary effort.

There may be times when the expressed or assessed needs of the parent and family are so great that they interfere with the child's attendance at school, development, and/or physical well-being. These issues may surface in multiproblem families where there is a complex interplay among capabilities, resources, and economics. Balancing professional roles with responsibilities to the child and the family can be difficult. Recently described case management models suggest identifying one member of the team as the individual whose role it is to establish linkages among nonschool agencies and resources and the family. Such a strategy limits the number of professionals calling on the family and offers greater potential for interagency coordination.

Professionals on teams serving school-age students will likely devote the greatest proportion of their time to direct services of the child at school, with indirect assistance provided to the child and family in the home. Infant and preschool teams are more likely to play a more direct role in teaching the child both at home and at school, while providing both direct and indirect support to the family. Interagency, as well as cross-disciplinary, collaboration will be important in the development of successful services at both age ranges. To the maximum extent possible, teams should invest decision-making responsibilities with the family and provide supportive guidance to parents/families in their efforts to function both adaptively and independently (Dunst et al., 1988; Kaiser & Hemmeter, 1989).

Treatment of Parents as Equal Team Members

Effective teams are typically those that employ creative problem-solving techniques and cooperative group process skills (e.g., Johnson & Johnson, 1986; Johnson, Johnson, Holubec, & Roy, 1984). There are four elements to cooperative learning (positive interdependence, individual accountability, collaborative skills, and group processing) that have direct implications for how we treat parents as team members. The ability of the team to work effectively (cooperatively and collaboratively) will require leadership, trust, communication, conflict management, and a commitment to work toward mutually agreed upon goals.

Johnson and coworkers (1984) suggested that skillful group members are made, not born. It is unrealistic to expect teams to function effectively if they lack knowledge and skills about the group process and collaboration. Teams, as units, and individual members are encouraged to identify their skills in each of the component areas mentioned above and develop activities to address deficiencies. Mentorships, in-service training, directed reading, continuing education coursework, and in vivo modeling by more experienced colleagues or parents are some of the more popular formal strategies for obtaining both informational and performance competence in this area. Supportive feedback from teammates is an essential, informal strategy that can significantly affect the cohesion of the team.

Clearly group process and collaborative team skills are but two of the elements needed to work effectively as a team. As indicated earlier in this chapter, attitudes, values, and beliefs also play an important role in how professionals and parents interact. Kaiser and Hemmeter (1989) provide a valuable framework for examining the relationship of values to educational decision making. In particular, they ask four questions related to interventions with children and families: "Does the intervention enhance community? Does the intervention strengthen the family? Does the intervention enable parents to do their jobs well? Does the intervention enhance individual development and protect the rights of individual family members?" (p. 78). The necessity of including parents' in the decision-making process is obvious in light of such questions. In a preliminary attempt to operationalize the four values-based elements, Kaiser and Hemmeter offered an 18-item checklist that addresses intervention plans and how they might affect the family.

Kroth (1978) stressed the importance of values clarification and assessment as a necessary tandem to conferencing skills. In related work, he recommended several resources for professionals wishing to assess their own and others' values (Kroth & Simpson, 1977; see Simon, Howe, & Kirschenbaum, 1972, for techniques).

Support and Promotion of Self-Sufficiency and Development of Families Through Integrated and Normalized Resources

Children do not exist in a vacuum; consequently, how a family functions affects children's performance at school. If schools expect children to do well, they must also promote the well-being of families. Schools and professionals can respond proactively by acting in ways that foster the self-sufficiency and independence of families. Actions that devalue single parents, those whose primary language is not English, those whose child-rearing beliefs are different from the beliefs of the majority, and those whose jobs compete for time with their family, are counterproductive to the development of collaborative home-school relationships.

Schools have an obligation to extend their educational expertise to families as well as to children. This can mean that team members function in the community in a variety of roles. For example, members of transdisciplinary teams may serve as consultant teachers/therapists to integrated community-based day care and pre-school programs (Tempelman, Fredericks, & Udell, 1989). With proper supports and training, generic agencies can be adapted to appropriately meet the needs of students with disabilities. In the process, parents are afforded the opportunity for more normalized resources and less dependence upon specialized, segregated services (Salisbury, 1986).

If schools view their boundaries broadly as encompassing home, school, and community environments, then instruction can and should occur in a variety of settings with or on behalf of the child. When families request support or information concerning their child at home, it is incumbent upon therapists and educators to respond with practical, minimally invasive recommendations in a timely manner. For example, parents may express frustration with their child's behavior in the home and/or in the community. Baker and Brightman's (1989) latest revision of *Steps to Independence* offers parents and teachers sound, practical advice for teaching specific social and self-help skills to children with disabilities at home. It is an excellent resource that can also serve as a text in in-service training and parent education workshops.

Rich's (1988) text, *MegaSkills*, is based on the premise that parents play a critical role in supporting their child's learning at school and at home. The book is a powerful compendium of concrete, practical strategies for promoting the values, attitudes, and behaviors that determine success in and out of school. "Tips" for integrating important life skills (many of which are "school skills") into activities that naturally occur in the home are provided for children at various age ranges. Additional chapters address special issues confronting the home-school partnership. Professionals will find many creative suggestions that should be of value in their work with parents and families.

SUMMARY

Parent inclusion on transdisciplinary teams is necessary for the development of a high-quality educational program for individual students. We must, however, be cautious about narrowly defining the roles and opportunities for parents and family members. There are many ways in which families support the learning needs of children, many of which do not require regular or sustained attendance at school. Because families, as well as children, present diverse needs and capacities, it is essential that professionals recognize and account for these differences in the design, development, and implementation of parent involvement opportunities within the educational context. This point becomes particularly salient when inclusion on transdisciplinary teams is at issue. Strategies exist, but their application must be prescriptive to the families we serve. For many, collaborating with parents and family members will require additional training, alterations of historical perceptions, and a commitment to inclusion. Commitment to a collaborative partnership must come first.

Two Sculptors

I dreamed I stood in a studio
And watched two sculptors there,
The clay they used was a young child's mind
And they fashioned it with care.

One was a teacher; the tools she used
Were books, music and art.
One, a parent who worked with a guiding hand
And a gentle, loving heart.

Day after day the teacher toiled
With touch that was deft and sure,
While the parent labored by her side
And polished and smoothed it o'er

And when at last their task was done,
They were proud of what they had wrought;
For the things they had molded into the child
Could neither be sold nor bought

And each agreed he would have failed
If he had worked alone,
The parent and the school,
The teacher and the home.

Author Unknown

REFERENCES

Allen, D.A., & Hudd, S. (1987). Are we professionalizing parents? Weighing the benefits and pitfalls. *Mental Retardation, 25*(3), 133–139.

Altheide, M., & Livermore, J.R. (1987). Supporting families of augmentative communication users. *Physical and Occupational Therapy in Pediatrics, 7*(2), 95–106.

American Occupational Therapy Association. (1989). *Guidelines for occupational therapy services in early intervention and preschool services.* Rockville, MD: Author.

Bailey, D.B., Simeonsson, R.J., Winton, P.J., Huntington, G.S., Comfort, M., Isbell, P., O'Donnell, K.J., & Helm, J.M. (1986). Family-focused intervention: A functional model for planning, implementing, and evaluating individualized family services on early intervention. *Journal of the Division for Early Childhood, 10,* 156–171.

Baker, B.L., & Brightman, A.J. (1989). *Steps to independence: A skills training guide for parents and teachers of children with special needs* (2nd ed.). Baltimore: Paul H. Brookes Publishing Co.

Barnard, K.E., & Kelly, J.F. (1990). Assessment of parent-child interaction. In S.J. Meisels & J.P. Shonkoff (Eds.), *Handbook of early intervention* (pp.278–302). New York: Cambridge University Press.

Bazyk, S. (1989). Changes in attitudes and beliefs regarding parent participation and home programs: An update. *American Journal of Occupational Therapy, 43*(11), 723–728.

Beckman, P. (1984). Perceptions of young children with handicaps: A comparison of mothers and program staff. *Mental Retardation, 22,* 176–181.

Bricker, D.D., & Cripe, J. (1989). Activity based intervention. In D.D. Bricker (Ed.), *Early intervention for at-risk and handicapped infants, toddlers, and preschool children* (pp. 251–274). Palo Alto, CA: VORT.

Bricker, D.D., & Squires, J. (1989). The effectiveness of parental screening of at-risk infants: The infant monitoring questionnaires. *Topics in Early Childhood Special Education, 9*(3), 67–85.

Bricker, D.D., & Veltman, M. (1990). Early intervention programs: Child focused approaches. In S.J. Meisels & J.P. Shonkoff (Eds.), *Handbook of early intervention* (pp. 373–399). New York: Cambridge University Press.

Brinckerhoff, J.L., & Vincent, L.J. (1986). Increasing parental decision making at the individualized educational program meeting. *Journal of the Division for Early Childhood, 11*(1), 46–50.

Bronfenbrenner, U. (1979). *The ecology of human development: Experiments by nature and design.* Cambridge: Harvard University Press.

Brown, L., Nietupski, J., & Hamre-Nietupski, S. (1976). The criterion of ultimate functioning and public school services for severely handicapped students. In M.A. Thomas (Ed.), *Hey, don't forget about me: Education's investment in the severely, profoundly, and multiply handicapped* (pp. 197–209). Reston, VA: Council for Exceptional Children.

Campbell, P.H. (1987). The integrated programming team: An approach for coordinating professionals of various disciplines in programs for students with severe and multiple handicaps. *Journal of The Association for Persons with Severe Handicaps, 12*(2), 107–116.

Carney, I.H. (1987). Working with families. In F.P. Orelove & D. Sobsey, *Educating children with multiple disabilities: A transdisciplinary approach* (pp. 315–338). Baltimore: Paul H. Brookes Publishing Co.

Cervone, B.T., & O'Leary, K. (1982). A conceptual framework for parent involvement. *Educational Leadership, 40*(2), 48–49.

Cutler, B.C. (1981). *Unraveling the special education maze.* Champaign, IL: Research Press.

Dunst, C.J., Trivette, C.M., & Deal, A.G. (1988). *Enabling and empowering families: Principles and guidelines for practice.* Cambridge, MA: Brookline Books.

Epstein, J. (1987). Parent involvement: What research says to administrators. *Education and Urban Society, 19*(2), 119–136.

Ford, A., Schnorr, R., Meyer, L., Davern, L., Black, J., & Dempsey, P. (Eds.). (1989). *The Syracuse community referenced curriculum guide for students with moderate and severe disabilities.* Baltimore: Paul H. Brookes Publishing Co.

Geismar, L. (1971). *Family and community functioning: A manual of measurement for social work practice and policy.* Metuchen, NJ: Scarecrow Press.

Gilliam, J.E., & Coleman, M.C. (1981). Who influences IEP committee decisions? *Exceptional Children, 47,* 642–644.

Goldstein, S., Strickland, B., Turnbull, A.P., & Curry, L. (1980). An observational analysis of the IEP conference. *Exceptional Children, 46*(4), 278–286.

Gradel, K., Thompson, M.S., & Sheehan, R. (1981). Parental and professional agreement in early childhood assessment. *Topics in Early Childhood Special Education, 1,* 31–39.

Greenspan, S.I. (1990). Comprehensive clinical approaches to infants and their families: Psychodynamic and developmental perspectives. In S.J. Meisels & J.P. Shonkoff (Eds.), *Handbook of early intervention* (pp. 150–172). New York: Cambridge University Press.

Greenspan, S., & Budd, K.S. (1986). Research on mentally retarded parents. In J. Gallagher & P. Vietze (Eds.), *Families of handicapped persons: Research, programs, and policy issues* (pp. 115–128). Baltimore: Paul H. Brookes Publishing Co.

Guralnick, M. (1989). Recent developments in early intervention efficacy research: Implications for family involvement in PL 99-457. *Topics in Early Childhood Special Education, 9*(3), 1–17.

Humphry, R. (1989). Early intervention and the influence of the occupational therapist on the parent-child relationship. *American Journal of Occupational Therapy, 43*(11), 738–742.

Johnson, D.W., & Johnson, R.T. (1986). Mainstreaming and cooperative learning strategies. *Exceptional Children, 52*(6), 553–561.

Johnson, D.W., Johnson, R., Holubec, E., & Roy, P. (1984). *Circles of learning.* Alexandria, VA:

The Association for Supervision and Curriculum Development.

Kaiser, A.P., & Hemmeter, M.L. (1989). Value-based approaches to family intervention. *Topics in Early Childhood Special Education, 89*(4), 72–86.

Kroth, R. (1978). Parents as powerful and necessary allies. *Teaching Exceptional Children, 10*(3), 88–90.

Kroth, R., & Simpson, R. (1977). *Parent conferences as a teaching strategy.* Denver: Love Publishing Co.

Lucca, J.A., & Settles, B.H. (1981). Effects of children's disabilities on parental time use. *Physical Therapy, 61*(2), 196–201.

Lynch, E.W., & Stein, R.C. (1987). Parent participation by ethnicity: A comparison of Hispanic, Black, and Anglo families. *Exceptional Children, 54*(2), 105–111.

MacDonald, T.D., & Gillette, Y. (1986). Communicating with persons with severe handicaps: Roles of parents and professionals. *Journal of The Association for Persons with Severe Handicaps, 11*(4), 255–265.

MacMillan, D.L., & Turnbull, A.P. (1983). Parent involvement with special education: Respecting individual preferences. *Education and Training of the Mentally Retarded, 18*(1), 4–9.

Mahoney, G., O'Sullivan, P., & Dennebaum, J. (1990). Maternal perceptions of early intervention services: A scale for assessing family focused intervention. *Topics in Early Childhood Special Education, 10*(1), 1–15.

Mahoney, G., & Powell, A. (1988). Modifying parent-child interactions: Enhancing the development of handicapped infants. *Journal of Special Education, 22*, 82–96.

Mink, I.T. (1986). Classification of families with mentally retarded children. In J. Gallagher & P. Vietze (Eds.), *Families of handicapped persons: Research, programs, and policy issues.* (pp. 25–44). Baltimore: Paul H. Brookes Publishing Co.

Mink, I.T., Nihara, K., & Meyers, C.E. (1983). Taxonomy of family life styles I: Homes with TMR children. *American Journal of Mental Deficiency, 87*(5), 484–497.

Minuchin, S. (1974). *Families and family therapy.* Cambridge: Harvard University Press.

Morgan, D.P., & Rhode, G. (1983). Teachers' attitudes toward IEPs: A two year follow-up. *Exceptional Children, 50*(1), 64–67.

Nihara, K., Mink, I.T., & Meyers, C.E. (1981). Relationship between home environment and school adjustment of TMR children. *American Journal of Mental Deficiency, 86*(1), 8–15.

Powell, D.R. (1989). *Families and early childhood programs.* Research monograph of the National Association for the Education of Young Children. Washington, DC: NAEYC.

Rainforth, B., & Salisbury, C. (1988). Functional home programs: A model for therapists. *Topics in Early Childhood Special Education, 7*(4), 33–45.

Rainforth, B., & York, J. (1987). Integrating related services in community instruction. *Journal of The Association for Persons with Severe Handicaps, 12*(3), 190–198.

Rich, D. (1988). *MegaSkills.* Boston: Houghton-Mifflin.

Salisbury, C. (1986). Generic community services as sources of respite. In C. Salisbury & J. Intagliata (Eds.), *Respite care: Support for persons with developmental disabilities and their families* (pp. 195–216). Baltimore: Paul H. Brookes Publishing Co.

Salisbury, C. (1987). *Parental perceptions of home and school relationships.* Binghamton School Partnership Project Technical Report #1. Binghamton: Center for Education and Social Research, State University of New York at Binghamton.

Salisbury, C. (1991). Mainstreaming during the early childhood years. *Exceptional Children, 58*(2), 146–155.

Salisbury, C., & Evans, J.M. (1988). Comparison of parental involvement in regular and special education. *Journal of The Association for Persons with Severe Handicaps, 13*(4), 268–272.

Salisbury, C., McLean, M., & Vincent, L.J. (1990). *Family participation in communication programming.* Unpublished manuscript, State University of New York, School of Education and Human Development.

Salisbury, C., & Vincent, L.J. (1990). "Criterion of the next environment" and "best practices": Mainstreaming and integration 10 years later. *Topics in Early Childhood Special Education, 10*(2), 78–89.

Salisbury, C., Vincent, L.J., & Gorrofa, S. (1987). *Involvement in the educational process: Perceptions of parents and professionals of dual sensory impaired children.* Unpublished manuscript, State University of New York at Binghamton.

Sameroff, A., & Fiese, B.H. (1990). Transactional regulation and early intervention. In S.J. Meisels & J.P. Shonkoff (Eds.), *Handbook of early intervention* (pp. 119–149). New York: Cambridge University Press.

Scanlon, C.A., Arick, J., & Phelps X. (1981). Participation in the development of the IEP: Parents' perspective. *Exceptional Children*, 47(5), 373–374.

Seitz, S., & Provence, S. (1990). Caregiver-focused models of early intervention. In S.P. Meisels & J.P. Shonkoff (Eds.), *Handbook of early intervention* (pp. 400–427). New York: Cambridge University Press.

Shevin, M. (1983). Meaningful parental involvement in long range educational planning for disabled children. *Education and Training of the Mentally Retarded*, 18(1), 17–21.

Silber, S. (1989). Family influences on early development. *Topics in Early Childhood Special Education*, 8(4), 1–23.

Simeonsson, R.J., & Bailey, D.R. (1990). Family dimensions in early intervention. In S.J. Meisels & J.P. Shonkoff (Eds.), *Handbook of early intervention* (pp. 428–444). New York: Cambridge University Press.

Simon, S.D., Howe, L., & Kirschenbaum, H. (1972). *Values clarification: A handbook of practical strategies for teachers and students.* New York: Hart.

Snell, M. (Ed.). (1987). *Systematic instruction of persons with severe handicaps* (3rd ed.). Columbus, OH: Charles E. Merrill.

Summers, J.A., Behr, S., & Turnbull, A.P. (1989). Positive adaptation and coping strengths of families who have children with disabilities. In G.H.S. Singer & L. K. Irvin (Eds.), *Support for caregiving families: Enabling positive adaptation to disability* (pp. 27–40). Baltimore: Paul H. Brookes Publishing Co.

Tempelman, T.P., Fredericks, H.D., & Udell, T. (1989). Integration of children with moderate and severe handicaps into a day care center. *Journal of Early Intervention*, 13(4), 315–328.

Turnbull, A.P., & Turnbull, H.R. (1986a). *Families, professionals, and exceptionalities.* Columbus, OH: Charles E. Merrill.

Turnbull, A.P., & Turnbull, H.R. (1986b). Stepping back from early intervention: An ethical perspective. *Journal of the Division for Early Childhood*, 10(2), 106–117.

Turnbull, A.P., & Winton, P.J. (1984). Parent involvement policy and practice: Current research and implications for families of young,

severely handicapped children. In J. Blacher (Ed.), *Severely handicapped young children and their families* (pp. 377–397). Orlando: Academic Press.

Tyler, N., & Kogan, K.L. (1972). The social by-products of therapy with young children. *Physical Therapy* 52(5), 500–513.

Vadasy, P.F. (1986). Single mothers: A social phenomenon and population in need. In R.R. Fowell & P.F. Vadasy (Eds.), *Families of handicapped children* (pp. 221–252). Austin, TX: PRO-ED.

Vincent, L.J., Laten, S., Salisbury, C., Brown, P., & Baumgart, D. (1980). Family involvement in the educational processes of severely handicapped students: State of the art and directions for the future. In B. Wilcox & R. York (Eds.), *Quality education for the severely handicapped: The federal investment.* Washington, DC: U.S. Department of Education.

Vincent, L.J., & Salisbury, C. (1988). Changing economic and social influences on family involvement. *Topics in Early Childhood Special Education*, 8, 48–59.

Vincent, L.J., Salisbury, C., Brown, P., Gruenewald, L., & Powers, M. (1980). Program evaluation and curricular development in early childhood special education: Criteria of the next environment. In W. Sailor, B. Wilcox, & L. Brown (Eds.), *Methods of instruction for severely handicapped students* (pp. 303–308). Baltimore: Paul H. Brookes Publishing Co.

Vincent, L.J., Salisbury, C., Laten, S., & Baumgart, D. (1979). *Designing home programs for families with handicapped children.* Unpublished manuscript, University of Wisconsin, Department of Rehabilitation Psychology and Special Education, Madison, WI.

Vincent, L.J., Salisbury, C., Strain, P., McCormick, C., & Tessier, A. (1990). A behavioral-ecological approach to early intervention: Focus on diversity. In S.J. Meisels & J.P. Shonkoff (Eds.), *Handbook of early intervention* (pp. 173–195). New York: Cambridge University Press.

Walker, R. (1989). Strategies for improving parent-professional cooperation. In G. Singer & L. Irvin (Eds.), *Support for caregiving families: Enabling positive adaptation to disability* (pp. 103–119). Baltimore: Paul H. Brookes Publishing Co.

Walsh, S., Campbell, P.H., & McKenna, P. (1988). First year implementation of the federal program for infants and toddlers with handicaps: A view from the states. *Topics in Early Childhood Special Education, 8*(3), 1–22.

Warren, S.A., & Kaiser, A.P. (1986). Incidental language teaching: A critical review. *Journal of Speech and Hearing Disorders, 51,* 291–299.

Winton, P.J., & Bailey, D.B. (1988). The family focused interview: A collaborative mecha-

nism for family assessment and goal setting. *Journal of the Division for Early Childhood, 12*(3), 195–207.

Yoshida, R.K., Fenton, K.S., Kaufman, M.J., & Maxwell, J.P. (1978). Parental involvement in the special education pupil planning process: The school's perspective. *Exceptional Children, 44*(7), 531-534.

II

Designing Individualized Education Programs

T HE NEXT FOUR CHAPTERS, SECTION II OF THE BOOK, DELINEATE STRATEGIES TO DESIGN
individualized education programs (IEPs) in which related services are integral
components. This section of the book focuses on students' programs, including curriculum, assessment, IEPs, and instruction. To help illustrate how the program components
evolve, two students with severe disabilities are introduced here and followed throughout Section II.

Kristen is 5 years old. She lives in a suburban community with her parents and her
7-year-old sister, Julie. Kristen has generalized severe developmental delays and cerebral
palsy with spastic diplegia. Kristen's family describes her as cute and lovable, but a little
stubborn. She enjoys all kinds of activities, especially if her dad helps her do them. Currently, she communicates primarily by vocalizations and gestures (desires by reaching,
negation by pushing away), which sometimes escalate into tantrums. Kristen is starting
to develop speech, and has a vocabulary of about 10 words. She seems to prefer playing
with people, especially adults, rather than toys. Her ability to manipulate objects is
somewhat limited, however, since she uses primarily a palmar grasp. She has just recently started walking. Kristen is graduating from an early childhood special education
program, and will enter a public elementary school in the fall. Her parents have requested that she be placed in a regular kindergarten class at their neighborhood school.
The school district has agreed. Although the preschool team knows many of Kristen's
needs, the professionals on the kindergarten team do not know Kristen so well, and
the kindergarten placement will present new demands and opportunities. Therefore,
Kristen's team will be designing a new program.

Jamal is 17 years old and lives in an urban community. On weekends, he lives with
his mother and sister, Keesha. During the week, he lives in a small group home with two
other young men. Jamal likes the same kinds of things as other youths his age: Nintendo,
MTV, cars and motorcycles, and Coke and french fries. Jamal is labeled profoundly mentally retarded. He has spastic quadriplegia, with slight head control, occasional active
movement with his right arm, and many contractures. He communicates preferences

with his eyes and facial expressions. After attending segregated programs for many years, Jamal entered an integrated educational program 3 years ago. Currently, he attends the public high school in his community, where he is part of the junior class. Jamal's team, including family, friends, teachers, and therapists, have worked together for some time to develop a comprehensive program comprised of activities at school and in the community. Since many components are in place, Jamal's team concentrates on "fine tuning" and preparing Jamal for graduation, with transition to a postsecondary program based largely in the community. The next four chapters describe only two parts of Jamal's program, which illustrate some of the variations and opportunities available at the secondary level. One part of his program builds on learning opportunities in a general education Spanish class, while the second occurs in a community-based work site.

In summary, Chapters 4 through 7 present a collaborative team approach to program development and implementation. Program components will be illustrated through representative aspects of Kristen's program at home and at school and Jamal's program at school and in the community.

4

An Ecological Model of Curriculum
A Natural Context for Therapy

CURRICULA ARE OFTEN CONSTRUED AS commercial packages of activities and materials, used primarily by teachers, with little relevance to other educational service providers. It is more accurate, however, to view a curriculum as a theoretical model, that represents beliefs about the scope and sequence of an appropriate education (Eisner, 1979). This view suggests several reasons that knowledge of curriculum is important for the entire educational team, including therapists. First, the curriculum guides decision making, particularly about selection of student goals and objectives for the individualized education program (IEP). Since therapists provide related educational services, they are necessarily contributors to the design and content of the IEP. Second, when students have disabilities that affect development of sensorimotor and communication abilities, therapists contribute to the curriculum by determining whether and how the curriculum scope and sequence need to be modified. Finally, a unifying theoretical model is an important foundation for effective teamwork (Johnson & Johnson, 1987). Educational teams often encounter problems because they have not consciously addressed curriculum in a collaborative manner. Without a curricular framework, teams may resort to prescribed activities and isolated interventions, spend excessive time inventing program content, or provide programs with little relevance or consistency. Without agreement about theoretical curricular models, teams lack a consistent basis for making decisions and members are more likely to experience ambivalence and conflict. A curriculum provides the framework and direction—a road map of sorts—so that all members of the educational team have a clear understanding of the educational program.

APPROACHES TO CURRICULUM

Three common approaches to curriculum in special education programs for students with severe disabilities are the developmental approach, the functional approach, and the ecological approach. Each approach is discussed below.

A Developmental Curriculum Approach

The traditional model for both special education curricula and pediatric habilitation has been a developmental approach, based on the scope and sequence of normal development of young children (see Ayres, 1972; Bloom & Lahey, 1978; Bobath & Bobath, 1972; Bricker & Bricker, 1974; Chapman & Miller, 1980; Frostig & Horne, 1973; Gesell & Amatruda, 1947; Miller, 1977). The theory underlying this model is that development of typical children progresses in a predictable sequence, which should be taught to students with disabilities. Teaching the normal sequence is expected to remediate delays and prevent deviations that would lead to greater delays and disability. A thorough understanding of normal child development is considered a fundamental competency in teacher and therapist training programs and is valuable for planning effective instructional strategies (see, e.g., Pratt & Allen, 1989). Numerous weaknesses have been identified in the developmental model, however, especially if it is used as the only or the primary approach to curriculum for students with severe disabilities (L. Brown, Nietupski, & Hamre-Nietupski, 1976; Orelove & Sobsey, 1991; Reichle & Karlan, 1985; Reichle & Keogh, 1986).

First, normal development presents the very sequences through which students with severe disabilities have failed to progress. Rigid adherence to achieving normalcy can become a barrier to learning achievable functional skills. Some teachers and therapists have focused for years on the next skill in a normal developmental sequence (e.g., prereading skills, babbling, rolling segmentally), and discouraged working on more meaningful skills because they are considered to be at a higher developmental level. Attention is focused on form rather than function, and alternative forms or adaptations to achieve desired functions are not part of the model (e.g., wheelchair or tricycle rather than

walking). Second, normal development does not actually prescribe a clear and valid teaching sequence. Although the presence or absence of "normal" behaviors may be significant, some behaviors are neither necessary nor desirable to teach, particularly for older students with disabilities (e.g., cry when separated from parent, gaze at mirror image). Recent research has demonstrated that typical children develop skills in a variety of sequences and patterns, which often differ from accepted norms (Loria, 1980; Van Sant, 1988). Even if existing sequences did prove to be generally valid, few developmental assessments or curricula present either a clear linear progression of skill development or the "lattice" (Bricker & Iacino, 1977) that is desirable to achieve more complex skills. Finally, and perhaps most important, using developmental curricula encourages teachers and therapists to view students with severe disabilities as "developmentally young" and to use educational activities and materials that are more appropriate to infants than to older children, adolescents, or adults. This limits opportunities to acquire more age-appropriate skills, creates a perpetual cycle of incompetence, and negatively affects others' perceptions of and expectations for students with severe disabilities (Bates, Morrow, Pancsofar, & Sedlak, 1984). Curricula referenced only to normal development fail to provide information about the contexts and functions that are most important for an individual student to participate more fully in everyday life.

A Functional Curriculum Approach

Having recognized the shortcomings of a pure developmental approach, many teams serving children and adults with severe disabilities have adopted a functional approach to curriculum. The philosophy of this approach is that students with severe disabilities need to acquire age-appropriate and functional skills. Two general strategies have been used to operationalize this philosophy. The first strategy is still referenced to normal child development, but items in developmontal assessments (or curricula) are analyzed to identify the significant component behaviors. For example, shaking a rattle for several seconds demonstrates beginning abilities to maintain a palmar grasp, to dissociate arm movement from the rest of the body, to use an object for a particular purpose, and to sustain intentional activity. If the team determined that any or all of these behaviors were deficient but needed by the student, they would identify functional contexts and age-appropriate materials for teaching the component behaviors. For a 10-year-old boy with severe disabilities, the same component behaviors might be taught as he learns to feed himself, brush his teeth, erase the chalkboard at school, or assist with snack preparation (e.g., shake chips from their box into a bowl). This approach is acceptable to many teachers and therapists because it both acknowledges typical sequences of skill development and, by having identified activities that appear more functional and age-appropriate, enables the student to achieve greater independence and social acceptance.

The second strategy to establish functional curricula is based on criterion-referenced assessment of independent living skills. This approach is especially familiar to occupational therapists, since it is the basis for much of their work in adult rehabilitation (see, e.g., Breines, 1984; Harvey & Jellinek, 1981; Klein & Bell, 1982). In special education, numerous packaged curricula have been developed to teach skills deemed necessary for participation in adult environments (e.g., activities of

daily living and vocational curricula). The scope and sequence of skills and the task analyses that comprise these curricula are typically identified and deemed "functional" because they contain activities performed: 1) by people without disabilities or 2) in programs or environments that serve only people with disabilities.

The functional approach to curriculum has one major advantage over a strictly developmental approach. It reflects higher expectations for students with severe disabilities and promotes opportunities to acquire age appropriate skills. The major weakness of the functional approach is that there is no clear organizational framework. Although there is an underlying presumption of functionality and age appropriateness, the content of the curriculum is largely idiosyncratic, and there are no established criteria for determining what is actually functional and relevant for an individual student. Many functional curricula have been field tested and formally validated with children and adults with disabilities. "Validation" can be defined in numerous ways, however, and it may only mean that users found the package useable and the content achievable. Validation does not necessarily mean a curriculum leads to successful participation in integrated environments (see, e.g., Brown et al., 1987). Furthermore, validation for a specific population of students does not ensure that the skills are relevant, important, or properly sequenced for an individual. As a result, the functional approach may produce programs that are inappropriate and nonfunctional for individual students as those devised using the developmental approach.

An Ecological Curriculum Approach
In an effort to ensure a more appropriate and relevant curriculum for individual

students, L. Brown and coworkers (1979) delineated a strategy known as an ecological approach (also referred to as an environment-referenced or community-referenced approach). With many years of use and refinement, the ecological approach to curriculum is considered a "best practice" in educating students with severe disabilities (see, e.g., Williams, Fox, Thousand, & Fox, 1990).

Ecology refers to the study of relationships between people and their environments (Webster's, 1987). Therefore, an ecological approach to curriculum reflects characteristics of both the individual student and the environments in which his or her participation is desired. The team for each student generates an individualized curriculum that encompasses the skills, activities, and environments that are most relevant and important for that student. The specific content evolves continually as the student's needs, goals, and opportunities change, as described in the next section.

The ecological approach respects the strengths of other curriculum models, but also has several advantages. It promotes teaching skills that are age appropriate and relevant to an individual's daily life, while it respects the need to teach skills in order of progressive refinement and complexity. It also encourages use of adaptations to accommodate disability or simplify task demands. Many teams find that an ecological curriculum expands the options for their students, including options for participation in less restrictive environments. For collaborative teams, an advantage of the ecological curriculum model is that it tends to unify rather than fragment team member efforts because the environments and activities identified as priorities for each student provide a natural context for

integrating occupational, physical, and speech/language therapy services (Giangreco, Cloninger, & Iverson, 1990).

There is an extensive body of literature on an ecological approach to curriculum. This chapter outlines steps and strategies to develop an ecological curriculum, with particular reference to the contributions of occupational, physical, and speech-language therapists. Readers who desire a more thorough examination and guide to developing an ecological curriculum are referred to Falvey (1989) and Ford et al. (1989).

DEVELOPING THE ECOLOGICAL CURRICULUM

L. Brown et al. (1979) conceptualized an ecological curriculum organized around four life domains: domestic, vocational, community, and recreation/leisure. More recently, educators have recognized the need to include school as a domain because school comprises a substantial element of the lives of all children and youth (York & Vandercook, 1991). School can be considered as either a fifth domain or a major division within the community domain. These domains provide the framework for the ecological curriculum.

An ecological curriculum is designed by conducting ecological inventories, in which team members identify: 1) the home and community environments that are important for an individual, 2) the priority activities that occur in those environments, and 3) the skills the individual needs to participate in those activities (L. Brown et al., 1979). As teams have used this analytical process, often they have also used a more intuitive process to identify some skills as priorities for individual students. Such skills might be important for a student to participate in many relevant activities (e.g., hand use), or to expand and enrich participation in many environments (e.g., making choices). In recognition of these priorities, the Brown et al. (1979) process has been modified over time to include a parallel step to identify important *embedded* skills, which are used in a variety of contexts (Ford et al., 1989; York & Vandercook, 1991).

The ecological curriculum process has also been influenced by two recent innovations in how education and human services agencies plan for people with disabilities (Mount & Zwernik, 1988; O'Brien, 1987; O'Brien & Lyle, 1987; Vandercook, York, & Forest, 1989). First, family members, friends, and neighbors are assuming important roles in educational planning, not because of legal mandates, but because of growing self-advocacy and self-determination movements and because growing numbers of professionals recognize the critical value of their input. Second, many educational teams now start their planning by envisioning a desirable future for the student with disabilities, and then focusing on ways to achieve or approximate the vision as they design the educational program (O'Brien, Forest, Snow, & Hasbury, 1989; Vandercook et al., 1989; York & Vandercook, 1991).

The major steps in designing an individualized ecological curriculum are described below, and depicted in Figure 4.1. Although clarity necessitates describing the process as linear, with a sequence of discrete steps, it is more accurate to characterize the components as interwoven and the process as flexible and evolving. Teams are urged to conceptualize and use the process with that understanding. The results of this process are presented at the end of this chapter for two students, Kristen and Jamal, who were introduced at the beginning of Section II.

Establish the Planning Team

The first and most important member of the planning team is the student with severe disabilities, who is encouraged to participate in planning to the greatest extent possible. The student's parents, general education teacher(s), special education teacher, and related services professionals typically form the core of the educational planning team. Although parent and professional perspectives are essential to plan an appropriate program, their views can be complemented and expanded by including friends, other family members, and even neighbors or other significant people. Additional team members are included as appropriate for a student's educational priorities. For example, a job coach, employer, and coworkers may be included in planning for an older student who receives the majority of his or her instruction in a community vocational site. Classmates and coworkers without disabilities offer great insights about actual (versus hypothesized) opportunities, requisites, and supports to participate in school, work, and community environments. When students with severe disabilities first enter new program settings, regular class teachers, typical peers, employers, and coworkers may not feel comfortable participating in planning immediately. Given time to get acquainted with the student and given support and encouragement to participate in the planning process, however, many become active and insightful members of planning teams for students with severe disabilities. When selecting planning team members, it is most important to ensure involvement by people who know the student and who have a sincere interest in designing and imple-

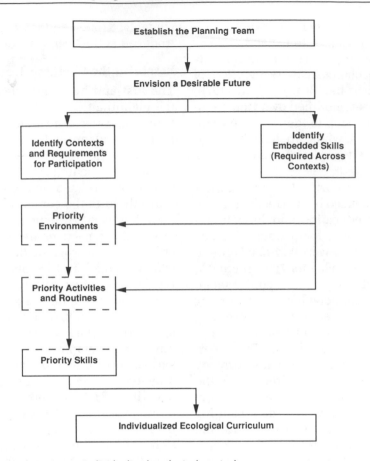

Figure 4.1.   Steps in designing an individualized ecological curriculum.

menting a program that produces successful life outcomes. Participation in implementing the plan is enhanced greatly by
active involvement in the design process
(Kruger, 1988).

Envision a Desirable Future

Several strategies have been used to generate visions of desirable futures for people
with disabilities (Mount & Zwernik, 1988;
O'Brien et al., 1989; Vandercook et al.,
1989). A common theme in these strategies
is that a desirable future is one in which a
person with disabilities is a participating
member of a family and an integrated com-

munity. In an educational program, the
team's vision of where and with whom a
student will live, go to school, work, spend
leisure time, and use other community facilities sets the context for deciding what
to teach in the educational program. Until
this vision or context is established, the
team has no clear direction and cannot ensure relevance of the curriculum for the individual student.

Envisioning a desirable future requires
knowledge of individual student characteristics, in a holistic sense: interests, assets, challenges, needs. The student is not
defined by test scores or by the skills and

deficits revealed through formal assessment. While addressing relevant challenges is important, building on capacities and interests is central to designing an educational program. Planning team members can generate a vision of a desirable future by discussing the following questions together: *pre meeting , overall*

Who is the student?

What are the student's interests and strengths?

What are the student's greatest challenges?

What is a desirable future . . . the dream for this student?

What is the nightmare . . . the future to be avoided?

What are this student's greatest needs?

(Adapted from Forest & Lusthaus, 1987; Vandercook et al., 1989.)

Kristen's team and Jamal's team used the questions above to help envision desirable futures for Kristen and Jamal. The resulting profiles are presented in Table 4.1 and Table 4.2, respectively.

A shared vision for a student helps team members maintain a holistic view of the student as a person, rather than a collection of deficits. Furthermore, having a shared vision about a student's future leads naturally to a more unified view of the purpose and design of the educational program. How should the program be designed to make the vision a reality?

Identify Environments for Participation

Within the domestic, school, vocational, community, and leisure domains, the educational team identifies the environments where it is most desirable for the student with severe disabilities to participate. The student's current home, school, and community environments are considered, and particular attention is placed on integrated or "typical" environments used by peers without disabilities, even if the integrated environments are not currently used by or available to the student. Before a student begins using integrated environments, the team can analyze future settings but can only speculate about exactly how the particular student will participate. (Some team members will speculate that the student will fail in integrated settings, but recent initiatives demonstrate that planning and support are better predictors of successful integration than student characteristics.) As the student enters these new environments, the opportunities for participation, the demands on the student, and the supports that are available there become more clear to the team. As students develop friendships in integrated environments, typical peers become invaluable team members who provide more relevant and accurate information about environmental demands and strategies for inclusion. Each of the life domains, including a range of environments for elementary, middle, and high school–age students, are described in more detail below. Readers are referred to Ford et al. (1989) for a more comprehensive discussion of the scope and sequence of activities comprising each domain.

Domestic Environments In this domain, the team considers the student's life in and around his or her actual home. If a family is considering an alternative community living setting, such as a supported home or supervised apartment, the team would inventory that environment also. If the student currently lives in a large residential facility, a small community residence would be identified as a future, more desirable, and less restrictive environment (Mallory & Herrick, 1987; Taylor, Biklen, & Knoll, 1987). Team members identify specific areas within and around the home (e.g., bedroom, bathroom, yard)

Table 4.1 Profile of Kristen

Who is Kristen?

•Our little girl
•Julie's younger sister (Julie is 7 years old)
•She's 5 years old, about to go to kindergarten
•Cute, but stubborn
•Happy and sad
•A little bit slow
•An important member of our family

What are Kristen's interests and strengths?

•Loves her dad; she likes him to tickle her
•Likes her dog, Duke
•Follows some short, simple directions, especially those associated with routine activities
•Has a wonderful smile that attracts people
•Sometimes initiates social play routines
•Can maintain play with an adult for several minutes
•Likes "The Little Mermaid" video
•Says a few words (e.g., Mom, Dad, Doo-wee/Julie, pop, ba/ball)
•Favorite toy is a soccer ball
•Favorite food is pizza
•She has a good appetite and eats by herself pretty well
•Usually well-behaved (except when frustrated, upset)
•Even though she's a little clumsy, she learned to walk, and we weren't sure she could do that

What are Kristen's greatest challenges?

•Cerebral palsy -- it's hard for her to walk, she trips a lot, she has trouble using her hands
•She can't tell us what she is thinking, so she gets really frustrated
•Tantrums when she gets really upset
•She just sits with nothing to do unless someone is right there playing with her
•Really frightened at the doctor, dentist
•She needs help with a lot of things that Julie could do for herself at this age -- dressing herself, helping a little
  with chores
•She is more interested in adults than in kids her own age

What is a desirable future . . . the dream for Kristen?

•She would go to the same school as her sister, and go on the same bus
•She would have friends who would invite her over to play and invite her to birthday parties; they would look
  out for her and teach her things; they'll know how sweet she is
•She could run and swing and laugh and play like other kids
•She would participate in some of the things that are really important parts of our family -- reading, or just
  listening to stories; helping make Christmas cookies, learning to cook
•When she grows up, I don't know if she could live by herself, but I don't think Julie should have to take care of
  her. I hope she'll be able to take care of herself
•She'll be able to talk and tell us everything she is thinking
•She'll be able to go everyplace with us (church, museums)
•She'll have her own interests

(continued)

Table 4.1 (continued)

What is the nightmare?

•She'll end up in an institution
•Her tantrums will get worse and she'll become an uncontrollable adult
•When her parents are gone, nobody will watch over her
•She'll remain highly dependent on others for her self-care needs
•She won't have any friends
•She'll never learn to talk to express herself

What are Kristen's greatest needs?

•Learn to communicate to express herself (vs. tantrum)
•Be toilet trained
•Have friends; be more interested in and enjoy kids her own age
•Get around better (walking)
•Learn to take care of herself, like dress herself and take a bath
•Learn to entertain herself
•Learn to play with other kids
•Cooperate at the doctor
•Be part of the kindergarten, do what the other children do

Questions adapted from Forest and Lusthaus (1987) and Vandercook, York, and Forest (1989).

Note: Kristen's profile was compiled by Kristen's parents, her older sister, and teachers and therapists from the elementary school program she will enter in the fall. It is expected that Kristen will make friends in kindergarten, and the friends will help expand Kristen's profile next spring.

where greater student participation is desired.

School Environments For students between the ages of 5 and 18, general education classrooms and other integrated school environments would be among the most relevant current or future educational environments (Vandercook et al., 1989; York & Vandercook, 1991). The grade level and classroom environments that are appropriate for the student's chronological age are identified in the inventory process. Table 4.3 identifies the routines and activities of a general education kindergarten class. Kristen's team used this inventory to identify the activities and skills that are age appropriate for and important to teach to Kristen, and the opportunities that are already available to her to address priority motor and communication needs in the classroom. At the secondary level, when students change classes every 45 to 50 minutes, the team selects a variety of specific classes to inventory, based on individual interests and needs. There are additional school environments besides regular classes that also may be priorities for individual students of all ages. These include the library, office, nurse's room, hallways, playground, bus area, and so on.

For children younger than 5, integrated preschools and day care settings would be among the age-appropriate school environments (McLean & Odom, 1988). For young adults between 18 and 21 who are still entitled to educational services, classrooms and other facilities at a community college might be included in the inventory (Wilcox & Bellamy, 1982). When determining priority environments in which to provide

Table 4.2 Profile of Jamal

Who is Jamal?

- Pleasant
- Nice
- Good sense of humor
- 17 years old, junior in high school
- Stubborn streak when it comes to food
- "Favorite" family member, son, big brother to Keesha (age 10), cousin to Michael (age 14) and Jiles (age 17)

What are Jamal's interests and strengths?

- Enjoys high school friends David and Jerome, especially before school (gazes toward friends he sees in the hall, vocalizes, and smiles), during study hall (smiles and vocalizes when friends greet him, sit down near him, or look at a magazine with him), at lunch (will not begin eating unless a friend is near him), after school ("screeches" his approval when friends are nearby at sporting events and when they cheer at sporting events)
- Likes to watch and be physically assisted to play Nintendo
- Makes choices between presented objects (e.g., Nintendo cartridges , favorite foods, people, clothing, positions) with his eyes (when his head is secure)
- Likes french fries (fast food type), Coke, soft serve ice cream
- Enjoys looking through magazines (*Cycle World*, *Cosmopolitan*, *Road and Track*)
- Likes upbeat music (shows this by smiling, screeching, and getting tense),epecally MTV, but radio OK too
- Prefers doing activities with or alongside other people rather than by himself
- Enjoys drives downtown at night, likes walks through the zoo - seems curious about the animals, gets excited to see kids on amusement rides
- Likes to stretch out on the floor
- Is flexible about changes in routine as long as he is with people he likes
- Attractive, "good body" (muscle definition), stylish clothes
- Lightweight - it is easy for friends and family to help him get around (in/out of car, push around in wheelchair)
- Hard worker when he is with favorite people; he works hard to turn his head to deflect a cheek switch to turn on electronic leisure activities/devices and appliances (he does get tense when appliances make a lot of noise)
- Can bear some body weight through legs by rigid extension (no balancing - serves a pivot/prop function only)

What are Jamal's greatest challenges?

- His body does not move well and he has difficulty achieving optimal body alignment...
  ...labeled as having spastic quadriplegic cerebral palsy
  ...holds up head for about ten seconds with his shoulders stabilized; requires head support to stabilize head enough to point with eyes; head tends to fall back into extension, but with head supported, he can turn his head about 45 degrees
  ...gets tense with intentional movement attempts, but relaxes into flexion when his body is supported and no active movement is attempted
  ...has a mild curve and a "hunch" in his spine and his hips are becoming dislocated which interferes with proper positioning
  ...arm movements consist of rigid extension, some lateral sliding of rigid arm when wrist is stabilized on tray

(continued)

Table 4.2 *(continued)*

•Difficulty communicating

  ...communication limited to use of eye movements and facial expressions (hand use for choice selection has been restricted due to inaccuracy in touching small targets)
  ...no means of "formal" communication using symbols/words
  ...initiates/asserts his choices involving two or three objects using eye gaze, but eye gaze is inconsistent for choicemaking involving yes/no cards or pictures
  ...unfamiliar people do not address him or include him

What is a desirable future . . . the dream for Jamal?

•Small home or apartment, close to an accessible community, 1 or 2 roommates/housemates, paid live-in support
•Paid work in an integrated environment --- i.e., some place where there are people around to interact with him...maybe in a day care center or library as a "reader" for story time for kids; maybe as an assistant for running errands (carrying items with an adapted chair); advocate for inclusion in collaboration with high school friends
•Ongoing relationships with friends and family
•Regular weekly involvement in community groups with people who share common interests

---

What is the nightmare?

•Alone - no consistent caring relationships, lack of meaningful communication
•Isolated - confined to limited array of environments
•Restricted participation in fun or risky activities because of physical challenges
•Stranded or vulnerable to dependence on others for physical care
•Deteriorating physical condition causing progressive limitations, pain, and threats to health

---

What are Jamal's greatest needs?

•Friends - David and Jerome...maybe a girlfriend?
•Active social life
•Family relationships and activities, especially with cousins, sister, and mom
•Schedule to accommodate physical needs (alternative positions, opportunities for relaxation, passive and assisted movement of body parts) and self-care needs so that interactions with classmates and fun time with friends is not infringed upon
•Assistance with physical and self-care needs
•Opportunities to indicate choices and needs about daily activities and routines
•Expansion of present communication abilities and a consistent mode of communication (with exploration of switch controls and scanning methods and devices)
•Exploration of power mobility via switch controlled by head movement or limited arm movement
•Ability to direct caregivers
•Planning for his life after high school...home, school, and community (including social life)
•Team members who help Jamal realize an integrated community life...now and in the future
•Circle of friends who share responsibility and support for Jamal and to which Jamal can contribute

Questions adapted from Forest and Lusthaus (1987) and Vandercook, York, and Forest (1989).

Table 4.3 Kindergarten routine and activities

8:30   Arrival and Free Play
Children walk from their bus and find their classroom. They hang their coats and bags in their cubbies. The aide checks to see who needs to use the bathroom. (Many kindergarten children need help with dressing, using toilet paper, flushing the toilet, and washing their hands.) The room has several areas where the children can play (blocks, house, etc.) or they can choose from the toy shelves. Children check the job board.

9:00   Opening Group (at tables)
Children sit at tables for attendance, calendar, weather, and review of the schedule for the day. (Activities each day follow a unit theme.) Job assignments for the day are reviewed.

9:20   Story (on rug)
Children listen to a story and participate in a discussion.

9:45   Gross Motor / Perceptual Activity (on rug) [a]
Activities teach body awareness, concepts of size and space.

10:15   Fine Motor / Perceptual Activity (at tables) [a]
Hands-on activities involving size, shape, color, number, and use of senses and leading to reading, writing, and counting.

10:45   Snack
Children wash hands and then try a variety of healthy snacks, help make their snack, work on sharing and manners, and help clean up.

11:10   Free Play
Children have their choice of activities (see 8:30). The group goes outside sometimes, weather permitting. This is also a time to finish class jobs or projects from small group. Children use the bathroom, wash up, collect their things, and get dressed to go home.

11:25   Dismissal
Children line up and walk to the bus.

---

[a] Or Art, Music, Library, Gym (on a rotating basis, 2 to 3 times weekly). Children walk in line to other areas of the school and work with other teachers.

instruction, a useful guideline is to first identify the environments used by same-age peers who do not have disabilities. Segregated schools or special classes in regular public schools would not be identified as priority environments, since neither offers opportunities to learn to participate in integrated settings.

Vocational Environments The community-based vocational training model (as opposed to a segregated prevocational model) provides the greatest opportunity for secondary school–age students with severe disabilities to achieve social integration and to perform real work (L. Brown et al., 1987). Using this model, the team identifies environments where people of the same age without disabilities work. For children at the elementary school age, the vocational domain usually is subsumed in the home and school environments, where children have chores and class or school jobs. At the middle school level, students sample a variety of jobs in community businesses, including stores, offices, motels, hospitals, and industries. The team selects vocational environments based on student interests, family preferences, opportunities for interactions with nondisabled peers, and geographic location. A student may sample five or more jobs during the middle (junior high) school years, which provides additional information about preferences and aptitudes. In high school, the team identifies vocational environments that offer the most plausible and enjoyable opportunities for supported work after graduation. Within any vocational environment, the team identifies the actual work area, as well as other areas the student would need to use successfully in the course of the workday, such as the cafeteria or breakroom, rest rooms, storage rooms, main office, and hallways. Coworkers may join the student's team to help create the vision, and a specific plan for how the student can participate as a member of the work force.

Table 4.4 shows a weekly schedule for Jamal, a high school student with severe disabilities. Jamal's schedule was designed to include regular instruction at a community vocational site, in addition to instruction in several environments at his high school and other community settings. (More information about Jamal's activities in these settings is presented later in this chapter.)

Community Environments Community environments include transportation systems, streets and sidewalks, and all businesses, services, and facilities in the community. Because of the number of possible training environments, priorities are clearly needed. For children at the elementary school age, public school environments have priority over other community environments. Therefore, children might

receive instruction related to riding the bus and crossing streets. Other community training would occur only if a family identified particular needs that could not be addressed in typical school environments. At the middle school level, priority environments might include fast food restaurants, grocery stores, department stores, community recreation facilities, and bus systems. Specific environments would be identified according to student interests and preferences, peer preferences (e.g., age-appropriate community hangouts, preferred activities), family preferences, opportunities for social interaction, and proximity to home, school, or vocational training site. During the high school years, environments would be selected to reflect the solidifying vision of postsecondary community participation for the individual student. In addition to environments identified previously, these might include a bank, express teller stations, laundromat, barber or hairdresser, more formal restaurants, and other environments used by adults who live and work in the community.

Leisure Environments Some leisure environments will overlap with environments identified previously because leisure activities occur at home, school, work, and in many locations in the community. Leisure environments at home may be the bedroom, den, and yard. Homes of friends and relatives would also be considered. At school, areas such as the playground, cafeteria, student lounge, hallways, rest rooms, club areas, and athletic areas might be included. At work, the cafeteria or employees' lounge, or an area outside the job site, may be an important leisure environment. The community offers many leisure opportunities, including parks, public organizations such as a community center, private health and country

Table 4.4 Jamal's weekly schedule

	MONDAY	TUESDAY	WEDNESDAY	THURSDAY	FRIDAY
Before school 7:00-7:45	Regular bus to school Rest room •7:30-7:45				
Homeroom 7:45-8:00	HOMEROOM	HOMEROOM	HOMEROOM	HOMEROOM	HOMEROOM
Period 1 8:05-8:55	SPANISH CLASS	SPANISH CLASS	SPANISH CLASS	SPANISH CLASS	SPANISH CLASS
Period 2 9:00-9:50	COMMUNITY PREP •9:00-9:15 COMMUNITY WORK •9:15-12:00	COMMUNITY PREP •9:00-9:15 COMMUNITY MOBILITY TRAINING	COMMUNITY PREP •9:00-9:15 COMMUNITY WORK •9:15-12:00	COMMUNITY PREP •9:00-9:15 COMMUNITY MOBILITY TRAINING	COMMUNITY PREP •9:00-9:15 COMMUNITY WORK •9:15-12:00
Period 3 9:55-10:45	Rest room •10:15-10:30	Rest room •10:15-10:30	Rest room •10:15-10:30	Rest room •10:15-10:30	Rest room •10:15-10:30
Period 4 10:50-11:40		CHOIR		CHOIR	
Period 5 11:45-12:35	LUNCH •12:20-12:50	COMMUNITY FAST FOOD RESTAURANT	LUNCH •12:20-12:50	LUNCH •11:45-12:15 Rest room •12:15-12:30	LUNCH •12:20-12:50
Period 6 12:40-1:30	ERRANDS •12:50-1:15 Rest room •1:15-1:30	Rest room •12:40-12:55 MEDIA CENTER •library •computer	ERRANDS •12:50-1:15 Rest room •1:15-1:30	MEDIA CENTER •library •computer	ERRANDS •12:50-1:15 Rest room •1:15-1:30
Period 7 1:35-2:25	HOME ECONOMICS	HORTICULTURE	HOME ECONOMICS	HORTICULTURE	HOME ECONOMICS
After school				After-school activity •swim team manager	

clubs, churches, museums, libraries, theaters, arcades, and malls. Selection of leisure environments would reflect interests and preferences of each student with severe disabilities. Selection may also be highly dependent upon interests and priorities of family members and typical peers, since they ultimately enable the student to access the environments.

Factors in Selecting Priority Instructional Environments When considering the range of current and potential least restrictive environments for a student, teams frequently identify more environments than can be addressed instructionally in any given school year. Therefore, it becomes necessary to set priorities. One strategy for prioritization is to project a time frame for each identified environment: 1) high priority for this year, 2) will become a priority within the next three years, and 3) will not be a priority until 3 or more years from now. In ranking priorities, teams are cautioned about assigning low priority to environments simply because students do not yet use them. This can become a self-fulfilling prophecy. Frequently students are provided access to new environments only when the environments are given high priority.

Another strategy for setting priorities evolves naturally from involving peers without disabilities as "experts" on the team. Children in kindergarten, middle and high school students, and adult co-workers are far more knowledgeable about participation in their respective spheres than most parents or professionals. When they participate in personal futures planning for their friend with a disability, typical peers often identify the most relevant needs and help teams determine workable strategies to address priorities. Implied in the discussions above are that high priority will be given to environments that are ap-

propriate to the student's chronological age and that promote social integration.

Identify Priority Activities and Routines

Once priority instructional environments have been identified, the team identifies the activities and routines that typically occur in those environments. At first, team members will need to visit the actual environments and observe, participate, and interview others who use the environment. Conducting this part of the environmental inventory is expedited as information is compiled about a widening assortment of integrated environments used by various students on a regular basis. The team identifies the activities and routines that are priorities for an individual student by considering the student's chronological age, preferences, and abilities, the family's preferences, the activities that offer the greatest opportunity for active inclusion in integrated environments now, and the possibilities for the future. (Criteria for selecting priorities are discussed in greater depth in Chapter 6.)

Identify Priority Skills

As priority activities and routines are identified, the team also identifies the skills that are typically required for participation. A designated team member (or members) go to the actual environment and perform an activity analysis (much like an extensive task analysis). This delineation of tasks and skills serves as the guide for assessing student performance in the environments (described in detail in Chapter 5). Included in the activity analysis is identification of common components of routines, as well as specific skills.

Common Components of Activities and Routines When conducting environmental inventories, it is important to consider the range of components that comprise functional activities and routines, rather than focusing narrowly on only the core components. For example, ordering a meal at a fast food restaurant involves more than just saying "I'd like a hamburger, small fries, and a chocolate shake." Students must appropriately initiate, prepare for, and terminate the ordering sequence. Similarly, activities in general education classrooms are defined more broadly than completing core academic tasks (e.g., math problems) while sitting at a desk. Students need to receive instructions, get materials, form work groups, perform core academic tasks, ask for assistance, check and turn in work, clean up, and prepare for the next class or activity. Considering only the core reading, writing, or computing tasks would limit options for participation and learning.

F. Brown, Evans, Weed, and Owen (1987) conducted a *component analysis of functional routines*, which provides a framework for examining complete activities. Brown et al. differentiated components as *core skills* (which typically define participation in an activity/routine), *extension skills* (required to perform a task independently), and *enrichment skills* (not required for independence, but desirable for social acceptance and pleasure). For our purposes, it is useful to designate components as either sequential or interwoven, as delineated in Table 4.5.

As an example of the process, consider the activity of using a bank to deposit or withdraw money, as performed by an adolescent or young adult who does not have a disability. *Initiation* of the activity might occur through the natural cues of receiving an allowance or paycheck, or participating in a discussion about an event for which money is needed (e.g., taking a trip, buying a birthday gift). The person might an-

nounce plans, ask permission, or respond to questions or suggestions to go to the bank. *Preparation* might include collecting money (if making a deposit), bankbook, and bus pass; putting on outerwear; walking to the bus stop; boarding the correct bus; riding the bus; buzzing the driver at the correct stop; exiting the bus; walking to the bank; and entering. The *core* component of the activity would include getting a deposit or withdrawal slip; filling it out and signing it; standing in line until called; giving the deposit/withdrawal slip, bankbook, and money to the teller; waiting for a receipt or money; and leaving the window. *Termination* of the activity would include telling companion(s) of plans to leave the bank; and returning to work, school, or home.

The interwoven components would occur throughout the activity. *Movement* might include the mobility for traveling to the bus, entering and exiting the bus, and continuing on to the bank; and the manipulation for opening doors, writing, and handling money. (Movement was not one of the components identified by Brown et al. [1987]. It was added by the authors of this book.) *Preferences* might include making choices about how much money to deposit or withdraw; whether a companion would go to the bank, and if so, who that would be; where to sit on the bus; and whether to make any other stops during the trip. *Communication* could be directly related to other components of the activity, such as asking the bus driver at which stop to get off, requesting assistance to access the deposit or withdrawal slips, or asking for a particular denomination of money. *Social interactions* might include greeting the bus driver, offering a seat to another passenger, talking with others about upcoming events or about scenery during the bus ride, and thanking the teller. *Problem*

Table 4.5 A component analysis of functional routines

Sequential Components

Initiation
>   communicate need, desire, intent to engage in activity
>   ask permission for activity
>   respond to natural cues to perform activity

Preparation
>   gather materials, go to location for activity

Core
>   perform central part of activity
>   (tasks that are the usual focus of instruction)

Termination
>   signal the end of the activity
>   put away material, clean area

Interwoven Components

Movement
>   for postural control, mobility, and manipulation of materials

Preferences
>   regarding activities, materials, other participants

Communication
>   about activity, participants, other events

Social Interactions
>   sharing, taking turns, helping

Problem solving
>   incidental opportunities as they arise
>   intentional or arranged opportunities

Monitor quality of performance
>   completeness, accuracy, need for assistance

Monitor tempo of performance
>   latency, duration, rate

Adapted from Brown, F., Evans, I., Weed, K., & Owen, V. (1987). Delineating functional competencies: A component model. *Journal of The Association for Persons with Severe Handicaps, 12* (2), 117-124.

solving could occur as incidents arise naturally (e.g., missing the bus, deciding in which line to stand, finding no deposit slips) or could be arranged (e.g., student is not reminded to take his jacket). *Monitor quality* could refer to clothing being coordinated and fastened appropriately, legibility of handwriting on the deposit slip, agreement between cash and amount on the deposit slip, or intelligibility of speech to strangers. *Monitor tempo* could refer to the amount of time it takes to walk to the bus stop, an acceptable rate to fill out forms or move in line, or the duration of waiting in line before tiring or becoming impatient.

The component analysis construct illustrates that the opportunities for participation and instruction extend far beyond the core of an activity or routine. In fact, components other than the core may comprise the most important and generalizable targets for instruction throughout a student's public education. As teams conduct environmental inventories, the components they include are likely to be influenced by both a typical person's routine, the abilities and needs of the particular student for whom they are planning, and the discipline perspectives of the team members who conduct the analyses. Participation by occupational, physical, and speech-language therapists increases attention to the range of sensorimotor and communication demands and opportunities presented by various activities. After the team members identify priority activities and analyze the activity routines, they will conduct a discrepancy analysis, in which they compare the actual performance of the student with the desired or typical performance. (This step is part of the assessment process and is discussed further in Chapter 5.) For students with severe disabilities, the discrepancy analysis is important not so much to show what they *cannot* do, but more to discover ways that students *can* actively participate in the routine. All steps in the activity and discrepancy analyses will not translate into IEP objectives, but the steps do suggest normalized routines to follow in various settings, and they identify natural opportunities for distrib-

uted practice and generalization of priority skills (Mulligan, Lacy, & Guess, 1982).

Priority Skills within Activities In addition to identifying common components in the activity analysis, the team identifies skills that are required within the context of those activities. The skill areas considered by the team are similar to those addressed in developmental curricula: sensorimotor, communication, social, self-care, and cognitive or academic. The distinction is that, in a developmental curriculum, skills are considered priorities because they are next in the developmental sequence. In the ecological curriculum, skills are considered priorities because they are components of functional routines, and because acquiring or improving the skills would enhance the student's participation in priority activities and environments. Following this logic, Ford et al. (1989) recommended viewing sensorimotor and communication skills as *embedded* within daily activities, where both assessment and instruction are more meaningful and valid than when these skills are approached as isolated entities.

Individual teachers and therapists are each likely to take more responsibility for some skill areas than others, since professional education, training, and experience promote knowledge and skills in specific areas. This does not sanction team members to assign or assume sole responsibility or authority for particular skill areas. All team members offer important perspectives, and the student needs comprehensive integrated services to acquire the clusters of skills embedded within activity routines. With this precaution in mind, the areas of sensorimotor skills and communication skills are discussed, with the perspective that these are the areas in which occupational, physical, and speech-language therapists bring considerable expertise. Because students with severe disabilities are so frequently excluded from meaningful instruction, the discussion of embedded skills includes numerous examples to illustrate the feasibility of teaching sensorimotor and communication skills within activity routines.

Sensorimotor Skills Therapists are concerned with quantitative and qualitative aspects of motor performance and the sensory processing that influences performance. In relation to activity routines, it is useful to look first at the quantifiable, functional outcomes of sensorimotor skills for transitions, positioning, hand use, eating, vision, and activity-specific motor participation (Rainforth, Giangreco, & Dennis, 1989; York, Giangreco, Vandercook, & Macdonald, 1992; York & Rainforth, 1991; York, Rainforth, & Wiemann, 1988).

Transitions refer to the mobility skills that students use when travelling from one area to another within the home, classroom, school, workplace, or community. Although many students with severe disabilities lack independent mobility, providing students with a means to move themselves increases their control over the environment and decreases "learned helplessness" (Seligman, 1975). Hulme, Poor, Schulein, and Pezzino (1983) found that young children with physical disabilities became more active and interested participants in environmental events when they achieved a means of independent mobility. York (1989) found that adults with physical disabilities typically used two or more types of mobility (e.g., walking, wheeling a chair, crawling/scooting on the floor), and were selective about where they used the various forms. Robinett and Vondran (1988) found that actual environmental demands for independent mobility varied tremendously among people, and that physical therapists needed to look beyond

the rates and distances on "independent living scales" if they were to be successful in rehabilitation of adults with disabilities. These findings emphasize the importance of looking at mobility within the context of the student's daily environments, and teaching a variety of types of mobility.

Options for independent mobility include walking, pushing or driving a wheelchair, riding a bicycle or tricycle (with adaptations if needed), creeping on hands and knees, crawling on the stomach, and rolling. Most teachers and therapists are familiar with the practice of whisking students from one area of the school building to another, from the classroom to the therapy room for example, and then creating artificial situations to assess and teach mobility skills. An inventory of the school day reveals many opportunities to address transition and mobility skills in functional contexts. Arrival from the bus, transitions between classrooms, transitions from one area to another within a classroom, and departure are natural situations in which mobility skills increase options for participation and in which students may be most motivated to use their skills. Expectations can be individualized in numerous ways. Students who walk or wheel without assistance can increase their rate or endurance by systematically increasing the distance or decreasing the time for transitions. For example, Brian was extremely motivated to go outside after lunch, so he was expected to wheel his chair the full 100 feet from the cafeteria to the door. (Brian's friends understood that he was to do this himself, but that once he reached the door, they could push his chair.) During transitions between other activities and classes, Brian was pushed to within 25 feet of the classroom, with 3 minutes to reach the door before the other students

began to change classes. Within his classroom, David was learning to creep reciprocally (rather than bunny hop) and rise to
stand/lower to kneel reciprocally during
free play time. He also worked on rising
from a chair and cruising during transitions in the classroom. During transitions between classrooms, he worked on
walking with a walker and ascending/
descending stairs.

Even students with the most severe disabilities can "partially participate" (Baumgart et al., 1982; York et al., 1988) in transitions. Missy has severe spastic quadriplegia
and poor head control. In order to get to the
table for a snack, a teacher or aide facilitated Missy through four cycles of segmen-
tal rolling, ending at her chair. Missy's objectives during this transition were to
maintain normalized tone, to rotate her
head actively in the direction she was rolling, and to reach to touch her chair. To
transfer out of her wheelchair, Missy was
expected to stay relaxed, keep her neck
flexed forward, and move her head in the
direction of the transfer. When Missy was
carried with total support at the trunk and
shoulders, she was to maintain her head in
an upright position with minimal support.

The examples above reflect typical sequences of motor development, where
those sequences represent logical progres-
sions of movement control and complexity
for the individuals. The examples also reflect adaptations in sequence and mode to
maximize current functional participation
while facilitating a quality of movement
that will improve functional participation
in the future.

Positioning refers both to the postural
control a student uses to assume and maintain upright positions and to the positions
used during various activities. The functional outcome of both supported and independent positioning is that students

with severe disabilities are able to participate most efficiently in some activity.
Appropriate positions are selected by considering the student's current postural
control, typical positions for each activity,
and the demands of participation in the activity. Although the typical position for
many school and work activities is sitting,
typical children and adults also move continually from sitting upright to leaning and
reaching to kneeling and standing, interspersed with walking, running, and even
jumping, in the course of a school or work
day. In contrast, students with severe disabilities are often dependent upon others
to change positions. When students sit, or
maintain any particular position, for several hours each day, they have a high risk
for developing irreversible deformities and
decubitus ulcers. An effective strategy to
avoid these problems is to develop a positioning plan for each student with severe
physical disabilities. The plan would include at least two different positions and
provisions to change positions at least
once per hour. Since contractures at the
hip and knee are common, it is beneficial
for the selected positions to incorporate
changes between hips and knees being
flexed (e.g., sitting) and extended (e.g.,
standing, lying). When students have poor
head and trunk control, it is advantageous
to alternate between upright and reclined
positions to avoid scoliosis secondary to
fatigue.

Typical positions for activities reflect a
combination of social norms and activity
demands. For example, people usually
stand to cook and wash dishes. When Rick
stood at the counter to prepare food, however, hip and knee flexion contractures and
poor coordination caused him to slowly
droop toward the floor. Sitting at a table
gave him insufficient mechanical advantage to cut or stir. A parapodium stander in

the home arts classroom enabled Rick to stand with his legs properly aligned and to use his hands for food preparation. Rosemary might have washed dishes sitting in a wheelchair at an accessible sink or with dishpans on a table, but a prone stander allowed her to reach the basin and faucets easily, practice standing, and take a break from her usual position of sitting. In Todd's middle school art class, typical students sit at long tables. Todd could hold a marker and draw most successfully when sidelying, however, so his team proposed that Todd be positioned sidelying at the end of an art table where typical students also sat. With a rationale provided, the typical students were quite comfortable with this arrangement, which they understood as merely another accommodation to facilitate Todd's inclusion and participation.

Like mobility, postural control reflects typical sequences of skill acquisition and refinement, in the context of functional participation. Tracy was developing head and trunk control. During story time, she was expected to sit on the rug leaning on her arms. When positioned in her adapted wheelchair, Tracy was expected to maintain her head in an upright position without the aid of a headrest. When Tracy ate, used her hands, or rode over uneven surfaces, however, she was provided with external trunk and head support, since the movement demands of the situations exceeded her current abilities. Many of Tracy's classmates learned when she needed her headrest put in place and when she could stabilize her head independently. Quite unobtrusively, they were the ones who most often assisted with removal and replacement of her headrest. Tracy's activities and abilities were reassessed regularly to ensure that she was challenged to use and improve her postural control, and to ensure that positioning enabled her to participate successfully in a variety of activity routines.

Hand use refers to the patterns of reach, grasp, manipulation, and release required for participation in activities. Once again, a developmental sequence serves as a useful guide, particularly when the sensorimotor components of tasks are identified and applied to age-appropriate tasks with age-appropriate materials. Putting pegs in a board is not inherently important, but the ability to use a fingertip grasp, precise placement, and controlled release are. The student's ability to perform these movements separately or in combination can be assessed and taught within a variety of functional activities. Grooming, for example, requires similar hand use in the course of face washing, toothbrushing, hair brushing, shaving, and applying makeup. Table 4.6 presents a task analysis of shaving with an electric shaver with a corresponding movement analysis to illustrate both the requirements and the teaching possibilities within any task.

Although hand use is an appropriate focus for functional outcomes, the movement analysis denotes the student's need for a foundation of control and movement at the shoulder and trunk. The student may provide this foundation internally, or it can be augmented externally through positioning equipment or dynamic support and facilitation. For example, during hair brushing, Sandra needed trunk support, assistance to grasp the brush, and assistance to bring the brush to her head. A standard wheelchair provided adequate trunk support. The teacher facilitated grasp by holding the wrist in a neutral or slightly extended position, and facilitated the upward reach by facilitation at the wrist and just above the elbow. When Sandra's tone increased, strokes with the brush were interspersed with relaxation

Table 4.6 Task analysis and movement analysis of shaving with an electric razor

Position: Sitting in wheelchair in front of mirror, electric razor on counter

Task Analysis	Trunk	Shoulder	Elbow	Forearm	Wrist	Fingers/Thumb
1. Reach to pick up electric razor	Slight forward flexion	60° flexion, neutral rotation	Full extension	Pronation	Neutral	Extension Abduction
2. Grasp electric razor	Same	Same	Same	Same	20° extension	Flexion Adduction
3. Bring razor to right cheek	Extension	45° flexion 60° external rotation 30° abduction	140° flexion	Neutral	20° extension Ulnar deviation	Same
4. Shave right cheek	Same	Alternate +/- 10° from above	Same	Same	Same	Same
5. Move razor to neck	Same	45° flexion 30° external rotation 75° horizontal abduction	Same	Same	Same	Same
6. Shave neck	Same	Same	Same	Same	Alternate ulnar and radial deviation	Same
7. Move razor to chin/upper lip	Same	45° flexion 30° external rotation 30° horizontal abduction	130° flexion	Supination	Ulnar deviation	Same
8. Shave chin/upper lip	Same	Alternate +/- 5° from above	Same	Same	Same	Same
9. Transfer razor to other hand	Same	0° flexion 15° external rotation	90° flexion	Neutral	Neutral	Extension Abduction
10. Repeat 3 - 8 to shave left cheek with other hand						
11. Put razor on counter	Slight forward flexion	60° flexion Neutral rotation	Full extension	Pronation	20° extension	Same

Note: Joint angles are approximations to illustrate position changes.

90

techniques, consisting of rhythmic movement alternating between reach away from the body (shoulder horizontal abduction with elbow extension) and reach overhead (shoulder flexion–external rotation with slight elbow flexion). Another student, Tim, used an immature palmar grasp when using his fingers to eat, and would not allow an adult to physically prompt a fingertip grasp throughout his meal. A better alternative was to fabricate a small splint to cross the web space of Tim's hand, which was sufficient to facilitate the more mature grasp.

Adaptations are an important consideration when analyzing how a student with severe disabilities might participate in an activity. Some students may be unable to achieve controlled grasp and release as a generalized skill, but might learn to reach in specified planes and positions to increase participation in specified activities. Some students may need adaptations to substitute for hand use. Bruce, Paul, and Sara are students for whom such adaptations were needed (York & Rainforth, 1991). Bruce learned to press a switch with the back of his hand to activate a variety of leisure materials when he was positioned sidelying. Although he could maintain a prone standing position with moderate ease, effort, and control, attempts at directed reach in this position exceeded his current abilities. Paul, who had only limited use of one arm, learned to collate papers while lying on his back. He activated a switch to move collating trays and "picked up" papers by putting his splinted hand, with Plasti-Tac on the tip, in the appropriate trays. Sara has congenital anomalies that prevented her from holding her own finger foods. Her team devised a food holder from a butterfly hairclip mounted on a stand and secured to the table, which enabled Sara to feed herself without using her hands. Sara also offers an excellent example of a student with severe disabilities who, having acquired the means to participate in a meaningful activity, surpassed the professionals' expectations. After some months of feeding herself with the sandwich holder, Sara decided she preferred the independence and efficiency of holding the sandwich in her own hands rather than using the sandwich clip. Given her improved hand use at mealtime, her team quickly reassessed her hand use in a variety of activities to maximize opportunities for improvement.

Vision refers to the use of orientation, gaze, scanning, and tracking as needed to participate in priority activities. As with other motor skills, students with severe disabilities often are required to practice vision skills in isolated contexts before teams identify or offer instruction in naturally occurring situations in which students actually need to use vision skills. Rather than have Jack orient to and track a flashlight, Jack's team involved him in leisure activities using a Light-Bright and battery operated cars with sirens and flashing lights, which motivated him to use his limited vision. During leisure and other activities, Jack was taught to focus on an object at midline and track it to the table, focus on and track a second object, scan the two, and gaze at his preference. Goetz and Gee (1987) cautioned teams to carefully analyze tasks to ascertain that vision is actually needed for accurate and efficient performance. For example, Loretta would not scan the school bathroom to find the soap dispenser, paper towels, and garbage can. When team members observed Loretta, they realized she (and most other students) found these items easily without looking. The team determined that visual scanning was required for participation in other environments that were not so familiar or predictable.

Eating refers to the oral-motor aspects of consuming liquid and solid foods, including sucking, sipping, biting, chewing, and swallowing, which are often considered prespeech skills as well. Self-feeding requires the skills of both eating and hand use. Most people recognize the functional contexts for eating; the precaution here is to avoid overloading mealtime with instruction. One team decided to stress oral-motor skill development during a snacktime in the classroom. During the integrated lunch period in the elementary school cafeteria, they used good but unobtrusive feeding facilitation techniques, and stressed the social aspects of mealtime. These alternatives are even more important for a family of a child with severe disabilities. A harried mother once warned a therapist to pare down the hour of prefeeding and feeding instruction to something manageable—that is, something she could do while preparing dinner, handling two other young children, greeting her husband, and having a pleasant meal with her family. With the support of other team members, therapists are encouraged to carefully weigh the numerous needs related to eating and mealtime, and evaluate the cost-benefit ratio of all intervention strategies. For example, if proper spoon placement is as effective alone as when combined with jaw control and facilitation to the lips, the former is preferable since it is simpler. If systematic guided toothbrushing and face washing are as effective to reduce oral sensitivity as 10 minutes of brushing and icing techniques, the former would be preferable since it is a natural part of the daily routine and addresses other needs simultaneously.

Activity-defined motor participation refers to the unique sets or combinations of motor skills used in activities such as swimming, dancing, or horseback riding, in which movement characterizes the activity core. Because they are so unique, the cores of these particular activities often are approached as therapeutic programs. As with other activities, teams are reminded to analyze the entire activity routine, however, to identify other sequential and interwoven components, and to determine which skills are priorities for instruction. Another example of activity-specific motor participation is found in the task of putting chairs on desks each afternoon and on the floor the next morning. When John was assigned this class job, it appeared that motor planning problems interfered with his performance. John was physically guided through lifting, turning, and placing approximately 100 chairs over several days, after which he spontaneously devised his own strategy to perform the task. Although John was still considered to have motor planning problems, he had learned to plan and execute the motor skills for this particular job.

Qualitative aspects of motor task performance, such as sensory integration, normalized tone, pelvic stabilization, and glenohumeral dissociation, are the focus of much therapeutic intervention. Therapists receive extensive training in assessing the presence and effects of sensory and perceptual motor dysfunction, and this information is invaluable to educational teams. While quality is always an important consideration, it becomes an intervention priority only when specifically referenced to participation in current and future activities and environments. This does not devalue attention to sensorimotor quality; it challenges all members of the educational team to examine how quality affects performance now and how it might do so in the future.

When a team determines that quality is an intervention priority, they are compelled to design and use interventions in the activities and environments where participation has been compromised. For example, Alan has severe spastic diplegia, and by the age of 5 he had already had hip adductor releases. Despite aggressive intervention, Alan continued to use bunny-hopping as his primary mobility, he used his arms rather than his legs to hoist himself to standing, and his hips were becoming tighter. Rather than provide intervention for circumscribed portions of the day, Alan's team decided on a more comprehensive approach. In addition to intensive relaxation and elongation each morning, they physically intervened whenever Alan started pulling to stand, guiding his legs through a reciprocal kneel to half-kneel to stand pattern. To provide additional opportunities for pelvic-femoral dissociation, the team also arranged for Alan to ascend and descend a flight of stairs at least once daily to do errands or travel to other activities. The team reasoned that these motor skills were both a means and end for maintaining hip joint flexibility.

Carl's team established a sensory integration program to decrease tactile defensiveness. After several weeks he was more tolerant of the sensory integration tasks, yet remained resistant to physical assistance during dressing, grooming, and eating. The team found that Carl's defensiveness decreased dramatically when, rather than performing tasks on him, they engaged his attention, told him what was about to happen, and assisted him to participate. They also infused opportunities to make choices during each routine (e.g.,

which item to start with, which position to use).

Communication Skills Some traditional models of communication development and instruction have emphasized discrete components (e.g., phonology, syntax, semantics) as the basis for assessment and intervention. Such abstract approaches have been unsuccessful for many students with severe disabilities, especially when programs occurred in isolation from everyday contexts for communication. Other communication models have emphasized behavioral prerequisites (e.g., visual attending, discrimination, compliance) or cognitive prerequisites (e.g., object permanence, means-ends relationships), and have relegated many students with severe disabilities to years of "getting ready" to communicate. Strict program entry criteria (e.g., reliable yes/no responding) and service eligibility criteria (e.g., significant discrepancy between mental and language developmental ages) have completely excluded other students from speech and language services.

Fortunately, speech-language therapists now recognize the integral relationship of communication with cognitive and social behaviors, the importance of the environment as a context for meaningful communication, and the role of others in facilitating communication development (Norris & Hoffman, 1990). The resulting models of communication development and intervention have positively influenced how speech-language therapists serve students with the most severe disabilities.

Pragmatics—the study of language usage and its relationship to the structure of language (Prutting & Kirchner, 1987)—has emerged as a useful model for communication development and instruction.

In the applied pragmatics model, assessment and intervention are most concerned with three areas: function, form, and context for communication. What are the pragmatic *functions*, or how does the student want to affect the environment (e.g., requests for attention, refusal to participate, greeting)? What *forms* does the student use to express each function (e.g., tap shoulder to request attention, say "no" to refuse participation, vocalize to greet)? What *contexts* (e.g., people, daily routines, places) are used for communication now, or could be used to expand the number and quality of communicative interactions? Within this model, "all learners possess a communicative repertoire" (Halle, 1988, p. 158). It is the responsibility of the educational team to ensure that every student has something motivating to communicate about, someone to communicate with, and a means to communicate.

Pragmatic approaches do not set the "prerequisites" for communication instruction that previously excluded many students. Emphasis on prerequisites for communication development has waned as a result of: 1) lack of empirical evidence supporting the need for cognitive prerequisites, and 2) recognition that such approaches frequently cannot meet immediate communication needs. According to current thinking, the only prerequisite to communication development is the availability of opportunities to communicate (Mirenda, Iacono, & Williams, 1990). Intent to communicate is viewed as a result of, rather than exclusively a prerequisite to, communicative interactions.

Infant development research shows that caregivers routinely assign communicative intent to their infants' behavior, although they do not believe such intent actually exists. For example, a caregiver interprets an infant's flailing reach to mean "I want the toy you are holding." The caregiver responds by presenting the toy and saying, "Here it is." Repeating such interactions exposes the infant to routines with social, cognitive, and language components that will eventually be differentiated and understood. The quality and quantity of these interactions seems to influence language learning in infants (Norris & Hoffman, 1990). For students with severe disabilities who demonstrate limited communication skills, Siegel-Causey and Guess (1989) advised educators to observe, interpret, and respond to student behaviors as expressive and meaningful, whether or not the behavior seems intentional. The listener's response teaches the student that the behavior has an effect, and thereby teaches meaning.

Use of formal symbols (e.g., signs, pictograms) no longer is considered necessary for communication to occur. Instead, intervention often focuses on teaching others in the student's environment to recognize, acknowledge, reinforce, and expand both nonsymbolic and symbolic communication functions and forms. For example, Dan had fewer than 10 words in his symbolic communication repertoire. Dan's teacher was taught to recognize and record additional less complex communication forms and functions. In one day of intermittent observations, the teacher saw Dan express five functions (greeting, farewell, emotions, comments, requests) by using eight specific forms (including vocal, verbal, tactile, and gestural). Dan's teacher was surprised by the extent of Dan's nonsymbolic communication repertoire, which previously had been dismissed as meaningless or annoying behaviors. With this new perspective, Dan's teacher worked with the speech-language therapist to reinforce and expand Dan's communication forms and functions, and to move him toward more spontaneous and complex means of communication. As shown in this example, communication intervention can build upon a well-identified nonsymbolic communication repertoire, rather than identified deficits, when students lack formal symbol systems (Mirenda et al., 1990).

Within a pragmatic theoretical framework for language development and instruction, it is useful to organize the embedded communication targets around three general communication outcomes: social interaction, comprehension, and expressing wants and needs (Mirenda & Smith-Lewis, 1989; Reichle & Keogh, 1986; Siegel-Causey & Guess, 1989).

Social interaction refers to a broad range of communicative functions, including attention to persons and activities in the environment, reciprocal interactions, and social conversation. Social aspects of communication may also include matching communication style and content with persons, activities, and environments.

Initially it may seem that some students with severe disabilities give little or no attention to their environment. Careful observation, however, usually reveals some reactions to people, activities, and living conditions. Crying, quieting, and even "tuning out" are very basic responses to the environment, which can become the basis for communication instruction. Participation with a communication partner in reciprocal interactions, such as taking turns in early social games, moves beyond these basic responses to environmental conditions. Van Dijk (1986) recognized that reciprocal interactions were an early form of intentional communication by infants, and applied this principle to his work with children classified as deafblind. Curricula based on van Dijk's work have been developed to teach reciprocal interactions to students with profound

handicaps (cf. Feiber, 1975; Robinson, 1975; Sternberg, Ritchey, Pegnatore, Wills, & Hill, 1986). More recently, Siegel-Causey and Guess (1989) and Writer (1987) extended the application of van Dijk's strategies from instruction in isolated contexts to communication instruction throughout daily routines. Siegel-Causey and Guess (1989) provided extensive guidelines and examples for how to recognize, support, and teach nonsymbolic communicative interactions in the context of daily routines.

As students acquire more formal modes of communication, they establish and maintain social interactions by labeling objects, people, and events, which develops into social conversation. Reichle and Keogh (1986) emphasized the need to differentiate between the social functions of labeling or describing and the requesting function. In one situation, a student may point to a friend to share thoughts about the friend. In another situation, pointing to a friend may be a request for a partner. Team members need to consider the context to interpret the intent of students' spontaneous communications properly and to determine which function to teach.

Other social aspects of communication include etiquette, such as saying "please" and "thank you," and greeting friends, familiar adults, and strangers in different ways. In secondary school programs, teams often find it important to teach students with severe disabilities to use certain vocabulary and nonverbal communication skills, so the students can "hang out" in ways consistent with the culture of the school.

Comprehension refers to understanding situations and language, which is inferred from some type of student response. Consistent demonstration of comprehension, or receptive communication, often is considered the prerequisite for teaching formal modes of expressive communication. Traditionally, comprehension has been assessed and taught to students with severe disabilities through series of adult-directed command-response and question-answer tasks. Although this format is convenient for instructors, it is inherently problematic. Consider Martha, who consistently followed directions and answered questions. When Martha reached the age of 17, her team realized that she rarely engaged in any communications or activities unless she was verbally directed to do so. The team established the priority of teaching Martha to make requests and initiate activities in response to natural cues. In contrast, Henry had no recognized mode of communication, so he could not answer questions. He rarely followed directions, and became violent when adults tried to control his actions. When adults began to watch Henry more closely, they realized that he clearly understood many things in his environment, and he responded to natural cues in appropriate ways.

For students like Henry, with no means to communicate their wants and needs, traditional interventions to "improve comprehension" do not produce functional outcomes. Teams now recognize that emphasis on receptive communication skills (e.g., following directions) encourages student dependence on artificial cues, limits student outcomes of communication, sometimes reduces motivation to communicate, encourages students to use undesirable behavior to communicate, and unnecessarily delays instruction on expressive communication. Instead, communication professionals increasingly focus on expressive communication needs first, and then assess and teach receptive communication skills as integral to expressive communica-

tion interactions. Several examples are presented below.

Expressing wants and needs refers to conveying desires, needs, and protests. Even when students demonstrate no reliable receptive communication skills, opportunities can be arranged for students to learn to control their environment by conveying preferences (Siegel-Causey & Guess, 1989). George seemed oblivious to his surroundings, and cried or slept for much of the school day. His team suspected that he was often uncomfortable, and devised an object communication system in which objects signified lying down, drinking water, and being changed. When George began fussing, team members interpreted his needs, guided him to touch the corresponding item, and immediately addressed the need. Not only did George begin to express these needs himself, but as a result of his needs being addressed, he started attending to other activities in his daily routine. Henry presented serious behavior problems, as described previously. Henry's team learned to interpret his behaviors from an ecological perspective and then taught him to express his needs with pictograms. Henry's acquisition of new expressive communication skills had the added benefits of reducing his use of inappropriate behavior for communication and his being described as "more manageable."

Jessica, a first grader with severe disabilities, only communicated basic emotions at school. When she continually refused to eat at lunch time, her team tried to make Jessica's food more appetizing and they arranged for her to eat in a calm, quiet area. Jessica still refused lunch. The team then hypothesized that her rejection of food was one of the few means she had to control her environment at school. Team members from school talked with Jessica's parents and found that she used her eyes in regular and reliable ways to communicate with family members. Although this was a rudimentary form of communication and she needed careful positioning for success, Jessica's communicative intents were clear. When the team consistently gave Jessica similar ways to control routine events throughout the day at school, she began eating her lunch.

Jessica and the other students discussed above demonstrated efforts to communicate. One means of improving the success of their efforts is to increase awareness and responsiveness of others in the environment to the communicative functions being expressed. Another complementary means is to address qualitative aspects of their communication.

Qualitative aspects of communication relate to mode, form, content, and rate. As with motor skills, the importance of qualitative features such as clear articulation, appropriate grammatical structure, and vocabulary size is determined through analysis of the function and context for communication (Browder, 1991). For example, Nick could point to and clearly name scores of objects when asked, but only began using his vocabulary for meaningful communication when the team provided opportunities for Nick to request materials when needed in daily routines.

Another student, Maria, had no verbal language but demonstrated her receptive language skills by following directions throughout the school day. In the context of daily routines, there were many indications that she could recognize pictures of people, actions, and objects. Her team was anxious to develop a formal communication system for her, but when "prerequisite" training tasks of pointing to pictures were presented, Maria did not seem to attend visually and randomly touched any picture. Nevertheless, Maria's immediate needs to communicate in daily routines were examined, and on this basis a communication board was designed. When meaningful opportunities for daily use were introduced, Maria was successful immediately. Her knowledge of language and pictures had no impact on her expressive communication development until a purpose or function for communication was evident to her.

Yolanda learned 20 manual signs at school to communicate her wants and needs. Her team then struggled with the fact that few people outside of Yolanda's school and home environments could understand her manual communications. Although she displayed an ability to master this mode of communication, its function for her in a wide range of environments was questionable.

Joe has a severe physical disability and a strong desire to communicate. He was learning to produce two distinct sounds: "hi" to greet people, and "hey" to gain attention. Once Joe initiated interactions with these verbalizations, he communicated needs and preferences with pictures and symbols. Because he had poor control of his head and both arms, Joe's team engaged in ongoing evaluation of the optimal means for him to convey his selection of symbols (e.g., gaze versus direct touch versus scanner).

Just as with sensorimotor skills, communication skills for students with severe disabilities can be addressed in the context of the ecological curriculum. The task of all team members, including related service providers, is the integration of their expertise for development of meaningful learning experiences within prioritized environments, activities, and daily routines.

AN INDIVIDUALIZED CURRICULUM

As the team identifies priority environments, activities, and skills for each student, an individualized curriculum begins to take shape. Kristen's and Jamal's teams used an "IEP worksheet" to begin identifying and organizing priorities for their respective curricula (see Table 4.7 and Table 4.8), following the steps outlined in this chapter. The format is intentionally called a "worksheet" because each team member receives a copy and is free to write and revise his or her own thoughts about priorities as the team discussion takes place (York & Vandercook, 1991). The worksheet is divided into two sections. The top section provides space to list environments, activities, and routines corresponding with life domains in which the student's participation is desired. Skills or other targets that are anticipated as important in a specific situation can be included in parentheses. The domains are not mutually exclusive, and many items could be written in more than one column. The bottom of the worksheet also lists skills the student needs to acquire, but these skills may apply to many activities and environments. The term "embedded skills" reflects that these skills are important not in isolation, but rather within the context of various activities and routines. The worksheet format presented here is one of many ways a team can organize the individualized ecological curriculum content. Perhaps the most important function of the worksheet is to focus all team members' attention on the same curricular content and process. Therefore, format adaptations are encouraged to meet varying team and student needs.

Initially, teams may fear that the curriculum for each student will be so diverse that it will be impractical to implement for one student, and impossible for more than one. In reality, there is overlap and meshing of priority environments and activities for many students, with the greatest diversity occurring in selection of skills to teach. Another concern is that establishing an ecological curriculum "from scratch" for every student is extremely time-consuming. Teams are reminded that adoption of an ecological curriculum is a *process,* which occurs over a period of time and which gradually replaces existing approaches to curriculum development. Although there are published versions of ecological curricula and assessments that may serve as models (see Freagon, Wheeler, McDaniel, Brankin, & Costello, 1983; Renzaglia & Aveno, 1986), these tend to reflect local circumstances. A variation is an "activity catalogue" that provides an extensive list of domain-referenced activities, which users abstract and expand to reflect local opportunities and student priorities (Kleinert & Hudson, 1989; Wilcox & Bellamy, 1987).

Whether working from an existing ecological curriculum model or starting from scratch, early curriculum development provides the foundation for later work. When a team identifies priority school or community environments and achieves access for one student, the process is established for the future. As the team delineates components of an activity routine for one student, their task is simplified for subsequent students. As new students enter the program, they participate in typical activities until assessments and IEPs are completed, just as they would with any other curriculum. In our experience, teams who adopt an ecological curriculum consider the benefits to outweigh the costs. Students receive more relevant and successful instruction and, as a result, team members find their own work more mean-

Table 4.7 IEP Worksheet for Kristen

Life Domains: Environments, Activities, and Routines

Home	School	School (continued)	General Community
Bedroom •choose clothing •ask for help •dressing -raise/lower pants -hold out arms/legs •select story •listen to story **Bathroom** •raise/lower pants •use toilet •wash hands •take a bath **Kitchen** •hold cup without handle •express preferences •use "more" and "all done" **Family room/backyard** •play alone •more interest in objects/toys •play with sister •develop social routines (e.g., soccer ball)	**Bus** •travel without parents **Hallways** •walk in halls (mobility) •find gym •find lunchroom **Classroom** •transitions •follow directions •follow routines •communicate with others **Play Areas** •select play materials •play with toys •interact with peers **Restroom** •raise/lower pants •use toilet •wash hands	**Art, Music, Library** •transitions •follow routines •cooperate with other teachers •listen to story •follow directions •get/put away materials •clean up **Gym** •follow group directions •work with peers •perform specified actions	**Doctor, Dentist, Hairstylist** •cooperate **Church** •interact with other children •participate in Sunday school activities **Restroom** •raise/lower pants •use toilet •wash hands **Fast Food Restaurant** •express preferences •use "more" and "all done" **Library** •select story •follow routines **Grocery Store** •select favorite cereal •follow routines •walking **YMCA** •follow routines •swim with adult •dressing -raise/lower pants -hold out arms/legs

Embedded Skills

Motor	Communication	Social	Other
•walk without falling •climb stairs •pincer grasp •reciprocal rise to stand	•express wants and needs (alternative to tantrums) •make choices	•take turns in play and other social routines	•play with toys •functional use of objects

Adapted from York, J., & Vandercook, T. (1991). Designing integrated education through the IEP process. *Teaching Exceptional Children, 23* (2), 22–28.

Table 4.8 IEP Worksheet for Jamal

Life Domains: Environments, Activities, and Routines

School	School (continued)	Community	Recreation/leisure	Domestic	Vocational (work experience >12 mos)
Homeroom •greetings •choice of magazines •choice of partner •head control •signal to turn page (vocalize) **Horticulture (T,Th)** •identify materials •plant watering (adaptation) •choice of partner **Home economics (M,W,F)** •identify materials •select recipe cards •operate appliances (with switch) •choice of correct partner •head control •eating •push recipe items away on tray to signal use **Lunchroom** •identify materials •select location •head control •eye gaze/scan for next bite	**Hallways** •choice of peer partner •mobility training with peer and walkman •transport materials on wheelchair **Media center (T,Th)** •explore computers, library use •choice of partner •games with peer **Choir (T, Th)** •identify materials •relaxation •music appreciation (taped to replay at home) **Spanish** •locate partners/group •activate prerecorded messages •participate in all cooperative learning group activities •team scorekeeper	**Bus stop** •greetings **Fast food** •identify materials •greet waitperson •select seat •picture request **Sidewalk & mall** •mobility training •select store (health/beauty aides vs. clothing) •select direction **Church** •relaxation •greetings •select location	**After school sports** •appreciation, enjoyment •greetings •swim team manager **Movie rental/MTV** •indicate desire •select snacks •operate appliance (milkshakes) **Community center/pool hall (VFW)** •select beverage •select activity •select partner/group **Mall wheeling** •mobility •greetings	**Kitchen (home)** •choice of drink, food •operate appliances •forward head position for spoon/cup •eye gaze/scan for next bite •indicate "done" **Bedroom** •choice of clothes •scan/eye gaze •call for attention upon waking (radio alarm) **Bathroom** •indicate order of grooming activities	**Inclusion specialist** •co-present slide series about school and community inclusion to high school students **Nursing home** •deliver mail •book cart •visit •escort residents to game room •carry items for residents **Insurance agency** •greetings •mobility practice during mail delivery •date stamping

Embedded Skills

Motor	Communication	Other
•explore power mobility using control switch adapted for head turning or gross arm movement •head or hand movement to deflect switches for activating simple electronic devices, communication •maintain/increase functional upper extremity use for specific tasks using adaptations •improve/maintain head and neck control during transitional movement sequences in selected positions and when eating/drinking •increase/maintain range of motion during transfers and in selected positions after relaxation and facilitation	•give directions (eye gaze) •direct attention to identifying information •self-determination: indicate wants, needs, and choices throughout daily routines (using eye gaze) to choose actual objects, people, locations •explore use of switch to indicate choices when objects are manually scanned (1 situation initially) •initial exposure to pictures for communication in the context of daily activities (no choice making) •vocalize to get attention (drop head, open mouth, vocalize)	•extend arm to press name stamp adaptation •transport materials on wheelchair

Adapted from York, J., & Vandercook, T. (1991). Designing integrated education through the IEP process. *Teaching Exceptional Children, 23* (2), 22-28.

ingful, enriching, and rewarding. More positive and extensive collaboration often occurs between school personnel and families because design and implementation of an individualized ecological curriculum requires significant family input. As to our purposes here, the ecological curriculum offers teams a unifying focus for their work. The curriculum encourages team members to view sensorimotor and communication skills as components of educational activities, and thereby facili-

tates implementation of an integrated therapy approach.

Given the legal requirement to develop an IEP prior to placement, initial goals and objectives may be projected as teams identify priorities for the curriculum. Prior to finalizing goals and objectives for the IEP, however, teams must assess student performance in the environments and activities they identified as priorities. The next chapter describes such an assessment process.

REFERENCES

Ayres, A.J. (1972). *Sensory integration and learning disorders.* Los Angeles: Western Psychological Services.

Bates, P., Morrow, S.A., Pancsofar, E., & Sedlak, R. (1984). The effect of functional vs. nonfunctional activities on attitudes of nonhandicapped college students: What they see is what we get. *Journal of The Association for Persons with Severe Handicaps, 9*(2), 73–78.

Baumgart, D., Brown, L., Pumpian, I., Nisbet, J., Ford, A., Sweet, M., Messina, R., & Schroeder, J. (1982). The principle of partial participation and individualized adaptations in educational programs for severely handicapped students. *Journal of The Association for Persons with Severe Handicaps, 7*(2), 17–27.

Bloom, L., & Lahey, M. (1978). *Language development and language disorders.* New York: John Wiley & Sons.

Bobath, K., & Bobath, B. (1972). Cerebral palsy. In P.H. Pearson & C.E. Williams (Eds.), *Physical therapy services in the developmental disabilities* (pp. 31–185). Springfield, IL: Charles C Thomas.

Breines, E. (1984). The issue is. . . . An attempt to define purposeful activity. *American Journal of Occupational Therapy, 38*(8), 543–544.

Bricker, D., & Iacino, R. (1977). Early intervention with severely/profoundly handicapped children. In E. Sontag, J. Smith, & N. Certo (Eds.), *Educational programming for the severely and profoundly handicapped* (pp. 166–176). Reston, VA: Council for Exceptional Children.

Bricker, W., & Bricker, D. (1974). An early language strategy. In R.L. Schiefelbusch & L. Lloyd (Eds.), *Language perspectives: Acquisition, retardation, and intervention* (pp. 431–468). Baltimore: University Park Press.

Browder, D. (1991). *Assessment of individuals with severe disabilities: An applied behavior approach to life skills assessment* (2nd ed.). Baltimore: Paul H. Brookes Publishing Co.

Brown, F., Evans, I., Weed, K., & Owen, V. (1987). Delineating functional competencies: A component model. *Journal of The Association for Persons with Severe Handicaps, 12*(2), 117–124.

Brown, L., Branston-McLean, M.B., Baumgart, D., Vincent, L., Falvey, M., & Schroeder, J. (1979). Using the characteristics of current and future least restrictive environments in the development of curricular content for severely handicapped students. *AAESPH Review, 4*(4), 407–424.

Brown, L., Nietupski, J., & Hamre-Nietupski, S. (1976). Criterion of ultimate functioning. In M.A. Thomas (Ed.), *Hey, don't forget about me!* (pp. 2–15). Reston, VA: Council for Exceptional Children.

Brown, L., Rogan, P., Shiraga, B., Zanella Albright, K., Kessler, K., Bryson, F., Van Deventer, P., & Loomis, R. (1987). *A vocational follow-up evaluation of the 1984 to 1986 Madison Metropolitan School District graduates with severe intellectual disabilities.* Seattle, WA: The Association for Persons with Severe Handicaps.

Chapman, R.S., & Miller, J.F. (1980). Analyzing

language and communication in the child. In R.L. Schiefelbusch (Ed.), *Nonspeech language and communication: Analysis and intervention* (pp. 159–196). Baltimore: University Park Press.

Eisner, E.W. (1979). *The educational imagination: On the design and evaluation of school programs.* New York: Macmillan Publishing Co.

Falvey, M. (1989). *Community-based curriculum: Instructional strategies for students with severe handicaps* (2nd ed.). Baltimore: Paul H. Brookes Publishing Co.

Feiber, N.M. (1975). *Movement in communication and language development of deaf-blind children.* Unpublished paper, Southwest Regional Center for Deaf-Blind Children, Sacramento, CA.

Ford, A., Schnorr, R., Meyer, L., Davern, L., Black, J., & Dempsey, P. (Eds.). (1989). *The Syracuse community-referenced curriculum guide for students with moderate and severe disabilities.* Baltimore: Paul H. Brookes Publishing Co.

Forest, M., & Lusthaus, E. (1987). The kaleidoscope: Challenge to the cascade. In M. Forest (Ed.), *More education/integration* (pp. 1–16). Downsview, Ontario: G. Allan Roeher Institute.

Freagon, S., Wheeler, J., McDaniel, K., Brankin, G., & Costello, D. (1983). *Individual student community life skill profile system for severely handicapped students.* DeKalb, IL: DeKalb County Special Education Association.

Frostig, M., & Horne, D. (1973). *The Frostig program for the development of visual perception* (rev. ed.). Chicago: Follett.

Gesell, A., & Amatruda, C.S. (1947). *Developmental diagnosis.* New York: Harper & Row.

Giangreco, M., Cloninger, C., & Iverson, V. (1990). *COACH: Cayuga-Onandaga assessment for children with handicaps.* Stillwater, OK: National Clearinghouse of Rehabilitation Training Materials.

Goetz, L., & Gee, K. (1987). Functional vision programming: A model for teaching visual behavior in natural contexts. In L. Goetz, D. Guess, & K. Stremel-Campbell (Eds.), *Innovative program design for individuals with dual sensory impairments* (pp. 77–98). Baltimore: Paul H. Brookes Publishing Co.

Halle, J.W. (1988). Adopting the natural environment as the context of training. In S. Cal-

culator & J. Bedrosian (Eds.), *Communication assessment and intervention for adults with mental retardation* (pp. 155–185). Boston: College Hill Press.

Harvey, R.F., & Jellinek, H.M. (1981). Functional performance assessment: A program approach. *Archives of Physical Medicine and Rehabilitation, 62*(9), 456–460.

Hulme, J.B., Poor, R., Schulein, M., & Pezzino, J. (1983). Perceived behavioral changes observed with adapted seating devices and training programs for multihandicapped, developmentally disabled individuals. *Physical Therapy, 63*(2), 204–208.

Johnson, D.W., & Johnson, F. (1987). *Joining together: Group theory and group skills.* Englewood Cliffs, NJ: Prentice-Hall.

Klein, R.M., & Bell, B. (1982). Self-care skills: Behavioral measurement with Klein-Bell ADL scale. *Archives of Physical Medicine and Rehabilitation, 63*(7), 335–338.

Kleinert, H., & Hudson, N. (Eds.).(1989). *Model local catalogue and curriculum process for students with moderate and severe handicaps.* Lexington: Kentucky Systems Change Project, Interdisciplinary Human Development Institute, University of Kentucky.

Kruger, L. (1988). Programmatic change strategies at the building level. In J.L. Graden, J.E. Zins, & M.J. Curtis (Eds.), *Alternative educational delivery systems: Enhancing instructional options for all students* (pp. 491–512). Washington, DC: National Association of School Psychologists.

Loria, C. (1980). Relationship of proximal and distal function in motor development. *Physical Therapy, 60*(2), 167–172.

Mallory, B., & Herrick, S. (1987). The movement of children with mental retardation from institutional to community care. *Journal of The Association for Persons with Severe Handicaps, 12*(4), 297–305.

McLean, M.B., & Odom, S. (1988). *Division for early childhood white paper: Least restrictive environment and social integration.* Reston, VA: Council for Exceptional Children, Division for Early Childhood.

Miller, J. (1977). On specifying what to teach: The movement from structure, to structure and meaning, to structure and meaning and knowing. In E. Sontag, J. Smith, & N. Certo (Eds.), *Educational programming for the severely and profoundly handicapped* (pp.

378–388). Reston, VA: Council for Exceptional Children.

Mirenda, P., Iacono, T., & Williams, R. (1990). Communication options for persons with severe and profound disabilities: State of the art and future directions. *Journal of The Association for Persons with Severe Handicaps, 15*(1), 3–21.

Mirenda, P., & Smith-Lewis, M. (1989). Communication skills. In A. Ford, R. Schnorr, L. Meyer, L. Davern, J. Black, & P. Dempsey (Eds.), *The Syracuse community-referenced curriculum guide* (pp. 189–209). Baltimore: Paul H. Brookes Publishing Co.

Mount, B., & Zwernik, K. (1988). *It's never too early, it's never too late: A booklet about personal futures planning.* St. Paul, MN: Metropolitan Council.

Mulligan, M., Lacy, L., & Guess, D. (1982). Effects of massed, distributed, and spaced trial sequencing on severely handicapped students' performance. *Journal of The Association for the Severely Handicapped, 7*(2), 48–61.

Norris, J., & Hoffman, P. (1990). Language intervention in naturalistic environments. *Language, Speech, and Hearing Services in Schools, 21*(2), 72–84.

O'Brien, J. (1987). A guide to life-style planning: Using The Activities Catalog to integrate services and natural support systems. In B. Wilcox & G.T. Bellamy, *A comprehensive guide to The Activities Catalog: An alternative curriculum for youth and adults with severe disabilities* (pp. 175–189). Baltimore: Paul H. Brookes Publishing Co.

O'Brien, J., Forest, M., Snow, J., & Hasbury, D. (1989). *Action for inclusion.* Toronto, Ontario: Frontier College Press.

O'Brien, J., & Lyle, C. (1987). *Framework for accomplishment.* Decatur, GA: Responsive Systems Associates.

Orelove, F.P., & Sobsey, D. (1991). *Educating children with multiple disabilities: A transdisciplinary approach* (2nd ed.). Baltimore: Paul H. Brookes Publishing Co.

Pratt, P.N., & Allen, A.S. (1989). *Occupational therapy for children* (2nd ed.). St. Louis: C.V. Mosby Co.

Prutting, C., & Kirchner, D. (1987). A clinical appraisal of the pragmatic aspects of language. *Journal of Speech and Hearing Disorders, 52*(2), 105–119.

Rainforth, B., Giangreco, M., & Dennis, R. (1989). Motor skills. In A. Ford, R. Schnorr, L. Meyer, L. Davern, J. Black, & P. Dempsey (Eds.), *The Syracuse community-referenced curriculum guide for students with moderate and severe disabilities* (pp. 211–230). Baltimore: Paul H. Brookes Publishing Co.

Reichle, J., & Karlan, G. (1985). The selection of an augmentative system of communication intervention: A critique of decision rules. *Journal of The Association for Persons with Severe Handicaps, 10*(3), 146–156.

Reichle, J., & Keogh, W. (1986). Communication instruction for learners with severe handicaps: Some unresolved issues. In R. Horner, L. Meyer, & H.D. Fredericks (Eds.), *Education of learners with severe handicaps: Exemplary service strategies* (pp. 189–219). Baltimore: Paul H. Brookes Publishing Co.

Renzaglia, A., & Aveno, A. (1986). *Manual for administration of an individualized functional curriculum assessment procedure for students with moderate to severe handicaps.* Charlottesville: University of Virginia.

Robinett, C.S., & Vondran, M.A. (1988). Functional ambulation velocity and distance requirements in rural and urban communities. *Physical Therapy, 68*(9), 1371–1373.

Robinson, P. (1975). *An educational approach utilizing developmental sequencing and the coactive movement theory.* Unpublished paper, Northern Regional Service Center, South Bend, IN.

Seligman, M. (1975). *Helplessness: On depression, development, and death.* San Francisco: W.H. Freeman.

Siegel-Causey, E., & Guess, D. (1989). *Enhancing nonsymbolic communication interactions among learners with severe disabilities.* Baltimore: Paul H. Brookes Publishing Co.

Sternberg, L., Ritchey, H., Pegnatore, L., Wills, L., & Hill, C. (1986). *A curriculum for profoundly handicapped students.* Rockville, MD: Aspen Publishers.

Taylor, S., Biklen, R., & Knoll, J. (Eds.) (1987). *Community integration for persons with severe disabilities.* New York: Teachers College Press.

Vandercook, T., York, J., & Forest, M. (1989). The McGill action planning system (MAPS): A strategy for building the vision. *Journal of The Association for Persons with Severe Handicaps, 14*(3), 205–215.

van Dijk, J. (1986). An educational curriculum for deaf-blind multi-handicapped persons. In D. Ellis (Ed.), *Sensory impairments in mentally handicapped people* (pp.375–382). London: Croom-Helm.

Van Sant, A.F. (1988). Age differences in movement patterns used by children to rise from supine position to erect stance. *Physical Therapy, 68*(9), 1330–1338.

Webster's Ninth New Collegiate Dictionary. (1987). Springfield, MA: Merriam-Webster, Inc.

Wilcox, B., & Bellamy, G.T. (1982). *Design of high school programs for severely handicapped students.* Baltimore: Paul H. Brookes Publishing Company.

Wilcox, B., & Bellamy, G.T. (1987). *The Activities Catalog: An alternative curriculum for youth and adults with severe disabilities.* Baltimore: Paul H. Brookes Publishing Co.

Williams, W., Fox, T., Thousand, J., & Fox, W. (1990). Level of acceptance and implementation of best practices in the education of students with severe handicaps in Vermont. *Education and Training in Mental Retardation, 25*(2), 120–131.

Writer, J. (1987). A movement-based approach to education of students who are sensory impaired/multihandicapped. In L. Goetz, D. Guess, & K. Stremel-Campbell (Eds.), *Innovative program design for individuals with dual sensory impairments* (pp. 191–224). Baltimore: Paul H. Brookes Publishing Co.

York, J. (1989). Mobility methods selected for use in home and community environments. *Physical Therapy, 69*(9), 736–747.

York, J., Giangreco, M.F., Vandercook, T., & Macdonald, C. (1992). Integrating support personnel in the inclusive classroom. In S. Stainback & W. Stainback (Eds.), *Curriculum considerations in inclusive classrooms: Facilitating learning for all students* (pp. 101–116). Baltimore: Paul H. Brookes Publishing Co.

York, J., & Rainforth, B. (1991). Developing instructional adaptations. In F. Orelove & D. Sobsey, *Educating children with multiple disabilities: A transdisciplinary approach* (2nd ed.) (pp. 259–295). Baltimore: Paul H. Brookes Publishing Co.

York, J., Rainforth, B., & Wiemann, G. (1988). An integrated approach to therapy for school-aged learners with developmental disabilities. *Totline, 14*(3), 36–40.

York, J., & Vandercook, T. (1991). Designing an integrated education for learners with severe disabilities through the IEP process. *Teaching Exceptional Children, 23*(2), 22–28.

5

Collaborative Assessment

Beverly Rainforth, Cathy Macdonald,
Jennifer York, and Winnie Dunn

STUDENTS WITH SEVERE DISABILITIES ARE evaluated for numerous purposes, including determination of service needs, identification of program content, and evaluation of program effectiveness (Bailey & Wolery, 1989; Browder, 1991). Public Law 94-142 and Public Law 99-457 require that a multidisciplinary team conduct a comprehensive evaluation to determine whether a child has exceptional educational needs that warrant special services. If special education is warranted, a comprehensive evaluation must be conducted at least once every 3 years for the duration of services. The student also must be assessed at least annually to determine his or her present level of educational performance, to ascertain progress on the current individualized education program (IEP), and to establish IEP goals and objectives for the next year. Additionally, effective instructional practices require frequent and ongoing assessment of student performance on IEP and individualized family service plan (IFSP) objectives, as the basis for instructional decision making and responsive program modification (Browder, 1991).

Eligibility for special education services has not been an issue for students with severe disabilities, and assessment to ascertain eligibility is not discussed here. This chapter presents assessment strategies related to the triennial evaluation, the annual review, and ongoing assessment as integral to daily instruction. The strategies described here presume that: 1) an ecological curriculum model has been (or is being) adopted, and 2) educational team members collaborate in the assessment process. The assessment process includes four main steps: 1) planning, 2) assessing student performance in natural environments, 3) analyzing performance discrepancies and generating hypotheses, and 4) conducting diagnostic assessment.

Since the steps in the process are nominally familiar to most teachers and therapists, it is important to note some distinctions. In traditional approaches, individual team members conduct independent assessments using a variety of formal and informal instruments. Often a disability in one area (e.g., movement) limits performance in another area (e.g., communication) without professionals from the respective disciplines recognizing or adjusting for this interaction effect. Or different professionals may collect information about similar skills (e.g., teacher, occupational therapist, and physical therapist all assess sensorimotor skills). Although varied perspectives are important for collaborative planning, parallel efforts tend to result in duplicated efforts. In traditional approaches, each discipline completes a separate report, so overall results might be redundant, conflicting, irrelevant, or incomplete. Furthermore, multidisciplinary assessment is very costly, and does not necessarily lead to effective program planning. W.A. Bricker and Campbell (1980) analyzed recommendations made by multidisciplinary teams who conducted educational assessments of 17 students with multiple disabilities. While 397 recommendations were made, only 30% were directly related to educational programming, appropriate for the designated student, and specific enough to be implemented. Only 11% of the recommendations were ever implemented. This is especially disappointing when one considers that the conservative cost estimate for these assessments was $1,500 per student in 1980. Similar assessments cost far more today.

Some of the shortcomings of traditional multidisciplinary and interdisciplinary assessment are addressed by the "arena" approach, in which the entire team assembles to observe the student's performance (Connor, Williamson, & Siepp, 1978). The assessment process is planned, team member participation is coordinated, and observations and conclusions are integrated. In a pilot study of arena assessment, parents reported increased satisfaction with this approach, which they considered more thorough and more likely to produce an ac-

curate picture of their child (Wolery & Dyk, 1984). Staff found that arena assessment increased parent participation, produced more accurate pictures of preschool-age children with severe handicaps, and resulted in more positive interactions, fewer miscommunications, and more team consensus than the interdisciplinary assessment process they had used previously.

Although the arena approach addresses many weaknesses of traditional assessments, it still establishes artificial settings and contrived tasks, which do not promote accurate assessment of students with severe disabilities. More recently, Linder (1990) described a "transdisciplinary play-based assessment" (TPBA) for young children. This variation on arena assessment recognizes play as a normal activity for young children, which provides a natural context for assessment. Because some aspects of the formal TPBA might be artificial for some children, Linder also encouraged teams to apply the strategy to other activities and environments that would be more relevant for individual children.

In the collaborative assessment process described in this chapter, observation of students performing typical activities in natural environments precedes more formal assessment by specific disciplines for several reasons. Aside from the problems discussed previously, starting with formal and discipline-specific assessment leads to preconceived notions about what a student *cannot* do, and tends to deny opportunities for participation in normalized activities and environments. Many students with severe disabilities have surpassed professionals' expectations when presented with real-life tasks in natural situations. Furthermore, it is performance in natural environments that is most significant. If a student points to the pictures of preferred food items at McDonald's, but will not point to the same pictures in the speech therapy room or in the formal assessment arena, an instructional need has not been identified. If a student can rotate and retrieve toys from the floor while sitting on a therapy ball, but does not reach down to get materials from a shelf in the classroom, a need exists. This need exists within the context of the typical activity in the classroom, however, and cannot be assessed accurately in another situation.

Finally, the disciplinary expertise of each team member can be used to the greatest advantage when it focuses on determining why a student has specific performance problems and how that performance can be improved. In traditional assessment, individual team members often perform this diagnostic assessment intuitively and fail to articulate conclusions or the bases for these to other team members. When team members see performance problems only from their own disciplinary perspective and plan interventions accordingly, conflict and confusion are likely. Therefore, it is essential that team members discuss their respective hypotheses prior to drawing conclusions. It is during the processes of assessment and program development that team members draw upon their store of scientific, theoretical, and practical knowledge to analyze situations and hypothesize solutions. Since it would be impractical and impossible to share all of this knowledge, we do not advocate role release to the extent that any relevant discipline would be eliminated from the assessment team. We do advocate that team members share information during the process, however, since this enables everyone to perform more effective assessment. The extensive information sharing, coordination, and coopera-

tion among team members throughout the assessment process lays the groundwork for designing comprehensive and integrated programs for students with severe disabilities.

THE ASSESSMENT PROCESS

The assessment process consists of four main steps: 1) planning the assessment, 2) assessing student performance in natural environments, 3) analyzing performance discrepancies and generating hypotheses, and 4) conducting diagnostic assessment. Although each step in the process is described below as a separate entity, an actual assessment proceeds at varied rates, and steps may overlap. For example, priorities or logistical constraints may result in a team completing almost all steps of an assessment at school before beginning assessment in community settings. As team members become skilled in the process, they are also likely to start collecting some diagnostic information while observing the student in routine activities. Examples of the process for an initial or triennial evaluation and for ongoing program development are presented for Kristen and Jamal, who were introduced in Chapter 4. The flow chart in Figure 5.1 provides an overview of steps in the assessment process.

Planning the Assessment

When using a collaborative team approach and an ecological curriculum model, coordination of assessment is challenging. It is desirable for all team members to assess student performance in every priority environment, but logistically, it usually is not possible to arrange this before instruction begins. Therefore, parent and professional members of the educational team must set

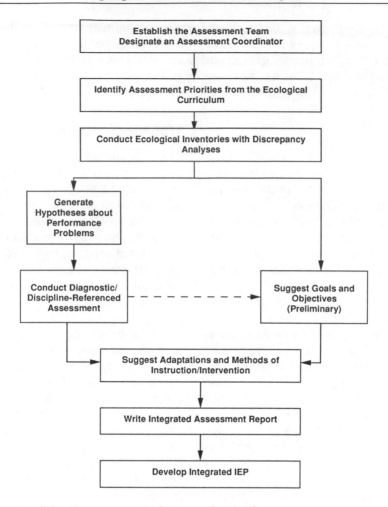

Figure 5.1. Steps in collaborative assessment to design an educational program.

priorities regarding the order of environments and activities in which the student will be assessed, and determine which team members will participate in each stage of the assessment.

The first step in planning is to establish the assessment team. As with any other assessment, the student's known and presumed needs determine team composition, and other members are added as new needs are identified. (Considerations for selecting specific team members are discussed in Chapter 8.) Once established,

the team designates an assessment coordinator. Typically this is the teacher since she or he has the most frequent contact with the student, family, and other school personnel. The teacher also manages the student schedule and knows the support staff schedules, which expedites coordination. The assessment coordinator develops a chart to organize and document the assessment process for each student. Examples of Ecological Assessment Planning Charts for Kristen and Jamal are presented later in this chapter (see Tables 5.3 and

5.8). Across the top of the chart are listed all the disciplines on the student's team. Down the left side are listed the environments and activities or routines in which ecological assessment will occur. Using this chart as a guide, the team meets to identify the initial environments for assessment. The highest priorities are identified and the team decides which team member(s) will assess the student's performance in these environments first. Dates are entered in the corresponding spaces to indicate when the assessments will be conducted. As reflected in Kristen's and Jamal's Planning Charts, it may take several days to complete ecological assessments in the limited number of environments that are designated highest priority. Since assessment in all environments is a long-term venture, it is better to think of ecological assessment as a process rather than an event.

The environments and activities where the assessment will occur are derived from the IEP worksheets and individualized ecological curriculum, as described in Chapter 4. Decisions about initial priorities will depend upon where the student currently participates and where participation is desired, both immediately and in the future. Family members often identify home or community environments where needs exist, and they may also have definite ideas about priority school environments. Family members are encouraged to identify their priorities first, after which professionals might add environments and activities they believe are priorities. At school, students are usually assessed first in environments and activities that comprise typical routines. As additional environments and activities are identified to meet individual needs, the team expands their assessment to those areas. When students reach middle and high school age,

community environments assume increasing importance. Considerations in scheduling the assessment include choosing the time when priority activities occur most naturally and when the child's perfor mance will be most representative. Strategies that allow flexibility for team members to work with students in a variety of environments are presented in Chapter 8.

Teams are urged to recognize that all members cannot conduct meaningful assessment of student performance in all environments and activities during the first month of school. Priorities must be set. For example, a team may decide that the occupational therapist and speech-language therapist should be the first ones to assess a student at his job site. The special educator will assess the student there eventually, but that team member's first priority may be to assess him in two integrated high school classes. Deciding which team members will be involved in initial assessments will depend on student needs, family priorities, and staff schedules. All team members might not need to observe the student in all activities, but they do need to observe representative performance in priority areas. For example, it may be important that the speech-language therapist assess the student's communication in individual, small group, and large group activities, or where the student has particular success or difficulty. It is also highly desirable for two or more team members to observe the student together, for more reliable and multifaceted interpretations of performance. For therapists to participate in this way, block scheduling is recommended (see Chapter 8). Teams are cautioned to limit the number of observers at any one time, however, to minimize the confusion, congestion, and artificial effects produced when too many adults are present.

There are special considerations for planning an assessment when a new student is entering a program. It is most appropriate for the assessment to start with observation in a familiar environment such as the home, day care center, or another education program. Observation in familiar environments and routines yields more valid information on performance, provides a general baseline for measuring growth, introduces the student to school personnel in a less stressful way, and offers bases for understanding or assessing the student's behavior at school. A team usually identifies one or two members to perform the ecological assessment at home. Considerations in selecting assessors include family preference, perceived needs, and staff schedules.

Many students demonstrate different abilities and personalities at home, and most perform under different expectations and limits than they do at school. Therefore, periodic re-assessment at home or in a day care setting can also be helpful. Factors such as geography, staffing, and program policies and procedures influence each team's ability to make home visits and preplacement visits. In some cases, alternative strategies, such as videotaping, can provide useful baseline information.

Assessing Student Performance in Natural Environments

The student's daily schedule and participation in priority environments provide the context for assessment of abilities and needs relevant to the educational program. Prior to the assessment, team members conduct inventories of priority environments and activities. An ecological inventory delineates the performance expected by a person of about the same age who does not have a disability. Depending upon the abilities and needs of the student

being assessed, the steps in the inventory may be expanded or condensed (Black & Ford, 1989). For example, the team considered Kristen's age, her prior educational experiences, and the nature of her disabilities when they based her inventories on performance of typical 5-year-olds, with steps added to emphasize motor and communication skills. For Jamal, a high school student with severe disabilities, some of the motor skill sequences were shortened for his assessment at work. The team had previously made systematic and concerted efforts to increase Jamal's motor participation in removing his jacket, yet he continued to need full assistance. Team members agreed that this performance probably would not improve significantly, so they did not break down this task. They carefully analyzed other motor skill sequences relevant to Jamal's job, however.

As inventories are developed, the student is observed during naturally occurring activities to determine how he or she performs without assistance. Assistance is given, of course, when failure to do so would endanger the student or completely preclude performance. An important aspect of assessment when students are not able to demonstrate a necessary skill is an initial attempt at intervention. Team members engage the student in designated activities, using a variety of teaching and intervention strategies to elicit optimal performance. Otherwise the assessment results would merely indicate whether or not the student performed the task but would provide no information about possible interventions. Using the environmental inventory as the guide for assessment, team members record whether the student performed designated activities independently, how the student participated, and what type of assistance elicited optimal performance. Examples of ecological inventories and corresponding assessments of Kristen and Jamal are presented later in this chapter (see Tables 5.5, 5.10, and 5.12).

Part of Jamal's ecological assessment was conducted in the general education classes in which he was integrated. Some students with severe disabilities develop a strong interest in a particular secondary curriculum area (e.g., biology), but require modifications in scope and quality of performance. As students with severe disabilities grow older, however, their learning priorities tend to become more discrepant from the priorities for students without disabilities. For example, in the Spanish or Home Economics classes in which Jamal was enrolled, his learning priorities had little to do with the core curricular content so it was inappropriate to design ecological assessments that focused exclusively on the core curriculum. Routines in general education classes present many other types of demands and learning opportunities that frequently are priorities for students with severe disabilities, and it is important to conduct ecological assessments of these opportunities (York & Vandercook, 1990). Browder (1991), Brown, Evans, Weed, and Owen (1987), Meyer and colleagues (1985), Thousand and colleagues (1986), and Williams, Hamre-Nietupski, Pumpian, McDaniel-Marx, and Wheeler (1978) offer strategies that apply to analysis of general education classroom environments. Based on a review of these sources, the "Assessment of Student Participation in General Education Classes" (Macdonald & York, 1989) was developed to assess student participation in two major areas: classroom routines and activities, and social and communication skills (Figure 5.2). Jamal's ecological assessment for Spanish class, presented later in this chapter, was based on this approach.

When multiple team members partici-pate in an assessment, it is helpful to designate roles. The facilitator engages students in routine activities, eliciting both typical and optimal performance. Observers watch and suggest alternative strategies to the facilitator. Recorders take notes on what the student does, how the student does it, and what he or she does not do. A complete assessment usually takes several sessions, and in the course of the assessment, each team member would alternate among the roles of facilitator, observer, and recorder. Parents participate in each of these roles as they feel comfortable and as the team (including the parents) deems appropriate. Experienced teaching assistants often participate actively in assessment.

Even within one assessment session, a team member may assume all three roles. For example, during snack time at school, a teaching assistant worked with Kristen on finger feeding. When the occupational therapist observed difficulties, he asked the assistant to seat Kristen on a higher chair, support her feet with a large block, and prompt at the elbow. Kristen responded well to each change. Then the occupational therapist stepped in as facilitator to see how he could prompt a fingertip grasp. He modeled one method for the assistant, who then resumed working with Kristen. The occupational therapist made notes about the situation as he continued to observe.

Analyzing Discrepancies and Generating Hypotheses

After performance information is recorded and the assessment is completed for a specific environment, discrepancies are identified between the way in which designated activities are performed by the student and the way in which they are performed by a person without disabilities. For each discrepancy, team members begin

Assessment of Student Participation in General Education Classes

Student: _____

Classroom Teacher: _____

Assessment Completed by: _____

Grade, Subject, and Class Period: _____

Prep Periods: _____ Room Number: _____ # of Students in Class: _____

Date: _____

Instructions:
1. After the student attends the specific general education class for approximately one week, the team reviews all the skills identified in Sections I and II of this assessment tool.

Score.	+	for items that student consistently performs;
	+/-	for items that student does some of the time but not consistently;
	-	for items that student never or very rarely performs; and
	NA	for items that are not appropriate for the student/class

2. Circle about 5 items that the team identifies as priorities for instructional emphasis for the individual student.
3. Write objectives for each of the circled items, then design related instructional programs.
4. Review student progress on all items at least 2 more times during the school year. Revise as needed.

I. CLASSROOM ROUTINES AND ACTIVITIES

Date: _____

	Date:		
1. Gets to class on time.			
2. Gets seated in class on time.			
3. Performs transitional activities during class in response to situational cues (e.g., changes in seating, activity)			
4. Begins tasks.			
5. Stays on task.			
6. Participates in some regular class activities without adaptations.			
7. Terminates tasks.			
8. Tolerates out-of-the-ordinary changes in classroom routine			
9. Follows class rules.			
10. Locates / brings materials to class as needed.			
11. Shares materials with peers when appropriate.			
12. Uses materials for their intended purpose.			
13. Puts materials away after use.			
14. Uses classroom materials and equipment safely.			
15. Works cooperatively with a partner.			
16. Works cooperatively with a small group.			
17. Performs competitive learning tasks.			
18. Readily accepts assistance.			
19. Evaluates quality of own work (given a model).			
20. Copes with criticism / correction without incident and tries an alternative behavior.			

II. SOCIAL AND COMMUNICATION SKILLS

Date: _____

21. Interacts with peers:
   a. responds to others
   b. initiates

22. Interacts with the classroom teacher:
   a. responds to the teacher
   b. initiates

23. Uses social greetings:
   a. responds to others
   b. initiates

24. Uses farewells:
   a. responds to others
   b. initiates

25. Uses expressions of politeness
(e.g., please, thank you, excuse me):
   a. responds to others
   b. initiates

26. Participates in joking or teasing
   a. responds to others
   b. initiates

27. Makes choices and indicates preferences:
   a. responds to others (cue or question)
   b. initiates

28. Asks questions
   a. asks for help
   b. asks for information (e.g., clarification, feedback)

29. Follows directions
   a. for curricular tasks
   b. for helping tasks/errands
   c. given to the student individually
   d. given to students as a group

30. States or indicates:
   a. don't know / don't understand
   b. when finished with an activity

31. Orients toward the speaker or other source of input.

32. Secures listener attention before communicating.

33. Maintains eye contact with the listener when speaking.

34. Takes turns communicating in conversation with others.

35. Gives feedback.
   a. gives positive feedback
   b. gives negative feedback

36. Uses appropriate gestures and body movements when
interacting with others.

37. Uses appropriate language / vocabulary / topic of
conversation.

38. Uses intelligible speech (volume, rate, articulation, etc.)

Comments:

Figure 5.2. Classroom assessment tool. (From Macdonald, C., & York, J. [1989]. Regular class integration: Assessment, objectives, instructional programs. In J. York, T. Vandercook, C. Macdonald, & S. Wolff [Eds.], *Strategies for full inclusion* [pp. 83–116]. Minneapolis: University of Minnesota, Institute on Community Integration; reprinted by permission.)

113

to hypothesize about factors that may contribute to the student's performance difficulties. As individual team members accumulate information about what the student does and does not do in a variety of situations, each begins to categorize his or her observations, and draw conclusions about the student's abilities, disabilities, and needs. The processes of analyzing discrepancies and generating hypotheses have tremendous influence on how teams design instructional programs, but rarely are these processes conducted in a collaborative manner. Although each team member's experience and discipline perspective is an important contribution to the process, it can also constrain or negatively bias the analysis. Conflict may arise when different team members ascribe different causes to the same behavior and then recommend different types of intervention. Consider, for example, a student with severe disabilities who starts crying soon after starting lunch in the cafeteria. Different observers might attribute this to various factors, such as sensory overload in the loud and busy cafeteria, fear or discomfort with ineffective feeding techniques, frustration with inability to communicate likes and dislikes, or underlying emotional disorders.

It is essential that team members identify and discuss the bases for their interpretations. An effective strategy to resolve differences among professional views is for the team to identify one or more performance problems, observe the student together, and brainstorm possible explanations and contributing factors. Observing the student together increases the likelihood that team members will agree on what they saw and, therefore, that they will understand and respect the perspective of other disciplines. During brainstorming, team members generate as many ideas as possible and refrain from judgments, since this limits creative thinking. After considering a variety of possibilities, the team eliminates those that are not supported by many other aspects of the student's performance. In the situation of the student crying in the school cafeteria, for example, the team might rule out an underlying emotional disorder, because the student is happy and cooperative in almost all other situations. The team might also note that the student is not distressed in other busy, noisy routines, such as when several classes are changing classrooms, during the beginning of a school assembly, or during the school's afternoon dismissal. The team will still be left with several possibilities, however, which they formulate into questions. Team members then devise systematic strategies to test the various hypotheses. Examples of how this process was used with Kristen and Jamal are presented later in this chapter.

Parents or special education programs sometimes refer students with severe disabilities to other agencies for independent or specialized assessments to complement those conducted by the educational program staff. Educational teams are often disappointed that the resulting assessment reports tell them little more than what they already knew. Frequently, school-based teams can elicit more satisfactory and enlightening results if they go through the process of hypothesis generation, formulate specific questions, and send their written questions to the outside assessment team.

Conducting Diagnostic/ Discipline-Referenced Assessment

It is after performance discrepancies in educational environments are identified and initial discrepancy analyses are performed that assessment by individual disciplines can produce the most useful information. This step in the assessment process has been termed "diagnostic assessment" (Hupp & Donofrio, 1983), because it analyzes the nature of and relationship among specific aspects of performance. The first purpose of the diagnostic assessment is to answer the questions raised during hypothesis generation, using a variety of informal and formal strategies. Informal diagnostic assessment consists of systematically testing the influence of various factors on the student's performance. In the case of the student crying in the cafeteria, the team might learn that the student also cries when eating at home and during toothbrushing at both home and school. Then team members try a variety of strategies, one at a time, to see if the student accepts the food more easily if given different prompts around the mouth, if told more about what is going to happen, if given time to smell the food before eating, if given choices between foods, if given foods of more consistent flavor or temperature, and so on. Because testing multiple factors at the same time tends to mask the positive, negative, and neutral effects of each factor, only one possibility is tested at a time.

For formal diagnostic assessment, Hupp and Donofrio (1983) recommended the identification and use of numerous assessment instruments, or portions of instruments, each with slightly different applications. Commercial tools that are useful for analyzing sensorimotor and communication performance are described below. *It is emphasized that the tools listed below offer diagnostic guidance. They do not have to be administered in totality.* Furthermore, the information needed to complete most items can be obtained in routine school and community activities, rather than through isolated testing. Finally, commercial assessment tools provide only one piece of information for the team to consider when designing instruction.

The second purpose of diagnostic/discipline-referenced assessment is to gather additional information that any team member considers important, but that was not available or appropriate for assessment during routine home, school, and community activities. This can also be done using formal or informal assessment strategies. For example, a speech-language therapist may formally assess receptive language using a standardized instrument to establish a baseline for later comparison or to fulfill school district requirements. After informally gathering information about functional range of motion during routine activities, a physical therapist might want to assess range of motion formally and record exact measurements for a student who has spasticity. When collaborative teams adopt an ecological curriculum, the diagnostic/discipline-referenced assessment focuses on performance difficulties that have already been identified as educational priorities by the team. This differs significantly from traditional, isolated assessments that serve as the initial and primary basis for determining program content.

Sensorimotor Assessment The areas considered here for sensorimotor assessment parallel the functional outcomes of sensorimotor skills identified in Chapter 4. Several tools that might support formal assessment of sensorimotor skills for students with severe disabilities are described in this section.

Postural Control and Mobility The Assessment of Behavioral Components (ABC) (Hardy, Kudar, & Macdonald, 1988) is a criterion-referenced assessment for children with severe motor disabilities related to cerebral palsy. The assessment has three sections: Tone and Range of Motion (17 items), Reflexes (10 items), and Gross Motor Development (65 items). The Gross Motor Development section has six subdivisions: Head and Trunk Control, Prone Position, Supine Position, Rolling, Sitting, and Standing. Organization of gross motor items by position is particularly useful to assess students whose development is uneven or who use only certain positions. An instructional manual describes important considerations for assessment of children with cerebral palsy, and uses a self-study format to prepare professionals, parents, and paraprofessionals to administer the assessment accurately. Each of the 92 items has jargon-free directions for testing, a description and illustration of the normal response, and descriptions and illustrations of other responses that might be observed when a child has cerebral palsy. Many items have separate descriptions of performance associated with high or low tone. Scores from 1 (normal) to 4 (severely abnormal), defined behaviorally for each item, correspond with small increments of change. A self-graphing score sheet has space for results of 12 test administrations to show trends over time. The ABC has been field tested with professionals, parents, and paraprofessionals with high levels of interobserver and test-retest reliability. The ABC has not been normed and does not yield a total motor performance score, which limits its utility for program evaluation or research (Campbell, 1989), but this does not affect its use for diagnostic assessment. Since the ABC is based primarily on infant development, it should be used cautiously with older children. The large number of items for fundamental gross motor skills, the organization of gross motor items by position, and the unique scoring system make the ABC particularly useful for assessment of students

with severe motor disabilities. Although not used widely yet, the ABC offers several advantages over other available assessment tools.

The *Peabody Developmental Motor Scales* (Folio & Fewell, 1983) is one of the very few assessments that examines early stages of gross motor development extensively (with 70 items up through the initial stage of walking) and is standardized. According to the examiner's manual, the scales have high levels of interrater and test-retest reliability, and good ethnic, concurrent, construct, and predictive validity. Others have raised concerns about test construction, content, administration, and scoring, however (see Hinderer, Richardson, & Atwater, 1989). Although the scales are normed, the authors also discuss their use as a criterion-referenced assessment and item adaptations for children with known handicaps. The Gross Motor scale has five subscales: Reflexes, Balance, Nonlocomotor, Locomotor, and Receipt and Propulsion (of a ball). The authors recommend that interpretation of results include comparison of performance on the various subscales. Although this has appeal, especially from a diagnostic perspective, the construct examined by each subscale is not defined by the authors. Users might define the scope of each subscale for themselves, but occupational and physical therapists may be troubled by some item placements (e.g., righting reactions included with primitive reflexes rather than balance). Hinderer et al. (1989) raised concerns about clarity of directions and criteria for scoring, but found these problems surmountable. Activity cards, intended to promote development of deficient skills, offer some useful suggestions but need to be referenced to activities in natural environments. Since the scales and activity cards were developed with children under

7 years of age with no known disabilities, users are cautioned about use with children who are older and/or present severe disabilities. In spite of the limitations, the Peabody Developmental Motor Scales offer a comprehensive scope and sequence of typical gross motor development that may be useful for diagnostic purposes.

The *Brigance Diagnostic Inventory of Early Development* (Brigance, 1978) is a criterion-referenced assessment with a unique organization of motor skills. The Pre-Ambulatory Motor Skills and Behaviors section delineates sequences separately for the supine, prone, sitting, and standing positions. This facilitates more careful assessment within positions, and is particularly useful for students who display uneven development or predominant use of certain positions. The Gross Motor Skills and Behaviors section delineates separate sequences for 13 different areas, including walking, climbing, and running. This organization can help teams focus on skill areas deemed important for individual students. The Brigance is not standardized, and performance criteria are not always defined clearly. Since the Brigance is referenced to the normal development of children from birth to 7 years, it should be used cautiously with older students with severe disabilities.

Hand Function The Erhardt Developmental Prehension Assessment (EDPA) (Erhardt, 1982) is a 100-item scale designed to assess prehension of children with developmental delays or motor disabilities. The items were derived from integration of normal child development literature and field testing with children with disabilities, and the EDPA is not considered a standardized tool (Erhardt, 1982). Despite this limitation, the EDPA seems to have advantages for use with students with severe disabilities. Items focus on posture

of the hand, arm, and body, rather than infant tasks. Illustrations and behavioral descriptions are provided for all items in the scale. The specified materials are not inherently functional (e.g., dowels), but they neither encourage use of infant materials nor seem to preclude substitution of materials deemed age appropriate and functional for an individual student. A videotape on administration and a book including case studies are also available from the publisher.

The *Peabody Developmental Motor Scales* (Folio & Fewell, 1983) are important to mention here because they offer a standardized measure of fine motor development. (Standardization of the Peabody Scales was discussed in the section on Postural Control and Mobility.) The Fine Motor Scale is divided into four subscales: Grasping, Hand Use, Eye-Hand Coordination, and Manual Dexterity. Unfortunately, the construct for each subscale is neither defined nor evident from examining the items, with similar items sometimes appearing in two or more subscales. The scales focus on tasks and materials for infants and preschoolers, further limiting utility for diagnostic assessment of older students with severe disabilities.

The *Assessment, Evaluation, and Programming System (AEPS) for Infants and Children: Vol. 1, AEPS Measurement for Birth to Three Years* (Bricker, 1992) is designed for use with children up to 6 years of age who function at a developmental age of between 1 month and 3 years. Recent studies indicate that the AEPS is reliable and valid, but it is more useful for assessing children with mild and moderate disabilities than for children with severe disabilities (Bricker, Bailey, & Slentz, 1990). As a criterion-referenced assessment, it includes "only skills that may enhance the child's ability to cope with and adapt to the demands of the social and physical environment" (Bricker, Gentry, & Bailey, 1985, p. 10). The assessment is not intended as a diagnostic tool, however, and the limited number of items in the Fine Motor domain is a shortcoming. Advantages of the Fine Motor domain are that instructions encourage use of optimal positioning, a context of functional tasks, and attention to generalization; therefore, teams just starting ecological assessment may find it helpful. Cautions about performance using abnormal movement patterns are included with several items, which can assist occupational and physical therapists to communicate with other team members. The Family Report is also available to assist families to participate in the assessment and evaluation of their children's skills and abilities.

Vision The *Erhardt Developmental Vision Assessment* (EDVA) (Erhardt, 1986) is a unique test of vision in that it examines visual-motor development rather than acuity. The EDVA is based on development of normal vision patterns through the age of 6 months, the age at which fairly mature functional components are achieved. The EDVA is designed to assess reflexive visual patterns (i.e., pupillary, doll's eyes, and eyelid reflexes) and voluntary eye movements of children with motor disabilities. Each item has both an illustration and a behavioral description of the motor performance. Initial field testing indicates that the content of the EDVA is useful and the instructions are clear, with high levels of interrater reliability (Erhardt, Beatty, & Hertsgaard, 1988). A videotape on administration and a book including case studies are also available from the publisher.

Informal Assessment of Sensorimotor Skills When students have severe disabilities, informal assessment strategies often yield more meaningful information

than formal assessment tools. Therapists can devise a task analysis of virtually any motor task, similar to the task analysis in Chapter 4 (see Table 4.6), as the basis for assessment of priority skills. In this type of assessment, emphasis is on whether and how the student performs the component movements, rather than where the student's performance is in relation to a normal developmental sequence. Dunn (1991) suggested a worksheet to analyze some of the qualitative considerations related to motor components of task performance (Figure 5.3).

Another important consideration in assessment is how the student's sensory systems receive, transmit, and interpret stimuli, both from the environment (e.g., touch, temperature, light, sounds, smells) and from the student's own body (e.g., head position in space, joint position, muscle tension). Dunn (1991) described these sensory systems and illustrated how they can influence performance of many tasks in typical daily routines. She recommended analyzing the sensory characteristics of routine tasks and determining task adaptations that might increase successful performance by a student who has difficulty processing sensory stimuli. Figure 5.4 shows a worksheet in which the sensory characteristics are analyzed and adaptations suggested for a student with severe disabilities who is working on face washing at the sink in a classroom that includes other children and adults without disabilities. This type of informal assessment adds information that is vital for effective program planning and cannot be obtained through more traditional formal approaches to sensorimotor assessment.

Communication Assessment Assessment of communication abilities has valuable prescriptive functions whether or not a student communicates with symbolic

Motor Characteristics of Task Performance

Routine/Task Motor Characteristics		General Status of Individual	Status During this Task	What adaptations are likely to improve functional outcome?
Muscle Tone	Hypertonic			
	Hypotonic			
	Other pattern			
	Reflexive patterns			
Physical Capacity	Strength			
	Endurance			
	Range of motion			
	Structural limitations			
Postural Control	Accomplishes alignment			
	Maintains alignment			
	Adaptability (e.g., restore equilibrium)			
Movement Characteristics	Efficient			
	Effortful but functional			
	Ineffective			
	Use of compensatory actions			
Essential Skills	Looking			
	Vocalizing			
	Reaching			
	Manipulating			
Cognition Requirements				

Figure 5.3. Worksheet for analysis of motor performance. (From Dunn, W. [1991]. The sensorimotor systems: A framework for assessment and intervention. In F. Orelove & D. Sobsey, *Educating children with multiple disabilities: A transdisciplinary approach* [2nd ed.] [p. 75]. Baltimore: Paul H. Brookes Publishing Co.; reprinted by permission.)

Sensory Characteristics of Task Performance

Routine/Task: Washing face

Sensory Characteristics	What Does The Task Routine Hold? A	B	C	What Does The Particular Environment Hold? (classroom sink)	What adaptations are likely to improve functional outcome?
Somatosensory					
light touch (tap, tickle)	X				Turn water off to decrease splashing
pain					
temperature (hot, cold)	X				Try alternative water temperatures
touch-pressure (hug, pat, grasp)	X				Pat face instead of rubbing cloth on face
variable	X				Pat large face area
duration of stimulus (short, long)	L				
body surface contact (small, large)	L				Try washing one part only; begin with chin area
predictable	X				
unpredictable					(Note: make sure routine is consistent day to day)
Vestibular					
head position change	X				Alter water source so don't have to bend head down (e.g., in a pan or tub)
speed change					
direction change	X				Keep head up so don't have the down-up pattern
rotary head movement					
linear head movement	X				Keep head up; if need arousal, place items on counter to encourage more head turning
repetitive head movement - rhythmic					
predictable	X				
unpredictable					
Proprioceptive					
quick stretch stimulus	X				Move objects to decrease head control requirements
sustained tension stimulus	X				
shifting muscle tension					
Visual					
high intensity					
low intensity					
high contrast					
high similarity (low contrast)	X			X Other objects	Use dark washcloths and light soap; use dark container on light counter; remove extra items from counter
competitive	X			X on sink	
variable				X counter change day to day	
predictable	X				If arousal is needed, vary placement of items
unpredictable				X	
Auditory					
rhythmic	X				Prepare wet cloth; don't have running tap water
variable	X				Use tub of water instead of running water
constant					
competitive				X Other students	Move child to the bathroom alone
noncompetitive					
loud	X			X Teacher's voice	Provide physical prompts and decrease talking
soft					
predictable	X				
unpredictable				X Unplanned	
Olfactory/ Gustatory					
mild	X				If arousal is needed, use strong smelling soap
strong					
predictable	X				
unpredictable	X				

Task Components   A=   B=   C=

Figure 5.4. Worksheet for analysis of task sensory components. Adapted from Orelove and Sobsey (1991).

120

language such as speech or sign language. Typical areas for communication assessment, regardless of student ability, are expression, comprehension, and opportunities to communicate in social and physical contexts of the environment. While the first two areas focus on student abilities, the third examines the extent to which the environment supports and promotes student efforts to communicate. The range of assessment considerations related to each of these three areas is outlined in Table 5.1. This table shows that specific considerations in communication assessment are much the same, whether the student uses nonsymbolic or symbolic communication.

Limitations of Formal Assessment Tools

Many commercial tests are available for assessment of communication abilities, al-though most are designed for individuals who use some symbolic language. Table 5.2 provides a list of assessment tools that can be used to assess students with severe communication disabilities. The tools are classified for use in assessing nonsymbolic, emerging symbolic, and symbolic communication. The Placement Checklist and Program for the Acquisition of Language with the Severely Impaired are actually components of communication intervention programs that can be adapted for use as criterion-referenced assessments. Of the seven tools listed, only three—the Communication and Symbolic Behavior Scales, The Nonspeech Test for Receptive/Expressive Language, and the Sequenced Inventory of Communication Development—have been standardized. Standard-

Table 5.1 Range of considerations for communication assessment

Nonsymbolic Focus	Symbolic Focus	
Student:		
Expressive Communication	**Expressive Language**	
Pragmatics	Pragmatics	
•function	•function	Syntax
•social rules	•social rules	Semantics
•relationships between	•relationship between	Articulation
communication and	communication and	Rate
behavior	behavior	Fluency
Form	Form	Volume
Quantity	Quantity	Vocal quality
Mode	Mode	
Intelligibility	Intelligibility	
Spontaneity	Spontaneity	
Comprehension	**Comprehension**	
For nonsymbolic language	For symbolic language	
For symbolic language	For nonsymbolic language	
Environment:		
Context	**Context**	
Social	Social	
Physical	Physical	

Table 5.2 Communication assessment tools for students with severe disabilities

Tool	Use
Communication and Symbolic Behavior Scales (Wetherby & Prizant, 1990)	Nonsymbolic, emerging symbolic
Environmental Language Inventory (J. MacDonald & Nickols, 1974)	Emerging symbolic
Environmental Pre-Language Battery (Horstmeier & J. MacDonald, 1975)	Nonsymbolic, emerging symbolic
The Nonspeech Test for Receptive/Expressive Language (Huer, 1983)	Nonsymbolic, emerging symbolic, symbolic
Sequenced Inventory of Communication Development (Hendrick, Prather, & Tobin, 1984)	Nonsymbolic, emerging symbolic, symbolic
Placement Checklist: Communication Training Program (Waryas & Stremel-Campbell, 1982)	Nonsymbolic, emerging symbolic, symbolic
Program for the Acquisition of Language with the Severely Impaired (PALS) (Owens, 1982a)	Nonsymbolic, emerging symbolic, symbolic

ization was conducted with normally developing children, but the first two tools were also field tested with children with disabilities, adding to their value when formal assessment of such children is required.

Unfortunately, few formal communication assessment tools yield relevant or functional information about students with severe disabilities. Available tests are generally inadequate for evaluation of students with limited symbolic language in that they are oriented toward speech for communication, are deficient in providing representative information about communication usage, and are unrelated to ultimate communication interventions (Browder, 1991). Because of these limitations, informal assessment methods using structured observations of the student during routine activities frequently are more applicable to answering the questions raised

in the hypothesis generation phase of program development.

Prescriptive Informal Assessment Blau, Lahey, and Oleksiuk-Velez (1984) found that more communication goals could be developed from a communication sample than from a formal test. Communication sampling procedures have been utilized for many years by speech-language therapists, and there are standard methods to analyze samples of symbolic communication. Symbolic language samples are evaluated for utterance length, syntax usage, pragmatic functions, semantic usage, articulation, and other quantitative and qualitative characteristics. Samples of communication for nonsymbolic communicators are usually analyzed from a pragmatic perspective, which emphasizes form, function, and context of communication. Kristen's and Jamal's assessments at the end of this chapter illustrate procedures for recording and analyzing samples of nonsymbolic and emerging symbolic communication use (see Tables 5.6 and 5.13). Excerpts from their assessment reports, also presented at the end of this chapter, provide examples of conclusions derived from pragmatic assessments.

When a student presents undesirable behaviors (e.g., aggression, self-injurious behavior, tantrums), the relationship between the student's lack of communication skills and undesirable behavior should be explored in the course of assessment. This involves formulating hypotheses about the communicative functions that undesirable behaviors serve for the student and designing interventions to teach new, more acceptable communication forms that serve the same functions. Excellent descriptions of this process can be found in Baumgart, Johnson, and Helmstetter (1990) and Donnellan, Mirenda, Mesaros, and Fassbender (1984).

Assessment of communication comprehension typically involves making verbal requests of students to perform a movement, act on an object, or interact with another person (Baumgart et al., 1990). During assessment, it is important to note what contextual cues (e.g., supporting gestural, temporal, and spatial cues) are present for future use in instruction. For example, as part of assessment, a student may demonstrate understanding of the suggestion, "Let's get a drink," when it is given after physical education class and near the drinking fountain, but not when the same words are used at a different time or environment. This would indicate the probablity that the student's understanding of the words, "Let's get a drink," is limited to a specific time and place. Language learners are thought to acquire comprehension skills through a process of "progressive decontextualization" (Bates, Benigni, Bre-

therton, Camaioni, & Volterra, 1979), gradually becoming less dependent upon specific nonverbal and verbal contexts for comprehension.

Informal assessment of basic comprehension skills for students with severe disabilities can be accomplished within daily routines through two strategies. The first is to use criterion-referenced measures, including requests for the student to look at, act on, or interact with people and things. The second is to observe the student's responses to communications from or among others in the same environment. Assessment for comprehension of verbal language and nonverbal communication can both be carried out through these means. During assessment, supporting gestures and other contextual cues are varied systematically and carefully recorded with performance data. The results of assessment consist of information about verbal and nonverbal communications understood by the student and the contextual cues needed for support. This approach enables the team to systematically enhance the student's communication comprehension throughout the day.

Communication is an interactive activity; that is, successful communication requires that at least two people participate, with one sending and the other receiving a message. For students with severe disabilities, communication development depends upon the participation of communication partners and the presence of other environmental conditions that encourage communication. Because essential conditions for successful communication extend beyond student abilities, meaningful assessment must include examination of representative communication environments. This type of assessment involves analysis of existing social and physical contexts that support communication and of changes in the environment that would better facilitate communication development. For example, assessment may show that an environment provides too few predictable routines for the student to learn to develop anticipatory responses, but that slight modifications would provide ample opportunities. Or assessment might show that potential communication partners do no not recognize or reinforce student attempts to communicate, but that the situation could be corrected by providing information about nonsymbolic communication. Some formal tests have subsections to evaluate environmental contexts for communication (see e.g., Owens, 1982a). The Communication Environment Checklist (Figure 5.5) was designed for informal assessment of communication opportunities in the environment.

During informal assessment, the student is observed across priority environments and routines to obtain communication samples to determine how he or she communicates through speech, vocalization, gestures, or other behavioral means. Assessment also includes observations made about comprehension and about what and who in the environment supports or impedes communication efforts. Results of the informal assessment can be applied directly to program development, to expand communication forms and functions and to increase participation in priority activities and environments.

WRITING A TEAM ASSESSMENT REPORT

The natural outcome of a collaborative educational assessment process is one comprehensive and integrated assessment report, rather than separate reports from each team member. There are two approaches to writing a team report. In the first approach, the team describes each area of skill development and then relates it to performance in activity routines. This approach is more like the interdisciplinary approach with which most professionals are familiar, and may be easier for teams when they first adopt a collaborative assessment process. The first approach is illustrated in an excerpt from Kristen's assessment report, at the end of this chapter. In the second approach, the team describes the student's overall performance in activity routines, with corresponding discussions of embedded sensorimotor, communication, and other skills. This approach focuses on the activities as the unifying and functional application for a variety of skills, and thus it is consistent with the ecological curriculum design. The second approach is illustrated at the end of this chapter in an excerpt from Jamal's assessment report. The authors strongly recommend that teams move toward the second approach, since it is more consistent with an ecological curriculum design. Furthermore, the process of writing the integrated report reinforces adoption of a common curriculum as a unifying framework, and helps team members clarify their roles within the curriculum.

Whichever approach a team uses, considerable coordination is required. One strategy for writing the report is for team members to discuss their observations and diagnostic findings at a team meeting. Afterward, one person drafts a report, which is circulated for additions and corrections. Another strategy is for each person to draft portions of the report, which one person integrates. Personal preference of the team and logistical considerations guide this decision.

The team report includes a brief description of the student, a brief description of the assessment process, a description of data gathering techniques (e.g., interviews, ecological inventories, directed observa-

Communication Environment Checklist

Student _____

Environment _____

Rating Scale: 1 = Not provided in current environment; needs intensive intervention
2 = Provided on a limited basis; needs expansion and refinement
3 = Generally provided; needs some refinement
4 = Provided consistently; needs no intervention

Dates

I. OPPORTUNITIES: Something To Communicate About

1. Consistent routines are present to allow students to learn natural cues.
2. Communication opportunities are integrated into daily routines.
3. Multiple opportunities to communicate are provided within activities that have multiple or repetitive parts (e.g.,turntaking).
4. Natural opportunities to communicate are not eliminated by others in the environment (i.e., by guessing the student's wants and needs before they can be expressed).
5. Additional opportunities to communicate are created by delaying action on wants/needs and by interrupting daily routines.

II. MOTIVATION: The Desire To Communicate

6. Instructional routines and activities utilized have a high reinforcer value for the student, especially at first.
7. Instruction ensures the student is reinforced by natural consequences of communication acts.
8. Reinforcement is of high frequency and/or duration in order to provide success.

III. MEANS: Partners and Tools for Conveying Messages

9. Communication partners who are familiar with the student's means of communication are accessible at all times as listeners, conversation partners, and models.
10. There are many opportunities for communication with same-age peers in the environment.
11. Others in the environment recognize and respond to/reinforce alternate forms of communication used by the student (especially nonverbal).
12. If an augmentative means of communication is used by the student, it is accessible at all times.

IV. MAINTENANCE, GENERALIZATION, AND SPONTANEITY: Varying Contexts and Fading Cues

13. Spontaneous, initiated communication is agreed upon as the ultimate goal of communication.
14. Opportunities for practice of specific communication skills continue to be available even after skills are "mastered."
15. Cues and prompts are individualized and faded to "natural" cues as soon as possible.
16. Communication partners are familiar with the hierarchy of cues and prompts for an individual student and know the student's current level.
17. Partners use directives and questions sparingly to increase initiation, independence, and problem-solving.
18. Opportunities are available for practicing communication skills in a variety of environments and with a variety of people.

Figure 5.5. Assessment of the communication environment.

tions), and a list of formal assessment instruments used. The team describes the student's independent performance, as well as the conditions that facilitated and limited performance. The report is written in language that can be understood by all team members, including parents. When unfamiliar technical terms are needed, they are accompanied by a brief explanation or diagram. The report is signed by all participating team members.

ONGOING ASSESSMENT

When the IEP is developed, it must include "objective criteria and evaluation procedures and schedules for determining . . . whether instructional objectives are being achieved" (20 U.S.C. §1401 (a) (19) (E)). Thus, in addition to annual assessment for program planning, the team must conduct ongoing assessment of student performance on IEP objectives. The purpose of ongoing assessment is to determine effectiveness of intervention strategies and to guide timely program revision, both when intermediate objectives are achieved and when satisfactory progress does not occur. A good rule of thumb is to collect data on student performance at least once weekly. This yields sufficient data to make decisions without being unmanageable. A weekly interval also approximates the schedule of data collection for students without disabilities (i.e., grades on homework, quizzes).

Therapists traditionally have recorded progress and concerns through "running notes." Although anecdotal data are useful, they do not fulfill the need for objective measures of performance to evaluate student change and intervention effectiveness (Ottenbacher, 1986). Therefore the team will need to determine the type(s) of data that will reflect the most relevant as-

pects of performance for each IEP objective, and then devise strategies to collect, analyze, and make decisions based on these data. When therapists have difficulty measuring performance, it is often because the target skill is too broad or vague (e.g., cope with frustration). It is helpful for therapists to remember that behaviors selected for measurement are intended to represent salient performance parameters (e.g., request assistance with difficult tasks), not to show all possible occurrences of all related skill development (e.g., improve social skills).

Educational programs often record performance in terms of frequency, duration, latency, rate, portion correct, and performance scoring (reflecting the prompts needed to elicit desired performance). Permanent products, including written work and videotapes, are valuable to capture quantitative and qualitative aspects of performance that can be analyzed retrospectively. Examples of data collection strategies are infused into the instructional programs presented in Chapter 7. Readers are referred to Alberto and Troutman (1990), Browder (1991), and Ottenbacher (1986) for further guidance on strategies for data collection and analysis and responsive decision making.

EXAMPLES OF ASSESSMENT PROCESS

Two examples of the assessment process described in this chapter are presented in the following pages. Both examples include ecological assessment, diagnostic/discipline-referenced assessment, and a team assessment report. Representative aspects of each stage have been included for each student. Kristen's team is working on a comprehensive assessment, as conducted for an initial evaluation or triennial review. They also are working to move from a developmental to an ecological orientation to curriculum and assessment. Jamal's team has used an ecological approach for some time. Since a comprehensive assessment was completed within the last 3 years, Jamal's assessment this year updates his performance in areas continued from last year's program and conducts in-depth analysis of opportunities and performance in new program areas.

Initial Assessment: Kristen

Planning the Assessment For Kristen, planning began in the spring, when her school district held her annual planning and placement meeting. Kristen's team decided she would be placed in a regular kindergarten in September, and that her parents, a special education teacher, kindergarten teacher, speech-language therapist, and physical therapist (as primary motor therapist) would comprise her core educational team. An occupational therapist, nurse, psychologist, and social worker would be available for consultation, but would not serve on the core team. Shortly after the meeting, the special education teacher contacted Kristen's parents to start identifying their priorities. Home and school were quickly identified as priority environments, and the school team agreed to observe Kristen at her early childhood special education program (the program she was leaving) in the spring, at home during the summer, and in kindergarten (the program she was entering) in September. Kristen's Ecological Assessment Planning Chart reflects priorities for each of the three phases (Table 5.3). The chart also illustrates the fact that ecological assessment is a process rather than an event.

The kindergarten teacher and physical therapist observed Kristen at the early childhood special education program.

They noted abilities and difficulties in Kristen's performance, and they generated numerous questions about Kristen's communication skills. Because of these questions, and because the special education teacher had not yet observed Kristen, the team agreed that the speech-language therapist and special education teacher would assess Kristen at home. Kristen's parents identified mealtimes, using the toilet, grooming, playing alone, and playing with her sister as priority and representative activities for assessment, which could be observed during the early afternoon at home.

Ecological Assessment at Home The speech-language therapist and special education teacher observed Kristen at home and recorded her performance anecdotally for each activity. Although Kristen demonstrated many abilities, her mother expressed frustration with what typically occurred in the bathroom after meals. The teacher and therapist observed the following:

Kristen finished lunch. Mrs. F (Kristen's mother) told Kristen, "Time to go clean up." Mrs. F led Kristen to the bathroom, seated Kristen on the toilet (lid down), pulled off Kristen's shirt, and wiped her face and hands with a wet washcloth. Kristen whined more each minute, rocked back and forth with her hands near her face, and finally fell back and hit her head. Mrs. F dried Kristen's face and hands. Kristen cried, held her hands near her face, and tried to push her mother's hands away. Mrs. F talked to Kristen throughout (but not to prepare Kristen or to ask for participation). [Mrs. F says this is actually better than usual, but she is frustrated and embarrassed.] Mrs. F slid Kristen off the toilet, then saw that Kristen's pants were wet. Kristen's legs seemed stiff. Mrs. F held Kristen by her shoulders (previously she just held one hand). Mrs. F sighed and pulled down Kristen's pants, and seated Kristen on the toilet (with seat adaptor for size). Kristen sat with her trunk and arms flexed, legs extended, and head forward. Mrs. F reported some successes on the toilet, but lots of accidents and no consistent pattern.

Table 5.3 Ecological assessment planning chart for Kristen

Priority Environments and Routines Where Assessment Is Conducted	Parents	Kindergarten Teacher	Special Education Teacher	Physical Therapist	Speech-Language Therapist
Special Education Preschool		5/29/92 (done)		5/29/92 (done)	
Home Mealtime / Toileting / Grooming / Dressing / Play with sister	6/26/92 (done) ↓		6/26/92 (done) ↓		6/26/92 (done) ↓
School - Kindergarten Bus				9/14/92	
Hallways			9/14/92	9/14/92	
Classrooms (transitions)					
Bathroom					
Play area		9/11/92	9/11/92	9/21/92	9/21/92
Tables (opening)					
Rug (story)					
Rug (gross motor)					
Tables (fine motor)					
Tables (snack)					
Nurse's office					

After finishing in the bathroom, Mrs. F took Kristen to the bedroom to get dressed. Kristen sat in a small arm chair with her feet on the floor. Her trunk, arms, and legs appeared relaxed. As Mrs. F got clothes from the dresser, Kristen began singing and "dancing" in her chair. Mrs. F smiled and explained that she and Kristen sing a variation of "Pop Goes the Weasel" while dressing. Mrs. F sang as she positioned a T-shirt on Kristen's head and helped Kristen grasp the hem of the shirt. Kristen sang a clear "pop" as she quickly pulled the shirt down over her head, and again as she pushed each hand through the sleeve. The routine was repeated with underpants, shorts, and sneakers. When finished, Kristen reached toward her mother. Mrs. F sang a little more and snatched Kristen from her chair as they sang "POP goes Kristie." (Kristen sang "Pop o e-o.") Mrs. F and Kristen both laughed. Mrs. F lowered Kristen to stand, and told Kristen to go find her ball. Kristen walked toward the family room. She walked with her arms flexed with hands near her waist, her hips and knees bent slightly and turned inward, and her feet pronated (inner side turned down).

Hypothesis Generation The team noted the following strengths in Kristen's performance:

- When her trunk and feet are supported in a sitting position, she seems to have normal posture and movement.
- In the context of an enjoyable routine, she maintains near-normal muscle tone and relaxes quickly after episodes of excitement.
- She uses her hands and arms functionally when gross movements are required.
- She walks independently.
- She initiates and sustains a play routine for several minutes.
- In the context of a known routine, she takes turns and participates actively, anticipating the next step in the sequence.
- She is nearly independent in putting on pull-on clothing.
- She has some articulate and appropriate speech.
- She follows simple verbal directions.

The team suggested the following possible explanations for Kristen's performance problems during the toileting routine:

- She experienced tactile defensiveness and was irritated by having the shirt,

washcloth, and towel touch her face and hands.
- She was frightened because she was unsteady sitting on the toilet.
- She wanted to use the toilet and cried in an attempt to communicate that need.
- She was frustrated because she wanted to participate in the routine more actively.
- She did not anticipate events in the routine, and cried out of confusion.

The teacher and speech-language therapist discussed Kristen's strengths, with special attention to the interactive nature of Kristen's participation in the dressing routine. They also discussed possible reasons for Kristen's difficulties in the toileting routine, and suggested some strategies to improve the situation. Before drawing conclusions about Kristen's needs, however, the team would conduct ecological assessment at school.

Ecological Assessment at School Kristen was assessed in her new program after she began school in the fall. The kindergarten schedule, outlined in Table 5.4, is composed of many routines. The team delineated the typical participation of children without disabilities for each of these routines, creating ecological inventories that would be used to assess Kristen and other children with disabilities who joined the kindergarten class. The special education teacher and therapists also served two other children with disabilities in the kindergarten, which enabled them to schedule blocks of time with the class. (See Chapter 8 for scheduling strategies.) During the course of the assessment, team members would observe Kristen during all scheduled activities. During the first month of school, the physical therapist, speech/language therapist, and teachers assessed Kristen during arrival and the free play routine, using the ecological in-

Table 5.4 Kindergarten schedule

8:30	Arrival
	Bathroom
	Job assignments
	Free play at tables, gross motor area, or playhouse
9:00	Opening group at tables
9:20	Storytime on rug [a]
9:45	Gross motor / perceptual activity on rug [a]
10:15	Fine motor / perceptual activity at tables [a]
10:45	Snack
11:10	Free play at tables, gross motor area, playhouse, or outside
	Bathroom, cleanup, and gather belongings
11:25	Departure

[a] Or art, music, library, gym, or special activities.

ventory format. The Planning Chart shows that Kristen's assessment occurred over several days and that all team members did not participate in all parts of the assessment. Kristen's performance is summarized in Table 5.5.

Hypothesis Generation Although Kristen had steadily increased her participation in the arrival and play routine, she had persistent difficulties, as indicated in the Student Inventory with Discrepancy Analysis column of the ecological assessment. The team considered the following as possible reasons for Kristen's performance difficulties during arrival and the play routine in the classroom:

• She does not really understand routines.
• She prefers the attention of adult assistance over playing with other children.
• She knows adults will help her if she waits long enough.
• She does not enjoy social interactions and prefers to be by herself.
• She is distracted by the activity of the other children.

• She cannot "motor plan" transitions with so many children, toys, and pieces of furniture as obstacles.
• She cannot carry objects while walking.
• She is too unsteady to walk through the play area alone with the obstacles and activity of the other children.
• She does not hear the verbal directions in the noisy room. She does not understand the verbal directions.
• She does not use other children as models.
• She does not know how to initiate interaction with her classmates.

Diagnostic/Discipline-Referenced Assessment Based on the observation at home and many observations at school, team members eliminated some of their hypotheses by identifying circumstances and performance that did not support the hypotheses (e.g., they identified several instances when Kristen appeared to have good motor planning abilities). Other hypotheses seemed to be supported (e.g., there were many instances when Kristen watched but did not participate in busy en-

Table 5.5 Ecological assessment: Kindergarten arrival and play routine

Student: Kristen F.
Date: 9/11, 9/14, & 9/21/92
Team Members: Jill M. (Kdg), Cathy
R. (SpEd), Lisa S. (PT), Jan M. (Sp/Lang)

Scoring Key:	
+	performs consistently
+/-	performs sometimes or in other environments, but not consistently
-	performs rarely or never

Inventory for Person without Disabilities		Student Inventory with Discrepancy Analysis	Teaching and Adaptation Hypotheses
SUBENVIRONMENT: OUTSIDE SCHOOL BUILDING			
Skills:			
Say goodbye to bus driver	-	No, and does not acknowl-edge bus driver's goodbye	•Teach to respond to bus driver's goodbye with eye contact and wave •Train bus driver to reinforce or respond appropriately
Exit bus	-	Carried down steps and lifted up curb	•Teach to descend steps holding rail •Step up on curb holding hand
Walk to building entrance	+	Follows other students with gestural and verbal cues from teaching assistant	
SUBENVIRONMENT: SCHOOL HALLWAY			
Skills:			
Walk to classroom	+	Walks independently	
Carry tote bag	-	Tries to carry bag, but falls	•Wear backpack
Locate classroom	+/-	Gets lost, but recognizes classroom	•Backward chain
SUBENVIRONMENT: KINDERGARTEN CLASSROOM			
Skills:			
Greet teacher at doorway	-	No, and does not acknowl-edge the teacher's greeting	•Teacher add physical compo-nent to her greeting routine •After establish routine, gradu-ally add delays to teacher initiation of greeting and use sequence of prompts for Kristen to initiate
Locate cubby	-	Goes to cubbies, doesn't find name	•Match name from card •Photo cue of Kristen next to name at first
Put bag in cubby		Leaves on base	•Assist to remove backpack and place in cubby

(continued)

Table 5.5 *(continued)*

Inventory for Person without Disabilities	Student Inventory with Discrepancy Analysis	Teaching and Adaptation Hypotheses
Remove coat	- Full assist with zipper and first sleeve, independent with second sleeve	•Teach to ask for help by touching a picture mounted in her cubby •Prompt to unzip and take off
Hang coat in cubby	- Full assist to hang	•Prompt to grasp and lift
Go to play area	- Stands and looks, must be led, did not follow general or direct verbal instructions	•Clear path to area •Use prompt sequence •Teach to follow peer •Instruct partner on least congested route
Select materials from shelves	- Watches others, did not stoop and retrieve; prefers social games to toys	•Prompt to kneel •Begin with daily observations recording object preferences •Give two choices for play by holding objects out to her in two hands •Assist to put on counter
Take materials to proper area	- Full assist to carry and find space	•Ask peer for assistance by giving object to peer •Have peer carry material •Teach to follow peer to play space
Play (solitary, parallel, or cooperative)	- Watches others	•Teach to use various materials near and with other children •Start with simple social games (e.g., ring-around-the-rosey), gradually add the functional use of objects (e.g., find the ball and throw to peer)
Clean-up time	- Full assist	•Backward chain
Transition to tables for opening group	- Won't walk during the commotion of clean-up time	•Leave before clean-up starts or after finished •Choose a peer partner to follow during transition •Instruct partner on least congested route •Hold partner's hand

vironments). The Teaching and Adaptation Hypotheses column of the ecological assessment shows that the team was already testing a variety of hypotheses through informal strategies. The team was still left with the following questions regarding Kristen's performance and effective instructional strategies:

- To what extent does Kristen understand and anticipate task sequences in routines? How quickly does she learn new routines?
- Should task sequences be more predictable?
- To what extent does Kristen attend to and imitate other children as models?
- What is Kristen's understanding of oral language?
- How well does Kristen hear verbal directions under different background noise conditions?
- To what extent is Kristen distracted by visual and auditory stimuli?
- What types and sequences of prompts are most effective to improve Kristen's responding?
- What expressive communication behaviors does Kristen demonstrate?
- When and how can more intentional communication be elicited?
- What mode(s) of expressive communication should be taught?
- To what extent does poor coordination/spasticity interfere with Kristen's abilities to walk, change position, and use her hands?
- Are there new motor skills that Kristen needs to learn to increase participation?
- What handling and facilitation strategies are effective to improve Kristen's motor participation?
- In which routine tasks could Kristen use peers for assistance?

Team members determined that they could gather the information needed to answer most questions during routine activities, using more focused behavioral observation strategies. The speech-language therapist, for example, conducted an informal Pragmatic Communication Assessment (see excerpt in Table 5.6). She conducted informal hearing assessment under a variety of environmental conditions and arranged for formal hearing tests. She also thought it appropriate to conduct an *Environmental Pre-Language Battery* (Horstmeier & MacDonald, 1975) to learn more about Kristen's receptive and presymbolic expressive language, and an informal assessment to learn more about her expressive communication use. The physical therapist chose to record her observations about motor skills on the ABC and the EDPA (through consultation from the occupational therapist). As part of the ABC, she measured the range of motion at Kristen's hips, knees, and ankles, areas where she was at risk for developing contractures. More formal testing (Environmental Pre-Language Battery, range of motion) was performed in the classroom, usually when the class went to an outside activity.

Assessment Report The team chose to organize their report around skill areas, but made sure to relate their findings to performance in routine activities. The following are excerpts from their report.

Initial Assessment
STUDENT: Kristen F.
DATE OF BIRTH: 4-29-86
DATE OF REPORT: 10-1-91
TEAM MEMBERS: Mr. & Mrs. F. (parents), Jill M. (Kindergarten), Cathy R. (SpEd), Jan M. (Sp/Lang), Lisa S. (PT), Jim D. (OT)

Kristen is a 5-year, 5-month old girl with generalized developmental delays and spastic cerebral palsy. She entered the kindergarten at Richmond Elementary School in September, 1991. Kristen's team observed her participating in routine activities at the Special Preschool Program (May 29, 1991), at home (June 26, 1991), and at the Richmond kindergarten (September 9–28, 1991). Ecological inventories were completed in kindergarten during arrival and free play routines. The following assessment tools were also used:
Assessment of Behavioral Components (9-14-91)

Table 5.6 Kristen: Pragmatic communication assessment (excerpts)

Date & Time	Context	Form	Message Expressed (Intent)	Pragmatic Function	Consequence	# Times Observed
9-21-92	**KINDERGARTEN CLASSROOM: SNACK**					
10:45 AM	Students were excused from previous activity to wash hands one table at a time. Kristen and Leah sat together waiting. Leah tried to get Kristen to play pat-a-cake (Kristen passively let Leah prompt motion, but was attentive.) A friend started to talk to Leah; Leah turned away from Kristen and terminated hand play.	Kristen reached toward Leah and pulled at her hand.	More pat-a-cake.	Request continuation of event	Leah said, "Oh, you want to play more. Wait just a second, Kristen."	II
10:48 AM	Kristen followed others from her table to the sink without cues. She stood near the sink watching the others. Teacher asked, "Kristen, are you going to wash, too?"	Looked at teacher when heard her name and then said "No" clearly.	"No" (verbal).	Comment/ response to question	Teacher approached and provided physical guidance for handwashing.	I
10:52 AM	Teacher took Kristen to the snack table and asked, "What kind of cookie do you want? Choose one," while holding a cookie out in each hand.	Reached and took the cookie to her right.	That one.	Comment/ response to question	Teacher said, "That one looks good."	I
10:54 AM	After Kristen picked her cookie, the teacher said, "Now, get some juice."	Kristen looked toward the 15 or so cups filled with juice and began to whine.	Help me get my juice.	Feeling / frustration, request for assistance	Teacher carried Kristen's cup of juice to her table for her. Kristen followed.	I
11:00 AM	A classmate (Joe) at Kristen's table began to make faces while eating. Other children at the table laughed.	Kristen giggled with others.	Funny.	Feeling / happy	None observed.	II

134

Time	Behavior	Verbalization	Function	Consequence	
11:02 AM	Joe chewed his snack with his mouth open saying, "Yum, yum." Verbalization: "um-um."	Yum, yum.	Comment/ social interaction with others	Classmates continued to laugh and giggle.	=
11:10 AM	Teacher had just announced that it was time for free play. Classmates started to transition to play area. Kristen headed in the opposite direction from the rest of the class and stood by the cubbies, then looked back at class.	I want to go outside. or I'm ready to go home.	Request for attention	Teacher walked over to Kristen and said, "No, we're going to play inside now."	–
11:12 AM	Teacher attempted to guide Kristen back to the play area. Kristen slipped down to the floor, whining.	No, I want to go now.	Reject event	Teacher left the cubbie area to let Kristen "cool down."	–
11:17 AM	Teacher returned to cubbie area (Kristen still on floor) and said, "Kristen, come see the new toy with me," and tried to assist her to stand. Kristen's body stiffened and she whined again.	No.	Reject event	Teacher said, "Ok, but you'll miss play time."	–
11:25 AM	Teacher returned again to Kristen and said, "Kristen, it's time to go home now." Kristen sat up and reached out her arms for support to stand.	OK, I'm ready. Help me get up.	Comment, request for assistance	Teacher helped Kristen get up, saying "Let's go get your bag."	–

Erhardt Developmental Prehension Assessment (9-28-91)

Environmental Pre-Language Battery (9-21-91)

Kristen's gross motor development is delayed, and flexor tone in her legs and trunk interferes with normal movement patterns. Kristen sits on a stool or chair with relatively normal posture as long as her feet are supported, but with increased tone and poor posture when her feet are not supported. For table activities, she needs a large chair with added back and foot supports so she can sit at a proper height relative to the table. When playing on the floor, she tends to W-sit, which carries over to a persistent pattern of hip flexion-adduction–internal rotation in tall kneeling and standing. Her range of motion is within normal limits at all joints. She rises to stand and lowers to kneel in a symmetrical pattern, by straightening or bending both knees while rolling over the insides of her ankles as she pulls up/lowers on furniture. The more normal reciprocal pattern (one foot at a time) can be facilitated easily by holding one ankle and tapping her opposite knee. She walks with a "scissor" pattern (one knee crosses in front of the other). She can step over objects or climb stairs only with both hands held. Kristen's tone increases when she is excited or upset, or when there are high levels of visual and auditory stimulation. As a result, Kristen seems reluctant to move in some school situations. For example, she walks freely through the classroom and hallways when there are few children present or they are engaged in quiet activity. During transitions and noisy activities, however, Kristen sits or stands in one place, and moves only when led by an adult. On three occasions, another child was asked to hold Kristen's hand during a transition; Kristen and her friend both seemed to like this alternative. Although Kristen tends to W-sit on the floor during free play, she responds positively to tone reduction (brief rocking while seated straddling adult's lap) followed by physical prompts to sidesit, kneel, half-kneel, and rise to stand. After prompting to change position several times during free play, Kristen will walk approximately 10 feet unassisted in transition to the next activity. This strategy can be generalized to other transitions in the classroom. For transitions to other areas of the school, it seems appropriate to give Kristen a head start until she is more adept at classroom transitions.

Kristen's fine motor development also is delayed, with posture and movement of her arms and hands influenced by flexor tone. She typically holds her elbows close to her sides with all joints flexed, and her hands held near her waist or the upper part of her chest. When walking, she often holds her hands up near her shoulders (high guard position), especially when excited. During arrival and play, she holds her bag and large toys with two hands, but only carries them 4 or 5 steps before dropping the object or falling. When performing routine tasks in familiar situations (e.g., put arm in shirt/coat sleeves), she is able to extend her elbows and wrists completely. When playing with a ball, she extends her elbows, wrists, and fingers to hold the ball, but alternates between extremes of flexion and extension when she tries to throw and catch. Although flexor tone (including shoulder internal rotation and forearm pronation) tends to interfere with reach and grasp, physical prompts just above the elbow (to flex the shoulder) are effective to elicit reach and grasp in several contexts (e.g., take paper towel from dispenser, take toys off shelf). She uses a palmar grasp to hold most objects (crayons, spoon, sandwiches, paper), but can use a lateral pinch or thumb-fingertip grasp to hold small objects when given physical prompts to hold her wrist in extension and to hold the space between her thumb and first finger open. Kristen can release only against resistance (e.g., hang coat on hook), with her wrist stabilized (e.g., heel of hand pressed on table), or when her fingers are stabilized so she can pull them into extension. Although she can eat finger foods independently, Kristen tends to hold food in her palm and then press her hand against her face to open her fingers—a messy strategy. Kristen's oral-motor skills appear satisfactory for eating a variety of whole foods. Kristen does not yet isolate her index finger, but she does use her arm to point to people/objects in the distance and the thumb-index finger portion of her hand to point to objects in her reach. Although Kristen is cooperative and seems willing to try almost any motor task once, she tends to give up or tantrum when unsuccessful.

Kristen does not play with toys, except balls. She uses a limited number of objects, such as a spoon, cup, ball, and brush (to help brush her dog), in functional rather than symbolic acts. She shows little interest in using blocks, cars, dolls, or other toys found at home or in the kindergarten classroom, although she watches other children play. Kristen seems to prefer simple social games and routines with adults; she will initiate games, sustain interaction for several minutes, take turns, and anticipate events in a play routine. Kristen's mother reported that Kristen is more likely to play with her older sister if an adult is involved (e.g., roughhousing with Dad), but the two girls do chase the dog around together and laugh. At school Kristen has not initiated interactions with other children, but she is starting to respond to and sustain interactions that they initiate.

Kristen appears to prefer predictable routines. When predictable routines are changed or have not been established, she participates much less, sometimes refusing to participate or even having tantrums. Informal and formal testing suggested that Kristen is dependent on contextual cues in routine activities for language comprehension. During classroom observation, Kristen responded appropriately, given contextual and gestural cues, to the following directions: "give me," "come here," "stand up," "go get," and "let's go to the bathroom now." Formal testing of receptive language abilities did not yield additional useful information. Kristen's mother reported that she follows simple directions for some routines at home. Kristen's hearing is within normal limits for awareness of environmental sounds. The influence of background noise on Kristen's hearing could not be assessed. Given her current language comprehension abilities, however, it is most appropriate for adults to work in close proximity to Kristen, using the same strategies as if background noise interference were confirmed.

Information gathered about Kristen's understanding of pictures was inconclusive. Kristen reportedly enjoys a particular children's videotape and the Sesame Street TV show, but representational images may not be the salient feature; Kristen may be attracted to other features such as color, movement, and/or music. At home, Kristen likes to look at a set of cards depicting Sesame Street characters, but she has no interest in a magazine depicting the same characters. Her mother reported that Kristen enjoys looking at the family photo album and points to pictures of immediate family members and the dog when asked "Where is . . . ?" In formal testing she identified a picture of a baby (from a choice of two images), but was unsuccessful on other items.

Kristen did not respond to formal expressive language assessment items requiring verbal production. She did imitate some gestures accompanied by verbal cues (e.g., waves when adult waves and says "bye"). During informal pragmatic communication assessment, Kristen used communication 18 times (during 1 hour) with functions for greetings, feelings, requests, rejections, and comments. Use was evenly distributed among functions, except for greetings, for which there were fewer opportunities. Classroom observation suggested a connection between behaviors defined as tantrums and Kristen's lack of communication skills. Kristen's mother and teachers all reported that she tantrums to reject activities and when she cannot get what she wants. This strategy is successful for her at least part of the time, because adults are making appropriate efforts to interpret and respond to Kristen's nonsymbolic communication.

Expressive communication included a variety of forms, such as smiling, reaching for another person, whining, going to the location of an activity, laughing, alternating gaze, reaching for food, and two verbalizations: "no" and "um-um" (for "yum-yum"). She was observed to imitate peers' communication twice, once laughing and once approximating yum-yum. Kristen's spoken vocabulary includes the following words and approximations: *Mom, Dad, Doowee* (Julie), *Doot* (Duke, the dog), *pop, no, ba* (ball), and *Nana.*

Conclusions and Recommendations
[Excerpts]

1. The quality of Kristen's gross and fine motor skills needs improvement to enable her to participate more successfully in daily routines at home and at school. Kristen also needs to develop more ad-

vanced patterns of grasp, manipulation, and release for play, academic, and self-care activities.

2. Kristen expresses herself through a few spoken words and a variety of nonverbal forms and functions, but she needs to expand these, particularly to direct the behavior of others. With consistent communication opportunities and appropriate prompting sequences, routines at home and school offer excellent contexts for this type of instruction. Additional opportunities should be created to use and expand existing single-word verbalizations. Use of pictures for communication in their actual contexts also should be explored.

3. Kristen's tantrums seem to reflect frustration with inabilities to perform motor tasks, to direct the behavior of others, and to understand changes in routines. At this time, tantrums should be addressed only through positive means, by interpreting her wishes, providing assistance, and modeling more appropriate ways to express requests and rejections. The team will need to devise a strategy to help Kristen understand changes in routines and to deal with her spontaneous requests and rejections when they conflict with home/school goals.

4. Although Kristen's social development is delayed, this is undoubtedly influenced by her motor disability, which previously would have limited her success with toys and typical children's play routines. Instruction in play needs to include attention to motor, communicative, and social abilities.

Annual Assessment: Jamal

Planning the Assessment   During Jamal's spring IEP conference, his team discussed his interests and needs and identified priority environments, activities, and skills, as discussed in Chapter 4. On this basis, they outlined a schedule of activities for the next school year (Table 5.7). Since entering high school, Jamal's schedule had reflected increasing participation in general education classes and community en-

vironments. The fall schedule included two new opportunities: a high school Spanish class and a work experience program. The Spanish class was chosen for Jamal because he frequently heard Spanish in his own home, especially when his grandmother visited; the structure of the class offered many opportunities for Jamal to participate; and the Spanish teacher had expressed interest in opening his classroom to students with diverse abilities and interests. The work experience at the Metro Insurance Agency was designed to prepare Jamal for his transition to adulthood and would require him to spend increasing amounts of time away from school. Although the team projected goals and objectives related to these new environments, they knew they would need to modify those goals and objectives in the fall after ecological assessments were conducted in actual learning environments.

Early in the fall, Jamal's core team met to plan his assessment. The core team included Jamal and those individuals with whom he would have the most contact across learning environments: his mother, community residence coordinator, special education teacher, occupational therapist, speech-language therapist, special education teaching assistant, and transition specialist. Because Jamal would be enrolled in general education classes, his homeroom teacher was selected as the representative for general education. His other teachers indicated that they wanted to provide information relevant to assessment and to learn strategies to support Jamal in their classes, but they preferred not to participate directly in the actual assessment. A nurse, psychologist, physical therapist, and county case manager (social worker) were available for consultation but were not part of the core team. After considering the highest priorities for assessment, Ja-

Table 5.7 Jamal's weekly schedule

	MONDAY	TUESDAY	WEDNESDAY	THURSDAY	FRIDAY
Before school 7:00-7:45	Regular bus to school Restroom •7:30-7:45				
Homeroom 7:45-8:00	HOMEROOM	HOMEROOM	HOMEROOM	HOMEROOM	HOMEROOM
Period 1 8:05-8:55	SPANISH CLASS	SPANISH CLASS	SPANISH CLASS	SPANISH CLASS	SPANISH CLASS
Period 2 9:00-9:50	COMMUNITY PREP •9:00-9:15 COMMUNITY WORK •9:15-12:00	COMMUNITY PREP •9:00-9:15 COMMUNITY MOBILITY TRAINING	COMMUNITY PREP •9:00-9:15 COMMUNITY WORK •9:15-12:00	COMMUNITY PREP •9:00-9:15 COMMUNITY MOBILITY TRAINING	COMMUNITY PREP •9:00-9:15 COMMUNITY WORK •9:15-12:00
Period 3 9:55-10:45	Restroom •10:15-10:30	Restroom •10:15-10:30	Restroom •10:15-10:30	Restroom •10:15-10:30	Restroom •10:15-10:30
Period 4 10:50-11:40		CHOIR		CHOIR	
Period 5 11:45-12:35	LUNCH •12:20-12:50	COMMUNITY FAST FOOD RESTAURANT	LUNCH •12:20-12:50	LUNCH •11:45-12:15 Restroom •12:15-12:30	LUNCH •12:20-12:50
Period 6 12:40-1:30	ERRANDS •12:50-1:15 Restroom •1:15-1:30	Restroom •12:40-12:55 MEDIA CENTER •library •computer	ERRANDS •12:50-1:15 Restroom •1:15-1:30	MEDIA CENTER •library •computer	ERRANDS •12:50-1:15 Restroom •1:15-1:30
Period 7 1:35-2:25	HOME ECONOMICS	HORTICULTURE	HOME ECONOMICS	HORTICULTURE	HOME ECONOMICS
After school				After School Activity •swim team manager	

mal's core team completed an Ecological Assessment Planning Chart (Table 5.8).

Ecological assessment was planned for each environment that was part of Jamal's school day. Since Jamal had not previously participated in Spanish class or work at the Metro Insurance Agency, the team gave high priority to assessing him in these two environments so appropriate objectives and instructional routines could be estab-

Table 5.8 Ecological assessment planning chart for Jamal

Priority Environments and Routines Where Assessment Is Conducted	Team Members Conducting Assessment			
	Parents	Special Education Teacher	Occupational Therapist	Speech-Language Therapist
Home				
Kitchen	9/10/92	9/10/92		
School				
Arrival				
Hallways		9/18/92		
Rest room				
Homeroom				
Spanish class		9/18/92	9/25/92	9/25/92
Choir				
Lunchroom				
Media center				
Home economics				
Horticulture				
Locker room				
Pool area				
Community				
Work experience (Metro Insurance Agency)		9/18/92	9/25/92	9/25/92
Shopping mall				
Fast food restaurant				

lished as soon as possible. These two environments have been selected as representative examples for Jamal's assessment. Both inventories include a discrepancy analysis describing Jamal's actual performance. Jamal's participation in the two learning environments was observed and recorded in order to clarify and validate instructional needs, priorities, and necessary supports.

Ecological Assessment in Spanish Class The Spanish teacher followed a fairly regular routine of tasks, which served as the inventory for persons without disabilities for the ecological assessment (Table 5.9). Jamal's team did not expect him to master Spanish core curriculum objects (i.e., learn Spanish), but the class was an excellent setting to address other individualized learning priorities. The team selected items from the Assessment of Student Participation in General Education Classes, presented earlier in this chapter (Figure 5.2), for an ecological inventory of the Spanish class that corresponded with priorities the team had pre-

Table 5.9 Spanish class routine

8:05 - 8:15	**Class opens with greeting exercise**
	•choose partners
	•introduce selves (Hola, Señor John!)
	•teacher indicates a context for conversation using specific vocabulary from a previous lesson listed on blackboard daily (e.g., One student is a baker and the other a customer. The customer asks, "Do you have any fresh bread?")
	•required to write up the greeting conversation in Spanish and turn in at the end of class; usually 2-3 sentences
8:15 - 8:25	**Jokes of the day**
	•different student is assigned to tell an English joke in Spanish each day
	•teacher usually comments on the joke's translation and if it would be considered funny in Spanish
	•teacher tells a Spanish joke after the student and the English translation is discussed
8:25 - 8:45	**Daily lesson and oral practice** [a]
	•whole group instruction
	•use of scripts in textbook or a worksheet
	•teacher first introduces new vocabulary, work forms, etc.
	•choral responses to teacher with new words, forms, etc.
	•conversational practice
	-teacher provides situational context and vocabulary list
	-teacher circulates in the classroom to comment and answer questions
	-pre-recorded lesson on a tape recorder sometimes used
8:45 - 8:55	**Closing and competency measures** [a]
	•group game with teams; keeps pressure off individuals
	•score kept for teams
	•beanbag thrown for responses
	•crossword puzzles
	•fill-in-the-blank poetry (rhyming words omitted)
	•poem and story writing
	•other word games

---

[a] With daily variation.

viously identified. The resulting assessment focused on Jamal's participation in classroom routines and activities and in social and communication interactions. The completed ecological assessment is presented in Table 5.10.

Ecological Assessment of Community Work Experience Jamal's community work experience at Metro Insurance Agency was scheduled for three mornings per week. Immediately after Spanish class, Jamal rode to work in a van with a crew of two other workers from his school and a special education teaching assistant. The three students worked in an area near secretarial staff for the insurance agency, which had about 30 employees. The first student opened, stapled, and stacked incoming mail. Jamal stamped the date on the mail, and the third student sorted the mail for delivery around the office. The sequence of events in the community work experience routine offered many opportunities for Jamal and the other students to learn skills (Table 5.11).

Prior to the ecological assessment, Jamal had made several short visits to the work site to become familiar with the environment. He did not spend the entire morning at the work site because he was unable to perform his work tasks without adaptive devices and/or personal assistance. Thus the primary purpose of the assessment was to determine opportunities for participation and instruction and strategies for teaching and adaptation. The completed ecological assessment is presented in Table 5.12.

Hypothesis Generation The completed assessments show that both Spanish class and the work experience offered many opportunities for Jamal to participate in routine activities and to work on embedded social, communication, and sensorimotor skills. Although the Student Inventory with Discrepancy Analysis col-

umn of the assessment in Spanish class shows that Jamal already participates in the routine, the Teaching and Adaptation Hypotheses column shows that new skills would increase the amount and quality of his participation. The assessment at work shows that Jamal currently is unable to perform many of the skills required for participation, and will need instruction, adaptations, and personal assistance. Unlike the hypotheses generated for Kristen earlier in this chapter, the team knew Jamal very well and spent less time on conjecture about why he performed a certain way and more on how he performed and what adaptations could be made to facilitate increased participation. Generally this will be true for older students with whom team members have had extensive experience. Teams are cautioned about becoming complacent, however, and encouraged to use the triennial review as an opportunity to take a fresh look at their students.

After completing their ecological assessments, Jamal's team developed a long list of ideas for teaching and adaptations, but still had questions that would be best addressed through diagnostic assessment. The following needs, identified in Spanish class and at Metro Insurance Agency, require further investigation by the team.

In Spanish class, Jamal continued giggling long after "the joke of the day" was over, detracting from the next task for all students in the class. Some team members thought Jamal might not be able to control his giggling once initiated. Others thought giggling may have been one of the few means Jamal had to participate in Spanish class, and that it might become less important to him if he had more ways to communicate.

At Metro Insurance Agency, Jamal's participation was also severely limited by his lack of communication abilities. Assess-

Table 5.10 Ecological assessment: Spanish class [a]

Student: Jamal W.
Date: 9/18 & 9/25/92
Team Members: Trish G. (Spanish),
John K. (SpEd), Jake S. (teaching
assistant), Ann E. (Sp/Lang), Lisa W. (OT)

> **Scoring Key:**
> + performs consistently
> +/- performs sometimes or in other environments, but not consistently
> - performs rarely or never

Inventory for Person without Disabilities	Student Inventory with Discrepancy Analysis	Teaching and Adaptation Hypotheses
SUBENVIRONMENT: SPANISH CLASS		
I. CLASSROOM ROUTINES AND ACTIVITIES		
3. **Performs transitional activities during class in response to situational cues (e.g., changes in setting, activity)**	- J cannot maneuver his w/c due to lack of space, movement required within the classroom for activities daily. Follows situational cues to change activities in other environments.	•Peer assistance to move within the classroom •Teach to request peer assistance to move during transition times •Request that teacher use consistent daily routine when possible •Learn situational cues to change activities
7. **Terminates task without extra direction**	+ Keeps giggling after "joke of the day"; usually not a problem for other activities.	•A competing task built into the routine may help terminate
9. **Follows class rules**	+/- Needs to quiet down after "joke of the day"; gets silly; quiet conversation is encouraged and teacher reports he is usually fine.	•See above (#7)
15. **Works cooperatively with a partner**	+ Repeatedly chooses his friend David as a partner. Attends to group activities.	•Greeting exercise - could be a 3rd partner in groups of 2 •Choose what group he will be in and request •Encourage J to join a group that doesn't include David
16. **Works cooperatively with a small group**	+ Attends to group activities.	•Flip score card for competitive games •Classmates write one response/day for J to give w/cues •Switch on/off tape recorder when used
19. **Copes with criticism / correction without incident and tries an alternative behavior**	+/- Usually OK, but after "joke of the day" did not quiet down to three requests by teacher.	•See above (#7)

(continued)

Table 5.10 *(continued)*

Inventory for Person without Disabilities	Student Inventory with Discrepancy Analysis	Teaching and Adaptation Hypotheses
II. SOCIAL AND COMMUNICATION SKILLS		
21. Interacts with peers **a. responds**	+ a. Uses facial expressions/ vocalizations, body posture.	•New augmentative system being developed •Instruct teacher and classmates on best ways to communicate with J •Initiate Spanish greetings •Initiate requests for assistance
b. initiates	+ b. Usually vocalizes for attention or greeting.	
23. Uses social greetings **a. responds to others**	+ a. Uses facial expressions/ vocalizations, body posture.	•Initiate Spanish greetings
b. initiates	+ b. Same as above.	
26. Participates in joking or teasing **a. responds to others**	+ a. Loves "joke of the day."	•Use peer support and a written joke when it is his turn to present a joke •Carry over "joke of the day" to the work setting with coworkers
b. initiates	+/- b. Limited motor and communication, sometimes pretends is asleep to joke.	
27. Makes choices or indicates preferences **a. responds (cue or ?)**	+/- a. With objects, but new augmentative system being developed.	•Choose a friend to greet •Choose a partner
b. initiates	+/- b. Sometimes, can be facilitated within class routines.	
28. Asks questions **a. asks for help**	- a. No, can be facilitated within class routines.	•Ask for help to move w/c around classroom for activities •Needs to initiate request for help when uncomfortable
b. asks for information (clarification, feedback)	- b. Not a priority.	
29. Follows directions **a. for curricular tasks**	+/- a-d. Needs routine or situational cues, but can do if short, direct, and in close proximity (but consider physical capabilities).	•Instruct teacher and classmates on needs for following directions
b. for helping tasks/errands		
c. given to the student individually		
d. given to the students as a group		

[a] The items for this assessment were prioritized from the "Assessment of Student Participation in General Education Classes" (Figure 5.2).

Table 5.11 Community work experience routine

9:15	Arrive in parking lot in van and get out
9:20	Go to Metro Insurance Agency office
9:27	Greet coworkers
9:35	Go to coat rack and store belongings
9:40	Go to work area
9:42	Do work tasks
10:15	Go to rest room and use facilities
10:30	Go to break room and take break
10:43	Prepare to leave break room
10:48	Do work tasks
11:35	Prepare to leave work area
11:42	Go to coat rack and get belongings
11:48	Go to front office area and say goodbye to coworkers
11:53	Go to van in parking lot
12:00	Get in van and depart

Times vary slightly from day to day.

ments indicated that he initiated interactions frequently, but that he communicated primarily by facial expressions and vocalizations. The lack of progress in communication by Jamal and other students with severe disabilities had frustrated the speech-language therapist for a long time, so she took a short course on assessment and facilitation of communication for students who, like Jamal, had no symbolic means of communication. The speech-language therapist learned strategies to conduct a more thorough diagnostic assessment of Jamal's communication abilities and needs.

Another priority for Jamal was to learn to use his motor capabilities to maximize participation in all activity routines. This included learning to use his new power wheelchair, assuming responsibilities in Spanish class (i.e., turn tape recorder on and off, keep score), and performing work tasks at Metro Insurance Agency. Routines in Spanish class and at work required movement around the room, but the classroom and parts of Metro Insurance were too congested for him to drive his chair. Other tasks requiring motor performance seemed beyond Jamal's current abilities. Therefore, the occupational therapist

Table 5.12 Ecological assessment: Community work experience (excerpts)

Student: Jamal W.
Date: 9/18 & 9/25/92
Team Members: John K. (SpEd), Jake
S. (teaching assistant), Ann E. (Sp/Lang),
Lisa W. (OT)

Scoring Key:
+   performs consistently
+/- performs sometimes or in other environments, but not consistently
-    performs rarely or never

Inventory for Person without Disabilities		Student Inventory with Discrepancy Analyses	Teaching and Adaptation Hypotheses
SUBENVIRONMENT: BUILDING ARCADE (FIRST FLOOR)			
Activity: Arriving at work			
Skills:			
Scan store fronts	+	Yes	
Locate insurance agency	+/-	Sometimes vocalizes at destination	Use of vocalization and eye gaze to indicate entrance
Walk to entrance and enter through archway	-	Power w/c with assistance	Develop power w/c skills to cruise arcade and enter open arch
SUBENVIRONMENT: METRO INSURANCE AGENCY FRONT OFFICE AREA			
Activity: Greeting coworkers			
Skills:			
Walk to/by coworkers' desks	-	Space too small to maneuver given present w/c mobility skills	Teaching assistant wheels to agency coworkers
Establish eye contact	+	Yes	
Smile and say "hi"	-	Vocal approximation	
Initiates appropriate conversation	-	Initates requests for attention with vocal, but can't initiate topics	•Develop augmentative communication skills •Bring joke to tell from Spanish class
Respond to questions and comments	+/-	Uses facial expression	•Needs more augmentative communication skills for conversation •Instruct coworkers on best ways to communicate with Jamal
Depart after greetings	-	Needs assistance with w/c	Develop augmentative means to ask to go to coat rack
Scan for coat rack	+	Looks in direction	
Walk between desks to coat rack	-	Space too small to maneuver given present w/c mobility skills	Teaching assistant wheels to coatrack
Remove jacket	-	Full physical assistance	Teach to drop head as a way to remain relaxed

(continued)

Table 5.12 *(continued)*

Inventory for Person without Disabilities	Student Inventory with Discrepancy Analyses	Teaching and Adaptation Hypotheses
Hang up jacket	- Full physical assistance	Relaxation and facilitation for full range of motion reach
Scan for work area	+ Looks in direction	
Walk between desks to work area	- Space too small for present mobility skills	Teaching assistant wheel to edge of work area

SUBENVIRONMENT: WORK AREA

Activity: Stamping and stacking mail

Skills:

Walk to counter	- Power w/c with assistance	Develop power w/c skills for work area
Request date stamp	- Unable to communicate	Request date stamp by vocalizing and looking at photo
Walk to work station	- Power w/c with assistance	Develop power w/c skills for work area
Get opened mail from coworker	- Unable to communicate	Develop augmentative means to request work
Set stamp to correct date	- Full physical assistance	Usually already set by coworker
Walk to chair	- Power w/c with assistance	Develop power w/c skills to maneuver in work area
Get seated	+ Already seated	
Stamp top piece of mail	- Full physical assistance	Develop adaptation for stamping
Move stamped piece to finished work stack	- No, but can push the entire stack	Develop adaptation to allow for use of a sliding movement
Stamp next piece	- Full physical assistance	Adaptation for stamping
[repeat previous steps]		
Get up from chair and take finished work stack to coworker	- Unable to use hands to move paper stack	•Develop augmentative means to request that coworker pick up finished work and put on w/c tray •Drive power w/c to recipient of stamped mail
Get more opened mail from coworker	- Unable to use hands to get more work	Develop augmentative means to request more work from coworker
[repeat previous steps]		

Activity: Preparing for break

Skills:

Decide it is break time (10:15AM)	- Does not tell time	Set kitchen timer to ring at 10:15AM (J will go to break before others to allow for extra time in rest room)
Place work materials on counter in work area	- Full physical assistance	Develop augmentative means to ask for help

would investigate the feasibility of the ideas noted in the Teaching and Adaptation Hypotheses column of the ecological assessments.

The team quickly reached agreement regarding one aspect of Jamal's motor performance. For several tasks in Jamal's assessment at Metro, team members wrote "personal assistance" in the Teaching and Adaptation Hypotheses column. After years of professional efforts to teach Jamal tasks such as putting on and removing his coat, Jamal's team was satisfied that certain motor tasks were simply too difficult for Jamal to perform independently, with or without adaptations. Therefore the assistance and adaptations previously provided for these tasks would continue. Team members agreed that instructional time would be used more productively by focusing on participation in other components of work activities. Team members also recognized that Jamal would always need assistance with personal care, so teaching him to express specific interests, wants, and needs was a high priority as he approached adulthood. It is emphasized that legitimate decisions to abandon long-term efforts are made only on an individual basis, after concerted efforts with a variety of instructional strategies, after thorough consideration by the entire team, and when more appropriate priorities or strategies have been identified.

Diagnostic/Discipline-Referenced Assessment

Ecological assessments for the Spanish class and community work experience environments were representative of assessments done for other environments Jamal used during his school day. After considering this information along with additional observations, the team still had the following questions regarding Jamal's performance and instructional strategies for Spanish class and work environments:

- What communication forms and functions and what augmentative system(s) are the most appropriate learning priorities for Jamal at this time?
- What specifically is important to communicate in Spanish class?
- How can interactions be facilitated between Jamal and his classmates in Spanish class?
- Can Jamal control his giggling behavior voluntarily? Has similar behavior been a problem in other environments in the past?
- How can Jamal's giggling be addressed in a positive, nonpunitive manner without discouraging social interactions with his peers?
- What specifically is important to communicate in the workplace?
- How can interactions be facilitated between Jamal and insurance agency co-workers?
- Which workplace subenvironments would provide realistic practice for Jamal to maneuver his power wheelchair?
- What adaptations should be made to capitalize on Jamal's strengths and enable him to perform his job tasks?

The team determined that the occupational therapist and speech-language therapist would conduct the needed diagnostic assessments because the questions listed above were most related to their areas of expertise. Both therapists decided that the information the team was seeking could best be obtained through observation of Jamal's performance in the context of routine activities, and that formal tests would reveal few useful data for instructional purposes for a student like Jamal.

The occupational therapist focused her observations on how Jamal used his power wheelchair in various subenvironments, what positions allowed Jamal to participate most fully in motor tasks (e.g., using gross arm movements) in instructional environments, and how to maximize Jamal's motor participation in instructional tasks, especially for his job at the insurance agency. She gave particular consideration to simple adaptations to maximize outcomes from Jamal's limited arm movements.

The speech-language therapist conducted observations in various subenvironments to collect a nonsymbolic communication sample, which revealed communicative forms and functions already in Jamal's repertoire (Table 5.13). From this information communication forms and functions for instruction were selected to fit the needs of Jamal's specific learning environments. The Communication Environment Checklist, presented earlier in this chapter, was used as an informal assessment of conditions in instructional settings that either facilitated or hindered communication (see Figure 5.5).

Assessment Report   The following excerpts from Jamal's assessment report are consistent with the ecological curriculum design. Jamal's overall performance for activity routines is described along with a discussion of embedded motor, communication, and other broad skill areas for each priority environment. This arrangement of assessment information better accommodates variations in student performance related to the assortment of environments and people typically found in students' schedules, especially at the secondary level where instructional environments change every 45–50 minutes.

Annual Assessment
STUDENT: Jamal W.
DATE OF BIRTH: 6-1-74
DATE OF REPORT: 10-1-91
TEAM MEMBERS; Mrs. W. (Parent), John K. (SpEd), Ben G. (GenEd), Ann E. (Sp/Lang), Lisa W. (OT), Jake S. (SpEd Teaching Assistant), Sandy B. (Transition), Earl M. (Community Residence Coordinator)

Jamal is a 17-year-old junior at Central High School who enjoys school and friends and participates in school activities with determination and a sense of humor. He has generalized developmental disabilities, including spastic quadriplegic cerebral palsy and communication skills limited to the use of eye movements, facial expressions, and vocalizations. An augmentative communication system using scanning for objects and/or symbols is being considered. Anecdotal data about Jamal's communication behaviors have always suggested that his comprehension skills for language far surpass his expressive communication abilities. Jamal has received special education services since the age of 2, and has attended Harper City Schools since the age of 5. During Jamal's past 2 years at Central High School, he has spent an increasing amount of time participating in regular class and community environments. Team members evaluating Jamal for the assessment observed him in the context of daily routines at school, in a work experience, and in other relevant community environments.

Spanish Class
Jamal travels to Spanish class in his power wheelchair. He is learning to operate his wheelchair using a joystick. He needs assistance to relax his right arm and to secure his right hand to the joystick using a holding glove adaptation. Once Jamal is correctly positioned, the teaching assistant holds firmly around Jamal's right shoulder to provide stability. With this support, Jamal is developing greater control pushing the joystick in forward directions. His accuracy for travel in a straight line has increased dramatically since the start of school: he now drives up to 20 feet before hitting walls in hallways. He still requires full assistance to turn and to drive in reverse.

Jamal typically greets classmates spontaneously upon entry into the classroom. Classmates appear to enjoy Jamal and include him in a series of small group activities throughout the period. A communication sample indicates Jamal uses only nonsymbolic communication, with the majority of his expressive communication in Spanish class serving the functions of requesting assistance, objects, or activities (50%) and commenting (20%). Additional communication functions noted were greeting, rejecting,

Table 5.13 Jamal: Pragmatic communication assessment

Date & Time	Context	Form	Message Expressed (Intent)	Pragmatic Function	Consequence	# Times Observed
9-18-92	**SPANISH CLASS** (8:05 - 8:55 AM)					
8:00 AM	Friend David greeted with "Hey Jamal!" as he entered class.	Arm moved away from body, vocalization.	Hi.	Greeting	David looked at Jamal and put a hand on his shoulder.	I
8:05 AM	Teacher instructed students to find partners.	Looked toward David, then teacher, then David.	I choose David.	Request social event	David said, "Ok, Jamal, we can be partners again."	I
8:20 AM	Teacher told joke about red shoes.	Looked at Kelly and then his feet, moved his leg.	I have red shoes, too (red high tops).	Request for attention	Kelly said, "What are you so excited about, Jamal?"	I
8:21 AM	Jamal responded to Kelly.	Vocalization and continued leg movement.	I have red shoes, too.	Comment in response to question	Kelly said, "Oh, you have red shoes."	I
8:30 AM	Teacher said, "I wonder if Jamal can help us out today." Jamal didn't respond, so Kelly said, "Look at the tape recorder, Jamal."	Looked from teacher to tape recorder and back to teacher.	Wanted teacher to know he'd help switch on the tape recorder.	Comment	Teacher directs class-mate to set up tape recorder on Jamal's tray.	I
8:35 AM	Students practicing oral lesson for whole group instruction.	Repeated neck extension, throwing head back.	Seems to do this when bored or unable to do task.	Feeling / boredom	Nobody commented?	Many (3 min.)
8:45 AM	Leon asked, "Hey Jamal, are you ready to play the game?" (Not as active participant.) Students moving about.	Blank facial expression, no movement.	No.	Reject event	Ignored. Jamal was wheeled to group.	I
8:46 AM	When moved to group, foot got entangled in foot rest.	Vocalization, body stiff-ened.	Ouch, help.	Requests for attention and help	Leon approached to figure out what was wrong.	III
8:55 AM	Kelly said, "See you at the swim meet, Jamal."	Vocalization, looked at Kelly.	Yeah, goodbye.	Farewell	None.	I

150

9-18-92 — METRO INSURANCE AGENCY (Observation 9:15 AM)

Time	Context	Behavior	Message	Function	Partner Response	
9:15 AM	Jamal was assisted in moving his w/c off the van lift. Teaching assistant (Jake) asked, "OK, Jamal, now where do we go?"	Looked at Jake and then toward building entrance and back at Jake.	Go over there to the door.	Comment/giving information in response to question	Jake assisted Jamal in directing his power w/c to the building entrance.	I
9:17 AM	Jake was helping man the w/c controls with Jamal. Arcade hallway empty.	Pushed Jake's hand away from w/c controls and looked at his face.	I want to do it by myself.	Reject assistance	Jake said, "Sorry Jamal, I have to help until we get around this corner."	=
9:25 AM	Jamal stopped w/c near entrance to Metro Insurance Agency.	Looked back to Jake as he approached and vocalized.	Signaled arrival at destination.	Comment/giving information	Jake acknowledged.	=
9:27 AM	Jake wheeled Jamal to office coworkers.	Vocalization.	Hi.	Greeting	Two coworkers greeted Jamal.	=
9:28 AM	Coworkers asked Jamal if it was still raining outside.	Looked at Jake and vocalized.	Yes (?).	Comment in response to a question	Coworker acknowledged by talking about weather some more.	I
9:57 AM	Finished his first tray of work (with assistance). Jake asked, "What do we need now?"	Vocalized and looked toward student coworker.	Signaled done with worktray and needed more work from student coworker.	Request object	Jake cued student coworker to bring Jamal more work.	I
10:15 AM	Timer went off for Jamal's break time.	Vocalized and got excited (body stiffened).	Signaled break time.	Comment on event	"Oh, it's break time for Jamal."	I

(continued)

Table 5.13 (continued)

Date & Time	Context	Form	Message Expressed (Intent)	Pragmatic Function	Consequence	# Times Observed
10:20 AM	In restroom. Jake gave urinal/toilet for choices (as reported by Jake).	Looked at urinal.	I need the urinal.	Request object	Jake assisted with urinal.	I
10:31 AM	In break room with coworkers and Jake. Jake asked, "Do you want a drink today, Jamal?"	Smiled and looked at vending machine with juice.	Yes, juice.	Request object	Jake assisted Jamal to vending machine to make choice of juice.	I
10:32 AM	Jamal and Jake at vending machine. Jake pointed to juice boxes behind Plexiglas in the machine one at a time, saying, "Which one?"	Vocalized (when Jake was pointing to apple juice).	I want apple juice.	Request object	Jake pressed button for apple juice.	I
11:00 AM	Jamal was doing the stamping task with physical assistance, and the rubber was coming loose from the handle of the stamp.	Vocalized and banged on his tray, tried to get free of Jake's assistance.	Look, the stamp needs to be fixed.	Request for attention and help	Jake told Jamal to stop fooling around and get back to work. Jamal whined and Jake took a closer look and discovered the problem.	II

152

and expressing emotions. Jamal uses vocalizations, body posture, eye gaze, and limb movement in various combinations to get the attention of others. About one third of the time, he used his nonsymbolic communication to specifically direct the behavior of others.

Students who are most familiar with Jamal are better at interpreting his nonsymbolic communications and responding to them. Other students do not provide Jamal with enough response time to interact and tend to provide assistance before he signals for it. More opportunities for communication could be facilitated by informing classmates about how to recognize Jamal's nonsymbolic communications, how to provide appropriate levels of assistance and time delays, and how to take advantage of natural opportunities for Jamal to communicate.

The Spanish teacher reported that Jamal continues to giggle after the "joke of the day" activity, often disrupting the next scheduled activity for class. Observations did not indicate that this behavior was beyond Jamal's voluntary control, and therapists conducting the assessment both recommended that initial intervention strategies emphasize teaching and/or eliciting alternative behaviors that are incompatible with giggling.

Community Work Experience

Jamal travels to his community work site three times per week (MWF). He displays the same skills for power wheelchair use as in other environments (e.g., Spanish class). The location of his work experience program in an office building with power doors and long hallways provides many excellent opportunities to practice wheelchair mobility skills. He does not currently receive instruction on driving his power wheelchair in outside environments.

At the time of the assessment, Jamal was not spending the projected 2½ hours on site because of his inability to complete work tasks without task adaptations. (Adaptations are now being developed based on results of this assessment. Jamal's use of the adaptations will be assessed as soon as they are available.) Jamal was dependent upon the special education teaching assistant for communication interactions and motor assistance during the observation. Coworkers appeared friendly, but needed instruction to recognize Jamal's nonsymbolic communications, to provide appropriate assistance, and to identify natural opportunities for Jamal to communicate within work routines.

Jamal's nonsymbolic communication at the work site was similar to that found for Spanish class. The communication sample revealed the communication functions of requesting (40%) and commenting (33%), with the remaining 27% of the sample distributed between greeting, rejecting, and expressing emotions.

Summary [Excerpt]

Communication intervention is needed to increase Jamal's use of the five communication functions presently in his repertoire, expanding his use of communication forms that direct the behaviors of others. Intervention will also focus on the introduction of an augmentative means of communication that uses scanning as a means of selecting objects/symbols on a display board. The new system will be designed to meet specific communication needs in a variety of environments. In the environments sampled for assessment, the number of recognized and successful communication attempts was up to 50% greater in settings where a person familiar with Jamal's nonsymbolic communication forms was present. This indicates a clear need to instruct communication partners as an integral part of Jamal's communication intervention, to ensure sufficient learning opportunities.

Maintaining and improving Jamal's motor abilities is important to ensure maximal involvement in priority daily environments and activities. Specific motor targets to be addressed across his day are: 1) mobility using a wheelchair, with efforts to control a power wheelchair; 2) positioning to provide optimal alignment and stability for active participation, and to prevent contractures and deformities; and 3) active and assisted movement, especially of the head/neck and arms, to promote participation and control in daily routines. Handling procedures to achieve appropriate alignment will be instituted immediately prior to: 1) positioning changes to achieve/maintain optimal alignment in new positions (e.g., prior to positioning in standing, kneeling, and sidelying equipment);

2) facilitating active use of arms/hands, such as when reaching to obtain his coat, deflecting microswitches, indicating choices, or driving his power wheelchair; and 3) facili-

tating active head/neck movement during position/equipment changes, such as during transfers in/out of his wheelchair.

REFERENCES

Alberto, P.A., & Troutman, A.C. (1990). *Applied behavior analysis for teachers* (3rd ed.). Columbus, OH: Charles E. Merrill.

Bailey, D.B., & Wolery, M. (1989). *Assessing infants and preschoolers with handicaps.* Columbus, OH: Charles E. Merrill.

Bates, E., Benigni, L., Bretherton, I., Camaioni, L., & Volterra, V. (1979). *The emergence of symbols: Cognition and communication in infancy.* New York: Academic Press, Inc.

Baumgart, D., Johnson, J., & Helmstetter, E. (1990). *Augmentative and alternative communication systems for persons with moderate and severe disabilities.* Baltimore: Paul H. Brookes Publishing Co.

Black, J., & Ford, A. (1989). Planning and implementing activity-based lessons. In A. Ford, R. Schnorr, L. Meyer, L. Davern, J. Black, & P. Dempsey (Eds.), *The Syracuse community-referenced curriculum guide for students with moderate and severe disabilities* (pp. 295–311). Baltimore: Paul H. Brookes Publishing Co.

Blau, A., Lahey, M., & Oleksiuk-Velez, A. (1984). Planning goals for intervention: Can a language test serve as an alternative to a language sample? *Journal of Childhood Communication Disorders, 7*(1), 27–37.

Bricker, D. (Ed.). (1992). *Assessment, evaluation, and programming system (AEPS) for infants and children: Vol. 1, AEPS measurement for birth to three years.* Baltimore: Paul H. Brookes Publishing Co.

Bricker, D., Bailey, E.J., & Slentz, K. (1990). Reliability, validity, and utility of the "Evaluation and Programming System for Infants and Young Children" (EPS-1). *Journal of Early Intervention, 14*(2), 147–158.

Bricker, D., Gentry, D., & Bailey, E.J. (1985). *Evaluation and programming system for infants and young children (EPS-1).* Eugene, OR: University of Oregon, Center on Human Development.

Bricker, W.A., & Campbell, P. (1980). Interdisciplinary assessment and programming for multihandicapped students. In W. Sailor, B. Wilcox, & L. Brown (Eds.), *Methods of in-*struction for severely handicapped students (pp. 3–45). Baltimore: Paul H. Brookes Publishing Co.

Brigance, A.H. (1978). *Brigance diagnostic inventory of early development.* North Billerica, MA: Curriculum Associates.

Browder, D. (1991). *Assessment of individuals with severe disabilities: An applied behavior approach to life skills assessment* (2nd ed.). Baltimore: Paul H. Brookes Publishing Co.

Brown, F., Evans, I., Weed, K., & Owen, V. (1987). Delineating functional competencies: A component model. *Journal of The Association for Persons with Severe Handicaps, 12*(2), 117–124.

Campbell, S. (1989). Review of "Assessment of Behavioral Components." *Physical and Occupational Therapy in Pediatrics, 9*(2), 155–156.

Connor, F.P., Williamson, G.G., & Siepp, J.M. (1978). *Program guide for infants and toddlers with neuromotor and developmental disabilities.* New York: Teachers College Press.

Donnellan, A.M., Mirenda, P., Mesaros, R.A., & Fassbender, L.L. (1984). Analyzing the communicative functions of aberrant behavior. *Journal of The Association for Persons with Severe Handicaps, 9*(3), 201–212.

Dunn, W. (1991). The sensorimotor systems: A framework for assessment and intervention. In F. Orelove & D. Sobsey, *Educating children with multiple disabilities: A transdisciplinary approach* (2nd ed.) (pp. 33–78). Baltimore: Paul H. Brookes Publishing Co.

Erhardt, R.P. (1982). *Developmental hand dysfunction: Theory, assessment, treatment.* Laurel, MD: RAMSCO Publishing Co.

Erhardt, R.P. (1986). *Erhardt developmental vision assessment.* Laurel, MD: RAMSCO Publishing Co.

Erhardt, R.P., Beatty, P.A., & Hertsgaard, D.M. (1988). A developmental visual assessment for children with multiple handicaps. *Topics in Early Childhood Special Education, 7*(4), 84–101.

Folio, M.R., & Fewell, R.R. (1983). *Peabody De-*

velopmental Motor Scales. Allen, TX: DLM Teaching Resources.

Hardy, M., Kudar, S., & Macdonald, J.A. (1988). *Assessment of behavioral components: Analysis of severely disordered posture and movement in children with cerebral palsy*. Springfield, IL: Charles C Thomas.

Hendrick, D., Prather, E., & Tobin, A. (1984). *Sequenced inventory of communication development* (2nd ed.). Los Angeles: Western Psychological Services.

Hinderer, K.A., Richardson, P.K., & Atwater, S.W. (1989). Clinical implications of the Peabody developmental motor scales: A constructive review. *Physical and Occupational Therapy in Pediatrics*, 9(2), 81–106.

Horstmeier, D., & MacDonald, J. (1975). *Environmental pre-language battery*. Columbus, OH: Charles E. Merrill Publishing Co.

Huer, M.B. (1983). *The nonspeech test for receptive/expressive language*. Wauconda, IL: Don Johnston Developmental Equipment, Inc.

Hupp, S., & Donofrio, M. (1983). Assessment of multiply and severely handicapped learners for the development of cross-referenced objectives. *Journal of The Association for Persons with Severe Handicaps*, 8(3), 17–28.

Linder, T. (1990). *Transdisciplinary play-based assessment: A functional approach to working with young children*. Baltimore: Paul H. Brookes Publishing Co.

Macdonald, C., & York, J. (1989). Regular class integration: Assessment, objectives, instructional programs. In J. York, T. Vandercook, C. Macdonald, & S. Wolff (Eds.) *Strategies for full inclusion* (pp. 83–116). Minneapolis, MN: University of Minnesota, Institute on Community Integration.

MacDonald, J., & Nickols, M. (1974). *Environmental language inventory*. Columbus, OH: Charles E. Merrill.

Meyer, L., Reichle, J., McQuarter, R., Cole, D., Vandercook, T., Evans, I., Neel, R., & Kishi, G. (1985). *Assessment of social competence (ASC): A scale of social competence functions*. Minneapolis: University of Minnesota

Consortium Institute for the Education of Severely Handicapped Learners.

Orelove, F.P., & Sobsey, D. (1991). *Educating children with multiple disabilities: A transdisciplinary approach* (2nd ed.). Baltimore: Paul H. Brookes Publishing Co.

Ottenbacher, K.J. (1986). *Evaluating clinical change: Strategies for occupational and physical therapists*. Baltimore: Williams & Wilkins.

Owens, R. (1982a). Caregiver interview and environmental observation. *Program for the acquisition of language in the severely impaired*. San Antonio, TX: Psychological Corporation.

Owens, R. (1982b). *Program for the acquisition of language with the severely impaired*. Columbus, OH: Charles E. Merrill.

Thousand, J., Fox, T., Reid, R., Godek, J., Williams, W., & Fox, W. (1986). *The homecoming model: Educating students who present intensive educational challenges within regular education environments*. Burlington: University of Vermont, Center for Developmental Disabilities.

Waryas, C., & Stremel-Campbell, K. (1982). *Placement checklist: Communication training program*. Hingham, MA: Teaching Resources Corporation.

Wetherby, A., & Prizant, B. (1990). *Communication and symbolic behavior scales* (research edition). San Antonio: Special Press.

Williams, W., Hamre-Nietupski, S., Pumpian, I., McDaniel-Marx, J., & Wheeler, J. (1978). Teaching social skills. In M. Snell (Ed.), *Systematic instruction of the severely handicapped* (pp. 281–300). Columbus, OH: Charles E. Merrill.

Wolery, M., & Dyk, L. (1984). Arena assessment: Description and preliminary social validity data. *Journal of The Association for Persons with Severe Handicaps*, 9(3), 231–235.

York, J., & Vandercook, T. (1990). Strategies for achieving an integrated education for middle school students with severe disabilities. *Remedial and Special Education*, 11(5), 6–15.

6

Collaborative Individualized Education Programs

T HE INDIVIDUALIZED EDUCATION PROGRAM (IEP) is the written document that outlines a child's abilities and needs, and defines the educational program designed to meet those needs. It is intended to be a planning document, which shapes and guides day-to-day provision of special education and related services. The IEP document is most useful to the student and team when it reflects the integrated approach to curriculum and instruction that emanates from the collaborative team process.

Initial guidelines for developing IEPs were established in the late 1970s and reflected the educational procedures of that time. Unfortunately, many educational teams have adhered to older models of curriculum, instruction, and teamwork, which are no longer considered good practice. As a result, many IEPs still contain separate lists of strengths and needs for discrete areas of skill development (e.g., fine motor, language), recommendations for episodic and isolated related services (e.g., 30 minutes three times a week), and goals that are too general to define the scope or priorities of the educational program (e.g., improve communication skills).

Frequently each discipline submits a separate list of objectives, which are stapled together, under the misconception that this creates a "team IEP" (Giangreco, 1986). When team members generate an IEP through this type of isolated, discipline-focused process, it is understandable that they will have difficulty in organizing and delivering integrated transdisciplinary services. Individual service providers may assume that they are not responsible for integrating the disparate pieces into a comprehensive, coordinated program, or that someone with a greater interest will assume the responsibility. When service providers fail to design and implement integrated and coordinated educational programs, however, they unwittingly delegate their responsibility to students with severe disabilities and decrease the likelihood of student success. If the planners cannot integrate and coordinate the program, the recipient of the program certainly will experience difficulty. When teams design collaborative IEPs, they lay the foundation for effective service provision.

Collaborative assessment, as described in Chapter 5, is the first step in developing a team IEP. The assessment provides team members with information about student performance in priority activities in integrated environments, including the student's specific strengths and needs for participation. From this information, the team can more easily reach consensus on educational program content, priority goals and objectives, and the type and amount of special education and related services required to address these priorities. This chapter presents strategies for: 1) identifying a single, comprehensive set of educational priorities, 2) writing goals and objectives that support transdisciplinary instruction and a curriculum referenced to activities in least restrictive environments, and 3) making service recommendations that promote efficient use of personnel and provision of integrated therapy services. The relationship among these three components is depicted in Figure 6.1.

Public Law 94-142 mandates that the IEP be developed by a team. The process will be more productive and the resulting document more meaningful when teams adopt principles of effective group decision making (e.g., Bolton, 1979; Johnson & Johnson, 1987). The first principle is that the group needs to have enough members

to provide the necessary information, but few enough so all members participate (usually between four and eight). For students who need input from more members, it is advisable to identify a core team that assumes primary responsibility for the IEP process, including day-to-day planning and instruction. The core team also assumes responsibility for seeking needed input from members of the extended team. Second, team members need to believe they have the power to make decisions about an individual student and that their decisions will not be overridden by an authority above the group. Third, members need to feel safe in discussions with their team, knowing that their input will not be negated or devalued by others. An open exchange of ideas will lead to a more inclusive and representative outcome when the group views its diversity as vital and negotiates resolutions rather than suppresses conflict. Finally, the group needs sufficient time to work through the decision-making process. Adopting any new approach initially takes more time than using familiar methods. It is also understandable that school personnel may want to work out some of their differences before meeting with parents, especially

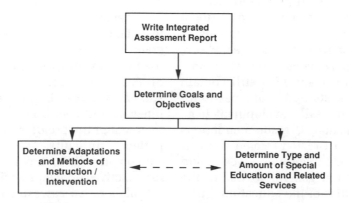

Figure 6.1. Relationship among components of an integrated IEP.

when staff are first adopting new roles, processes, and procedures. For all of these reasons, it may be appropriate and necessary for teams to have planning meetings before the formal IEP conference.

It is emphasized that the purpose of such planning meetings is not to develop the IEP. Furthermore, it is essential that parents be involved in informal planning and that they feel as influential in decision making as any other member of the team. Parents can be encouraged to participate in planning through ongoing written, telephone, and face-to-face communications with staff. Later, parents meet with the core team to finalize planning. Prior to the IEP meeting, staff "suggestions" are not written onto forms or typed, since this conveys finalization, and lessens the parents' perception of their own power to influence team decisions.

When parents and staff develop an IEP, use of collaborative problem solving (Bolton, 1979) and consensual decision making (Johnson & Johnson, 1987) strategies can produce a better IEP. The process includes the following steps:

1. Identify the problem or need.
2. Gather information.
3. Brainstorm options without clarification or evaluation of ideas.
4. Establish criteria to choose among options.
5. Apply criteria.
6. Act on decisions.
7. Evaluate outcomes.

The process is consensual when all team members contribute ideas and negotiate agreement on decisions (reach consensus), rather than vote or defer to an authority figure. This process is discussed in relation to group problem solving in Chapter 8. The steps in the consensual decision-making process are discussed here with specific

application to the major decisions that shape the IEP.

SELECTING PRIORITIES FOR THE IEP

As discussed in the previous chapters, identifying educational priorities begins long before the team meets to develop the IEP. Through the processes of completing the IEP Worksheet and the Assessment Planning Chart, the educational team works with the family to identify the integrated environments and activities in which the student's participation is most important. During the assessment, the team identifies the student's abilities and needs in specific educational activities, and gains information about how specific disabilities (e.g., cerebral palsy, visual impairment) may influence the student's overall performance. When the team engages in a collaborative assessment process and writes an integrated assessment report, a natural extension is a single, integrated list of the student's needs. Although this list is highly individualized, the team usually must make further determinations about which needs have the highest priority for the current year's IEP. Although this discussion focuses on making final decisions about what to include in the IEP, many considerations apply to the processes for determining priorities described in Chapters 4 and 5.

Students with severe disabilities often have several significant needs, in the areas of posture and mobility, hand use, receptive and expressive communication, functional academics, socialization, self-care and independent living, use of leisure time, community participation, work, and the like. Even with a collaborative team approach, it is necessary to set priorities to ensure relevance of the IEP and balance in the student's life. While students with severe disabilities have extensive needs, they also have finite time and energy to participate in education. Furthermore, each student is first and foremost a child and family member, and second, a student with disabilities (Benson & Turnbull, 1986). Every child needs opportunities for unstructured and self-directed activities in addition to adult-directed activities and instruction, both at home and at school. Finally, each child with severe disabilities has unique needs related to his or her individual disabilities. Rather than competing for student time and energy, seeking consensus on priorities enables teams to maximize student outcomes.

When first adopting a team approach, it is natural for service providers to see priorities from the vantage of their own discipline. A collaborative and consensual approach to determining priorities may be the most difficult aspect of designing the IEP, since it frequently requires one or more team members to let go of what they view as important from their discipline's perspective. As team members observe and work with students in integrated environments, consensus about priorities is usually achieved more easily because each team member sees the student in a functional context working to meet daily demands. Instead of asking questions like "How can we improve gross motor skills?" team members start asking "What is most important for this student to participate in this educational situation?" The context of the student's performance, rather than an isolated skill orientation, starts driving decisions about priorities.

The consensual decision-making process is used to establish priorities through the following steps. First, at the conclusion of the student's assessment, the team generates a list of specific needs without eval-uating the appropriateness or relative importance of individual items. Evaluation at this point tends to limit contributions. Next, the team establishes criteria to select the highest priorities from the list. It is not necessary for the team to generate new criteria for each student, but the relative importance of each criterion will vary from student to student, especially given variations in family values and perspectives. Numerous authors (Bricker & Campbell, 1980; Browder, 1991; Brown et al., 1988; Meyer & Evans, 1989; Orelove & Sobsey, 1991) have identified criteria for selecting educational priorities, which include the following:

1. Maintains health and vitality
2. Enhances participation in current and future integrated environments
3. Increases social integration, including interactions with peers
4. Has frequent or multiple applications across environments and activities
6. Is essential for further development
7. Is a student priority, including individual preferences or interests
8. Is a family priority
9. Is a priority of a significant person in a target environment

Needs meeting more than one of these criteria would be a high priority for translation into goals and objectives. Some programs use a weighting system in which needs are given points for meeting various criteria and are ranked according to their total number of points (e.g., Renzaglia & Aveno, 1986). When needs meet the criteria above, final selection or ranking might reflect the following considerations:

1. A majority of the team considers the need a priority.
2. People, materials, and time are available to address the need.

3. Real or simulated environments are available for instruction.
4. Real environments are available for validation of learning.
5. The student can achieve the goal relatively easily.

When needs are selected as priorities because they meet one or more of the criteria above, it is important that the resulting goals and objectives reflect the same criteria. For example, if independent mobility is a priority for a child with muscular dystrophy, different objectives might be written depending upon whether the determining criterion was "maintain vitality" or "participate in integrated environments" or both. Illustrative criteria are discussed below, with examples of goals and objectives.

Maintains Health and Vitality

For students with health impairments, this criterion usually determines the highest priorities because it reflects the minimum conditions necessary for those students to participate in education. Increasing fluid and caloric intake would be a high priority for a child with inadequate nutrition and hydration. Regular changes in position would be a high priority for a student who is at risk for decubitus ulcers, contractures, and constipation. These needs might be translated into the following goals:

David will improve oromotor patterns for eating and drinking.
Michelle will communicate discomfort and request position changes.

These student goals should not be confused with "passive" or "management" goals and objectives, such as:

David will receive a high-calorie dietary supplement.

Michelle's position will be changed every half hour.

Downing (1988) found that students with the most severe disabilities had a high proportion of passive objectives on their IEPs. When students have significant care and management needs, it may be important to record recommendations of this type on the IEP. It is most appropriate to record them as service objectives for the team, however, since they do not address student learning.

Occasionally this health criterion has the effect of limiting educational opportunities. Since most learning presents some element of risk, teams need to weigh the potential benefits against the potential risks, and recall that there is dignity in risk (Perske, 1988). It is certainly appropriate to ensure safety, but adults often discover that their fears were disproportionate with reality. One mother, who had been warned not to let her daughter participate in community activities, found that her daughter actually had fewer and less severe respiratory infections when she left the "protective" environment of the special school. Another mother was relieved to see that her child could eat solid foods fairly easily, with no more risk of choking than any other child. For a child with difficult-to-control seizures, the team was concerned that inclusion in general education classes would increase the likelihood of warning signs being missed. Instead, the student's close proximity to classmates resulted in ongoing, albeit inadvertent, monitoring of signs. Parents often desire a higher quality of life for their child, and understand that risks accompany such opportunities. Involving parents in the discussion of risks and benefits is essential; it increases the likelihood that students will be allowed to take reasonable risks, that safeguards will be adequate, and that individuals charged with implementation will feel sufficient support during new ventures.

Enhances Participation in Current and Future Integrated Environments

This criterion assists with selection of appropriate activities and materials, as well as specific skills and behaviors. It may be reflected in IEP goals such as:

Kristen will increase her participation in kindergarten activities.
Tom will participate in work routines in the middle school cafeteria.
Brian will select books and listen to stories in the school library.
Meg will play with her third grade friends for 15 minutes.
Jodi will partially participate in planning and cooking a meal.

Goals and objectives that meet this criterion are also likely to meet one or more of the other criteria discussed below.

Increases Social Integration

Related aspects of this criterion are that improved performance would both enhance the student's social status and increase social interactions with other students. When considering this criterion, it is often useful to include chronological age peers without disabilities in the decision-making process. Friends are generally pleased to offer social validation (Kazdin, 1977; Wolf, 1978)—that is, to evaluate whether proposed activities and materials are socially acceptable and desirable. For example, Meg's team agreed that a priority was for Meg to play with third grade friends. They considered the following objective:

Meg will dress and undress large dolls as a preferred leisure activity.

When Meg's friends explained that only Barbie dolls are acceptable at their age, the team needed to consider whether Meg could readily develop the dexterity to manage Barbie dolls, or whether another leisure task would better meet the criterion of increasing social integration.

Friends of Eric, a 7-year-old boy with severe intellectual and physical disabilities, identified two specific pieces of playground equipment on which Eric should play. Their recommendation was made not because Eric could play on the equipment independently, nor even because he might like it, but because all the 7-year olds used those two pieces of equipment.

Has Frequent/Multiple Applications

Tracy's need to improve communication skills was previously addressed through objectives to name objects when asked "What is this?" When the team considered the criterion of frequent/multiple applications, they established a new objective:

Tracy will request the following by pointing to and then naming:
a. preferred foods and drinks
b. preferred leisure materials
c. materials needed to complete assigned tasks (e.g., household chores, functional academics, clerical work).

Thus the skill has application to mealtimes, leisure activities, and a variety of other tasks at home, school, and work. Tracy also needs to improve her ability to manipulate small objects, which has frequent and multiple applications. The team specified the priority manipulation skills and materials in an objective:

Tracy will improve fine motor skills to perform the following tasks in her daily living routine:
a. button/unbutton her coat, fasten her shoes, fasten her belt

b. remove/replace toothpaste/shampoo cap, open soap/toothpaste cartons

c. open milk carton, straw, and utensil packs in the cafeteria

d. dial and touch numbers accurately on telephones to call home

When priority skills can be taught frequently in naturally occurring situations, there is little justification for removing students from integrated learning environments for isolated instruction.

Is Essential for Further Development

Some behaviors and skills are desirable primarily because they form the foundation for other skills or learning. Teams are cautioned about this criterion, however, because many persons with severe disabilities have spent their lifetimes working on "prerequisites" without opportunities to learn meaningful and useful skills. Furthermore, many skills in normal developmental sequences have proven not to be valid as "prerequisites" to further development or participation. Therefore teams must examine whether skills proposed to meet this criterion are really essential and whether teaching them would really provide greater opportunities for participation than alternative approaches such as task adaptations. While such skills may be legitimate prerequisites, this does not suggest they should be taught in an isolated fashion. Essential skills can be taught in the context of meaningful activities, and often meet the criterion of having frequent/ multiple applications. For example, Kim's physical therapist identified the need to improve Kim's head and trunk control. Some team members questioned this priority, since Kim already used her vision and hands functionally in a variety of tasks, and used good oromotor skills during mealtime, when positioned in her adapted wheelchair. After discussion, the team agreed that Kim might still achieve better control, which would increase her options for positioning, mobility, and task participation. They also agreed that objectives for improved head and trunk control could be incorporated into activities throughout the day.

Before Jamal's speech-language therapist attended a workshop on presymbolic communication, she assumed that students must display clear communicative intent (desire to communicate) before moving toward use of an augmentative system. As a consequence, she did not facilitate use of objects or pictures as symbols before a student established intent in a wide variety of daily events. From her new information on presymbolic communication, the therapist realized that instruction to develop communicative intent could take place within the context of existing daily routines and simultaneously with instruction to use objects and/or pictures as communication symbols. For example, she could teach a student to signal primitive intent (e.g., hold out a cup for more juice) and to signal more complex intent with symbols (e.g., touch a picture to get a snack) at the same time. The therapist learned that adhering to a strict progression from primitive to symbolic intent may just make it more difficult for students with severe disabilities to make the transition to more symbolic communication (Reichle, York, & Sigafoos, 1991). Furthermore, lack of demonstrated intent is not necessarily an indication that students are not ready to learn other types of communication skills. Lack of opportunities for students with severe disabilities to display intent often precludes such intentional behavior, such as when unresponsive listeners extinguish intent or caregivers provide so much assistance during daily routines that the student does not need to display intent (Baumgart, Johnson, & Helmstetter, 1990).

Is a Student/Family Priority

Some programs use this as their primary criterion, reaffirming that the child and family are the central focus of the IEP. A priority for Sandra's mother was for Sandra to crawl up and down stairs because the only bathroom at home was on the second floor and Sandra was hard to carry. The team arranged situations at school to teach Sandra to climb stairs, and worked with her mother on designing a home program. Rick had poor articulation due to athetoid cerebral palsy, but wanted to communicate via speech rather than a communication board. Although some team members doubted that Rick would ever speak intelligibly, the speech-language therapist agreed to provide intensive training on articulation.

In contrast, Jeremy's mother wanted the team to focus on toilet training. For 2 years, team members disagreed about this priority and failed to put it on the IEP because some members considered it unrealistic. Finally, in the third year, toilet training was made a priority. After a couple of months, Jeremy's mother reported that she saw no progress, and thought they should move on to other needs. Some readers may conclude that the professionals finally "beat" this unrealistic parent, but another view is that the team might have achieved a unified effort 3 years earlier if they had started by honoring the mother's priority. Controversies often can be resolved with less conflict if the team agrees to implement an intervention, records objective data, and then evaluates results of the actual intervention, rather than continuing to speculate about possible outcomes.

Is a Priority of a Significant Person in a Target Environment

Many students with severe disabilities are being educated in integrated school and community settings. General education teachers, employers, and others may express priorities for student performance while in integrated environments. Some teachers place great importance on students working cooperatively and assisting each other; others want students to raise their hands and wait for assistance. Similarly, some work environments are arranged to require solitary work while others promote regular opportunities for coworkers to interact for work tasks and social events. Successful placements in integrated settings require identification of these preferences, responsive instructional priorities, and thoughtful placement decisions.

WRITING GOALS AND OBJECTIVES

Public Law 94-142 specifies that an IEP "shall include . . . a statement of annual goals, including short-term instructional objectives, . . . and appropriate criteria and evaluation procedures and schedules for determining, on at least an annual basis, whether instructional objectives are being achieved" (20 U.S.C. §1401 (a)(19)). Within these specifications, there are numerous variations on how to write goals and objectives for an IEP. Typically, goals describe general performance while objectives outline either a scope or a sequence of skills that comprise the goal. Frequently, goals and objectives are written in ways that make it difficult to determine exactly what performance is desired, how performance is to be evaluated, and whether progress is being made (e.g., improve gross motor development as judged by therapist). Mager (1984) recommended that objectives include: 1) the target behavior(s) defined in observable and measurable terms, 2) conditions under which the behaviors are performed, and 3) objective criteria to evaluate achievement. Behavioral objectives improve communication among team members and facilitate systematic and responsive instruction.

Therapists often struggle with behavioral objectives because they are concerned with qualitative aspects of performance. Although it is sometimes difficult to conceive of quality components in behavioral terms, the desired outcomes of improved quality usually can be defined. The following objectives address quality first by defining the desired performance as clearly as possible, and then by specifying conditions or criteria under which the desired quality occurs. The first two objectives define quality by using social validation as an evaluation strategy (Kazdin, 1977; Van Houten, 1979; Wolf, 1978):

Rick will make verbal requests that can be understood by five out of five friends.

Rick will make verbal requests that can be understood by three out of five persons unfamiliar with his speech.

The next two objectives address quality partly by defining what the desired performance will look like and partly by specifying the performance conditions—that is, the type, location, and amount of prompting (or facilitation) necessary to achieve the desired performance:

After 1 minute of tone reduction and while given physical guidance at the elbow and wrist, Sonja will reach to her communication board five times without pulling back, for 3 consecutive days.

With a verbal cue to relax and with maintained support at the shoulder, Sonja will reach for and grasp her electric toothbrush without pulling her shoulder up and back, for the first 2 minutes of toothbrushing on 3 consecutive days.

When writing behavioral objectives, team members' diverse perspectives are helpful to determine whether desired performance is defined clearly and to identify considerations most relevant to performance quality.

The criterion for any objective contains two components. The first reflects the standard of accuracy or fluency in any given day or evaluation period, such as "80% correct on a weekly quiz," "for 5 minutes," or "during the first 2 out of 3 opportunities each day." The second component reflects the consistency of performance over time to confirm that performance is typical rather than chance, such as "on 3 out of 5 days" or "for 4 consecutive days." Unfortunately, some computer-generated IEPs have predetermined that one criterion (e.g., "80% correct for 4 out of 5 days") is proper for all students and tasks. Like all other aspects of an IEP, the standards for both accuracy and consistency must be determined individually based on the student's current level of performance, the time frame for achievement, and social validity considerations (Browder, 1991).

Incorporating the Ecological Curriculum

The importance of an ecological curriculum as a "best practice" and context for integrated therapy services was discussed in Chapter 4. Because an ecological curriculum is the basis for educational priorities, the corresponding goals and objectives must maintain an ecological orientation. Therefore, IEP goals and objectives should identify the priority environments and activities in which priority skills will be used. There are two general approaches to writing such goals and objectives on the IEP.

Approach #1: Goals Specify Priority Skills; Objectives Specify Contexts for Performance Some teams find this approach easier when first moving from a developmental or functional skills curriculum to an ecological curriculum. Each goal identifies a skill or skill area; the corresponding objectives identify the educational contexts (activities and environments) in which the skill must be performed. The contexts must be derived from an ecological analysis of actual demands in priority environments, not from guesses or presumptions about functional activities. Goals and objectives organized in this way tend to remain discipline referenced—that is, each team member can easily write and locate the sets of goals and objectives most relevant to his or her discipline. Since the priorities of each discipline are easier to identify, so is their role in the educational program. The familiarity of this approach can be reassuring for educational team members as they adopt other changes in their model of service provision.

Examples of this approach include the following:

GOAL

Brian will improve positioning of his posterior walker to perform functional activities.

OBJECTIVES

1. When given visual cues and verbal reminders, Brian will align his walker next to the cafeteria counter and walk through the line, for 3 consecutive days.
2. When given visual cues and verbal reminders in homeroom, Brian will position his walker behind his chair and pivot into his seat, using his seat back for support, for 3 out of 4 days.
3. When given visual cues and verbal re-

minders, Brian will position his walker to the left of his locker, open the door, and remove and hang his coat, for 3 out of 4 days.

GOAL

Missy will improve visual scanning and focusing to make and convey choices in daily routines.

OBJECTIVE

When positioned in her chair with her head stabilized and presented with two objects at eye level, Missy will look at each object for 1 second and focus on her preference for 5 seconds, in 3 out of 4 trials, on 3 consecutive days, in each of the following situations:

1. mealtime (choose between food and drink)
2. free time (choose between toys for microswitch)
3. grooming (choose sequence from washcloth, toothbrush, hairbrush)

Kristen's IEP, at the end of this chapter, is written using this format for goals and objectives. Kristen's mother and other team members were most familiar with a developmental approach, and felt most comfortable when the IEP goals outlined priorities for skill development.

Although this is a vast improvement over traditional approaches that do not specify contexts for performance at all, there is danger of remaining in a discipline context rather than adopting an environmental context. If the starting point for generating priorities varies among team members, the resulting program will still be fragmented. There is also danger of contriving "functional" contexts and losing site of those environments and activities in which performance was originally desired. Thus opportunities to address skills might determine the activities in which students participate, and limit attention to skills that support participation in integrated school and community environments and activities. For these reasons, we encourage teams to move on to the approach described below.

Approach #2: Goals Specify Priority Environments and Activities; Objectives Specify Component Skills Many team members find this format difficult at first, especially for young children and children with profound/multiple disabilities. Teams become more comfortable with this approach as they focus on the team goal of teaching students to participate in integrated community environments and as they become more versed in using an ecological approach to assessment. In the examples below, goals specify priority environments and activities; objectives outline a cluster of skills required to reach the goal. Goals and objectives organized in this way are the natural extension of an ecological curriculum and assessment.

GOAL

Becky will water plants at home.

OBJECTIVES

1. After being assisted once with facilitation at the pelvis, Becky will push to stand from half-kneeling, with controlled weight shift while using support from the sink edge.
2. Becky will maintain symmetrical upright trunk alignment without reminders, while standing at the sink to fill the watering can.
3. Becky will use two hands to support the watering can while kneewalking from the sink to the family room.
4. Becky will follow a left-to-right sequence to water plants, with visual cues, and pour for a count of 3.

Criteria for all objectives: 8 out of 10 opportunities in 1 week

This goal-objective format also matches well with the organization of secondary-level programs, when students typically change classes every 45–50 minutes. Goals reflect the various learning environ-

ments (classes) and objectives reflect the priority skills relevant for class participation.

GOAL

Tess will participate in a sixth-grade science class.

OBJECTIVES

1. Tess will read "science" from her schedule and print "science" next to the model, without overlapping letters, for 1 week.
2. When given a verbal reminder, Tess will tell other students in her science group, "I can do this, thanks," or "I need help, please" on 80% of opportunities for 1 week.
3. At the end of class, Tess will converse with a friend in a turntaking routine by answering the friend's question and then asking a question about the preceding science activity, daily for 1 week.

Jamal's IEP, at the end of this chapter, is written using this format. His team has fully adopted an ecological curriculum and assessment strategy, and finds that this is the logical model for IEP development. It might be noted that each goal on Jamal's IEP has some objectives unique to the learning environment identified in the goal as well as some objectives that are similar across learning environments.

MAKING SERVICE RECOMMENDATIONS

A major challenge for teams adopting a transdisciplinary and integrated therapy model is how to determine which services are necessary, how frequently, and for how long. One difficulty is that traditional service recommendations, such as "30 minutes of OT 3 times a week," lock therapists into rigid schedules that prevent effective integration of related services into educational programs. Many students who need occupational, physical, or speech-language therapy have been referred from early intervention or medical rehabilitation programs in which therapy is a *primary* service rather than a related service. Through these primary services, the "30 times 3" approach may inadvertently be established as the only "correct" model. Additionally, in a primary service model, children typically receive physical therapy if they demonstrate any gross motor disabilities, occupational therapy for any fine motor or perceptual difficulties, and speech-language therapy for any communication problems. In educational programs, children receive these as related services, if deemed necessary to achieve IEP goals and objectives. When children move from early intervention and rehabilitation systems into educational systems, parents may view digression from the primary/direct service model as decreasing the intensity of their child's services.

Therefore, the challenge to educational teams is to make related service recommendations that ensure: 1) the desired scope, intensity, and coordination of services; 2) the flexibility for therapists to work in a variety of school, home, and community settings; and 3) accountability to students and fellow team members. Strategies to determine and document the type, amount, and form of related services are examined in the following sections. In Chapter 8, broader considerations in scheduling to meet the needs of multiple students are discussed.

Type of Related Service

Some states and school districts have criteria for eligibility for related services, which specify the type and degree of disability a student must have to qualify for a particular service (see, Carr, 1989). Such criteria may be useful to identify students whose disabilities are mild enough that they do no not interfere with educational performance. Therapists are cautioned against using the criteria to disqualify students with severe or multiple disabilities, judging that they are too disabled to benefit or that related services are unnecessary if (limited) motor or communication performance is consistent with overall educational performance. Such interpretations are clearly contradictory to the intent of Public Law 94-142, which gave highest priority to services for students with the most severe disabilities. This priority was recently reaffirmed in the case of *Timothy W. v. Rochester, NH, School District* (1989). Furthermore, a policy clarification from the U.S. Department of Education, Office of Special Education Programs states that such eligibility criteria cannot usurp the IEP team's authority and responsibility to determine student need for related services (Rainforth, 1991).

In general, teams will determine which related services to recommend by matching the student's priority needs with the personnel who can meet those needs. If a student needs to improve oromotor skills for eating, for example, a team member with expertise in feeding facilitation needs to be identified. It cannot be assumed that every speech-language therapist and occupational therapist will have the necessary skills, or that a physical therapist, teacher, or nurse does not possess the skills to address this need. If no one on the team has the required expertise, the team will need to access outside resources to expand the skills of one or more team members.

When therapists have similar skills, program coordination and efficient resource allocation can be maximized if the team agrees on an occupational therapist or a physical therapist as the primary motor therapist. For example, Kristen needs to learn normalized movement patterns for posture, mobility, and manipulation of materials. Both the occupational therapist and the physical therapist available to support Kristen report that they could address most of these needs. After discussing the interrelationship and relative importance of Kristen's needs, the therapists' overlapping and separate skills, and considerations such as program coordination and therapist scheduling, the team determined that the physical therapist would be the primary therapist for Kristen. In addition, the occupational therapist would consult with the physical therapist for specific needs related to hand use. By arranging for the occupational therapist to offer consultation, rather than a separate service, the physical therapist can integrate the occupational therapist's recommendations, devise comprehensive strategies, coordinate priorities across daily routines, and ensure more consistent program implementation.

The decision to use a primary therapist is based upon similarity or overlap of therapist skills and the need to coordinate strategies to achieve priority objectives. Personnel resources and student time are not used well when team members use different strategies to achieve the same outcome, use similar strategies to achieve different outcomes, or merely duplicate services. This does not mean that there is no time when the team draws upon every available resource. A high priority for Jamal is to use a communication system, but his team has not achieved much success on this goal. As the team makes decisions about types of communication systems, selection modes, positioning, prompting strategies, contexts for use, and vocabulary, input will be needed from many team members. Although they will address overlapping questions, each team member will bring unique perspectives and skills to the process. The need for input from a particular discipline during decision making does not necessarily mean the discipline will be needed to provide ongoing services, however.

This does not suggest that teachers who are highly skilled in addressing sensori-motor and communication needs should be encouraged to work without the support of therapists. Few teachers receive the same scope or intensity of training in these specialized areas as therapists. Even when teachers do have great expertise, it is inappropriate to place full responsibility for educating children with the most challenging needs on one staff member. The importance of teamwork in effective education for students with severe disabilities cannot be overemphasized.

Models of Related Service

A variety of terminology has been used to delineate the various models of service provision (see, e.g., Dunn, 1988). The choice of terms is not so important as making sure they are clearly defined and communicated to all members of the educational team. In this book, the terms "integrated therapy," "direct therapy," and "consultation" are used. Collaborative teamwork is necessary for any of these models to be truly effective.

Integrated Therapy　The key feature of the integrated therapy model is that therapy services are provided and then strategies associated with the disciplines providing therapy are used within the activities and environments the team deems a priority for a given student. Implementing this model requires direct, indirect, and transdisciplinary service components. Direct "hands on" services by the therapist are necessary while assessing the student, determining intervention strategies, training others to use specific strategies, solving implementation problems, and modifying programs. The therapist also provides indirect services, such as providing general training, observing program implementation, monitoring performance data, and developing equipment and materials. The transdisciplinary component occurs as therapists release parts of their roles to other team members so students can receive frequent and ongoing instruction on sensorimotor, communication, and other skills in priority educational contexts in the absence of the therapist. These are all ongoing processes. The importance of collaborative teamwork for implementing an integrated therapy model is clear.

Service recommendations specify the amount of time the therapist is needed to provide the direct and indirect services outlined above. The recommendation for each related service is in proportion to the priorities outlined in the IEP, and with consideration of which team member can competently address each priority. For example, the goals and objectives on Jamal's IEP (excerpts are at the end of this chapter) all reflect motor and communication needs, and require input from a speech-language therapist and an occupational and/or physical therapist. Motor and communication needs seem equal, but the team thought additional speech-language therapist time would be needed at the start of the year to develop Jamal's new communication system. The occupational therapist was selected as the primary motor therapist because this individual had more expertise than the available physical therapist to meet Jamal's greatest needs (adaptations, use of hands/arms). The therapists, special education teacher, and special education teaching assistant had worked as a collaborative team with Jamal and his family for some time, but Jamal would be working in new environments

with new general education teachers and new coworkers who would need education about Jamal's needs. Based on all these considerations, the team recommended 4 hours/month of integrated speech-language therapy, 4 hours/month of integrated occupational therapy, and 1 hour/month of physical therapy consultation. Rather than state time recommendations in minutes per day or week, a "block" of therapist time was recommended, to increase the therapists' flexibility to work with Jamal and other students in their routine activities. (See Chapter 8 for further discussion of block scheduling.)

When first changing from direct therapy to integrated therapy, the team may want to recommend the same amount of time but state it in terms of time per month. For example, Kristen had received speech-language therapy for 30 minutes three times a week, occupational therapy for 30 minutes twice a week, and physical therapy for 30 minutes twice a week in her previous program. This would translate to 6 hours/month for speech-language therapy, and 4 hours/month for both occupational and physical therapy. Kristen's parents had fought hard to get the services they thought she needed, so they were apprehensive about an unfamiliar service provision model. With explanation of the rationale for integrated therapy, assurance that therapists would be accountable for their services, and agreement that Kristen would receive the equivalent amount of therapist time, Kristen's parents agreed to try integrated therapy with the following block time recommendation: 6 hours/month integrated speech-language therapy, 6 hours/month integrated physical therapy, and 2 hours/month occupational therapy consultation. (The physical therapist was selected as the primary motor therapist.)

It might be noted that more time was recommended for Kristen's services than for Jamal's. Several factors entered into these decisions. Jamal's mother was more comfortable with the concept of integrated therapy and block time recommendations, since she has seen the benefits for her son in the past. Jamal's core team had worked together longer than Kristen's, so the members of Jamal's team were more skilled at collaborating with one another, infusing motor and communication instruction into educational routines, and educating others about Jamal's needs. Jamal's therapists had had more time to establish good rapport with his family. Over time Jamal's core team also had become more familiar with Jamal's abilities and needs and knew that he would not change as quickly as they did when he was younger. For all of these reasons, *Jamal's team was comfortable with recommending less therapist time than Kristen's team. Jamal's team did not consider Jamal less able to benefit from related services; his core team had become more efficient in the way they developed and provided services.*

Integrated therapy is considered the primary model of service for most students with severe disabilities because it provides the most educationally relevant services in least restrictive environments (Giangreco, York, & Rainforth, 1989). When teams recommend direct therapy for students with severe disabilities, it is as a support and supplement to integrated therapy.

Direct Therapy   Direct therapy generally refers to "hands-on" treatment that is episodic and provided in isolation, rather than in the context of the student's daily routine. Since synthesis and generalization of new skills cannot be assumed under these circumstances, direct services must be justified carefully and re-evaluated frequently. Some common reasons for considering direct services are discussed below. Note that some of the justifications initially seem appropriate, because they reflect familiar thinking about use of therapist time. When analyzed further, however, appropriateness must be questioned.

"Lizzie is changing so quickly right now that I must address new needs each time I see her."   In this situation, the therapist uses treatment time most efficiently to work directly with the child, rather than teach teammates new strategies that will be outdated immediately. Even in this situation, however, the therapist regularly works with other team members in applied contexts to ensure that student needs are being addressed effectively. The therapist also works to identify a set of strategies that teammates can begin to learn, with the goal of returning to transdisciplinary and integrated services as soon as feasible.

"I haven't figured out how to handle this need."   Some students present particularly challenging needs, so it may take longer to complete assessment and program planning. Or a therapist may be learning a new strategy to address a certain type of need, such as when Jamal's speech-language therapist first applied her new knowledge about nonsymbolic communication to develop a communication system for Jamal. While these may be legitimate concerns on a short-term basis, parameters must be established to avoid prolonged indecision or experimentation, which does not benefit the student.

"This needs to be done privately to maintain dignity."   It may be preferable to perform procedures such as postural drainage in a private area, such as a nurse's office. Privacy, typical activities, and acceptance of disability as an individual difference are all considered when making decisions, however. For example, Michael has a severe tongue thrust and loses a lot of food

when eating. The speech-language therapist has established oromotor procedures, and the team considered feeding Michael in the classroom until his eating improved. When they considered that it may be several years before Michael ate "neatly" and that he already ate in a variety of public settings, they decided he would eat lunch in the cafeteria. Michael seemed to enjoy being there, and most other students seemed to be unaffected by his eating habits. The teacher did overhear remarks about Michael's appearance, and talked with those students (and teachers!) about Michael's needs, and their discomforts.

"Chang is too distractible to work with in the classroom." Some students are highly distractible, but retreat to an isolated environment often addresses adults' short-term needs more than students' long-term needs. Since stimuli in the community resemble those of integrated school settings more than a quiet therapy room, the team as a whole faces the challenge of teaching students to participate and work in distracting settings. Teachers and therapists need to engage in joint planning to ensure that they coordinate with and complement one another, rather than compete for the student's attention in the classroom. If the team decides that there is a compelling reason to address a need in an isolated setting, criteria and strategies for bringing the student back to natural settings are established at the outset.

"Yolanda isn't ready to use this skill in her daily routine yet." Many students with severe disabilities have spent months and years "getting ready" for some unspecified application of prerequisite or component skills. In most cases, the student has not had the opportunity to learn the skill in the context of routine activities, but engages in those activities without good instruction on the target skill. If the team

does determine a legitimate need to teach a skill out of context first, it is essential that they also set objective, attainable, and valid criteria to initiate generalization and discontinue isolated skill instruction.

"I need to use special equipment and materials, which are only in the therapy room"/"I use specialized techniques, which are not appropriate to teach to others"/ "There is no meaningful context." In all of these situations, a compelling justification is needed to remove a student from priority educational activities and environments to receive services that cannot be applied to these priorities. By refocusing on the student's needs, the team can often determine alternative strategies that can be incorporated into the student's routine activities.

"I have extra time." It is difficult to imagine that therapists might make this claim, but if therapists find that they do have extra time, they might provide additional services. Occasional opportunities can be used to conduct a specialized assessment, fit a piece of equipment, or address some other circumscribed need. For more generalized needs, the student and therapist will achieve the greatest benefit when extra services are applied to the priorities identified by the team.

In summary, long-term direct therapy services are difficult to justify for students with severe disabilities, and the rationales for even short-term direct services must be examined carefully. When making decisions about service models, teams must remember that related services are provided to enable students to perform clusters of important skills with a variety of people in a variety of integrated activities and environments. Although direct services may be appropriate for some students for short periods, exclusive use of a direct therapy model limits students' opportunities for generalized learning. Furthermore, the rigid scheduling usually associated with the direct therapy model limits therapist flexibility to work with students in multiple contexts. Collaborative teams work together to ensure that, when direct services are recommended, services are well integrated in the student's overall program.

Consultation Consultation refers to a variety of services that are infrequent and of short duration. Upon request, a therapist may offer input, such as conferring with the teacher, observing the student, making general suggestions, and/or recommending referral for evaluation, on a student who does not receive a related service. A therapist may check at specified intervals (e.g., once per marking period) on students who previously received related services and students who are considered at risk but not currently in need of services. Therapists may also be "on call" for students who do not need related services but have adapted equipment that needs periodic adjustment or repair. School districts have widely varying policies and procedures on consultation, however, and teams may want to influence the type and amount of support available through consultation. As with the other models of service provision, collaborative teamwork increases the relevance of consultation as a related educational service.

Documenting Therapist Responsibilities

In traditional service provision models, each team member submits the goals and objectives for which he or she is responsible, and therapists address their respective objectives during a specific schedule of therapy. Since responsibilities are circumscribed, accountability seems clear. Actually, this system provides little account-

ability for achieving the ultimate goal of skill synthesis, generalization, and maintenance in applied contexts. Other systems have been devised to increase accountability for outcomes and provide clear documentation for the IEP. Two ways to document the need for related services and to document therapist responsibilities for the IEP are suggested below. Strategies to document day-to-day service provision are described in Chapters 7 and 8.

Goals State Required Services When IEPs are written so goals specify priority skills, a statement of the services required to teach those skills is included. For example:

Brian will improve positioning of his posterior walker to perform functional activities, through general education, special education, and integrated physical therapy services.

Missy will improve visual scanning and focusing to make and convey choices in daily routines, through general education, special education, integrated occupational therapy, and integrated speech-language services.

The disciplines identified in the goal are responsible for all of the corresponding objectives, since the objectives specify the contexts in which the student will perform the skill. Kristen's IEP at the end of this chapter is written in this format.

Objectives Are Followed by Required Services When IEPs are written so that objectives specify skills that are components of priority activities, each objective is followed by a notation of services required to teach the skill. If the IEP includes a space for "Methods and Materials," the services can be listed in that space. Separate columns can be added for each related service, with a check mark placed in the appropriate column after each objective.

A third option is to list the services at the end of each objective. For example:

Tess will read "science" from her schedule and print "science" next to the model, without overlapping letters, for 1 week. (SpEd, OT)

When given a verbal reminder, Tess will tell other students in her science group, "I can do this, thanks," or "I need help, please" on 80% of opportunities for 1 week. (GenEd, SpEd, Speech)

Jamal's IEP at the end of this chapter is written in this format.

EXAMPLES OF IEP DEVELOPMENT

The IEPs for Kristen and Jamal include service recommendations, goals, and objectives. Kristen's IEP contains a complete list of goals and objectives, whereas Jamal's includes only the goals and objectives established for Spanish class and work at Metro Insurance Agency. For brevity, neither IEP includes statements of current levels of performance, which would repeat the assessment results presented in Chapter 5.

INDIVIDUALIZED EDUCATION PROGRAM

STUDENT: Kristen F.
SCHOOL: Richmond Elementary
AGE: 5.2 years
MEETING DATE: 10/5/91
CORE EDUCATIONAL TEAM: Mr. & Mrs. F. (Parents), Jill M. (Kindergarten Teacher), Cathy R. (Special Education Teacher), Jan M. (Speech-Language Therapist), Lisa S. (Physical Therapist), Jim D. (Occupational Therapist)
SERVICES: Special education, 15 hours/week (8:30 A.M. – 11:30 A.M.); mainstreaming in kindergarten 15 hours/week (8:30 A.M.– 11:30 A.M.); integrated speech-language therapy, 6 hours/month; integrated physical therapy, 6 hours/month; occupational therapy consultation, 2 hours/month

Goals and Objectives

A.   Kristen will increase her independence in dressing and toileting through kindergarten, special education, integrated PT services, and a home program (developed in collaboration with family).

1.   After assisted to put her thumbs inside her waistband, Kristen will push down and pull up her pants independently.
    a.   for two out of four trips to the bathroom at home, on 4 out of 5 days
    b.   for three out of three trips to the bathroom at school, on 4 out of 5 days
2.   When taken to the toilet on a regular schedule at home and at school, Kristen will have no accidents for 10 consecutive days.
3.   When seated on a chair with feet and trunk supported, Kristen will remove and put on pullover tops, with prompts only at the upper arm, for 8 out of 10 opportunities during one week.
    a.   to wear sweatshirt outside at home and school
    b.   to change dirty shirt after lunch at home and school
    c.   at bath time at home, 5 out of 7 days

B.   Kristen will improve social, receptive language, and expressive language skills through special education, kindergarten mainstreaming, and integrated speech-language services.

1.   When the teacher delays an already established greeting routine, Kristen will say "hi" within 10 seconds for three out of three opportunities daily for 3 consecutive days.
    a.   at the doorway upon arrival
    b.   just prior to morning circle
    c.   upon approaching the snack table
2.   When given a verbal reminder, Kristen will say "all done" calmly and push her materials (or adult hands) away gently, on each occasion when she demonstrates frustration for 4 out of 5 days.
    a.   in kindergarten
    b.   at home
3.   When given a verbal cue during routine social games, Kristen will maintain a turntaking interaction using a toy/daily living materials with an adult/classmate/sister by requesting "more" for four out of six turns on 3 consecutive days.
    a.   free play time at school (three opportunities)
    b.   play or other daily routines at home (three opportunities)

4. Given a gestural cue and pictures placed in natural contexts in the classroom, Kristen will make requests by touching pictures representing her wants/needs 10 times/day for 4 out of 5 days. (Vocabulary: *cookie, cracker, cheese, drink, help with coat, help wash, ball, Ernie doll, and paint*)

5. Kristen will choose one of two items held out to her by reaching for one, four out of six times daily for 3 consecutive days.
   a. toys during free play (four opportunities)
   b. snack/drink (one opportunity)
   c. materials for fine motor activity (one opportunity)

C. Kristen will improve her fine motor skills from using a palmar grasp for all objects to using palmar, lateral pinch, and thumb-fingertip grasps appropriate for the object, through kindergarten, special education, integrated PT services, OT consultation, and a home program (designed with family).

1. When cylinders are presented in a vertical position, Kristen will use a palmar grasp and neutral forearm position, 8 out of 10 times daily, for 3 consecutive days.
   a. crayon, marker, or pencil during small group
   b. cup during snack/mealtime
   c. toothbrush, brush, and lotion during grooming

2. When reminded before presentation, Kristen will grasp cards/papers using a lateral pinch or thumb-fingertip grasp during circle and small group work, four out of five times daily, for 3 consecutive days.

3. After wearing her splint for the first 10 minutes of snack time, Kristen will use a pincer grasp (1 or 2 fingers) for finger foods, for 3 consecutive days.
   a. at school, four out of five bites
   b. at home, four out of five bites

D. Kristen will improve postural stability, trunk and lower limb mobility, and reciprocal patterns through kindergarten, special education, integrated PT, and a home program (designed with family).

1. When reminded before activities, Kristen will assume a sidesitting position on the floor, and maintain the position for a minimum of 3 minutes without additional cues, for three of three activities daily for 5 consecutive days.
   a. playtime at arrival
   b. morning circle
   c. playtime at departure

2. When holding stable objects and given tactile cues at the hip, knee, and ankle, Kristen will use a reciprocal pattern to ascend from and descend to the floor, for three of three activities daily for 5 consecutive days.
   a. playtime (five opportunities)
   b. storytime on rug (one opportunity)
   c. gross motor activity (two opportunities)

3. When physically assisted to position forearms in neutral with hands open, and when stabilized at the shoulders, Kristen will hold large objects with two hands and carry them at least 10 feet, four out of five times daily for 5 consecutive days.
   a. carry bag to cubby from classroom door
   b. carry toys (in bins) to play area
   c. carry materials for class job
   d. carry materials for snack
   e. carry book, shoes, ball, and so on during special activities

INDIVIDUALIZED EDUCATION PROGRAM

STUDENT: Jamal W.
SCHOOL: Central High School
AGE: 17 years
MEETING DATE: 10/08/91
CORE EDUCATIONAL TEAM: Mrs. W. (Parent), John K. (Special Education Teacher), Lisa W. (Occupational Therapist), Jake S. (Special Education Teaching Assistant), Ann E. (Speech-Language Therapist), Sandy B. (Transition), Earl M. (Community Residence Coordinator), Ben G. (General Education Teacher)
SERVICES: Special education, 35 hours/week; integrated speech/language therapy, 6 hours/month (decreasing to 4 hours/month on November 1); integrated occupational therapy 4 hours/month; physical therapy consultation 1 hour/month; general education integration, 15 hours/week (for homeroom, lunch, Spanish, choir, media center, horticulture, home economics)

Goals and Objectives

[excerpts for Spanish and Community Work Experience]

A. Jamal will participate in Spanish I class.

1. Jamal will vocalize to get the attention of others when he wants to communicate for at least three of four planned communication opportunities daily for 5 consecutive days. (GenEd, SpEd, Sp/L)

2. In response to a question, Jamal will chose a partner for group by maintaining gaze toward a selected classmate nearby for 10 seconds, two of two opportunities daily for 3 consecutive days. (GenEd, SpEd, Sp/L)

3. Jamal will make requests by scanning a communication display and selecting the desired object/symbol for four of four opportunities on 5 consecutive days. (GenEd, SpEd, Sp/L)

    a. to request assistance moving his supine stander during group transitions (two opportunities)

    b. to request the tape recorder to tape the joke of the day (one opportunity)

    c. to request assistance placing the joke cassette tape in his bag (one opportunity)

4. Jamal will turn on/off the tape recorder by deflecting a paddle switch for 100% of two or more opportunities/day for 3 consecutive days. (GenEd, SpEd, OT)

B. Jamal will participate in his community work experience at Metro Insurance Agency using work and work-related skills.

1. When provided with stability around his right shoulder, Jamal will operate an adapted joystick with his hand to drive his wheelchair down the hallway to/from the insurance agency within 3 minutes for two of two opportunities for 3 consecutive work days. (SpEd, OT)

2. Jamal will drop his head to remain relaxed while his jacket is put on/taken off for two of two opportunities on 3 consecutive work days. (SpEd, OT)

3. Jamal will vocalize to get the attention of others when he wants to communicate for 100% of at least 10 planned communication opportunities daily for 3 consecutive work days. (SpEd, Sp/L)

4. Jamal will make requests by scanning a communication display and selecting the desired object/symbol at least 10 times daily for 3 consecutive work days. (SpEd, Sp/L)

    a. to request the tape recorder to play the joke of the day from Spanish class (two opportunities)

    b. to request assistance to initiate/maintain/terminate various work tasks (at least eight opportunities)

5. Jamal will turn on/off the tape recorder to tell a joke by deflecting a paddle switch for 100% of at least two opportunities per day for 3 consecutive work days. (SpEd, OT)

6. When given stabilization around his right shoulder, Jamal will raise and lower his forearm to depress an adaptive device to date stamp mail, stamping mail at a rate of two pieces/minute for 2 of 3 work days. (SpEd, OT)

REFERENCES

Baumgart, D., Johnson, J., & Helmstetter, E. (1990). *Augmentative and alternative communication systems for persons with moderate and severe disabilities.* Baltimore: Paul H. Brookes Publishing Co.

Benson, H.A., & Turnbull, A.P. (1986). Approaching families from an individualized perspective. In R.H. Horner, L.Meyer, & H.D. Fredericks (Eds.), *Education of learners with severe handicaps: Exemplary service strategies* (pp. 127–157). Baltimore: Paul H. Brookes Publishing Co.

Bolton, R. (1979). *People skills: How to assert yourself, listen to others, and resolve conflicts.* Denver: Love Publishing Co.

Bricker, W.A., & Campbell, P.H. (1980). Interdisciplinary assessment and programming for multihandicapped students. In W. Sailor, B. Wilcox, & L. Brown (Eds.), *Methods of instruction for severely handicapped students* (pp. 3–45). Baltimore: Paul H. Brookes Publishing Co.

Browder, D. (1991). *Assessment of individuals with severe disabilities: An applied behavior* approach to life skills assessment (2nd ed.). Baltimore: Paul H. Brookes Publishing Co.

Brown, L., Shiraga, B., Rogan, P., York, J., Zanella Albright, K., McCarthy, E., Loomis, R., & VanDeventer, P. (1988). The "why" question in programs for people who are severely intellectually disabled. In S.N. Calculator & J.L. Bedrosian (Eds.), *Communication assessment and intervention for adults with mental retardation* (pp. 139–153). Baltimore: Paul H. Brookes Publishing Company.

Carr, S.H. (1989). Louisiana's criteria of eligibility for occupational therapy services in the public school system. *American Journal of Occupational Therapy, 43*(8), 503–506.

Downing, J. (1988). Active versus passive programming: A critique of IEP objectives for students with the most severe disabilities. *Journal of The Association for Persons with Severe Handicaps, 13*(3), 197–201.

Dunn, W. (1988). Models of occupational therapy service provision in the school system. *American Journal of Occupational Therapy, 42*(11), 718–723.

Giangreco, M.F. (1986). Delivery of therapeutic services in special education programs for learners with severe handicaps. *Physical and Occupational Therapy in Pediatrics, 6*(2), 5–15.

Giangreco, M. F., York, J., & Rainforth, B. (1989). Providing related services to learners with severe handicaps in educational settings: Pursuing the least restrictive option. *Pediatric Physical Therapy, 1*(2), 55–63.

Johnson, D.W., & Johnson, F. (1987). *Joining together: Group theory and group skills* (2nd ed.). Englewood Cliffs, NJ: Prentice Hall.

Kazdin, A.E. (1977). Assessing the clinical or applied importance of behavior change through social validation. *Behavior Modification, 1*(4), 427–451.

Mager, R. (1984) *Preparing instructional objectives* (2nd ed.). Belmont, CA: Lake Publishing Co.

Meyer, L.H., & Evans, I.M. (1989). *Nonaversive intervention for behavior problems: A manual for home and community.* Baltimore: Paul H. Brookes Publishing Co.

Orelove, F., & Sobsey, D. (1991). *Educating children with multiple disabilities: A transdisciplinary approach* (2nd ed.). Baltimore: Paul H. Brookes Publishing Co.

Perske, R. (1988). *Circles of friends: People with disabilities and their friends enrich the lives of one another.* Nashville, TN: Abingdon Press.

Rainforth, B. (1991, April). OSERS clarifies legality of related services eligibility. *TASH Newsletter, 16*(4), 8.

Reichle, J., York, J., & Sigafoos, J. (1991). *Implementing augmentative and alternative communication: Strategies for learners with severe disabilities.* Baltimore: Paul H. Brookes Publishing Co.

Renzaglia, A., & Aveno, A. (1986). *Manual for administration of an individualized, functional curriculum assessment procedure for students with moderate to severe handicaps.* Charlottesville: University of Virginia.

Timothy W. v. Rochester, NH, School District, 875 F.2d 954 (First Cir. 1989).

Van Houten, R. (1979). Social validation: The evolution of standards of competency for target behaviors. *Journal of Applied Behavior Analysis, 12*(4), 581–592.

Wolf, M.M. (1978). Social validity: The case for subjective measurement or how applied behavior analysis is finding its heart. *Journal of Applied Behavior Analysis, 11*(2), 203–214.

7

Collaborative Instructional Design

THE PREVIOUS CHAPTERS IN THIS SECTION have addressed team tasks that lay the foundation for the team's ultimate responsibility: providing instruction. As used in this chapter, the term "instruction" refers to the intervention methods associated with each of the various disciplines, as well as the more multifaceted interventions designed by an educational team collectively. In educational settings, the instructional strategies associated with each discipline are among the most significant contributions team members make in the collaborative teamwork process. Because integration of multiple and varied perspectives increases the magnitude of instructional effectiveness, a team's diversity truly is its strength. The collaboration and interdependence required for intentional planning, systematic decision making, role release, and ongoing role support are challenging, particularly for new teams. Professionals who previously worked autonomously must reach consensus with others from varied personal and professional backgrounds representing different philosophies and experiences. As discussed in other chapters, the ultimate goal of education for students with severe disabilities is to enable them to participate in a variety of home, school, and community routines, with a variety of people, using the supports and responding to the cues that occur naturally in those settings. Therefore, the benefits of professional contributions are maximized when a team assumes responsibility for integrating instructional strategies from the component disciplines into a coordinated approach that can be applied in a variety of natural environments and activities.

To ensure normalization for students with severe disabilities, the philosophy of "only as special as necessary" must guide decisions about instruction (Taylor, 1988). To understand the practical implications of this tenet, it is useful to consider some of the dimensions along which instruction may vary in educational environments. Understanding the continuum of "best practices" found in general education and special education will enable collaborative teams to design interventions that are both effective and acceptable, and therefore normalizing. Collaborative teams that are planning integration of students with severe disabilities into general education programs will benefit from efforts to learn the specific instructional philosophies and current best practices that are accepted in the "target" environments of those students.

Although it may initially appear that there are significant differences between the approaches used in general education and in special education, there is growing understanding of the similarities between the two fields. For example, special educators have "borrowed" cooperative learning strategies (Johnson & Johnson, 1987) from general education, and have found that these strategies are highly effective in facilitating both integration and learning for students with a variety of disabilities. Special education's community-referenced instruction was conceptualized in much the same way as general education's whole language instruction and experiential learning strategies. Building upon these similarities helps to promote acceptance of students with severe disabilities into the general education community.

Differences between general education and special education philosophies may arise around issues of who directs learning experiences, who is the source of knowledge, and how the learning environment is structured. For example, typical early childhood settings often have stimulating environments where children direct their own learning through processes of experience and discovery (Yonemura, 1986). Adults arrange the environment to facilitate learning and cooperative relationships among children, but play very subtle roles in instruction. Although secondary academic classes often exemplify the adult-centered, expository approach in which teachers lecture while students take notes, there is increasing recognition that student-centered, self-directed, cooperative, and experiential learning are best practices in both elementary and secondary education (Goodlad, 1984).

In contrast, direct and systematic instruction is considered a best practice in special education. In its original form, adults controlled most aspects of the learning situation, including task selection, preparation of materials, use of prompts, determination of acceptable performance, and schedules of rewards. Special educators have identified difficulties inherent in this approach, however. After intensive use of direct and systematic instruction, students with severe disabilities often need additional instruction to respond to natural cues and correction procedures (Ford & Mirenda, 1984). When programs are less structured and use incidental teaching procedures, young children with disabilities spend more time engaged in learning activities, which translates into greater achievement (McWilliam, Trivette, & Dunst, 1985). Self-direction is now seen as an essential element of effective intervention programs for students with severe behavior problems (Meyer & Evans, 1989). At the same time, systematic instruction has proven necessary and effective for teaching children and adults who were once considered "ineducable" (Kauffman, 1981; Snell, 1987). Collectively, this information indicates that systematic instruction is an important teaching technology for students with severe disabilities, but it must be used cautiously with careful attention to the least restrictive alternative for each individual student.

Systematic instruction and data-based decision making also represent an analytical approach to education as a "science." In contrast, the "art" is evident when a master practitioner acts intuitively, sometimes leaving observers awestruck at the master's apparently magical abilities (Watts, 1983; Yonemura, 1986). The artist is highly creative, easily devising new strategies, making decisions about what strategy will be effective under which circumstances, and solving problems before a problem is even evident to others. While analytical approaches to instruction have been criticized as too rigid and technocratic, intuitive approaches have been criticized as too idiosyncratic. After working with and observing scores of practitioners, the authors have concluded that the most effective members of educational teams use a combination of intuitive and analytical approaches. Analytical approaches enable practitioners to define needs and possible solutions and to evaluate the effectiveness of those instructional solutions; intuitive approaches are necessary when solutions are not predictable and when traditional solutions are not effective. The combination enables team members to expand their current practice and discover more effective strategies, but also enables them to analyze what did or did not work and why. The latter is particularly important when a *team* of people is responsible for supporting students. In contrast with autonomous practitioners, individuals working as members of a collaborative team must be able to identify and communicate the reasoning and subtle cues that influenced their decisions, the specific steps that elicited the desired participation from a student with learning difficulties, and the precise distinctions between the strategy that worked and the ones that did not. Only when this occurs can a collection of people operate as a team that consistently guides students with disabilities, rather than confuses them.

Although individual learning styles become evident during assessment and instruction, generally it can be assumed that students with severe disabilities will have difficulty learning to participate in activities when given only natural cues, loose structures, and intermittent instructional opportunities. Therefore, educational teams must make deliberate decisions about instructional design, such as how often to provide instruction, which cues or prompts to use, and when to fade the cues or prompts. This chapter provides an overview of principles and strategies of systematic instruction, and illustrates how they can be combined with strategies associated with the disciplines of occupational therapy, physical therapy, and speech/language therapy. Examples also incorporate strategies rooted in general education instructional design, such as self-direction, incidental teaching, and cooperative learning, which are effective as well as normalizing for students with severe disabilities. Albano (1983) found that written instructional procedures and student performance data were essential tools for communication among members of collaborative educational teams. To facilitate such communication, this chapter provides a variety of formats for writing procedures and recording data. Figure 7.1 shows the steps that collaborative teams follow in designing instructional programs.

This chapter provides only an introduction to the extensive information currently available on systematic instruction. Readers are referred to other sources such as Bailey and Wolery (1989), Browder (1991), Ford et al. (1989), Ottenbacher (1986), Powell et al. (1991), Reichle, York, and Sigafoos (1991), and Snell (1987) for more thorough discussions of instructional strategies, data collection and analysis procedures, and other formats for recording this information.

PRINCIPLES OF SYSTEMATIC INSTRUCTION

Considerations in design of systematic instruction include how often and where instruction will occur, how the student will be prepared for instruction, what system and type of cues and prompts will be used

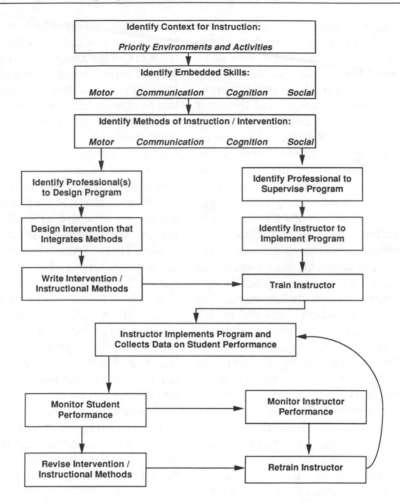

Figure 7.1. Steps to design comprehensive instructional programs.

to elicit the desired performance, what adaptations will be used to enhance performance, and how performance will be assessed. Guidelines for making decisions about who will provide instruction and how instructors are prepared to provide collaborative instruction are presented in Chapter 8.

How Often and Where Will Instruction Occur?

As discussed in Chapter 2, students with severe disabilities tend to learn new skills slowly and have difficulty transferring learning to new situations. The conclusion of that discussion was that, to be effective, instruction must be provided frequently in natural situations. The traditional approach of providing *massed trials* (many repetitions in a short time period, e.g., 30 minutes) addresses the need to accelerate learning, but usually occurs in artificial contexts and thus hampers application and generalization of skills. *Distributed trials* (repetitions spread over a longer time period, e.g., a day) supports instruction in a variety of applied settings, and are as effective as massed trials to promote skill acquisition if equal numbers of learning opportunities are provided (Mulligan, Lacy, & Guess, 1982). When planning instruction is based on distributed trials, however, there is danger that instruction on priority skills may get lost in the bustle of the daily routine and will not receive sufficient attention. Therefore, the team must plan intentionally to ensure sufficient instruction. An effective planning strategy is to construct a matrix in which skills corresponding to individualized education program (IEP) objectives are listed on one axis, the day's schedule of activities are listed on the other axis, and instructional opportunities and considerations are noted in the matrix (Guess & Helmstetter, 1986). An activities-skills matrix for Kristen shows when and where she will receive instruction on all her IEP objectives (Table 7.1). Kristen's team found the matrix invaluable to get the "big picture" of how her IEP would be implemented during her daily routine.

For any activity or routine, the team may wish to examine opportunities or priorities more closely, and begin planning for instruction. One strategy is to use the same activity or task analysis as was used for the ecological inventory and student assessment (see Chapter 5). Another strategy is to use a Related Services Planning Sheet to focus particular attention on the general outcomes of occupational, physical, and speech-language therapy, which were discussed in Chapter 4. The Planning Sheet contains columns to note transitions, positions, participation, comprehension, expression, and social interactions for one student in multiple activities or multiple students in one activity. The Planning Sheet is particularly useful when teams are either trying to increase the type and amount of instruction during an activity or trying to establish balance among competing needs. Kristen's team used the Planning Sheet to examine the morning arrival and play routine, which presented so many opportunities for instruction that there was a danger of trying to do too much. Besides Kristen, there were also children with mild disabilities who received instruction during these routines, so the Planning Sheet helped the team keep a perspective on the needs of all the children. The priorities to be addressed during this routine are shown in Table 7.2.

How Will the Student Be Prepared for Instruction?

Preparing the student might entail physical preparation such as ensuring the student is properly positioned for participation. Students with physical disabilities need to have regular opportunities to change position and need to use positions that match the physical demands of activities (Rainforth & York, 1991). Table 7.3 presents considerations in selecting positions and positioning equipment for students with severe disabilities, with examples for two students participating in leisure activities. By asking the questions listed in the table, Jamal's team realized that he spent his entire day sitting, and that some alternative positioning was necessary and feasible. In addition to position changes that were a natural part of Jamal's personal hygiene routine, the team determined that he could also use a sidelying position during Choir and a standing position during Spanish, Home Economics, and Horticulture classes. The team was not satisfied yet with the frequency or duration of alternatives to sitting, and agreed to continue looking for other opportunities. Table 7.4 shows Jamal's weekly schedule, in which information about positioning was inserted.

Table 7.1 Activities / skills matrix for Kristen [a]

							Objectives from IEP						
Time and Activity	Pants down/up	Use toilet	Pullover top	Say "hi"	Reject task	Request "more"	Make requests	Choose item	Palmar grasp	Pincer grasp	Side sit	Stand and kneel	Two hand carry
8:30 A.M. Arrival			X	X	I		help coat						bag
Bathroom	X	X			I		help wash						
Jobs					I								materials
Free Play					I	three times	Ernie, paint	four times (toys)			X	four times	toys
9:00 A.M. Opening				X	I	G	G	G	marker	X			
9:30 A.M. Story					I		G	G			X	one time	
9:50 A.M. Gross motor					I	G	G				G	two times	G
10:10 A.M. Bathroom	X	X			I		help wash						
10:20 A.M. Fine Motor					I	G	paint	one time	marker	X			G
10:45 A.M. Snack			X	X	I		cookie cracker grease artist	one time	cup	after wearing splint			materials
11:15 A.M. Bathroom	X	X	X		I		help wash		tooth-brush > brush				
Clean up							Ernie		lotion		X	one time	
11:30 A.M. Departure			G		G		help coat						G
Specials			G	G	G	G	G	G	G		G	G	X

[a]Key: X, provide instruction; I, as incidents arise; G, generalization opportunity.

Table 7.2 Related services planning sheet for three students in kindergarten

Teacher: Jill and Cathy **Activity:** Free play **Time:** 8:30-9:00

Students	Transitions	Positions	Participation	Interactions	Comprehension	Expression
Kristen	Ask another child to walk with Kristen to toy shelves to toy shelves; staff prompt her to kneel and stand correctly.	On floor: side-sitting; no W-sitting	Carry baskets and large toys with two hands.	Continue turn-taking by requesting "more" (involve other children).	Follow specific directions: "go get ___, give me ___, let's go to ___."	Choose one of two toys by reaching for preference (involve other children).
Turner		Discourage W-sitting (OK occasionally).	Use finger-tip grasp and refined release.	Encourage use of toys for representational play (e.g., for playing house, dress up, cars).	Respond to verbal directions given to the group.	Indicate choice of toys or next activity to playmate.
Rex					Respond to verbal directions given to the group.	Bring toy to peer and make request, "Want to play with ___?"

185

Table 7.3 Considerations in selecting positions and positioning equipment

Considerations	Ted - Baking cookies	Joan - Gardening
Proposed Position	**Sitting**	**Kneeling**
1. What positions do nondisabled peers use when they engage in the activity?	Usually standing/walking. Sometimes sitting (but with hips at height of table/counter).	Standing, stooping, kneeling/ hands and knees.
2. Which of these positions allow easy view of and access to activity materials and equipment?	Standing is better than sitting at table.	Kneeling seems most versatile. Could build raised garden bed to allow sitting on edge, transfer from wheelchair.
3. Do the positions allow for proximity to peers?	Yes, for sitting or standing. Peers will probably stand.	Yes, peers can garden in adjoining areas/rows.
4. Do the positions promote efficient movement as needed to perform the task?	Standing/walking much better than sitting/wheeling.	Once sitting or kneeling, Joan can plant/weed/harvest an area, then scoot to next.
5. What positions provide alternatives to overused postures or equipment?	Standing is best. Ted spends too much time sitting.	Kneeling is a good change. Joan sits for most activities.
6. If positioning equipment is required, is it unobtrusive, cosmetically acceptable, and not physically isolating?	Wheelchair and supine stander are both large. Could use kitchen chair but will lose mobility. When stander is vertical, Ted can stand close to counter, tables. Wheelchair allows mobility around kitchen.	Garden kneeling stool is unobtrusive, used by people without disabilities; may assist positioning and transitions.
7. Is the positioning equipment safe and easy to handle?	Positioning in stander requires adult. Then other children can handle safely and easily.	Yes, may need outriggers to prevent tipping.
8. Is the equipment individually selected and modified to match individual learner needs?	A supine stander with individualized adaptations was purchased for Ted.	Team will borrow garden kneeling stool to try it.
9. Is the equipment available in / easily transported to natural environments?	Stander available at home and school. Difficult to transport to other environments.	Garden kneeler is lightweight, easy to transport.
Final position	**Standing using equipment to assist.**	**Kneeling using equipment to assist.**

Table 7.4 Jamal's weekly schedule with positioning information

	MONDAY	TUESDAY	WEDNESDAY	THURSDAY	FRIDAY
Before school 7:00-7:45	Regular bus to school Restroom •7:30-7:45 (position transfer)				
Homeroom 7:45-8:00	HOMEROOM	HOMEROOM	HOMEROOM	HOMEROOM	HOMEROOM
Period 1 8:05-8:55	SPANISH CLASS (position: standing)	SPANISH CLASS (position: standing)	SPANISH CLASS (position: standing)	SPANISH CLASS (position: standing)	SPANISH CLASS (position: standing)
Period 2 9:00-9:50	COMMUNITY PREP •9:00-9:15 COMMUNITY WORK •9:15-12:00	COMMUNITY PREP •9:00-9:15 COMMUNITY MOBILITY TRAINING	COMMUNITY PREP •9:00-9:15 COMMUNITY WORK •9:15-12:00	COMMUNITY PREP •9:00-9:15 COMMUNITY MOBILITY TRAINING	COMMUNITY PREP •9:00-9:15 COMMUNITY WORK •9:15-12:00
Period 3 9:55-10:45	Restroom •10:15-10:30 (position transfer)	Restroom •10:15-10:30 (position transfer)	Restroom •10:15-10:30 (position transfer)	Restroom •10:15-10:30 (position transfer)	Restroom •10:15-10:30 (position transfer)
Period 4 10:50-11:40		CHOIR (position: sidelying)		CHOIR (position: sidelying)	
Period 5 11:45-12:35	LUNCH •12:20-12:50	COMMUNITY FAST FOOD RESTAURANT	LUNCH •12:20-12:50	LUNCH •11:45-12:15 Restroom •12:15-12:30 (position transfer)	LUNCH •12:20-12:50
Period 6 12:40-1:30	ERRANDS •12:50-1:15 Restroom •1:15-1:30 (position transfer)	Restroom •12:40-12:55 (position transfer) MEDIA CENTER •library •computers	ERRANDS •12:50-1:15 Restroom •1:15-1:30 (position transfer)	MEDIA CENTER •library •computer	ERRANDS •12:50-1:15 Restroom •1:15-1:30 (position transfer)
Period 7 1:35-2:25	HOME ECONOMICS (position: standing)	HORTICULTURE (position: standing)	HOME ECONOMICS (position: standing)	HORTICULTURE (position: standing)	HOME ECONOMICS (position: standing)
After school				After School Activity •swim team manager	

Although sidelying is not a "normal" position for school, the team found that Jamal appreciated the change and the position enabled him to "sing" in Choir. Because Jamal was prone to upper respiratory infections, the team was pleased that the position and activity improved his breathing, even if only temporarily. The Choir teacher was equally pleased that Jamal was able to participate. Once given an explanation, the other students were very accepting of and interested in how Jamal was positioned. Since transporting equipment through the school and changing Jamal's position was easier with extra people, the team recruited classmates for assistance. The occupational therapist and physical therapist established training activities to teach students to help lift and transfer Jamal safely. (See Inge and Snell [1985] for an example of a systematic instructional program that could be used in this way.) The Special Education teaching assistant who accompanied Jamal to Choir, Home Economics, and Horticulture was then able to ask for assistance from a student who had been taught to help lift Jamal. In addition to teaching students and staff a variety of lifting, transferring, and positioning strategies, the occupational and physical therapist devised checklists, diagrams, and/or photographs as reminders of how to use the strategies properly with various students. The reminders were attached to equipment or posted on walls unobtrusively in the areas where staff were likely to be repositioning students with physical disabilities.

Another way that students with physical disabilities might be prepared for instruction is by normalizing their tone (York & Wiemann, 1991). Most frequently, this means that a student with spasticity has his or her tone reduced by some type of slow, rhythmic movement. In isolated therapy models, therapists often have done this using special equipment such as bolsters or therapy balls. Both Kristen's team and Jamal's team found they could accomplish the same goal in a more integrated fashion. For example, one of Kristen's objectives was to rise to stand and lower to kneel by stepping up or down with one foot at a time. Without intervention, spasticity caused her to keep both knees together and push her weight over the inner side of her ankles to get on and off her feet. During the kindergarten play routine and other daily activities, Kristen frequently moved between kneeling and standing spontaneously, so the team needed an incidental teaching strategy to normalize her tone and facilitate reciprocal movement. The team agreed upon how they would prepare Kristen verbally for their physical intervention (e.g., "Kristen, let me help you stand up one foot at a time.") and how they would reinforce her (e.g., "That was great! That's a good way to stand up.") The physical therapist taught classroom staff to identify when Kristen was getting ready to change positions, separate Kristen's knees to facilitate a normal standing or kneeling position, reinforce the position by pressing down through her hips, hold her knees apart and shift weight as she changed position, and then reinforce the new position by pressing down through her hips (see Figure 7.2). In addition to stick figure diagrams, the physical therapist provided a data sheet to remind staff of the procedures, to record Kristen's performance, and to monitor the number of opportunities provided for Kristen to learn this new pattern (Table 7.5). When therapists develop useful diagrams, they may wish to file them for use with other students and staff. Commercial packages of diagrams

Steps 1, 2, & ✳   Steps 3&4   Steps 5&6   Steps 7, 8, & ✳

Figure 7.2. Stick figure diagrams to remind staff how to prompt Kristen to rise to stand. Steps 1 through 8 and * are detailed in Table 7.5.

to guide positioning and handling are also available (e.g., Jaeger, 1987; Ossman & Campbell, 1990).

Jamal was expected to improve use of his arms and hands for tasks such as turning on the tape recorder in Spanish class, stamping mail at Metro Insurance Agency, and driving his wheelchair. After working on these tasks for a few days, team members reported back to the occupational therapist that Jamal continued to be "stiff" and seemed to resist participation. In response, the occupational therapist established a "warm-up" procedure of tone normalization, stretching, and coactive movement to prepare Jamal to use his arms and hands (Table 7.6). To evaluate its effectiveness, the procedure included a system for data collection. As with Kristen, the warm-up was done as an integral part of the activities in which Jamal needed to use his hands. The occupational therapist worked with all staff members to ensure that they could use the procedure effectively. In the process, they reviewed the

written procedure, clarified terminology, and selected key words that would cue staff to remember the most relevant aspects of the procedure.

Another way students might be prepared for an activity is through communication about the day's schedule, upcoming transitions, choices available in an activity, and changes in the routine. Kristen's team determined that she was likely to become upset when she was confused about the sequence of activities, such as on days the class went to special activities. To help communicate these changes to Kristen, she was given a sweatband to wear to gym, bells to wear to music, or a smock to wear to art just prior to leaving for the activity. The team planned to incorporate these cues into a picture schedule when Kristen developed an association between the objects and corresponding events. Kristen's classmate, Brad (who was not identified as handicapped), often became upset during the transition from playtime to opening group. The team discovered that he did

Table 7.5 Performance scoring data sheet for Kristen

Student: Kristen F. **Program:** Kneel to stand
Initial Instruction: Kristie, go one foot at a time.
Prompts and Scoring:
 3 = spontaneous
 2 = touch / tap body part
 1 = grasp body part, passive move
 0 = grasp body part, resisted movement
Time Delay between Prompts:
        23 seconds

Movement sequence	Prompt at:	9/16	9/23	9/30	10/7	10/14	10/21	10/28
1. Hold furniture with two hands	No physical prompt	3	3	3	3	3	3	3
2. Kneel - Knees apart, hips straight	Inner side knees, top front and lower back of pelvis	1	1	1	2	1	2	2
* Reinforce position by pressing down on hips for 5 seconds.								
3. Shift weight over one knee.	Opposite hip	1	1	2	2	2	2	2
4. Lift opposite knee, place foot in front, keep knee out to side.	Back and inner side leg, just above knee	0	0	0	0	1	1	2
5. Shift weight over forward leg.	Both sides of pelvis	1	1	2	2	2	3	2
6. Straighten front hip and knee, keeping weight forward.	Top front and lower back of pelvis	1	2	2	3	3	2	3
7. Slide other foot forward and place.	Heel	2	2	2	2	3	3	3
8. Stand - Knees apart, hips and knees straight	Front and inner sides of knees, back of hips	0	0	1	2	1	2	2
* Reinforce position by pressing down on hips for 5 seconds.								
POSSIBLE SCORE= 24 TOTAL SCORE =		9	10	13	16	16	18	19
# TIMES TAUGHT TODAY		//// 4	++++ / 6	++++ /// 8	++++ /// 8	++++ /// 8	++++ // 7	++++ /// 8

Table 7.6 Generic preparation procedure for arm use for Jamal

Student:	Jamal
Date:	10-16-92
Contexts:	Drive wheelchair, stamp mail, clothing on/off, personal care activities, turn on/off tape recorder, and other hand/arm use.

Positioning

Jamal: Standing or sitting, as specified for activity. Right elbow and forearm supported on tray.

Instructor: Standing facing Jamal on his right side. Left hand cupped firmly around top outside part of Jamal's right shoulder. Right hand cupped firmly around underside of elbow and upper forearm.

Preparation

1. While maintaining a firm hold around Jamal's shoulder, gently shake the arm from the elbow until you feel a release of the muscle tension (usually about 2 to 5 seconds).

2. As the tension releases move the shoulder into a rounded forward position, the elbow into a straighter position, and the forearm into a position so the palm of the hand faces downward.

3. Hold the arm in this more forward and elongated position for 2 to 5 seconds. Then allow the arm to relax a little, but maintain a firm hold at the shoulder and elbow.

4. Repeat steps 2-3 until the arm remains in the forward and elongated position. Maintain control at the shoulder only (approximately 5 to 10 repetitions).

5. With your right hand, hold firmly under Jamal's wrist and hand. Shake the hand/wrist gently. As tension releases, continue to move wrist and fingers into a slightly extended position.

Active Movement

1. **Coactive practice:** Maintain firm hold around right shoulder. Initiate movement of his elbow into extension. Pause slightly (but maintain hold) to allow Jamal the opportunity to continue active extension himself. Guide completion of movement as necessary to perform the designated task.

2. Repeat 3 times.

3. **Active movement** (with maintained control at shoulder): Repeat practice sequence but remove control at elbow after Jamal starts to extend his elbow.

4. **Error correction:** Reinstate control from elbow and assist to complete facilitated movement pattern.

Data

1. **Preparation:** Number of repetitions required for relaxed and elongated position to be achieved.

2. **Coactive Practice:** Score (+) for the practice opportunities in which Jamal completes active elbow extension while instructor maintains hold.

3. **Active movement:** Score (+) for the opportunities in which Jamal completes active elbow extension without the instructor maintaining control at elbow.

4. **Function/application:** Score (+) for the opportunities that active extension results in sufficient movement to perform the designated task.

much better when he could anticipate the end of playtime by being told that clean-up would start in 1 minute, at which time a kitchen timer would go off. The team did not think a formal program was needed for either procedure; they simply implemented practices that seemed to assist Kristen and Brad. Both procedures enabled the students to anticipate upcoming events and participate actively rather than fight to control confusing events. In Brad's case, the team acted as a classroom support team, preventing the type of crisis that often results in student referral to special education (Hayek, 1987).

What System and Types of Cues and Prompts Will Be Used To Elicit the Desired Performance?

There are extensive combinations of verbal, visual, and physical prompts that can be individualized to meet the learning needs of each student. Although verbal prompts are often considered the least intrusive and physical prompts the most intrusive, the number, type, and sequence of prompts that are effective depends upon the task to be performed and the type of prompts to which the student responds (see Effgen, 1991; Powell et al., 1991). For example, the movement procedures outlined for Kristen and Jamal in Tables 7.5 and 7.6 rely on a range of physical prompts to elicit the desired performance. Although Jamal understands verbal directions and Kristen responds well to gestures, verbal and gestural prompts were not effective to elicit the desired movements, nor would they be easy to fade from tasks of this type. One of Kristen's communication programs (Table 7.7) used a sequence of a gesture, then an indirect verbal prompt and a gesture, and finally physical guidance. One of Jamal's communication programs (Table 7.8) used an indirect ver-

bal prompt ("Do you want to tell me something?") with a direct but complex verbal prompt ("When I touch what you want, look at my eyes."), followed by a direct verbal prompt ("Look at your board."). One of Jamal's student coworkers at Metro Insurance Agency, who had depended heavily on frequent verbal directions, was being taught to use a pictorial checklist as the least intrusive prompt to perform his job.

When using a sequence of increasing assistance, a good rule of thumb is to select two or three prompts for the prompting sequence. The first prompt would be as close as possible to a natural cue; the student may not respond to this prompt at the start of instruction but is expected to learn. The second prompt would provide greater assistance but would not consistently elicit the desired performance from the student at the start of instruction. The final prompt in the sequence would increase assistance but provide the minimum amount needed to ensure the desired performance. Using more than three prompts would make the student wait too long before experiencing success. Another component of a prompting sequence is a time delay, a brief waiting period before giving the next prompt (see Snell, 1987). A time delay may be as little as 1 second for a student who moves quickly and makes frequent errors. A student with a severe physical disability may need as long as 10 seconds to initiate a motor response. A time delay of between 2 and 5 seconds is appropriate for most students and tasks, but individualized decisions are needed even within this range. During initial learning, delays longer than 10 seconds are rarely effective since they encourage distractions. When students have learned skills but do not use them spontaneously, delays of 15 seconds have been used to elicit responses (Halle, Marshall, & Spradlin, 1979).

Table 7.7 Communication program for Kristen

Student: _____Kristen_____   **Date** : _10-6-92_____

Program:___Requests_____

Instructional Procedures

Setting, Grouping Positioning	• Adults and children should model use of pictures for communication with Kristen throughout daily routines. Classmates should be encouraged to talk about the pictures, touch them, match them to real objects, and so forth.
Equipment/Materials	• Pictures placed around the classroom where corresponding activities occur
Initial Instruction and Prompt	• Teacher announces the activity to all students (natural cue). • When Kristen approaches the activity associated with a picture, an adult directs her attention to the picture by pointing at it.
Correct Response	• Kristen touches the picture.
Time Delay and Correction	• Wait 5 seconds. If no response say, "Kristen, do you want _____?" and point to the picture. • Wait 5 seconds. If still no response, manually guide her hand to touch the picture.
Reinforcement	• Natural consequence-obtain object/activity • Social- Touch the picture while saying, "Great, you touched _____, so here's _____."
Frequency to Teach	• Daily, at least 10 opportunities throughout the day
Frequency of Data	• Tuesdays and Fridays
Type of Data	• Record type of performance for each opportunity provided -- (N)Natural cue only, (P)Point, (V)Verbal prompt, (G)Guide.
Criterion for Change	• Success of plan -- 10 times per day with pointing cue only for 4 out of 5 days • Failure of plan -- physical guidance needed on more than 50% of trials for 4 out of 5 days

Projected completion date: ___11-23-92_____
Actual completion date: _____
Comments:

Although it is best to individualize the prompting sequence to both the student and the objective, some students benefit from having a prompting sequence that can be used until specific instructional programs are developed. For example, Kristen's classmate Rex did not follow directions when expectations were not clear and consistent. After the third day of school, the team agreed to use the following prompting sequence with Rex:

Give a general verbal instruction to the group (e.g., "It's time to sit in the story circle on the rug.")
Wait 5 seconds

Table 7.8 Communication program for Jamal

Student:_____Jamal W._____   **Date** :__10-9-92_____

Program:_____Scanning_____

The emphasis of this objective is on learning to scan rather than initiation of communication, which will be addressed at a later date.

Instructional Procedures

Setting, Grouping, Positioning	• Spanish I class in supine stander or w/c, grouping varies with activity. • Daily after the opening exercise (request to move). • Daily after being repositioned for the joke of the day (request tape recorder). • Daily immediately after the joke of the day (request to put tape in bag). • Daily before the team activity (request to move).
Equipment/Materials	• Hinged Plexiglas display, that attaches to his stander or wheelchair, 4 clear plastic pockets attached to the display, object/symbol (e.g., a scrap of fabric from his bag and a picture of his bag) to put on the display
Instruction and Prompt	• Classmate stands near Jamal and announces the next activity. • "Jamal, do you want to tell me something on your board? When I touch what you want, look at my eyes." (Classmate gestures toward his/her eyes.) • Classmate points to the 4 plastic pockets one at a time (3 empty) manually, pausing for 3 seconds at each pocket.
Correct Response	• Jamal looks at the classmate's eyes when he/she touches the object/symbol.
Time Delay and Correction	• If Jamal looks up at the wrong time or doesn't look within three seconds say, "Let's try again, look at your board." Repeat scanning and say, "Here's (object/ symbol)," when the object/symbol is reached. • If Jamal still does not succeed, repeat the above cues along with a slight physi-cal prompt to his chin to lift his eyes to yours.
Reinforcement	• Natural consequences -- Classmate touches the object/symbol again, reiter-ates Jamal's message, and responds by touching the object/symbol and saying, "Oh you want some help with the tape recorder," and then assisting Jamal with the activity.
Frequency to Teach	• 4 opportunities daily
Frequency of Data	• Tuesdays and Thursdays
Type of Data	• Record type of performance for each opportunity provided -- (+) scanned correctly, (0) error or no response. • Note number correct per day.
Criterion for Change	• Success of plan -- 4 out of 4 correct for 5 consecutive days • Failure of plan -- $\leq$ 2 out of 4 correct for 5 consecutive days

Projected completion date:___11-9-92_____
Actual completion date: _____
Comments:

Face Rex at eye level; give a specific verbal direction (e.g., "Rex, please go sit on the rug now.")

Wait 5 seconds

Tell Rex you will help him; *gently* take his hands/shoulders and physically guide him if necessary

The team's intent was not to force compliance but to make sure their expectations were expressed clearly and consistently, enabling Rex to chose participation over resistance and confrontation. After 1 week Rex was responding to specific verbal directions. By the end of September, he was following group directions as consistently as other children in the class.

For his community work experience, Jamal needed varied types and levels of assistance to perform the steps in his job of stamping the mail. Rather than try to determine one prompting sequence for the entire task, the team determined the preferred prompt for each step in the task analysis and noted them on the data sheet (see Table 7.9). Periodically the team, including the teaching assistant who went to the worksite, reviewed Jamal's performance and updated the preferred prompt. Because the team was also concerned with Jamal's rate of production, the data sheet included space for this information.

There are countless formats for recording information about instructional procedures to ensure that all team members understand and use the same method to achieve an objective. In addition to the prompting sequence, procedures should include the type and schedule of reinforcement, the frequency with which to teach the skill, the frequency with which to collect data, the type of data to be collected, and criteria to revise the instructional procedure.

What Adaptations Will Be Used To Enhance Performance?

Adaptations can take many forms (Baumgart et al., 1982; York & Rainforth, 1991). The form most familiar to therapists involves modifying materials or providing special equipment. Jamal's team had an assistive device built to enable him to stamp mail at Metro Insurance Agency (Figure 7.3). A pictorial checklist enabled Jamal's coworker to perform his job independently. Jamal's and Kristen's augmentative communication systems were both adaptations. Another form of adaptation involves modification of task sequences so steps are skipped or completed with assistance. Jamal was expected to drive his power wheelchair in uncongested hallways, and he was given physical assistance as both an adaptation and a teaching strategy. In congested areas such as classrooms, someone else pushed Jamal's chair. Personal assistance can be given by family members, staff, or, in integrated settings, by peers without disabilities (Thousand & Villa, 1990). Jamal's coworkers at Metro Insurance Agency and his classmates were encouraged to provide needed assistance. They were also taught *when, how,* and *how much* to assist Jamal so he both completed the immediate task and improved his performance over time. Kristen had an IEP objective to carry objects with both hands. During playtime, however, the team opted both to teach this skill and to encourage her to hand materials to a peer who would carry them for her. Kristen's friends were taught to help make decisions about which situations were better for each approach. Table 7.10 provides other examples of adaptations that might be considered for a child with physical disabilities during play time in kindergarten.

Table 7.9 Community work program for Jamal

Student: Jamal Williams
Date: 10-9-91

Position: Sitting in wheelchair at work station
Materials: Date stamp, adaptation, mail, pictures of materials in plastic pockets

Procedure	Jamal's response	Date	Date	Date	Date
A. SCAN PICTURES TO OBTAIN MATERIALS					
1. **Say,** "Do you want to tell me something on your board? When I touch what you want, look at my eyes."	Scans for date stamp.				
	Scans for adaptation.				
2. **Point** to each of 4 pockets (3 empty), pausing for 3 seconds at each.	Scans for stack of mail.				
B. STAMP MAIL					
1. **Preparation:** Refer to generic preparation procedure for arm use. T maintains shoulder and elbow control.	Relaxes arm in elongated position.	# repetitions required ___	# repetitions required ___	# repetitions required ___	# repetitions required ___
2. **Coactive practice:** T initiates movement, maintains shoulder and elbow control.	Completes active movement into elbow extension.				
3. **Active movement:** T maintains shoulder control only.	Initiates and completes active movement into extension.				
4. **Depress stamping adaptation:** T places hand on adaptation, maintains shoulder control only.	Initiates and completes depression of adaptation.				
5. **Slide mail off adaptation:** T places hands on top of pieces of mail, initiates lateral movement, maintains shoulder control only.	Completes lateral movement to slide mail off pile.				
Repeat steps 4-5 until the pile of mail is stamped. If needed, repeat steps 1-30.					

196

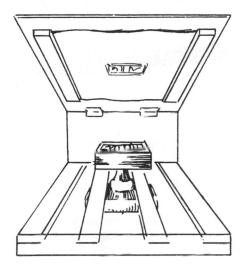

Figure 7.3. Stamping adaptation (developed by Kathy Zanella Albright). (From York, J., & Rainforth, B. [1991]. Developing individualized adaptations. In F.P. Orelove & D.J. Sobsey, *Educating children with multiple disabilities: A transdisciplinary approach* [2nd ed.] [p. 283]. Baltimore: Paul H. Brookes Publishing Co.; reprinted by permission.)

Although certain types of adaptations may be associated with particular disciplines, it is the team that decides whether an adaptation is warranted. York and Rainforth (1991) discussed the following considerations that can assist a team with decisions about adaptations:

Will the adaptation increase active participation in the activity?

Will it allow the student to participate in an activity that is preferred or valued by the student, friends, or family members?

Will it continue to be useful and appropriate as the student grows older and starts using other environments?

Will it take less time to teach the student to use the adaptation than to teach the skill directly?

Will the team have access to the technical expertise to design, construct, adjust, and repair the adaptation?

Will use of the adaptation maintain or enhance related motor and communication skills?

An adaptation is a strategy, like a prompt, that is one component of an instructional procedure. Therefore, when an adaptation is warranted, team members will provide instruction, assess performance, and conduct responsive program modifications (including modifications of the adaptation), just as they do with other instructional procedures. Furthermore, like other "artificial" strategies, adaptations are faded as soon as it is possible and efficient to do so.

How Will Performance Be Assessed?

Student performance on IEP objectives and the effectiveness of instructional procedures must be assessed regularly through ongoing data collection. During skill acquisition, data are usually collected at least once a week by the person who provides instruction. Team members other than therapists usually provide instruction involving motor and communication skills and would collect data on those programs. One way that therapists can monitor student performance is to review the data that other team members have collected. During their scheduled time with a class, therapists might also collect data as a reliability check. Thus regular data collection promotes communication about student performance and program effectiveness.

The data collected for an objective should provide relevant information about student performance. Duration, latency, frequency, distance, rate, and number correct all provide relevant information about some types of performance, but not all types. Several instructional procedures presented in this chapter provide information about the type of prompts needed to perform tasks successfully. When a score is assigned to each prompt, this type of

Table 7.10 Possible adaptations for a kindergarten student with physical disabilities during free play

Nondisabled Peer Activities	Typical Methods and Acceptable Alternatives		
	Transitions / Mobility	Positions	Participation
Looking at / reading books	TYP: Walk to shelves. ALT: Scoot, crawl, roll. Not much space but small equipment OK.	TYP: Sit on carpeted steps, sit or lie on floor. Children are physically very close, usually touching. ALT: Avoid use of equipment that isolates.	TYP: Manipulate books with hands, read/comment out loud. ALT: Most would be OK. Book holders, sticks to turn pages, taped books.
Talking with friends	TYP: Walk, run to carpeted steps, room corners. Small groups may change location to exclude peers or increase privacy. ALT: Floor method OK, small equipment OK.	TYP: Same as above. Positions may change to exclude peers or be more private. ALT: Avoid use of equipment that isolates, may need to work in position changes.	TYP: Talk, whisper, giggle, point, watch others, interrupt, leave if not included. ALT: Show pictures, activate prerecorded taped messages.
Showing toys to friends	TYP: Walk, skip to cubbies then return to play area. ALT: Floor method OK, scooter board difficult on surface change, wheelchair OK, friend could get toy.	TYP: Stand or sit on floor or steps, usually very close to each other and touching. ALT: Most upright positions OK.	TYP: Hold, show, exchange, manipulate items. ALT: Point to items, have friend help show item.
Climbing on carpeted stairs / seats	TYP: Walk, skip to steps. ALT: Any method OK, small equipment OK.	TYP: Stand to step, sit to scoot up/down. ALT: Could lie to roll down deep steps.	TYP: Stepping in standing position, scooting seated. ALT: Rolling down deep steps.

TYP, typical methods displayed by nondisabled peers; ALT, alternatives that may be acceptable.

data collection is termed "performance scoring." The advantage of performance scoring over simply recording the type of prompt is that performance on the complete task can be summarized with a numerical score. The total score does not provide information on specific aspects of performance; rather, it shows a trend in overall performance. The data sheet in Table 7.5 presents an example of perfor-

mance scoring. Once data are collected and summarized, graphing the data is recommended for accurate analysis and responsive program modification.

Deciding when to modify an instructional procedure is expedited by establishing two types of performance criteria. The "success criterion" indicates that the student has achieved an intermediate objective and a more challenging procedure or criterion should be established. The "fail-ure criterion" indicates that the instructional procedure has not been effective and must be revised. (*Note:* Since the special education team is responsible for designing effective instruction, it is the procedure that has failed, not the student.) These criterion lines are marked on the graph so it is easy to compare desired and actual performance. To be used for responsive decision making, data must be collected, graphed, and compared with criteria regularly (i.e., at least weekly). If data are collected only once a week, the frequency of data collection can be increased temporarily as a student approaches the criterion established by the team. The graph of Jamal's performance driving his power wheelchair illustrates that the first instructional procedure was not effective, but that he made steady progress after the team modified their approach (Figure 7.4).

A simple strategy for timely communication about student performance is to keep a supply of short fill-in-the-blank notes (see Table 7.11). When the teaching assistant who worked with Jamal on driving his wheelchair noticed that Jamal was not making satisfactory progress, he completed a Program Change note and put it in the occupational therapist's mailbox. When the therapist received the note, she made it a priority to observe this program during her next regularly scheduled time with the class. Based on observation and discussion with the teaching assistant, the therapist tried the "warm-up" procedure discussed earlier in this chapter, put the procedure in writing, and circulated the completed Program Change note to relevant team members. When Jamal reaches the success criterion, the teaching assistant will send another note to the therapist so the program can be revised quickly.

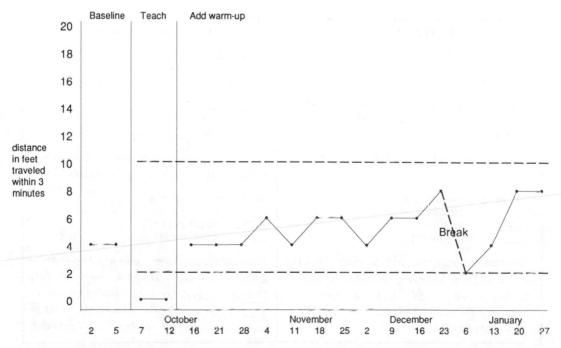

Figure 7.4. Graph of Jamal's performance driving his power wheelchair.

Table 7.11 Program change notes regarding Jamal

PROGRAM CHANGE NEEDED	PROGRAM CHANGE MADE
Date: 10 - 12 - 92	Date:
To: Lisa W. (OT)	To:
From: Jake S. (Teaching Assistant)	From:
Student: Jamal W.	Student:
Program: Driving wheelchair	Program:
Reason change is needed: _____ criterion met __X__ no progress _____ other (specify)	Reason change was met: _____ criterion met _____ no progress _____ other (specify)
Comments/suggestions: He's not doing as well as during baseline. He seems interested but he gets real stiff and seems to resist my prompts.	Comments/suggestions:

PROGRAM CHANGE NEEDED	PROGRAM CHANGE MADE
Date: 10 - 12 - 92	Date: 10 - 16 - 92
To: Lisa W. (OT)	To: Jamal W.'s team
From: Jake S. (Teaching Assistant)	From: Lisa W.
Student: Jamal W.	Student: Jamal W.
Program: Driving wheelchair	Program: Stamping mail, driving wheelchair, turning on tape recorder
Reason change is needed: _____ criterion met __X__ no progress _____ other (specify)	Reason change was met: _____ criterion met __X__ no progress _____ other (specify)
Comments/suggestions: He's not doing as well as during baseline. He seems interested but he gets real stiff and seems to resist my prompts.	Comments/suggestions: Jamal does much better when relaxed and stretched before asked to use his hands. I'll work with each of you to use warm-up procedure (attached)

WORKING WITH SYSTEMATIC INSTRUCTIONAL PROCEDURES

Establishing instructional procedures, collecting and analyzing data, and making responsive program modifications is an ongoing process. Teams should not expect to identify and write effective instructional procedures for the entire year for all students' priorities during the first few weeks of school. This is a long-term endeavor, much like the assessment process discussed in Chapter 5. For the same reason, procedures that have been effective are not discarded at the end of the school year, but are continued as long as appropriate to promote achievement of priority objectives.

Many therapists will find it challenging to establish systematic instructional procedures, since few therapists are formally trained for this task. One of the authors of this book required 3 months of instruction and support from a special education teacher on her team to write her first instructional program. Special educators who are knowledgeable about developing systematic instructional procedures and collecting and analyzing data are valuable resources to their teams. When team members pool their knowledge about curriculum, assessment, systematic instruction, and the specific strategies associated with each discipline, students with severe disabilities have greater opportunities for programs that are comprehensive, consistent, and effective.

REFERENCES

Albano, M.L. (1983). *Transdisciplinary teaming in special education: A case study.* Unpublished doctoral dissertation, University of Illinois at Urbana-Champaign.

Bailey, D.B., & Wolery, M. (1989). *Assessing infants and preschoolers with handicaps.* Columbus, OH: Charles E. Merrill.

Baumgart, D., Brown, L., Pumpian, I., Nisbet, J., Ford, A., Sweet, M., Messina, R., & Schroeder, J. (1992). The principle of partial participation and individualized adaptations in educational programs for severely handicapped students. *Journal of The Association for Persons with Severe Handicaps, 7*(2), 17–27.

Browder, D.M. (1991). *Assessment of individuals with severe disabilities: An applied behavior approach to life skills assessment* (2nd ed.). Baltimore: Paul H. Brookes Publishing Co.

Effgen, S.K. (1991). Systematic delivery and recording of intervention assistance. *Pediatric Physical Therapy, 3*(2), 63–68.

Ford, A., & Mirenda, P. (1984). Community instruction: A natural cues and corrections decision model. *Journal of The Association for Persons with Severe Handicaps, 9*(2), 79–88.

Ford, A., Schnorr, R., Meyer, L., Davern, L., Black, J., & Dempsey, P. (Eds.). (1989). *The Syracuse community-referenced curriculum guide for students with moderate and severe disabilities.* Baltimore: Paul H. Brookes Publishing Co.

Goodlad, J.I. (1984). *A place called school: Prospects for the future.* New York: McGraw-Hill Book Company.

Guess, D., & Helmstetter, E. (1986). Skill cluster instruction and the individualized curriculum sequencing model. In R. Horner, L. Meyer, & H.D. Fredericks (Eds.), *Education of learners with severe handicaps: Exemplary service strategies* (pp. 221–248). Baltimore: Paul H. Brookes Publishing Co.

Halle, J., Marshall, A., & Spradlin, J. (1979). Time delay: A technique to increase language use and facilitate generalization in retarded children. *Journal of Applied Behavior Analysis, 12*(3), 431–439.

Hayek, R.A. (1987). The teacher assistance team: A pre-referral support team. *Focus on Exceptional Children, 20*(1), 1–7.

Inge, K.J., & Snell, M.E. (1985). Teaching positioning and handling techniques to public school personnel through inservice training. *Journal of The Association for Persons with Severe Handicaps, 10*(2), 105–110.

Jaeger, L. (1987). *Home program instruction*

sheets for infants and young children. Tucson, AZ: Therapy Skill Builders.

Johnson, D.W., & Johnson, R.T. (1987). *Learning together and alone: Cooperative, competitive, and individualistic learning.* Englewood Cliffs, NJ: Prentice Hall.

Kauffman, J.M. (Ed.). (1981). Are all children educable? *Analysis and Intervention in Developmental Disabilities, 1*(1), 1–108.

McWilliam, R.A., Trivette, C.N., & Dunst, C.J. (1985). Behavior engagement as a measure of the efficacy of early intervention. *Analysis and Intervention in Developmental Disabilities, 5*(1), 59–71.

Meyer, L.H., & Evans, I.M. (1989). *Nonaversive intervention for behavior problems: A manual for home and community.* Baltimore: Paul H. Brookes Publishing Co.

Mulligan, M., Lacy, L., & Guess, D. (1982). Effects of massed, distributed, and spaced trial sequencing on severely handicapped students' performance. *Journal of The Association for the Severely Handicapped, 7*(2), 48–61.

Ossman, N.H., & Campbell, M. (1990). *Adult positions, transitions, and transfers: Reproducible instruction cards for caregivers.* Tucson, AZ: Therapy Skill Builders.

Ottenbacher, K.J. (1986). *Evaluating clinical change: Strategies for occupational and physical therapists.* Baltimore: Williams & Wilkins.

Powell, T.H., Pancsofar, E.L., Steere, D.E., Butterworth, J., Itzkowitz, J.S., & Rainforth, B. (1991). *Supported employment: Providing integrated employment opportunities for persons with disabilities.* New York: Longman.

Rainforth, B., & York, J. (1991). Handling and positioning. In F.P. Orelove & D. Sobsey, *Educating children with multiple disabilities: A transdisciplinary approach* (2nd ed.) (pp. 79–117). Baltimore: Paul H. Brookes Publishing Co.

Reichle, J., York, J., & Sigafoos, J. (1991). *Implementing augmentative and alternative communication: Strategies for learners with severe disabilities.* Baltimore: Paul H. Brookes Publishing Co.

Snell, M. (1987). *Systematic instruction of persons with severe handicaps* (3rd ed.). Columbus, OH: Charles E. Merrill.

Taylor, S. (1988). Caught in the continuum: A critical analysis of the principle of the least restrictive environment. *Journal of The Association for Persons with Severe Handicaps, 13*(1), 41–53.

Thousand, J., & Villa, R. (1990). Strategies for educating learners with severe disabilities within their local home schools and communities. *Focus on Exceptional Children, 23*(3), 1–24.

Watts, N. (1983). Eighteenth Mary McMillan lecture: The principle of choice. *Physical Therapy, 63*(11), 1802–1808.

Yonemura, M.V. (1986). *A teacher at work: Professional development and the early childhood educator.* New York: Teachers College Press.

York, J., & Rainforth, B. (1991). Developing instructional adaptations. In F.P. Orelove & D. Sobsey, *Educating children with multiple disabilities: A transdisciplinary approach* (2nd ed.) (pp. 259–295). Baltimore: Paul H. Brookes Publishing Co.

York, J., & Wiemann, G. (1991). Accommodating severe physical disabilities. In J. Reichle, J. York, & J. Sigafoos, *Implementing augmentative and alternative communication: Strategies for learners with severe disabilities* (pp. 239–256). Baltimore: Paul H. Brookes Publishing Co.

III

Implementation Strategies and Issues

THE SECOND SECTION OF THIS BOOK (CHAPTERS 4 THROUGH 7) FOCUSED ON STRATEGIES FOR designing individualized education programs for students with severe disabilities that facilitate current and future participation in integrated school and community environments. Central to the design was the integration of the perspectives, knowledge, and skills of various disciplines into one cohesive and comprehensive program, rather than an educational program composed of independent discipline-referenced segments (e.g., the physical therapy program, the communication program). Traditional service provision models must change in order for such integrated educational programs to be implemented.

There are both organizational and personal factors that influence the ability to develop new approaches to service provision. Organizationally, there must be a structure that allows team members to collaborate with one another and to work with students in the educational contexts that are of high priority for individual students. Personally, team members must share a common philosophy about education and teamwork, must be skilled in their own disciplines, and must demonstrate effective interpersonal collaboration skills.

The last section of this book (Chapters 8 and 9) focuses on these organizational and personal issues and strategies related to implementing the integrated curricular and instructional design described in Section II. Parallel practices that currently are evolving in general education and special education are discussed also. Chapter 8 presents a broad framework for collaboration based on a theory of positive interdependence among team members. Specific strategies and applications designed to promote collaboration are presented as well. Chapter 9 provides a summary of the shifts in educational service design and implementation for students with severe disabilities. Common shifts occurring in both general education and special education are identified. A discussion of current and future issues that are likely to influence the realization of collaborative team practices is provided as well.

8

Organizational Strategies for Collaborative Teamwork

JOHNSON AND JOHNSON (1989) DESCRIBED A theory of social interdependence that provides the construct from which to understand and subsequently design effective collaborative teamwork strategies. Basically, there are three ways in which people interact: individualistically, competitively, and cooperatively (Table 8.1). These ways of interacting are referred to as goal structures. In *individualistic* goal structures, people work independently; there is no interdependence (Johnson & Johnson, 1989). The outcome of one person's efforts has no effect on and is not affected by the actions of another person. Each person does his or her own work with students. Frequently, this is how members of educational "teams" function in a school setting. An individualistic goal structure is perpetuated by organizational structures, such as rigid scheduling of direct therapy times in isolated environments (e.g., physical therapy on Tuesday and Thursday from 10:00 to 10:30 A.M.). Individualistic structures also are perpetuated by interpersonal factors, such as the desire to work in isolation instead of working with other team members and in integrated settings.

In *competitive* goal structures, there is negative interdependence (Johnson & Johnson, 1989). For one person to achieve his or her goal (i.e., to win), another person must fail to do so (i.e., lose). Sometimes interactions among educational team members unintentionally take this form of win-lose competition. For example, when direct therapy time conflicts with reading class, the therapist and teacher are in competition for time with the student. Or, when the communication specialist is adamant that social interaction is the instructional priority for a 25-minute lunch period and the occupational therapist insists that promoting more efficient hand use skills is most important, they have competing goals. Lacking skills in conflict resolution and consensus decision making, many team members are destined for competitive interactions, frequently at the expense of what is best for the student. Failure to develop and work from a unifying curricular orientation also contributes to competition among team members because there is no shared vision of desired outcomes that can provide the common basis for making decisions jointly.

In *cooperative* goal structures, there is

Table 8.1 Goal structures that affect team interactions and outcomes

Competitive
   •win or lose
   •negative interdependence

Individualistic
   •work independently
   •no interdependence

Cooperative
   •help and support others
   •positive interdependence

Summarized from Johnson, D. W., & Johnson, R. T. (1989). *Cooperation and competition: Theory and research.* Edina, MN: Interaction Book Company.

positive social interdependence (Johnson & Johnson, 1989). Each person's work to achieve his or her goal both depends upon and enables other persons to achieve their goals. Team members "sink or swim" together. This reflects the underlying premise of collaborative teamwork. Cooperative interactions are promoted by structuring goal interdependence, resource interdependence, and reward interdependence (Thousand et al., 1986). *Goal interdependence* occurs when all members of the educational team commit themselves to achieving a mutually agreed upon goal. *Resource interdependence* occurs when team members commit their respective talents to achieving their mutual goal and when team members divide tasks in an efficient, fair, and agreed upon manner. *Reward interdependence* occurs when all team members share equally in benefits realized from accomplishing their mutual goal. For example, when a student with severe disabilities develops a friendship with a classmate for the first time, all team members share the feeling of accomplishment. To function as a collaborative educational team, positive interdependence must be structured through mutually agreed upon goals, contribution to goal attainment, and celebration of goal accomplishment.

Making the decision to work as a collaborative team and to design structures to promote positive interdependence does not result immediately in collaboration. Change to collaborative ways of interacting, like all change, involves an evolution in thinking and in behaving. Efficient and satisfying interactions among group members evolve through ongoing interaction opportunities and conscious effort to develop effective ways to collaborate. Tuckman (1965; Tuckman & Jensen, 1977) presented five phases through which groups evolve:

Forming is an initial phase of group interaction in which members try to determine their places in the group and to develop the procedures and rules of the group.

Storming is the period in which conflicts arise. Some members may resist the group influence or rebel against accomplishing the task.

Norming describes the period during which the group establishes cohesiveness and commitment. Members discover new ways to work together.

Performing describes the period in which the group becomes efficient at its work and develops more flexible ways of working together.

Adjourning describes the point at which the formal work of the group is completed, thereby removing the central mission. The result is dissolution of the group. This period sometimes involves elements of *mourning* as well.

Lacoursiere (1980) presented a similar chronology of group evolution with stages labeled as: orientation, dissatisfaction, resolution, production, termination, and negative orientation. In the work of Johnson and Johnson (1987), yet another derivation of group evolution is described, beginning with defining procedures and becoming oriented and moving through periods of conforming to procedures and getting acquainted, recognizing mutuality and building trust, rebelling and differentiating, committing to take ownership for goals, procedures, and other team members, and finally, reaching a period of functioning maturely and productively. Termination of groups occurs when the work of the group is completed. In the case of IEP teams, the work is rarely completed but terminations and new beginnings occur as members leave and as new members join. Changes in other group variables can result in recycling through various stages as well.

These variations of group evolution have been presented as an indication that the development of effective collaboration involves an active process. The purpose of this chapter is to present strategies that promote positive interdependence among team members and result in effective collaboration. Specifically, the following will be discussed: 1) moving toward a shared mission by clarifying the function of collaborative educational teams; 2) identifying team members for individual students; 3) structuring opportunities to collaborate, including scheduling related services personnel in integrated educational environments with students and arranging regular opportunities to interact with fellow team members; 4) developing collaboration skills, including exchanging skills among team members, solving problems, making decisions as a group, and resolving con-

flicts; 5) communicating with parents; and 6) developing a supportive environment for change.

CLARIFYING THE FUNCTION OF COLLABORATIVE EDUCATIONAL TEAMS

The primary function of collaborative educational teams is to support students to achieve integrated life outcomes through attainment of priority educational objectives identified in the individualized education program (IEP). Educational team members also provide support to one another. A major responsibility for related services personnel is to support teachers, paraprofessionals, and others who work closely with students on a daily basis.

Support Students To Achieve Integrated Life Outcomes

Before support of any kind can be provided, members of the collaborative educational team need to know what it is that they are supposed to support. The desired outcomes of educational service provision must be identified. Engaging in a discussion about desired educational outcomes is one way for team members to develop the shared goals necessary for them to interact in a collaborative way. The discussion can begin by each team member writing down and then sharing in a discussion their responses to the statement: "I believe that the educational program for students with severe disabilities should result in the following outcomes." Responses to this question usually include depictions of students enjoying and participating in family life, having friends and other stable relationships, making choices about small and large life issues, participating in community activities, and working or making other contributions to the community. In a recent concept paper developed by the National Center on Educational Outcomes (1991), life outcomes were defined in terms of presence, participation, accomplishment, contribution, and satisfaction across life domains. Broad statements about educational and life outcomes provide the framework from which specific and individualized objectives are identified for students through the curriculum development process (as discussed in Section II of this book). Clarity of desired outcomes is necessary before complementary implementation strategies, including how to provide support to students and fellow team members, can be developed.

Support Fellow Team Members

Different types of support that team members provide to one another include: 1) resource support (e.g., materials, funding, literature, people); 2) moral support (e.g., listening, encouraging); and 3) technical support (e.g., specific and individualized strategies, instructional methods, and adaptations) (York, Giangreco, Vandercook, & Macdonald, 1992). For support to be real, rather than perceived, the recipient of the support must feel supported. As team members work together to achieve desired student outcomes and to support one another, they should talk about specific actions that are supportive to students and to each other. Examples of practices that are likely to be supportive and those that are not likely to be supportive are presented in Table 8.2 (York et al., 1992).

The way in which support is operationalized into collaborative teamwork practices, and specifically into individual team member roles and responsibilities, will vary from team to team, building to building, and district to district. For individuals joining an already existing and effectively

functioning collaborative team, responsibilities and expectations can be communicated clearly in writing, through talking with fellow team members, and through observation and experience working as a member of the already collaborative work environment and team structure. For teams just initiating the change to collaborative teamwork practices, responsibilities and performance expectations frequently seem vague and poorly defined. Some support during this transition phase can be provided by external sources (e.g., individuals from other teams, written materials, outside consultants). Developing effective means of collaboration among the members of any specific team, however, involves a process and cannot be achieved exclusively through external support.

As team members work together, more effective and comfortable ways of interacting and supporting one another develop. When team members begin to understand more clearly their roles and responsibilities, job descriptions can be developed. The sample job description in Table 8.3 includes broad statements of educational outcomes and expectations, as well as operationalized physical/occupational therapist performance expectations. The checklist provided in Table 8.4 outlines competencies that are generic for most members of a collaborative educational team. The checklist can be used as a self-check, as a way to solicit feedback from fellow team members, or as a performance evaluation by an informed and involved supervisor.

The overriding responsibilities of each member of the collaborative educational team are: 1) to contribute knowledge and skills so that students achieve their educational outcomes; 2) to support fellow members of the collaborative team; and 3) to contribute to the overall development of inclusive school communities where all

Table 8.2 Examples of what support means . . . and does not mean

Support means . . .

..... helping students and families realize their own vision of a good life

..... listening to and acting on the support needs identified by students, families, and other team members

..... reallocating resources to support efforts to include students in regular school life, including resources for teams to learn and work together

..... remembering that the students are the "stars" and that the educational team members are the supporting actors

..... acknowledging the efforts of fellow team members

..... designing curricular and instructional methods that assist the student to be an active learner

..... designing curricular and instructional methods that assist the classroom teacher to effectively include the student

..... designing curricular and instructional methods that promote positive interdependence among students in the class

..... providing constructive feedback to fellow team members that results in more effective team member interactions and ultimately improved student learning

..... providing enough information, but not too much

..... being around and available enough, but not too much

Support does not mean . . .

..... conducting a classroom observation then writing and depositing notes on the teacher's desk with no opportunity for follow-up discussion

..... giving your opinions, advice, and recommendations then leaving before a discussion can ensue

..... requesting to meet with the classroom teacher during instructional time without making prior arrangements

..... presenting the classroom teacher with a list of skills or activities to be integrated into the classroom day

..... telling the teacher or family what to do

..... giving the classroom teacher a file folder of resources when she asked for problem-solving support

..... hovering near students with disabilities in the classroom

..... doing "therapy" in the back of the room

..... suggesting interventions that interfere with the classroom routine

..... providing more support than is needed

From York, J., Giangreco, M., Vandercook, T., & Macdonald, C. (1992). Integrating support personnel in the inclusive classroom. In S. Stainback & W. Stainback (Eds.), *Curriculum considerations in inclusive classrooms: Facilitating learning for all students* (p. 104). Baltimore: Paul H. Brookes Publishing Company; reprinted by permission.

Table 8.3 Sample physical / occupational therapist job description

JOB DESCRIPTION:
Physical / Occupational Therapist

The following job description delineates responsibilities for physical and occupational therapists who work with students who have moderate, severe, and multiple disabilities categorically referred to here as severe disabilities. This job description was predicated on the following tenets. Physical and occupational therapy services provided in educational settings must: 1) address the individual educational needs of each student; 2) be integrated throughout the regular education, domestic, recreation/leisure, community, and vocational environments in which students receive instruction and are expected to function; and 3) be coordinated with the services provided by other members of the educational team. Collaboration and communication across disciplines and with family members is essential.

Meeting the comprehensive, varied, and complex educational needs of students with severe disabilities presents a significant challenge for students, as well as team members. However, through a collaborative teamwork model, the educational team can move closer toward accomplishing the goal of maximal student participation in regular school and community environments. This job description is intended to present guidelines for the practice of physical/occupational therapists in educational settings such that achievement of this goal can be realized.

The Physical / Occupational Therapist Job Description is divided into four primary areas of responsibility: assessment, program planning, program implementation, and team process.

ASSESSMENT

1. The Physical / Occupational Therapist will participate in assessment of individual students to determine the need for and the type of therapy services that need to be delivered to support the educational program.

2. The Physical / Occupational Therapist will participate in initial assessments performed jointly by an Occupational Therapist and a Physical Therapist. Two types of assessment information will be obtained: environment-referenced information derived from an ecological inventory, and skill referenced information derived from diagnostic assessments. Both types of information can and should be obtained through observation and hands-on interaction in naturally occurring, functional situations to the greatest extent possible.

   a. Environment-referenced information addresses the ability of a student to interact and participate in educational activities under natural conditions. To obtain this information, the Physical / Occupational Therapist will observe students and perform hands-on assessment in the school, home, and community environments intended as priority educational contexts for each individual student. Examples of environments and activities in which assessment might take place include:

      School environments: classrooms, rest rooms, cafeteria, hallways and entryways, playgrounds, and bus loading/unloading areas

      Community environments: cars, public buses, grocery stores, shopping malls, restaurants, and work sites

      Home environments: walkways and entryways, yard, kitchen, family room, bathroom, and bedroom

(continued)

Table 8.3 *(continued)*

The information that will be obtained in the above environments will be related to the following activity components:

Transition: How does / should the student move between educational environments and activities?

Position: How does / should the student be positioned to enable maximal participation In the educational envlronments and activities?

Participation: How does / should the student move to engage in educational activities in an efficient and participatory manner?

Adaptation: What equipment, environmental modifications, or adaptive devices are available or could be built / obtained to enhance participation in educational environments and activities?

b. Skill-referenced information in each of the following areas will be obtained:

Gross motor skills, including: methods of mobility, postural control, balance / equilibrium responses, transitions and transfers between body positions, strength and endurance

Fine motor skills, including: functional and cooperative hand use, reach/grasp/release, eye-hand coordination, visual motor skills, tool use

Oral motor skills, including: drinking, sucking, swallowing, biting, chewing, and other components related to effective eating

Respiratory functioning, including: breathing patterns and efficiency, coughing

Overall neuromotor status, including: joint range of motion, muscle tone, muscle strength, endurance, coordination, efficiency, motor planning, quantity and quality of movement, interfering reflexes, sensorimotor integration and processing

3. The Physical / Occupational Therapist will determine and then share with other team members safe and efficient methods for transitioning, positioning, handling, facilitating movement, and transferring individual students. Methods will incorporate use of proper body mechanics to increase movement efficiency and to minimize physical strain on persons working with the students.

4. The Physical / Occupational Therapist will collaborate with other team members during the ecological assessment process. Because each team member analyzes the abilities and needs of students from a different point of view, a synthesis of observations and viewpoints provides a comprehensive and balanced analysis of student functioning in educational contexts. Therapists and teachers will jointly discuss synthesized analyses of assessment findings leading to collaboration in determining priority of educational goals and objectives.

5. The Physical / Occupational Therapist will contribute to the collaborative team assessment reports by detailing relevant environment-referenced and skill-referenced information. Skill-referenced assessment information that is pertinent to educational programming will be objectively and concisely summarized for parents, physicians, and other team members regarding each student's current motor abilities as part of every 3-year re-evaluation. Environment-referenced assessment information will be summarized as part of the collaborative team report on performance in educational environments and activities. This information will be organized into school, community, general community, domestic, recreation / leisure, and vocational areas of functioning. Specific activities assessed in each of these areas will be delineated and commented upon. The IEP goals and objectives will serve as the basis for documenting change In student abilities on an annual basis.

(continued)

Table 8.3 *(continued)*

6. The Physical / Occupational Therapist will engage in ongoing assessment of student abilities in educational environments and activities. This will include both observations of and hands-on interactions with students, as well as implementing and/or monitoring ongoing systems of data collection and analysis.

PROGRAM PLANNING

1. The Physical / Occupational Therapist will participate in a discussion with other team members to prioritize educational goals and objectives to be targeted for instruction during the school year. This requires delineation of educational needs identified during assessment, followed by team discussion of consensus decision making regarding the most important skills to receive instructional emphasis.

2. The Physical / Occupational Therapist will write educationally relevant goals and objectives that are stated in behavioral and measurable terms and that specify performance in educational environments and activities.

3. The Physical / Occupational Therapist will collaborate in the writing of instructional programs and procedures, many of which will be carried out on a regular basis by other team members. The instructional information contributed by the Physical / Occupational Therapist might include:
   - Equipment and adaptive devices required
   - The position of the student and a description of how to achieve the position
   - The movements expected of the student for participation
   - The position of the instructor
   - The assistance provided by the instructor
   - Other pertinent antecedents
   - Consequences, both error correction and reinforcement procedures
   - Data collection procedures

4. The Physical / Occupational Therapist will participate in scheduling student and class activities for the purpose of identifying opportunities throughout the week when mobility / transition, positioning, movement, and other movement expectations can be integrated into educational activites that occur in school, home, and community environments.

PROGRAM IMPLEMENTATION

1. The Physical / Occupational Therapist will observe, monitor, and re-evaluate student performance during educational activites in school, home, and community environments on a regular basis. The frequency, duration, and location of these interactions will be determined by the educational team based on individual student needs.

2. The Physical / Occupational therapist will provide direct and indirect services as appropriate for each student. To the greatest extent possible, intervention methods designed to improve mobility, posture, and efficient movement will be integrated as part of instruction that occurs on an ongoing basis in educational activities. When most intervention methods are integrated in the educational program, the therapist will still maintain direct, hands-on interactions with students on at least an intermittent basis. This direct interaction can and should occur in a consultative manner in educational contexts.

3. The Physical / Occupational Therapist will make or obtain necessary equipment and adaptive devices required for appropriate mobility, positioning, and optimal participation in educational activities.

(continued)

Table 8.3 *(continued)*

4. The Physical / Occupational Therapist will teach teachers, parents, instructional aides, and others methods of safe and therapeutic physical management of students, including methods for lifting, carrying, transferring and mobility, positioning and use of positioning equipment, normalizing muscle tone, facilitating efficient movement, and using adaptive devices.

5. The Physical / Occupational Therapist will document recommendations, feedback, and program changes after each observation of or interaction with a student in the context of educational activities. This information will be distributed to all team members.

6. The Physical / Occupational Therapist will collaborate with other team members in writing educationally relevant goals and objectives, instructional programs, and data-based assessment procedures. She or he will analyze performance and determine program changes needed based on systematically collected data.

7. The Physical / Occupational Therapist will perform temporary direct therapy services when:
   - Hands-on interaction is necessary to determine student progress and effective intervention procedures.
   - Highly specialized and high-risk handling procedures are required, such as immediately after surgery.
   - The functional status of a student is either rapidly progressing or deteriorating so as to warrant frequent direct interactions to determine changing needs. In every situation in which direct services are deemed appropriate, indirect service must be provided also.

TEAM PROCESS

1. The Physical / Occupational Therapist will participate in regularly scheduled team meetings for students when the therapist is a core team member. Participation includes problem solving and brainstorming related to all areas of educational programming. That is, participation is not limited to areas viewed as specific to the therapist's own discipline or areas of expertise.

2. The Physical / Occupational Therapist will be a supportive team member and participate in collaborative educational program planning and implementation as specified previously.

3. The Physical / Occupational Therapist will expand his or her knowledge and expertise in educational and therapeutic advances of relevance to the education of students with severe disabilities by attending inservice training activities, professional conferences, and workshops.

Adapted from York, J., Peters, B., Hurd, D., & Donder, D. (1985). *Guidelines for using support services in educational programs for students with severe, multiple handicaps* (pp. 48-49). DeKalb, IL: DeKalb County Special Education Association; revised and reprinted by permission.

students and adults are welcomed, valued, supported, and successful.

IDENTIFYING TEAM MEMBERS FOR INDIVIDUAL STUDENTS

In Chapter 2 the concept of a core team and a support team was discussed. Also mentioned was the need for flexibility in terms of who functions on the core team given the priority educational needs of a student at any given point in time. Core team members are those individuals who are most directly involved in designing and implementing or monitoring the daily educational program. The support team consists of individuals who are available on an as-needed basis but who do not have frequent and regularly scheduled interactions with students or members of the core team.

Table 8.4 Generic team member performance checklist

Collaborative Team Member Checklist

Team Member Name:————————————————————— Date:———————————

Checklist completed by: (check one)

___Teacher   ___Support Staff   ___Aide   ___Program Supervisor   ___Other

	High				Low	
	5	4	3	2	1	NA
Participates in the assessment of student abilities in the array of educational environments and activities determined as priorities for individual students:						
•School environments and activities	5	4	3	2	1	NA
•Home environments and activities	5	4	3	2	1	NA
•Community environments and activities	5	4	3	2	1	NA
Effectively communicates educationally relevant assessment information to other team members.	5	4	3	2	1	NA
Participates in writing educationally relevant team assessment reports.	5	4	3	2	1	NA
Participates in team collaboration for determining priority educational goals and objectives.	5	4	3	2	1	NA
Writes educational goals and objectives that are:						
•Educationally relevant	5	4	3	2	1	NA
•Functional	5	4	3	2	1	NA
•Chronologically age appropriate	5	4	3	2	1	NA
•Behavioral	5	4	3	2	1	NA
•Measurable	5	4	3	2	1	NA
Writes clear instructional programs and procedures, including evaluation information.	5	4	3	2	1	NA
When teaching other team members, provides a rationale for the procedures and clear instruction-supportive feedback.	5	4	3	2	1	NA
Incorporates behavior management practices into programs and procedures as appropriate.	5	4	3	2	1	NA
Effectively teaches other team members how to integrate their own expertise into student's daily programming.	5	4	3	2	1	NA
Requests information from other team members.	5	4	3	2	1	NA
Is organized, efficient, and directed during classroom and community consultations.	5	4	3	2	1	NA
Effectively monitors and observes student performance.	5	4	3	2	1	NA
Provides supportive and instructive feedback to other team members regarding expanded roles.	5	4	3	2	1	NA

(continued)

Table 8.4 *(continued)*

	High				Low	
	5	4	3	2	1	NA
Participates effectively and appropriately in team meetings.	5	4	3	2	1	NA
Participates effectively and appropriately in IEP meeting and annual reviews.	5	4	3	2	1	NA
Maintains a good rapport and interacts appropriately with students.	5	4	3	2	1	NA
Maintains a good rapport and interacts appropriately with family members of students.	5	4	3	2	1	NA
Maintains a good rapport and interacts appropriately with other team members.	5	4	3	2	1	NA
Presents him/herself as a learner and continually attempts to enhance his/her knowledge of educational and specialized professional practices.	5	4	3	2	1	NA
Supports overall development of educational excellence in the school community.	5	4	3	2	1	NA

ADDITIONAL COMMENTS

1. Areas of strength:

2. Areas for improvement:

3. I would like more of:

4. I would like less of:

Adapted from York, J., Peters, B., Hurd, D., & Donder, D. (1985). *Guidelines for using support services in educational programs for students with severe, multiple handicaps* (pp. 48-49). DeKalb, IL: DeKalb County Special Education Association; revised and reprinted by permission.

Many professional disciplines could contribute to the educational service provision of students with disabilities. Legislation has been enacted to ensure the availability of a variety of special education and related services professionals so that individual student needs can be met. However, when deciding specifically who should provide support to an individual student, as well as what, when, and how support should be provided, there are a number of factors that require thoughtful consideration given constraints in the real world of educational practice.

The number of individuals on a team is one factor that has an effect on collaboration. Theoretically, the more people that are involved the more diverse the expertise that can be brought to bear for any individual student. The more people who are involved, however, the greater the difficulty in coordinating schedules and enabling team members to have access to one another. Communication among all members of the team becomes more difficult. As groups get bigger, individual responsibility and contribution frequently diminish as well. Another factor that enters into team member selection it the likelihood of meaningful (e.g., frequent and engaged) access and involvement of the potential team member. In some districts, certain support staff (e.g., physical therapists) simply are not available, despite ongoing attempts to recruit and retain additional staff. Another selection factor is overlap in knowledge and skill demonstrated by potential team members. Roles and responsibilities of specific professionals and disciplines vary across districts, and even school buildings, given the specific makeup of staff involved in each location and the expectations that have been set historically.

The overriding issue of what is, in fact, supportive to students and to direct instructional staff needs to be discussed at the local level. A starting point for the discussion is for the team to determine the primary challenges experienced by an individual student in accomplishing his or her educational goals. Next, potential team members with the specific competencies needed to address those challenges and provide support to the student and his or her direct instructional staff are identified. Table 8.5 delineates a range of student challenges and respective individuals who might be able to provide support (York et al., 1992). Note that there are several possible support personnel options for each student challenge. For example, depending on the specific nature of the communication challenges experienced by an individual student, support could be provided by teachers, classmates, speech-language therapists, occupational therapists, psychologists, or family members.

In selecting the specific support personnel to function on the core team, consider the following guidelines:

1. If two or more potential team members have overlapping information and skills related to the challenge area, select only one of the team members to be involved.

For example: An individual audiologist and an individual speech-language therapist both are knowledgeable about how the classroom teacher can more effectively communicate with Henry, a student with a mild hearing impairment. The team decided that only one of these professionals needed to be involved in designing instructional adaptations for Henry. The other could be consulted on an as-needed basis, particularly in complex problem solving and long-range program development activities.

Table 8.5 Student challenges and respective support personnel

Student Challenge	Potential Support Personnel
Cognitive / learning process	
• Curricular / instructional adaptations or alternatives	General educator, special educator, speech-language therapist, occupational therapist, psychologist, vision or hearing specialists
• Organizing assignments, schedules	General educator, special educator, occupational therapist, speech-language therapist
Communication / interactions	
• Nonverbal communication	Speech-language therapist, special educator, family members
• Socialization with classmates	Speech-language therapist, special educator, psychologist, classmates
• Behaving in adaptive ways	General educator, special educator, psychologist, speech-language therapist, classmates
Physical / motor	
• Functional use of hands	Occupational therapist, physical therapist, special educator
• Mobility and transitions	Physical therapist, occupational therapist, orientation and mobility specialist, special educator
• Posture (body alignment)	Physical therapist, occupational therapist
• Fitness and physical activity	Physical therapist, adaptive physical educator, nurse
Sensory	
• Vision	Vision specialist, occupational therapist, orientation & mobility specialist
• Hearing	Audiologist, hearing specialist, speech-language therapist
Health	
• Eating difficulty	Occupational therapist, speech-language therapist, physical therapist, nurse, special educator
• Medications	Nurse
• Other health needs	Nurse, physicians, selected health care professionals
Current and future living	
• Career and vocational pursuits	Vocational educator, counselor, special educator
• Leisure pursuits	Special educator, occupational therapist, recreation personnel
• Support from home and community	Social worker, counselor, special educator, general educator

Adapted from York, J., Giangreco, M., Vandercook, T., & Macdonald, C. (1992). Integrating support personnel in the inclusive classroom. In S. Stainback & W. Stainback (Eds.), *Curriculum considerations in inclusive classrooms: Facilitating learning for all students* (p. 108). Baltimore: Paul H. Brookes Publishing Company, reprinted by permission.

2. If one potential team member is able to address multiple challenges or needs of an individual student, select that team member.

For example: Henry, the student with a mild hearing impairment, also had some difficulty interacting with classmates. The speech-language therapist has been very interested and involved in developing social skills curricula. The team therefore decided to have the speech-language therapist, instead of the audiologist, be more directly involved with Henry because she could address both his auditory and socialization challenges.

3. If two or more potential team members have similar competencies but one has more frequent or closer geographical access to the student's school, select the individual who has closer and more frequent access.

For example: Yolanda has a vision impairment that presents particular challenges during her community-based instruction. Both the vision specialist and orientation and mobility specialist have experience teaching students with vision impairments to access community environments. Neither professional currently serves students in the rural high school that Yolanda attends. The vision specialist, however, lives in that community. The team decided that the vision specialist should be part of Yolanda's core team because he would have more frequent access to Yolanda as a result of geographical proximity. The team also decided that the orientation and mobility specialist would consult informally with the vision specialist just prior to each bimonthly regional support group meeting for professionals serving low-incidence student populations.

4. If none of the potential team members has adequate knowledge and skills to address a challenge area, identify one team member who will obtain additional training and support either through student-specific technical assistance or through various forms of continuing education and in-service training (e.g., courses and workshops).

For example: Neither the occupational therapist nor the physical therapist nor the speech-language therapist have experience facilitating oral motor skills for complex eating challenges. Amy, a 6-year-old, experiences extreme gagging when attempting to eat. The occupational therapist has been extensively involved in teaching other students to feed themselves and has developed an increased interest in mealtime skills. Because of the occupational therapist's interest and current availability during mealtimes, the team decides that it makes sense for the occupational therapist to take a 3-day workshop on prespeech and eating skills offered at a regional therapy training institute. In the meantime, the administrator supports the team's recommendation to hire a consultant to provide initial and follow-up technical assistance to assist in the assessment and program development related to Amy's specific eating abilities.

5. If two professionals have similar but not overlapping knowledge and skill competencies, provide the opportunity for these two individuals to work together to train one another in complementary skill areas, with the ultimate goal being a divided caseload with each professional having more time to be involved with individual students. This is a capacity-building approach in that the capacity of one

professional to meet more diverse learner needs is being developed. Ultimately, this can result in greater efficiency because the number of people involved with any one student can be streamlined without significant loss of expertise.

For example: An occupational therapist and physical therapist have common competencies related to positioning, handling, and adaptive equipment. In addition, the occupational therapist has considerably more knowledge about hand use. The physical therapist has more experience facilitating mobility. For 4 months they work together with students who have hand use and mobility challenges to train and support one another. They also spend time together sharing resources on their respective new learning topics. After 4 months, they divide their caseloads so that either the occupational therapist or the physical therapist is providing primary "motor" support to students with comprehensive physical challenges (including hand use and mobility). They also schedule monthly opportunities to work together with the students.

Selections regarding specific core team members must balance efficiency (e.g., number of team members with whom to coordinate, logistical issues such as regular access and availability) and diversity of knowledge and skill. Selections always focus on matching student challenges and needs with the competencies of individual support personnel. Specific competencies are not ensured by a given discipline label. There is tremendous variability in the knowledge and skill among professionals with the same discipline label. Furthermore, there is tremendous overlap in the knowledge and skills of some professionals who have different discipline labels. In

making the best possible decisions regarding support personnel to meet individual student needs, myths about professional discipline labels must be dispelled. Some of these discipline myths are:

Myth #1: The most important requisite for team member effectiveness is competence within one's own discipline . . . for example, a clinically superb physical therapist will also be an excellent team member in a public school setting.

Myth #2: There are well-defined boundaries between disciplines . . . for example, there is no overlap between what teachers and occupational therapists know.

Myth #3: Each individual trained in the same discipline has the same competencies . . . for example, all speech and language therapists have competence in augmentative communication.

Myth #4: Professionals with a specific discipline label "own" their respective area of discipline expertise . . . for example, only the physical therapist can be knowledgeable about mobility. (York et al., 1992)

The purpose of presenting these discipline myths is to expose some of the perceived truths to which we hold in making decisions about support and personnel needs. Focusing on the labels of professionals instead of on the specific interests and competencies of an individual professional can create inefficiencies and inadequacies in service provision (just as adhering to the generalizations associated with the labels ascribed to children can result in overlooking individual assets and interests). Individual people with their unique contributions, only some of which relate to an ascribed discipline label, are what make collaborative teamwork effective. A game called "Discipline Myths and Truths" can be used as an icebreaker by exposing some discipline myths so that team members can begin talking about effective and efficient ways to work together to support students (Table 8.6).

Table 8.6 A game to elicit discussion about roles and responsibilities of various disciplines

---

Discipline Myths and Truths

<u>Instructions</u>: This is a screening tool for determining your *DISCIPLINE OUTLOOK*. For each of the following statements, mark "M" for MYTH or "T" for TRUTH. If you work with other people to discuss the statements, add an additional 5 points to your score. If you work in isolation subtract 5 points from your score.

____ There are well defined boundaries between disciplines. For example, there is no overlap between what teachers and occupational therapists know.

____ No single discipline encompasses sufficient knowledge and skills to effectively meet the needs of all students.

____ Many of the skills considered unique to a particular discipline can, in fact, be taught to people who do not have the particular discipline label.

____ There are genetic and identifiable brain differences between people with differing discipline labels.

____ The most important requisite for team member effectiveness is competence within one's own discipline. For example, a clinically superb psychologist will also be an excellent team member in a public school setting.

____ Each individual trained in the same discipine has the same competencies. For example, all speech-language therapists have competence in augmentative communication.

____ Disciplines involved in educational teams exist to support students to participate in and contribute to family, school, and community life . . . now and in the future.

____ Professionals with a specific discipline label "own" their respective area of discipline expertise. For example, only the occupational therapist can be knowledgeable about hand function; only a nurse can know about seizure disorders.

____ There are many areas of overlapping knowledge and skills among disciplines.

____ The most important consideration in determining who should provide support to a student is knowledge and skills, not discipline label.

DEVELOPING A STRUCTURE THAT PROMOTES COLLABORATION

When educational teams are just starting to design and implement a new collaborative approach to service provision, more time is needed to interact than in later stages of implementation. By definition, the acquisition stage of learning is inefficient and therefore requires more time and effort. One of the most frequently asked questions is "How are we supposed to function as a collaborative team when we have no time to interact?" The answer is simply, "You cannot." Team members simply must allocate time to work together. Because obtaining more work time is not a viable option in most circumstances, the task becomes that of making changes in how time is currently spent. To implement an integrated approach to the provision of related services, time must be allocated for therapists to work with students in integrated learning environments and to collaborate with other members of the educational team. During these interactions, efficiency is maximized by developing clear expectations and procedures. Strategies for scheduling time in integrated learning environments and with team members and for maximizing efficient interactions during these times are discussed here.

Schedule Related Services Personnel in Integrated Educational Environments

Traditional multidisciplinary or interdisciplinary service provision models involved each professional spending individual or small group time with students focusing on a specific challenge. For example, a physical therapist might have worked with a student on improving walking skills using parallel bars in a separate therapy room. Or a speech-language therapist might have spent individual time increasing a child's response to greetings by engaging in repeated practice trials in a one-on-one therapy session. Greater inclusion of students with disabilities in general education classes and other integrated learning environments has created the need for support personnel to change their traditional methods of service provision. Specifically, structures that allow support personnel to observe and work with students in the context of the ongoing educational programs is essential to ensure educational relevance of their support. This requires a flexible approach to scheduling so that support personnel can spend time in general education classes and other integrated school and community environments.

An alternative to traditional scheduling

of related services time (i.e., back-to-back direct therapy sessions of 30–45 minutes, twice a week, in a separate environment) is the use of *block scheduling* (Rainforth & York, 1987; York, Rainforth, & Wiemann, 1988). Block scheduling refers to allocating longer periods of time than usual (e.g., a half or full day instead of 30–45 minutes) to provide the time and flexibility needed to work in and move between the learning environments in which students with disabilities are integrated. The amount of time spent providing services using a block scheduling approach usually is about the same as in a more traditional approach to scheduling. For example, in a more traditional approach, a speech-language therapist might have spent a total of 12 hours a month with three students, seeing each student for 30 minutes, twice a week: (30 minutes/session) $\times$ (2 sessions/week $\times$ 4 weeks/month $\times$ 3 students/week = 12 hours/month). Using a block scheduling approach and assuming there are 6 hours of school/day, the same speech-language therapist might spend one half day per week or one full day every other week in an elementary school in which three students with intensive challenges are integrated. Each student will continue to receive 4 hours of service/month. The major difference between the approaches is not how much time is spent supporting students, but how that time is spent.

There are countless ways to design block schedules. The specific design will vary given the array of demographic, student, district, and team member variables. Typically, a block scheduling model results in less frequent interactions with students but longer periods of time available during each interaction. This longer time block provides the flexibility needed to allow the therapist to interact with students in a number of educational environments and activities. Two examples of how a block schedule might look for an individual therapist are provided in Figures 8.1 and 8.2.

In the first example (Figure 8.1), the schedule for Ms. Jackson, a speech-language therapist who works in an urban high school, is shown. There are two speech-

Ms. Jackson's Schedule for 1991-92 School Year

	Monday	Tuesday	Wednesday	Thursday	Friday
Week 1	A (freshmen) ·········· A (sophomores)	B	A (juniors) ·········· A (seniors)	B	A flex
Week 2	B	A (freshmen) ·········· A (sophomores)	B	A (juniors) ·········· A (seniors)	flex
Week 3	A (freshmen) ·········· A (sophomores)	B	A (juniors) ·········· A (seniors)	B	A flex
Week 4	B	A (freshmen) ·········· A (sophomores)	B	A (juniors) ·········· A (seniors)	flex

Central High School
•1,500 students grades 9-12

•80 students receiving speech-language support:
   60 students with mild disabilities or speech-language needs
   20 students with moderate/severe disabilities

•Caseloads of 2 full-time speech-language therapists:
   •Ms. Romando: 50 students with mild disabilities or speech-language needs
   •Ms. Jackson: A blocks - 20 students with moderate/severe disabilities and speech-language
                         needs (5 freshmen, 5 sophomores, 5 juniors [including Jamal], 5 seniors)
                   B blocks - 10 students with mild disabilities and/or speech-language needs

Figure 8.1. Sample block schedule for a speech-language therapist in an urban high school.

language therapists at the high school. One of the therapists has caseloads of students with mild disabilities and speech-language needs only. One of the therapists, Ms. Jackson, has 10 students with mild disabilities and 20 students with severe disabilities (students labeled as moderately, severely, or profoundly mentally retarded) on her caseload. Because most of Ms. Jackson's support of the students with severe disabilities occurs in integrated general education classes and off campus in community-based instructional sites, it is easier to develop Ms. Jackson's schedule by designating time blocks for students with severe disabilities (A) as different from time blocks for students with mild disabilities (B). There are five students with severe disabilities in each class (grade). One half-day block of time is allocated to each different class (e.g., freshmen, sophomores, juniors, seniors) to facilitate correspondence with staff assigned to the respective grade levels during the block of scheduled time. Because some of the high school classes meet every other day, the schedule rotates to provide opportunities to work with students on different days of the week. Two *flex* days are scheduled every month to provide the opportunity to work in environments missed during the regularly scheduled block times and to consult with other school and community personnel.

The second example (Figure 8.2) shows the schedule for Mr. Wiley, a physical therapist working as the *primary motor therapist* for a physical/occupational therapist team. (A primary therapist approach is described in greater detail below.) Mr. Wiley provides services in a three-county rural cooperative education district. Some of the same scheduling strategies are used for this rural-based therapist as for the urban high school therapist: allocate half- or full-day blocks of time for a designated group of students; add a rotating element to the schedule to allow work on different days; and add a "flex" time to get back to missed activities and to consult with other team members. Therapists in rural areas usually have smaller caseloads spread over large geographic areas, requiring considerable time for travel. Because of the low incidence factor, the scheduling options for this rural therapist were to see every student for a short block of time on a weekly basis, or to see every student for a longer block of time but less frequently—about every other week. The teams decided that longer blocks of time every other week were more desirable than shorter blocks of time every week. Note that because this full-time physical therapist is working as a *primary motor therapist*, his caseload is about half of what it would be if both the physical and occupational therapist tried to provide ongoing support to every student. The physical/occupational therapist team decided that, for most of the students, one therapist or the other could meet the sensorimotor needs.

Most frequently applied to the provision of occupational and physical therapy services, a *primary therapist model* involves designating either the physical or occupational therapist as the primary "motor" therapist for individual students. A physical therapist and occupational therapist are teamed to have ongoing access to one another. They work together during assessments and during initial team discussions about the design of the educational program and selection of educational priorities. Ongoing consultation and support to students and teachers is provided by one therapist or the other. Usually on a monthly basis, the physical therapist and occupational therapist are scheduled to work together on individual student issues or other relevant aspects of service provi-

Mr. Wiley's Schedule for 1991-92 School Year:

	Monday	Tuesday	Wednesday	Thursday	Friday
Week 1	HS (5 students)	MS (2 students) ••••••••• E1 (2 students)	E2 (2 students)	E3 (2 students)	flex
Week 2	E6 (1 student) •••••••••• E7 (1 student)	E1 (2 students) ••••••••• E8 (1 student)	E4 (2 students)	E5 (2 students)	flex
Week 3	E1 (2 students) •••••••••• MS (2 students)	HS (5 students)	E3 (2 students)	E2 (2 students)	flex
Week 4	E8 (1 student) •••••••••• E1 (2 students)	E7 (1 student) ••••••••• E6 (1 student)	E5 (2 students)	E4 (2 students)	flex

•Mr. Wiley functions as the primary therapist for an OT/PT team. Opportunities for Mr. Wiley and his OT complement are available on flex days and by overlapping schedules in the same regions on the same days.

•22 students in 10 different school buildings receive integrated motor support from Mr. Wiley:

Union Junior / Senior High School	(HS)	5 students
Wawiag Middle School	(MS)	2 students
East Wawiag Elementary School	(E1)	2 students
Central Elementary School	(E2)	2 students
Duncan Elementary School	(E3)	2 students
Farmington Elementary School	(E4)	2 students
Elliott Elementary School	(E5)	2 students
Horace Elementary School	(E6)	2 students
Grant Elementary School	(E7)	2 students
West Union Elementary School	(E8)	1 student

Figure 8.2. Sample of a block schedule for a physical therapist (functioning as a primary therapist for an occupational therapist/physical therapist team) in a rural cooperative district.

sion and support. Adoption of a primary therapist model of service provision is predicated on recognition that many physical therapists and occupational therapists have overlapping areas of expertise, particularly in the area of developmental disabilities. When areas of expertise do not overlap, they can learn from one another, just as when professionals learn new skills from members of their own discipline.

There are many advantages to a primary therapist model. First, teachers, parents, students, and other members of the teams know whom to consult when "sensorimotor" issues arise. Second, there are fewer team members among whom coordination must occur. Third, therapists can spend nearly twice the time with any one student because caseloads are condensed. Fourth, therapists are forced to look comprehensively at student's sensorimotor needs, the impact of those needs on educational performance, and priorities for instructional intervention and management. Fifth, therapists have an opportunity for ongoing professional growth and learning. Sixth, therapists have a way to structure ongoing (albeit infrequent) access to another therapist. This is particularly advantageous for therapists who are isolated from one another in rural areas. The primary disadvantage in the initial stages of implementing a primary therapist model can be somewhat lower knowledge and skill related to certain aspects of student performance. Short-term diminished expertise usually is considered a reasonable cost for long-term efficiency and effectiveness in meeting student needs.

On days that therapists have time blocked to spend with students, they typically work in a range of educational environments. Before school on a block scheduled day, usually the therapist meets briefly (10–15 minutes) with the teacher(s) of the students to be seen during the day to identify priorities for the therapist to address for each student, and to determine where the therapist needs to be and when in order to attend to the priorities. With priorities identified, a schedule for the block time is developed. Table 8.7 shows an example of one such schedule.

Activities engaged in during the block scheduled time can include: collaborating with teachers, the student, and paraprofessionals to establish priorities that need to be addressed; observing and working directly with students in educational contexts to determine the effectiveness of interventions and the need to make program changes, expansions, or deletions; providing support to primary instructors in terms of training, problem solving, and providing feedback and reinforcement; recording data on student performance; and documenting decisions made. Many teams designate regularly scheduled meeting times on some of the block scheduled days to reduce the time that therapists spend traveling between school buildings on any given day. Although meeting to establish priorities and plan interventions is essential for an effective collaborative team approach, team members are cautioned about letting meetings encroach on time that was originally allocated for working directly with students.

One challenge encountered when implementing a block scheduling approach is to develop an accountability or monitoring system so that priority needs of students are not inadvertently forgotten. Figures 8.3 and 8.4 provide two formats that can be used to keep track of priority student needs supported by the therapist. Figure 8.3 presents a worksheet format used to identify and monitor priority needs for each educational context. The specific example shows a partial listing of the priority

Table 8.7 Example of a blocked therapy schedule for a speech-language therapist assigned to high school students

Time	Location	Instruction	Students and Activities/Priorities for Therapist	
7:45–8:00	Homeroom (Room 106)	Nancy A. (teacher)	Andy:	Greetings Conversation book
			William:	Initiate and maintain conversation
8:05–8:55	Spanish (Room 247)	Trish G. (teacher)	Jamal:	Vocalize for attention Choose a partner Make requests by scanning
			Sue:	Initiate appropriate conversation Choose a partner Maintain conversation (turntaking)
9:15–12:00	Community Work Experience (Metro Insurance Agency)	Jake S. (teaching assistant)	Andy:	Greetings Conversation book Indicate need for assistance
			Jamal:	Vocalize for attention Make requests by scanning Tell a joke with the tape recorder
			William:	Initiate and maintain conversation Request assistance Indicate when work is finished
12:40–1:30	Art Class (Room 117)	Brian K. (teacher)	Denise:	Choose art materials Request assistance Show project to a classmate
			Sharla:	Greetings Follow directions for project tasks Secure listener attention before communicating
1:35–2:25	Home Economics (Room 106)	Jane M. (teacher)	Sue:	Initiate appropriate conversation Maintain conversation (turntaking) "Read" the list of ingredients in an adapted recipe to a classmate
			Sharla:	Greetings Secure listener attention before communicating Follow directions from a peer for a cooking task
			James:	Greetings Give color-coded utensils to a classmate upon request Maintain conversation by responding to a question from a classmate

Consultation/Monitoring Worksheet

School: Xavier High School   **Grade**: 11th (junior)
Students: JW, MR, YI, RJ, SN
Support Schedule: Week 1   Monday morning   **Support person**: Ms. Adams
                 Week 2   Tuesday morning   **Team meeting**: Week 3
                 Week 3   Monday afternoon   Monday 2:45 - 3:45 PM
                 Week 4   Tuesday afternoon

Student	Context	Priority	Comments	Student	Context	Priority	Comments
JW	School	Inside mobility		YI	School	Rate of mobility	
	Classes	Positions			School	Transfers	
	Classes	Movement sequence			School	Carrying belongings	
	Classes	Arm use			School	Locker use	
	Classes	Adaptation			School	Coat	
	Comm.	Other			School	Gym clothes change	
	Comm.	Outside mobility			School	Gym participation	
	Comm.	Arm use			School	Location in class	
	Comm.	Head/neck position			School	Organization of materials	
	Comm.	Other			Comm.	Rate of mobility	
	Work	Inside mobility			Comm.	Inclines	
	Work	Positions			Comm.	Doors	
	Work	Arm use			Comm.	Elevators	
	Work	Head/neck position			Comm.	Carrying	
	Work	Other			Comm.	Car transfer	
	Home	Positions			Comm.	Other	
	Home	Movement sequence			Home	Floor mobility	
	Home	Arm use			Home	Position transfers	
	Home	Adaptations					

Figure 8.3. Partial sample consultation/monitoring worksheet of educationally relevant priorities to be addressed by a physical/occupational therapist.

Consultation/Monitoring Worksheet

Date: _____   **Support by:** _____

Daily Kindergarten Schedule	Instructional Priorities Requiring Speech–Language Support for:			
	Kristen	**Yolanda**	**Turner**	**Rex**
Arrival and Free Play				
Opening Group (at tables)				
Story (on rug)				
Gross Motor/Perceptual Activity (or specials)				
Fine Motor/Perceptual Activity (or specials)				
Snack				
Free Play				
Dismissal				
Other				

Comments / notes: _____

_____

_____

_____

_____

Copy and disseminate to: _____

_____

_____

Figure 8.4. Sample consultation/monitoring worksheet for identifying instructional priorities supported by a speech-language therapist.

needs of students with severe disabilities in the Junior class (of which Jamal is a member) that will be addressed in collaboration with the physical/occupational therapist. This type of worksheet can be used as a guide for teachers and therapists to identify priorities for the therapist during each block scheduled time. For example, before school on the day that the therapist is scheduled to observe and work with the Xavier High School Juniors with severe disabilities, the therapist and teacher would meet and circle items on the worksheet that the were priorities for the therapist to observe on that day. The comments column provides space to write notes about the specific issues to address and about observations made or follow-up needed. On subsequent visits, the therapist and teacher can look back over past worksheets to determine which needs have not been attended to and should therefore be priorities for subsequent consultations/observations. Depending on the specific format used, the worksheets with comments can be copied and disseminated to other members of the team as well.

Figure 8.4 presents a different consultation/monitoring format, especially useful when more than one student with support needs is located in the same or an adjacent class. In this example, 4 of 22 students in Kristen's kindergarten class required the support of a speech-language therapist. Before school on block schedule days, the teacher and therapist identify needs to be addressed during that day using the chart as an organizational framework. There is room to write comments at the bottom of the worksheet. As with the other worksheet, this worksheet provides an organizational structure to cue team members as to priority needs to be addressed, provides space to write comments, and serves as an

ongoing way to monitor attention to priority needs.

Plan Opportunities for Team Members To Collaborate

Opportunities to collaborate occur informally throughout the block scheduled days and activities, as well as during regularly scheduled meetings with other team members (e.g., monthly team meetings, biweekly shared prep periods, breakfast or lunch meetings), special purpose meetings (e.g., IEP meetings), and staff development or training sessions. We recommend that at the beginning of each school year, a yearlong schedule for meetings be established. Meetings can always be canceled but they are very difficult to schedule when a number of people are involved. Many professionals respond negatively to the notion of regularly scheduled meetings. Much of this negative response stems from a history of meetings that do not result in useful outcomes. Questioning the benefit of these types of meetings is understandable. The purpose of regularly scheduled interactions among members of the collaborative educational team is to provide support to other team members in meeting the needs of students. As team members begin to realize benefit from the supportive interactions, they are usually less opposed to the regular interactions. In fact, many team members have come to enjoy and look forward to team member interactions because they provide a sense of community among coworkers.

Regular opportunities to interact are necessary. The way in which team members carve out this time depends largely on a range of local logistical factors. Certainly, the easiest structure from which to plan regularly scheduled team meetings is one in which students with severe disabilities attend self-contained special education classes. Team meetings can then address the needs of multiple students from the same class at the same time. As more students become fully included in general education and other integrated learning environments, however, meeting structures become more complex because of the decentralized student population, the increased number of team members involved (i.e, general education staff), and the great number of children with whom each general education teacher is involved. Allocating time to meet poses an even greater challenge at the secondary level than at the elementary level because of frequent class changes, dramatically increased numbers of service providers, and organization of teachers by curricular content area instead of by grade or class. Despite these challenges, or perhaps because of them, team members must work to find time to collaborate so that educational programs are designed and implemented in the most coordinated way possible. Some strategies that may be useful are presented here.

When initiating a change to greater inclusion of students with severe disabilities or to greater collaboration among staff, teams frequently will focus on one or two students as a pilot effort. Sometimes this has resulted in teams scheduling meetings to discuss only the targeted students. Certainly such intensive scheduling may be necessary during the transition process. It is rarely possible, however, to maintain such a high level of interaction for individual students when increasing numbers of students become involved. Therefore, it is suggested that preexisting interaction structures from which to expand be identified and/or interaction structures that will have maintenance potential be developed, because increasing numbers of students

will have needs that must be addressed in a collaborative way.

In some schools the focus of preexisting meeting structures has been expanded to include attention to the needs of students with disabilities. For example, many elementary and middle schools have regularly scheduled grade level team meetings. Special education and related services personnel should be part of these meetings. In this way, they learn more about general education and they can serve as a resource to a broader array of children. One special education or related services professional can be assigned to each grade level team to serve as a primary liaison. The special education and related services personnel may then meet on their own as a support team to exchange information across grade levels.

In addition to grade level interactions in elementary and middle schools, time is usually required to focus on issues specific to individual students or classrooms. These interactions usually occur between the classroom teacher, the special education support teacher, and depending on the needs of the student(s), select related service personnel. During the initial stages of working together, these meetings typically occur at least every other week. Sometimes the issues that involve related services personnel must be channeled through the special education teacher because of his or her more frequent access to the general education classroom teacher. At other times the nature of the discussions must involve the related services personnel directly. In general, classroom teachers seem more receptive to meetings when there is the potential to discuss issues related to more than just the labeled student with severe disabilities.

Scheduling regular meetings among team members at the secondary level presents a significant challenge because of the number of different teachers who may be involved with any particular student. It is helpful to develop a master schedule of prep periods for each of the general education classroom teachers. Frequently, the special education teacher meets with the general education classroom teachers during prep periods or for a few minutes before or after classes. The nature of these consultations is specific to the student's participation in the respective class. The flexibility offered through a block scheduling strategy and through the provision of flex days provides related services personnel with the opportunity to meet with classroom teachers during prep periods as well. To reduce fragmentation, especially at the secondary level, it is useful to conceptualize support teams that comprise special education and related services personnel. These support teams provide support to a number of students and general education teachers across classes and grades.

Once an array of collaboration opportunities have been identified, the next step is to maximize the productivity of the interactions. Meetings are student focused, with the primary outcomes being curricular, instructional, and social strategies to promote student success in the educational program. The following guidelines are offered to increase the efficiency of scheduled meetings:

1. Begin and end the meetings on time. When people arrive late, everyone's time is wasted. When people leave early, contributions are lost and momentum decreases.
2. Identify a facilitator and recorder for each meeting and rotate these roles among all team members. The facilitator's job is to elicit participation and to clarify discussion. The recorder is responsible for keeping minutes. Rotating these roles is one way to share responsibilities and leadership equally among team members. When meetings are scheduled in advance for a school year, facilitator and recorder responsibilities can be identified on the master schedule.
3. Generate an agenda prior to the meeting; then review and prioritize items at the beginning of the meeting. When submitting agenda items, the following should be included: a brief description of the item, the name of the person who submitted the item, preparation that is needed by other team members, the desired outcome of the discussion, and an estimated amount of time required to address the item. All team members can contribute items to the agenda. This can be accomplished by placing future agenda forms in a central location or by mailing or calling in agenda items to the facilitator prior to each meeting. It is the facilitator's responsibility to make copies of the agenda. Some teams choose to use the first few minutes of a meeting to converse or share interesting anecdotes. A sample agenda format is provided in Figure 8.5.
4. Limit meetings to a set period of time, usually 30–60 minutes. Concentrated collaboration for this range of time can be very productive, especially after teams have evolved to a more efficient mode of interaction. At the beginning of each meeting, the facilitator leads the team in a process of prioritizing agenda items so that the anticipated discussion lasts no longer than the allocated period of time.

Team Meeting Agenda

Team meeting for:_____ Date:_____ Time:_____

Location of meeting: _____

Facilitator:_____ Recorder: _____

Agenda Items and Description	Outcomes Desired	Time

Figure 8.5.   Sample team meeting agenda format.

5. For each item, delineate follow-up activities, assign people to be responsible for completion, and determine an appropriate timeline for follow-up. At the beginning of each meeting, follow-up responsibilities from previous meetings are reviewed by the facilitator. If necessary, the team can decide on follow-up alternatives required. A sample format for keeping minutes of the meetings is provided in Figure 8.6.

6. Copy and disseminate team minutes to each team member within a few days following the meeting. If possible, copies can be made immediately following the meeting and disseminated before team members leave.

DEVELOPING EFFECTIVE COLLABORATION SKILLS

An inherent assumption of collaborative teamwork is that an open exchange of information, made possible through effective communication, results in the best possible educational programs for individual students. A central question then becomes, what facilitates open communication? Trust among team members is essential. Trust behaviors include: expressing appropriate warmth and liking of others; expressing support and acceptance; lack of ridicule, rejection, put-downs, and silences; listening to others, and praising others (Thousand et al., 1986). Each team can establish its own set of ground rules for interaction by having each team member write down answers to the following question: "What would it take for me to feel safe communicating openly and honestly in this group?" The responses are compiled anonymously into a list of ground rules for the group. Effective communication also is enhanced when team members demonstrate both task and rela-

tionship skills required for collaboration (Kruger, 1988; Thousand et al., 1986) (see Table 8.8). To remain effective, collaborative educational teams must maintain a balance between accomplishing the work or tasks of the group and maintaining positive and reinforcing relationships among team members.

Collaboration skills are learned. Some team members may be more inclined to demonstrate collaborative tendencies, but all team members can learn specific collaboration skills given the commitment, support, and opportunity. Four types of skills frequently are required of collaborative team members: 1) exchanging information and skills (e.g., engaging in role release, teaching one another); 2) solving problems as a group; 3) making decisions by consensus; and 4) resolving conflicts. Surprisingly, very few team members have received information or training on these important elements of collaboration. Many times it is helpful for teams to have the opportunity to learn about and to initiate the development of these skills through exercises unrelated to the context of their day-to-day work (see Johnson & Johnson, 1987).

Exchanging Information and Skills

To implement an integrated approach to the provision of related services, information and skills are exchanged among team members. As discussed in Chapter 7, intervention methods are contributed from various team members and integrated into one instructional plan, usually for each educational activity. Implementation of the instruction is then carried out by a designated primary instructor, usually a teacher or paraprofessional. Effective implementation of the integrated instructional plans requires that team members become effective teachers of other adults on the team.

Team Meeting Minutes

Team meeting for:_____   Date:_____
                                                      Start time:_____ Finish time:_____

Participants: _____

_____

Facilitator:_____   Recorder:_____

Priority Sequence	Agenda Items and Key Points	Follow-up Needed: Who? What? When?
1. 2.	Anecdote: Follow-up:	

Next meeting:
Date/time: _____   Location:_____
Facilitator:_____   Recorder:_____
Agenda items:_____

Figure 8.6. Sample team meeting minutes format.

Table 8.8 Examples of task and relationship skills required for collaborative teamwork

Task Skills	Relationship Skills
•Offering information	•Encouraging participation
•Offering opinions	•Offering a tension reliever
•Acting as an information seeker	•Being a communication helper
•Acting as a summarizer	•Being a process observer
•Diagnosing group difficulties	•Being an active listener
•Coordinating work	•Offering support to ideas
•Acting as a recorder	•Offering personal support
•Acting as a timekeeper	•Being a praiser
•Giving help	•Being a harmonizer and compromiser
•Asking for help	•Being an interpersonal problem solver
•Asking questions	

From Thousand, J., Fox, T. J., Reid, R., Godek, J., Williams, W., & Fox, W. (1986). *The Homecoming Model: Educating students who present intensive educational challenges within regular education environments* (p. 36). Burlington, VT: University of Vermont, Center for Developmental Disabilities; reprinted by permission.

The likelihood of experiencing success in efforts to teach other team members is increased when many of the same positive approaches to teaching that we advocate for children are applied to adult learners as well. In the process of teaching other team members, several principles are important to keep in mind:

1. *Be supportive and approachable.* Welcome questions and assist the adult learner to formulate the questions when difficulty arises. Assume responsibility for unclear expectations. Do not be too serious—use humor. Be respectful but have fun.
2. *Communicate clearly and watch for signs of understanding.* Interventions

are learned and implemented most effectively when the adult learner knows not just the specific procedures and the desired student outcomes, but a rationale as well. Signs that the learner has a clear understanding of the expectations and rationale frequently are exhibited through nonverbal feedback (e.g., head nodding, smiling). Lack of understanding frequently is evident in facial expressions and body language as well.

3. *Use an experiential learning approach.* To the greatest extent possible, especially in early stages of learning new information, provide the adult learner with opportunities to understand through direct experience. It has

been estimated that people retain 10% of what they hear, 15% of what they see, 20% of what they see and hear, 40% of what they discuss with others, 80% of what they experience directly and practice, and 90% of what they teach to others (National Training Lab, date unknown). After an experiential basis is established, the adult learner has an emerging construct from which to apply new pieces of information.

4. *Provide meaningful reinforcement.* An errorless learning approach is advocated for children in order to maximize the self-esteem and confidence that accompanies success and to minimize the defeatist attitude that can accompany repeated failure. Many adults are uncomfortable when faced with a situation where new learning is required in the context of other adults. Reinforcing successive approximations and providing positive, meaningful feedback about performance creates a positive working relationship.

When therapists are unsuccessful in teaching others to use new skills, it is often due to two preventable situations. First, the recipient of training did not understand or share the therapist's intention or goal for the student. The need for shared goals and strategies for eliciting them has been discussed throughout this book. The second preventable situation is that the therapist did not teach effectively. Often therapists demonstrate strategies, ask trainees if they understand, and incorrectly assume that an affirmative response means teaching has occurred. Table 8.9 presents a multistep teaching sequence that the authors have found effective. This sequence can be adapted for individual circumstances.

Like all instruction, the specific strat-egies employed when team members teach one another intervention methods will depend on a number of variables, including the complexity of the skills to be taught, the risks involved in demonstration of the skill, the experience of the teacher, the experience of the learner in the skill area, and unique characteristics of the student with disabilities. The decision regarding when the team member in the role of learner is considered sufficiently skilled to implement interventions will depend on a number of factors as well. Ensuring the safety of both the team member who will implement the interventions and the student with disabilities is the most important consideration. Specific to meeting the physical and health care needs of students with disabilities, many professionals, professional organizations, and agencies set forth guidelines to assist in making such determinations.

Implemented in a supportive environment, exchanging information and skills among team members can be a source of positive personal and professional growth.

Solving Problems as a Group

Group problem-solving strategies are considered advantageous over individual problem-solving efforts for the following reasons: 1) more diverse knowledge and perspectives are brought to bear on the problem, 2) greater interest is stimulated in the problem as a result of attention by numerous individuals, 3) there is a cumulative effect of individual contributions, and 4) poorly conceived individual contributions are rejected (Johnson & Johnson, 1987; Kruger, 1988). There are a number of group problem-solving strategies. A five-step process developed by Johnson and Johnson (1987) is described briefly here (Table 8.10):

Table 8.9 A sample sequence for teaching other team members (role release)

1. Specify the desired student behavior/outcome and explain why the behavior is important for the student.

2. Outline the intervention sequence and provide a rationale for its design.

3. Explain the sequence and steps to the team member learner. Emphasize no more than two or three of the most important aspects of the intervention.

4. Demonstrate the intervention sequence in the situation in which the intervention will actually be used.

5. Ask the team member learner to review the demonstration and written sequence. Assist in reinforcing critical aspects of the intervention.

6. Provide an opportunity for the team member learner to demonstrate the intervention sequence at least three times. It may be helpful to try the intervention with another team member and/or in a simulated setting. For teaching to be complete, however, the learner must demonstrate the intervention with the student in the setting where support is required.

7. Provide instructive feedback and reinforce successive approximations. Provide specific and positive feedback about correct intervention procedures. Provide corrective feedback only on the critical aspects of the intervention that were not demonstrated correctly.

8. Review, discuss, and revise the written procedures so they function as a useful prompt for correct implementation of the intervention.

9. Ask if the team member learner has any questions or concerns or if s/he would like to demonstrate the procedures again.

10. Encourage the team member learner to initiate contact if questions or comments arise. Arrange for follow-up interactions.

Step 1: Define the problem. Before a problem can be addressed in an effective way, it must be clearly and completely defined in the most objective way possible. This requires specification of the desired state of affairs (including a concrete description of people, places, events, and other definitive aspects) and validation of the existing state of affairs. Commitment to solving the problem rests with agreement as to the existence of the discrepancy between current and desired circumstances and an understanding of its importance.

Step 2: Diagnose the problem. The next step is to diagnose, as accurately as possible, the causes for the problem. Why does the problem exist? It is useful to list the restraining forces (or barriers) that need to be overcome and the helping forces (or capacities) that can assist with problem resolution.

Step 3: Formulate alternative strategies. The third step is to formulate strategies aimed at reducing the restraining forces and/or at increasing the helping forces. Reducing the restraining forces such that existing helping forces can be applied usually is more effective than exclusive effort to increase helping forces.

Table 8.10 A process for group problem solving

Step 1:	Define the problem
Step 2:	Diagnose the problem
Step 3:	Formulate strategies
Step 4:	Decide and implement strategy
Step 5:	Evaluate the success of the strategy

Summarized from Johnson, D. W., & Johnson, K. P. (1987). *Joining together: Group theory and group skills* (2nd ed.). Englewood Cliffs, NJ: Prentice-Hall.

In group problem solving, one of the greatest restraining forces can be resistance of member(s) to change. Resistance usually is lessened when the member(s) are involved in problem diagnosis. During this step, group members should come up with as many ways as possible to reduce each identified restraining force as well as ensure at least maintenance of helping forces.

Step 4: Decide and implement strategy. To decide on which alternative strategy to implement, team members go through a process of discussing the benefits for each alternative, identifying resources (e.g., people, time, money) needed to implement each alternative, and discussing the likelihood of success. There are a number of decision-making approaches that teams can use for final selection of a strategy to implement. A consensus decision-making approach is advocated in most circumstances and is discussed below. A consensus decision-making strategy results in greater commitment by the team to follow through with implementation. Implementation of the strategy selected proceeds when specific actions, persons responsible, and timelines are developed.

Step 5: Evaluate the success of the strategy.

Evaluation involves determination of the success of the implementation process (was the strategy implemented correctly?) and the outcome (is the current state of affairs now closer to the desired state of affairs?). If the outcome is closer but not close enough, other alternatives may need to be considered.

In addition to identifying a process for problem solving, Johnson and Johnson (1987) discussed eight blocks to problem solving. These are: lack of clarity in stating the problem; not getting the needed information; poor communication within the group; premature testing of alternative strategies; a critical, evaluative, competitive climate; pressures for conformity; lack of inquiry and problem-solving skills; and inadequate motivation. When teams experience inefficient or ineffective problem-solving efforts, it is likely that the difficulty stems from one of these blocks.

Making Decisions by Consensus

Integral to solving problems is the ability of the collaborative team to make decisions. There are a number of different means by which decisions can be made including: by a person in authority (with or without group discussion), by a person considered an expert in the relevant area, decisions made by majority vote, by averaging the individual opinions of group members, by a minority composition of the group (e.g., an executive committee structure), and by consensus (Johnson & Johnson, 1987). For most decisions that are made by a collaborative educational team, consensus decision making is recommended. Consensus is generally considered to represent the collective opinion of the group, arrived at through open communication of perspectives and opinions. It is not always possible for *all* members to agree on a decision, but the greater the level of agreement the greater the shared commitment to implementation. Making decisions through consensus is a time-consuming activity and necessarily involves some degree of conflict, but the benefits of a high-quality decision resulting from the sharing of diverse perspectives and shared commitment to the decision and its implementation are worth the investment of time and energy for important team decisions.

Johnson and Johnson (1987) offered the following guidelines for making decisions through consensus among group members:

1. Avoid arguing blindly for your own opinions. Present your position as clearly and logically as possible, but listen to other members' reactions and consider them carefully before you press your point.
2. Avoid changing your mind *only* to reach agreement and avoid conflict. Support only solutions with which you are at least somewhat able to agree. Yield only to positions that have objective and logically sound foundations.
3. Avoid conflict-reducing procedures such as majority voting, tossing a coin, averaging, and bargaining.
4. Seek out differences of opinion. They are natural and expected. Try to involve everyone in the decision process. Disagreements can improve the group's decision because they present a wide range of information and opinions, thereby creating a better chance for the group to hit upon more adequate solutions.
5. Do not assume that someone must win and someone must lose when discussion reaches a stalemate. Instead, look for the next most acceptable alternative for all members.
6. Discuss underlying assumptions, listen carefully to one another, and encourage the participation of *all* members. (pp. 106–107)

As with attempts to solve problems, teams also can run into blocks to making decisions. The blocks identified by Johnson and Johnson (1987) include: lack of group maturity, conflicting goals of group members, failure to communicate and utilize information, egocentrism of group members, concurrence seeking within the group, lack of sufficient heterogeneity, interference, inappropriate group size, no need for deliberations, leaving work to others, power differences and distrust, premature closure and dissonance reduction, and lack of sufficient time. Readers interested in a more in-depth discussion and applications of consensus decision making are referred to Bolton (1979), Giangreco (1990), and Johnson and Johnson (1987).

Resolving Conflicts

Making decisions necessarily involves some degree of conflict. The quality of the decisions made depends largely on the ability of the team to address conflict in a healthy and productive manner. Johnson and Johnson (1987) presented guidelines for resolving conflicts such that a satisfactory outcome can be realized by all participants (Table 8.11):

Step 1: Confront the opposition. "A *confrontation* is the direct expression of one's view of the conflict and one's feeling about it and at the same time an invitation to the opposition to do the same" (p. 301). This initial step in conflict resolution provides an opportunity to better understand the issues raised in relation to the conflict and the nature of each participant's feelings about those issues.

Step 2: Jointly define the conflict. With views and feelings about the conflict expressed, the next step is for the involved participants to jointly define the conflict. First, the conflict is approached as a problem to be solved, instead of as a competition in which only one participant can win and the other must necessarily lose. Next, the conflict is defined

Table 8.11 A process for resolving conflict

Step 1:	Confront the opposition
Step 2:	Jointly define the conflict
Step 3:	Communicate positions and feelings
Step 4:	Communicate cooperative intentions
Step 5:	Take the opponent's perspective
Step 6:	Coordinate motivation to negotiate in good faith
Step 7:	Reach an agreement

Summarized from Johnson, D. W., & Johnson, K. P. (1987). *Joining together: Group theory and group skills* (2nd ed.). Englewood Cliffs, NJ: Prentice-Hall.

"in the smallest and most precise way possible" (p. 305). Small and precise conflicts are more easily managed than large and undefined conflicts.

Step 3: Communicate positions and feelings. As participants work together to understand more clearly each other's positions and to define the conflict, positions and feelings may change. These changes indicate movement and usually progress toward resolution of the conflict. It is only through ongoing communication about positions and feelings that the changing nature of the conflict can be determined and addressed accordingly.

Step 4: Communicate cooperative intentions. Communicating and being sincere in efforts to work cooperatively to resolve the conflict go a long way to reduce defensiveness and the need to be correct (to win)—both of which must be accomplished to reach a satisfactory agreement. Joining together (cooperating) in solving the problem (in this situation, a conflict) establishes a shared goal among the parties, whereas adhering to a win-lose orientation (competition) creates an atmosphere that works against satisfactory resolution. Knowing that one's position is heard and understood by the persons with opposing views provides the basis for continued healthy exchange of positions and feelings.

Step 5: Take the opponent's perspective. Knowing that one's position and feelings are recognized and acknowledged accurately allows the interaction to shift from ensuring recognition that opposing positions exist to that of understanding the reasons for the positions. By taking the perspective of another person, there is greater understanding of why each person maintains certain positions. This provides a greater information base from which to address the underlying concerns in the process of reaching resolution.

Step 6: Coordinate motivation to negotiate in good faith. The benefits of negotiating resolution must outweigh the costs—both personal and organizational. If the costs of negotiation and resolution outweigh the anticipated benefits for any participant, participation toward resolution may be thwarted. Similarly, if the benefits of maintaining the conflict outweigh the costs, resolution is thwarted as well. To move toward resolution, hidden agendas must be disposed of so that participants join together in good faith efforts to negotiate.

Step 7: *Reach an agreement.* The conflict is resolved when an agreement satisfactory to all parties has been reached. The agreement should be specified in terms of expectations for each involved party.

Perhaps one of the greatest barriers to effective resolution of conflict is the inability to communicate openly and honestly because of fear of being rejected because of one's opinions or feelings, or fear of failure in that one's positions ultimately are not adopted by the group as acceptable or correct. Maintaining an atmosphere of mutual respect where the safety and integrity of each individual is ensured is essential for effective communication to occur.

COMMUNICATING OPENLY WITH PARENTS

Parents, like most people, are highly influenced by their history and experiences. Frequently, parents' initial interactions with therapists are in a hospital or clinic setting, such as a clinic-based early intervention program. Some infants and toddlers receive therapies as their only early intervention service. Clinical settings typically define therapist roles such that therapists provide the traditional direct and isolated intervention and rarely work with children in naturally occurring daily routines. Although there is increasing emphasis on home-based early intervention

programs and integrating "therapy" interventions as part of family daily routines (Hinojosa & Anderson, 1991; Rainforth & Salisbury, 1988), many families reach public school programs with the experience of their child receiving only direct and isolated therapy. Interactions with classmates and participation in an ongoing schedule of educational activities is not the focus of clinical early intervention programs. Therefore, it is understandable that the introduction of a more integrated approach to therapy is not always embraced. Following are several recommendations for explaining and working through with parents a rationale for more integrated services in the educational program. A booklet developed to assist parents in understanding the difference between therapy in education environments and in clinical environments and to guide parents in obtaining appropriate school-based therapy services is available from ARC-Minnesota (1987).

Learn What Parents Want for Their Child

Parents of students with disabilities, like all parents, simply want what is best for their child. If they are asking for a particular type of service or program, the professional should realize that in almost every situation it is because they honestly believe what they are asking for would be best for their child. Focus on the desired outcomes first, not the process or method of service provision. Provide parents with the opportunity to state their opinions and desires before the professionals state their opinions. Ask parents to identify the outcomes they would like for their child as a result of therapy, or assist them to identify desired outcomes. Always emphasize where and in what activities (i.e., the context) they desire improved functioning of their child. For example, if a parent wants his son to use his hands better, identify the daily routines and activities in which improved hand use would facilitate greater participation and success. If a parent wants her daughter to articulate better, determine specific situations in which and people with whom improved communication would be especially beneficial. Some parents, like therapists, have learned to focus on improved skills without equal or greater attention to function in naturally occurring daily environments and activities.

Find Out the Specific Concerns about Integrated Therapy

Until the parents' specific concerns or fears about integrating therapy throughout daily routines are identified, it is impossible to address those concerns. Some of the most commonly expressed concerns of parents are that: 1) team members other than therapists do not have sufficient expertise, 2) intervention will be "watered down," 3) the therapy will not get done because of the other demands in the classroom, 4) the child needs isolated and direct intervention to really focus on improving skills, 5) therapists will not remain involved in the educational program, and 6) services are being reduced because potential benefit is being questioned. Some parents also believe that an integrated approach to therapy is actually an administrative move to decrease the number of therapists required. With the concerns identified, information can be provided and services designed to minimize the concerns.

Explain Why Integrated Therapy Frequently Is Appropriate and Least Restrictive

Therapy services provided through the public schools must be implemented so as to support the educational program. It is difficult, if not impossible, to determine

educational relevance when assessment and intervention occur in environments removed from the educational context. Therapy integrated into daily routines not only results in opportunities to learn and use new skills in functional situations, it also avoids removal of the child from his or her educational program. When students are removed to a therapy room, they miss participation with classmates in the typical, ongoing activities. For these reasons, integrating therapist knowledge and skill into the educational program is a logical *first choice* of service provision, whether or not isolated services are provided.

Share Information from Research about Various Models of Service Provision

Although there is an emerging research base for the effectiveness of interventions applied in contexts that are most relevant to daily life (Campbell, McInerney, & Cooper, 1984; Giangreco, 1986), there is very little research supporting either an isolated or an integrated approach to the provision of therapy services. Perhaps the most compelling research related to the effects of collaborative teamwork can be derived from an extensive body of literature (over 520 studies in the past 90 years) that indicates that cooperative goal structures provide many advantages over either individualistic or competitive goal structures (Johnson & Johnson, 1989). Clearly, effective collaboration among team members is a cooperative effort. (Research issues are discussed in greater detail in Chapter 9.)

Develop Clear Procedures To Ensure Accountability for Integrated Services

On the student's daily or weekly schedule, indicate the times when instruction will be provided to assist the student to move, use his or her hands, or communicate better. Outline the instructional methods to be used and the way in which performance data will be collected. Also indicate who will assist the student (e.g., the classroom teacher, paraprofessional, classmate) and when the therapist will be present to train and support the primary implementor. Share with parents the way that team members teach one another to implement intervention methods (see Table 8.9). The consultation/monitoring worksheets presented earlier in this chapter provide another means of demonstrating accountability. These are necessary implementation details to address and can be communicated to parents. The type and quantity (e.g., duration, frequency) of related services must be documented on the IEP as well (see Chapter 6).

If a Team Decides That Direct and Isolated Therapy Is Needed To Supplement Integrated Therapy, Clarify the Intent of the Service and Develop Criteria for Discontinuation

There are at least three circumstances in which the provision of short-term direct and isolated therapy may be appropriate for individual students. First, when a student is particularly challenging, a therapist may need to conduct an expanded and longitudinal assessment to determine interfering influences and successful intervention methods. A therapist cannot teach others how to work with students before he or she has had a chance to determine what will be effective. A second circumstance could involve a student just returning to school after undergoing orthopedic or oral surgery. Postoperative interventions can require a high degree of sophistication and evaluation during implementation. Safety of the student and ensuring continued progress are central to the decision making regarding type and amount of therapy support. A third circumstance in which direct and isolated therapy might be

considered is when a student is in a period of tremendous growth or regression, and therefore requiring frequent changes in intervention. It is important to note that in each of these circumstances there would still be people (who are not therapists) who interact with the students throughout the school day. Therefore, integrated therapy is always a support provided by therapists in educational settings. Short-term direct and isolated therapy services are decreased or eliminated when the mitigating circumstances no longer exist.

When Disagreements Arise, Implement a Data-Based Approach to Making Decisions

Occasionally, team members cannot resolve disagreements through discussion. There are simply opposing viewpoints that cannot, and arguably should not, be resolved through discussion and persuasion. In these circumstances, implementation of a data-based approach to making decisions can render a more objective and student-centered resolution. For teams that routinely implement a systematic and data-based instructional approach, disagreements can be easily addressed in this way. For teams that do not have such an approach instituted, assistance may be necessary to specify the desired student outcome, to operationalize the opposing intervention methods, and to design an implementation schedule that can result in reasonable attribution of change in student behavior (or lack of it) to one of the methods or a combination of the methods (see, e.g., Ottenbacher, 1986).

Invite Parents To Visit the Classroom and School

Part of parental concern about changing to an integrated model of service provision stems from a lack of experience with the new model and the resulting lack of clarity about what it would look like. For example, how could working on a transitional movement sequence from sidesitting to standing be integrated as part of the routine in reading class? Invite parents to visit, to see what their child's classroom is like and how their sons and daughters participate. A "come and see" attitude also reduces the fear that school personnel are hiding the "real reasons" for changing models of service provision. Many parents fear that school personnel have given up on their children and therefore are shifting to a less intense model of service provision. Some are concerned that the real reason behind an integrated approach to therapy is to diminish services and save money. By being open and welcoming, it becomes clear that there is nothing to hide. Because it is not yet commonplace for parents and other community members to be present and involved in schooling in general education, the only precaution with the "come and see" strategy is to avoid making visits obtrusive or uncomfortable for the student.

When Families Request Therapy Services That Are Not Educationally Relevant, Assist Them To Obtain Supplemental Services

Some families want their children to receive frequent, direct hands-on therapy by a therapist. Sometimes such service is not educationally relevant. (Questions that address the educational relevance of therapy services were provided in Chapter 2.) At other times, such services may be determined to be educationally relevant but, because removal from integrated learning environments would be necessary, families decide to arrange direct therapy services as after-school activity rather than remove the child from the program. In those situations in which therapy is not educationally relevant or is not an educational priority,

school personnel should assist parents in their search for supplemental services from local agencies or therapists in private practice. Parents have the right and responsibility to pursue activities they view as beneficial to their children, and school personnel should respect these pursuits.

DEVELOPING A SUPPORTIVE ENVIRONMENT FOR CHANGE

Developing a collaborative teamwork approach for addressing the educational needs of students with severe disabilities requires some degree of change for most team members. By definition, change involves behaving differently. Moving toward more collaborative ways of providing services involves making changes and taking risks in the midst of a variety of other people. This is not a comfortable position for most people. It is important, therefore, to pay specific attention to promoting an environment that supports team members during the change process. What is supportive of change?

Throughout this chapter, we have emphasized various aspects of support in the process of change to a more collaborative way of providing services by stressing the need for team members to work together, discussing ways to think about what support is needed and who should provide the support, and describing some of the skills required to work together. In posing a "participation approach to change," Kruger (1988) asserted that "the most ethical and efficacious manner in which to carry out a change program is to involve a group of people who can collaborate as a team in order to systematically plan and evaluate programmatic solutions" (p. 500). The individuals involved in and expected to implement change must also be involved in conceptualizing and developing the plan to change. Directives to "do collaboration" without providing opportunities to understand, plan, and therefore own the process will fail.

One simple process that has been used to assist teams in planning for change is a modification of the McGill Action Planning System (Forest & Luothaus, 1990; Vandercook, York, & Forest, 1989) (see Table 8.12). The process incorporates reflection on past and current practices and identification of capacities to work from, as well as challenges that must be overcome. Teams frequently forget to acknowledge their own strengths and capacities and become overwhelmed in focusing on all that must change. Selecting priorities for change is perhaps one of the most difficult but essential aspects of the planning process. By agreeing on priorities, the group gives "permission" to let go of the guilt associated with imperfection. This is especially important in early phases of the change process. While remaining aware of the continual change that must occur, team members must learn to celebrate their accomplishments. Team members desiring resources to assist in the evaluation of specific aspects of collaborative teamwork are referred to Institute on Community Integration (1991) and Thousand and Villa (1992).

SUMMARY

In this chapter, we have provided general strategies and specific examples related to some of the many organizational and interpersonal issues that arise in the process of changing models of service provision. The

Table 8.12 A process for planning change

Step 1:	Describe past and present collaboration
Step 2:	Develop a vision for collaboration
Step 3:	Identify concerns and risks
Step 4:	Identify capacities and strengths
Step 5:	Identify challenges
Step 6:	Select priorities for change
Step 7:	Develop an action plan

Adapted from Vandercook, T., York, J., & Forest, M. (1989). MAPS: A strategy for building the vision. *Journal of The Association for Persons with Severe Handicaps, 14* (3), 205-215.

reader is reminded that in the change process both the organizational and personal issues must be addressed. As team members work together to address these issues, the change process can be a source of great personal and professional growth.

One of the challenges encountered in providing strategies and examples is attempting to ensure relevance to the wide range of applications that would address the specific circumstances relevant to each reader. Furthermore, because our educational service systems are in the midst of such great change, the strategies and examples provided in this chapter undoubtedly will require change in conceptualization as well as specific application. In the next chapter, we will identify some of the current and emerging critical issues that are likely to influence the design and implementation of collaborative teamwork as a support in the provision of education and related services to students with severe disabilities.

REFERENCES

ARC-Minnesota. (1987). *A parent's guide to obtaining occupational and physical therapy services in the public schools.* Minneapolis: Author.

Bolton, R. (1979). *People skills: How to assert yourself, listen to others, and resolve conflicts.* Denver: Love Publishing Co.

Campbell, P.H., McInerney, W., & Cooper, M.A.

(1984). Therapeutic programming for students with severe handicaps. *American Journal of Occupational Therapy, 38*(9), 594–602.

Forest, M., & Lusthaus, E. (1990). Everyone belongs with the MAPS Action Planning System. *Teaching Exceptional Children, 22,* 32–35.

Giangreco, M.F. (1986). Effects of integrated therapy: A pilot study. *Journal of The Association for Persons with Severe Handicaps, 11*(3), 205–208.

Giangreco, M.F. (1990). *Effects of a consensus building process on team decision making: Preliminary data.* Burlington: University of Vermont, Center for Developmental Disabilities (manuscript submitted for publication review).

Hinojosa, J., & Anderson, J. (1991). Mothers perceptions of home treatment programs for their preschool children with cerebral palsy. *American Journal of Occupational Therapy, 45*(3), 273–279.

Institute on Community Integration. (1991). *Collaborative teamwork: Working together for full inclusion.* Minneapolis: University of Minnesota, author.

Johnson, D.W., & Johnson, R.T. (1987). *Joining together: Group theory and skills* (2nd ed.). Englewood Cliffs, NJ: Prentice Hall.

Johnson, D.W., & Johnson, R.T. (1989). *Cooperation and competition: Theory and research.* Edina, MN: Interaction Book Company.

Kruger, L. (1988). Programmatic change strategies at the building level. In J.L. Graden, J.E. Zins, & M.J. Curtis (Eds.), *Alternative educational delivery systems: Enhancing instructional options for all students* (pp. 491–512). Washington, DC: National Association of School Psychologists.

Lacoursiere, R. (1980). *The life cycle of groups: Group developmental stage theory.* New York: Human Sciences Press.

National Center on Educational Outcomes. (1991). *Definitions, assumptions, and a preliminary conceptual model for a comprehensive system of outcomes indicators for children and youth with disabilities.* Minneapolis: University of Minnesota, National Center on Educational Outcomes.

National Training Lab. (date unknown).

Ottenbacher, K. (1986). *Evaluating clinical change: Strategies for occupational and physical therapists.* Baltimore: Williams & Wilkins.

Rainforth, B., & Salisbury, C. (1988). Functional home programs: A model for therapists. *Topics in Early Childhood Special Education, 7*(4), 33–45.

Rainforth, B., & York, J. (1987). Integrating related services in community instruction. *Journal of The Association for Persons with Severe Handicaps, 12*(3), 193–198.

Thousand, J.S., Fox, T., Reid, R., Godek, J., Williams, W., & Fox, W.L. (1986). *The Homecoming Model: Educating students who present intensive educational challenges within regular education environments.* Burlington: University of Vermont, Center for Developmental Disabilities.

Thousand, J.S., & Villa, R. (1992). Collaborative teams: A powerful tool in school restructuring. In R. Villa, J. S. Thousand, W. Stainback, & S. Stainback (Eds.), *Restructuring for caring and effective education: An administrative guide to heterogeneous schools* (pp. 73–108). Baltimore: Paul H. Brookes Publishing Co.

Tuckman, B. W. (1965). Developmental sequence in small groups. *Psychological Bulletin, 63,* 384–399.

Tuckman, B.W., & Jensen, M.A.C. (1977). Stages of small group development revisited. *Group and Organizational Studies, 2,* 419–427.

Vandercook, T., York, J., & Forest, M. (1989). MAPS: A strategy for building the vision. *Journal of The Association for Persons with Severe Handicaps, 14*(3), 205–215.

York, J., Giangreco, M.F., Vandercook, T., & Macdonald, C. (1992). Integrating support personnel in the inclusive classroom. In S. Stainback & W. Stainback (Eds.), *Curriculum considerations in inclusive classrooms: Facilitating learning for all students* (pp. 101–116). Baltimore: Paul H. Brookes Publishing Co.

York, J., Peters, B., Hurd, D., & Donder, D. (1985). *Guidelines for using support services in educational programs for students with severe, multiple handicaps.* Dekalb, IL: Dekalb County Special Education Association.

York, J., Rainforth, B., & Wiemann, G. (1988). An integrated approach to therapy for school aged learners with developmental disabilities. *Totline, 14*(3), 36–40.

9

Moving Forward with Collaborative Teamwork

DEVELOPING STRATEGIES FOR COLLABO-rative teams to support students with severe disabilities to be more fully included in school and community life is just one of the many challenging issues that educators face today. The success achieved in moving toward full inclusion will be influenced by a number of significant issues currently facing the field of education. We must remain cognizant of both internal and external influences on our system of education and share in the commitment to create an educational system that is dynamic enough to meet the continually changing learning and social needs of today's children and youth. School communities that desire to remain isolated from their larger communities and that fight to maintain old models of service provision simply will not be effective. More than ever before, we must work together to restructure our educational systems to promote lifelong learning for all members of the school community, adults and children alike.

Given, at best, maintenance of the same level of fiscal and human resources in our public system of education, the broad approach to school restructuring can be con-ceptualized quite simply. We have two options. One option is to continue to support an antiquated system of education in which people work in isolation from one another and in which rigid bureaucratic structures prevent people from using common sense and making essential changes. The other option is to work together to build capacity in one system of education, general education, to support the diverse learning and social needs of all students. The choice must be to work together to build capacity in one system of public education. Together, two pivotal questions must be addressed: "What are the most essential skills for participation, contribution, and even survival in our current and future communities?" and "How can acquisition and application of these skills be best facilitated in our public schools?"

In most schools, classroom teachers struggle in isolation with how to best meet increasingly diverse student needs. Special educators and related services personnel remove children from regular learning environments to work in isolation on remediation of fragmented skill deficit areas. Only in rare circumstances are the structures in place that facilitate, encourage,

247

and support collaboration among teachers and other service providers so that sharing responsibility and resources to solve the increasingly complex problems is possible. If we do not restructure our systems of education so that all members of the school community—adults and children —work together, the resources needed for change will not be realized.

SHIFTS IN EDUCATIONAL SERVICE DESIGN AND IMPLEMENTATION

Many of the changes in educational service design and implementation that would best facilitate learning and participation of today's children and youth in increasingly complex and heterogeneous communities are the same for *all* students, regardless of abilities or challenges. Many of the issues raised in educating students with severe disabilities are more similar than different from issues raised in educating all students. Many of the shifts that are occurring in practices for educating students with severe disabilities parallel shifts that are occurring in general education for all students. As we join with educators of students with mild disabilities and educators of students without labels, similar struggles and strategies are evident.

In designing considered best educational practices for students with severe disabilities, special educators and related services personnel have been "freed up" from constraints experienced in the traditions of general education and the traditions of rehabilitation. The need to determine individualized functional priorities always has been evident because of the recognition that many children labeled as having *severe disabilities* experience great learning challenges, making relevance of each skill learned critical. The need for a

team approach always has been evident, although not always realized to such an extent that students truly benefit. In recent years, the need to provide instruction in meaningful contexts has become increasingly evident.

Some of the most significant shifts that have occurred in education and related services practices for students with severe disabilities involve location of services, curriculum, assessment, program planning, instruction, and teamwork. Table 9.1 presents these shifts and serves as a summary of the major tenets on which the content of this book has been based. The shifts identified reflect an evolution in our understanding of what works for meeting the learning and social needs of today's children and youth. It is only by implementing what we consider best practices today that we can advance even better practices for tomorrow.

THOUGHTS ABOUT TWO CRITICAL ISSUES

In this book we have focused on the design and implementation of educational services for children and youth with severe disabilities in inclusive school communities. More specifically, the emphasis has been on integrating the contributions of occupational, physical, and speech-language therapists into educational programs. Two critical issues not addressed directly in this book but that influence greatly the successful implementation of a collaborative team approach are research and preservice personnel preparation. Although it is beyond the scope and purpose of this book to engage in a comprehensive discussion of these issues, we mention them briefly here in recognition of their influence on collaborative teamwork practices in educational settings for students with severe disabilities.

Table 9.1 Shifts in the provision of education and related services for students with severe disabilities

Service Component	Past Practices	Current Practices
	Shift from:	To:
Location:		
Where should students go to school?	*Physical segregation*	*Physical integration and social inclusion*
Curriculum:		
What is most important for students to learn?	*Developmental focus; remediation of deficits; core curriculum/academic focus only*	*Ecological focus; attention to challenges and capacities; core curricular content and social focus*
Assessment:		
How do we know what students already know?	*Testing by separate disciplines in isolated environments*	*Observation and interaction in natural environments*
Program Planning:		
How are program priorities determined?	*Classroom "program" dominated by professionals*	*Individualized program with family/student focus*
Instruction:		
How do students learn most effectively?	*Isolated context; established cue hierarchies; adult directed*	*Natural context; cues referenced to environment; natural supports, including peers*
Teamwork:		
Who needs to be involved and how do they work together?	*Uni- and multidisciplinary; single agency; systems and professional driven*	*Transdisciplinary and collaborative; interagency; consumer driven*

Research

In every circumstance in which we discuss issues of collaboration and inclusion in the education of students with severe disabilities, someone inquires about the empirical basis of our work. Typically, this inquiry is raised in some variation of the following question: *What empirical, systematic, controlled, data-based, quantitative, longitudinal research supports what you are recommending?* To the best of our knowledge, we have provided references throughout the book that support the information presented. Much of the information, however, is based on our collective applied work as members of collaborative educational teams and as external facilitators with individuals currently working as members of teams in educational settings. Currently, there is extensive research both on effective collaborative group processes and on effective instruction of students with severe disabilities. In this book, we have indicated ways these bodies of research apply to integrating education and therapy in educational settings for students with severe disabilities. Unfortunately, there is very little empirical research that either supports or negates the specific practices set forth in this book. However, there is no empirical research that supports the traditional practices of direct, isolated therapy by members of loosely organized teams. Of one empirical pursuit we can be sure: No additional facts and figures are necessary to indicate that our educational systems are in need of dramatic change.

To define the arena from which to pose research questions of interest, we must ask, *What do we want to know?* To a large extent, the answer to this question is directed by our values, not by data. We are not interested in empirical pursuits directed at decisions that are, in fact, values based. For example, although extensive data do not exist to specifically support collaborative educational practices for students with severe disabilities, we believe that such collaboration is essential. Furthermore, we believe that collaboration will be necessary to an even greater degree as our world becomes more and more complex. Some people may disagree. As another example, we believe that children with diverse abilities and challenges must grow up and learn together in inclusive

school communities in order to best prepare all children for complex and heterogeneous community life. Some people may disagree.

The research questions of interest to us reflect a desire to learn how to collaborate best and how to educate students most effectively in inclusive school communities, not whether or not collaboration and inclusion are good practices to implement. *How can learning be maximized in heterogeneous and inclusive schools? How should we design and implement structures so that schools are environments in which adults and children maximize the human resource potential to learn and grow throughout life?* Based on our values and beliefs, each of us must decide the questions to ask and the direction to take to discover what works best. The questions about location of services, curriculum, assessment, planning, instruction, and teamwork posed in Table 9.1 broadly frame some major topical research questions.

One additional topic on which there exists little or no research indicating best practices is *how* to most effectively train professionals to function effectively as members of collaborative educational teams.

Preservice Personnel Preparation

Adults in college personnel preparation programs, like children and youth in the public schools, learn what they are taught. If personnel preparation programs maintain a single-discipline focus, students are not afforded the opportunity to observe collaboration in process or to experience the benefits realized from collaboration during their preservice training. College personnel preparation programs suffer from tradition in much the same way that public schools have. To redesign preservice training programs that best meet the future needs of their respective consumers, we pose questions similar to those used earlier in this chapter to frame a discussion of issues for restructuring public schools: *What are the most essential competencies for effective functioning on collaborative educational teams? and How can acquisition and application of these competencies best be facilitated in preservice training programs?*

To use the same curricular construct presented in Chapter 4, essential competencies in professional preservice training include core, extension, and enrichment skills. Core skills are those usually considered to reflect the unique aspects of each specific labeled discipline, even though there is considerable overlap in what each discipline identifies as core and unique. (Discipline overlap was discussed in Chapters 2 and 8.) Extension and enrichment skills include those required for effective interpersonal interactions and collaboration (e.g., creative problem solving, critical thinking, conflict resolution, organization, clear and direct communication), those required for lifelong learning, and those required for making connections with resources both internal and external to school communities. Regardless of specific discipline label, student-specific expertise and commitment (i.e., knowing a student and having a stake in his or her life success) is necessary as well. This means that the availability and investment of an individual team member in the life of each student and school community is just as important as the expertise considered core to the individual team member's discipline.

To address the question of how learning could be best facilitated in preservice preparation programs, we draw from what is currently understood about effective models of teaching and learning. We know that people learn and retain significantly more information through experiential learning methods than from predominantly auditory or visual methods of presentation. When students read about collaborative teamwork but experience only loosely organized multidisciplinary teams in both didactic instruction and practical application, it is unlikely that they will truly understand collaborative teamwork. Instruction in preservice preparation programs, therefore, should include modeling of collaborative practices in both classroom and practicum experiences and direct experience in being a member of a collaborative team. Given the similarity of extension and enrichment competencies across disciplines, collaboration could occur at least minimally through shared coursework and experience directed at these competencies. In fact, greater instructional efficiency could be realized if the same content were not taught separately in each preparation program but instead were taught by a team of faculty from numerous departments at colleges and universities.

In summary, to best prepare professionals to function effectively as members of collaborative educational teams, preservice training should incorporate opportunities for students in different disciplines to learn together, to learn about one another's disciplines, and to learn about the rationale and strategies for collaborative teamwork practices. This type of cross-disciplinary preservice preparation has been a priority in federally funded personnel preparation projects for more than a decade. There is, however, little evidence that this outcome has been achieved.

CONCLUSION

As the student population in school communities becomes more heterogeneous,

models for providing education and related services support will necessarily
evolve to meet increasingly diverse learning and social needs. As the issues facing
our public system of education become
more complex, collaboration will be even
more essential. Many of the recent education reform and school restructuring initiatives are aimed at developing capacity to
meet diverse learner needs at the local
school building level. This reflects the beginning of a shift to empower the people
closest to students, as well as the students
themselves, to make decisions about what
makes the most sense given the circumstances unique to each school community
and each student.

The move toward empowerment carries
with it risk that direct service providers
will, in effect, be empowered to decide to
maintain the status quo and to decide that
students who experience the greatest challenges are not worth the instructional effort. To minimize the risks involved in this
move, we must work quickly to establish
an understanding of why exclusion of any
child or youth from a supportive educational environment designed to maximize
learning ultimately will harm not only the
individual student but our larger communities as well. The safeguard against any
one individual not acting in a student's
best interest is the collaborative team support structure. Effective implementation of
a collaborative team structure results in a
number of adults keeping watch over each

individual student. If greater individualiz-
ation and relevance of learning is to occur,
our educational accountability systems
must shift from paper to people. There is
no way to reflect on paper the interactive
and complex process used by members of
the collaborative team to yield the most effective program decisions.

As we conclude this book, we offer a few
final words to those readers who make a
commitment to design and implement collaborative practices that result in all students being fully included and successful
in school communities. Congratulate yourself on selecting such an important area for
your life's work. Know that it is possible to
make a significant difference in the lives of
children and youth in our public schools.
Embrace the challenges that lie ahead; you
will experience great personal and professional growth in addressing the challenges. Continue to ask yourself, *What is
most important to teach students and how
do we do it most effectively?* Circle yourself with at least a few friends and colleagues to provide support, to enrich your
learning, and to have fun. Celebrate each
success. Keep clearly in mind the vision of
an inclusive community in which all people, regardless of unique challenges and
abilities, are valued and contribute in the
evolution of cooperative community life.
Through your collective efforts, successive approximations of this vision can be
realized.

Appendix

Blank Forms

What Does Your Family Consider Important About School Contacts?

Parents have different ideas about the kinds and amounts of information they want to get from school about their child. The list below contains different ways you and your child's teacher might communicate with each other. Please circle the number to the right of the phrase to show how important each type of contact is to you.

		NA	not at all					extremely	RANK	COMMENTS
1.	Written notes	0	1	2	3	4	5	6	____	
2.	School newsletters	0	1	2	3	4	5	6	____	
3.	Parent/teacher conferences or individualized education program (IEP) meetings.	0	1	2	3	4	5	6	____	
4.	Open house	0	1	2	3	4	5	6	____	
5.	Informal contacts	0	1	2	3	4	5	6	____	
6.	Parent / Teacher Organization (PTO) meetings	0	1	2	3	4	5	6	____	
7.	Classroom observation	0	1	2	3	4	5	6	____	
8.	Other, please specify:	0	1	2	3	4	5	6	____	

Using the above list, place the numbers 1, 2, or 3 next to the three most important ways of communicating between your family and your child's teacher.

A. How much contact do you want to have with your child's teacher after your child begins public school?
___Daily   ___Once a week   ___Once a month
___Once a semester   ___Other (specify)

B. Would you prefer
___to initiate most of the contacts with your child's teacher?
___the teacher to initiate contacts with you?
___or both?

Source: Unknown

What Is Important for Your Child To Learn at School?

Parents want their child to go to a classroom where he/she will make progress. Children can make progress in different areas, and some areas may be more important than others. The list below contains different areas your child may progress in next year. Please circle the number to the right of the phrase to show how important it is for your child to progress in this area next year.

	NA	not at all					extremely	RANK
1. Learn basic concepts such as colors, numbers, shapes, etc.	0	1	2	3	4	5	6	____
2. Learn prereading and reading skills such as letters.	0	1	2	3	4	5	6	____
3. Learn to use a pencil and scissors.	0	1	2	3	4	5	6	____
4. Learn to listen and follow directions.	0	1	2	3	4	5	6	____
5. Learn to share, and play with other children.	0	1	2	3	4	5	6	____
6. Learn to be creative.	0	1	2	3	4	5	6	____
7. Learn more communication skills.	0	1	2	3	4	5	6	____
8. Learn confidence and independence.	0	1	2	3	4	5	6	____
9. Learn to work independently.	0	1	2	3	4	5	6	____
10. Learn to climb, run, and jump.	0	1	2	3	4	5	6	____
11. Learn self-care such as toileting, dressing, feeding.	0	1	2	3	4	5	6	____
12. Learn to follow classroom rules and routines	0	1	2	3	4	5	6	____

Using the above list, place the numbers 1, 2, and 3 next to the three most important areas for your child to progress in next year.

Source: Unknown

Assessment of Student Participation in General Education Classes

Student: _____

Classroom Teacher: _____

Assessment Completed by: _____

Grade, Subject, and Class Period: _____

Prep Periods: _____ Room Number: _____ # of Students in Class: _____

Date: _____

Instructions:

1. After the student attends the specific general education class for approximately one week, the team reviews all the skills identified in Sections I and II of this assessment tool.

Score.	+	for items that student consistently performs;
	+/-	for items that student does some of the time but not consistently;
	-	for items that student never or very rarely performs; and
	NA	for items that are not appropriate for the student/class

2. Circle about 5 items that the team identifies as priorities for instructional emphasis for the individual student.
3. Write objectives for each of the circled items, then design related instructional programs.
4. Review student progress on all items at least 2 more times during the school year. Revise as needed.

I. CLASSROOM ROUTINES AND ACTIVITIES

Date: _____

1. Gets to class on time.				
2. Gets seated in class on time.				
3. Performs transitional activities during class in response to situational cues (e.g., changes in seating, activity)				
4. Begins tasks.				
5. Stays on task.				
6. Participates in some regular class activities without adaptations.				
7. Terminates tasks.				
8. Tolerates out-of-the-ordinary changes in classroom routine				
9. Follows class rules.				
10. Locates / brings materials to class as needed.				

Date: _____

11. Shares materials with peers when appropriate.				
12. Uses materials for their intended purpose.				
13. Puts materials away after use.				
14. Uses classroom materials and equipment safely.				
15. Works cooperatively with a partner.				
16. Works cooperatively with a small group.				
17. Performs competitive learning tasks.				
18. Readily accepts assistance.				
19. Evaluates quality of own work (given a model).				
20. Copes with criticism/correction without incident and tries an alternative behavior.				

II. SOCIAL AND COMMUNICATION SKILLS

Date: _____

Date: _____

21. Interacts with peers:
    a. responds to others
    b. initiates

22. Interacts with the classroom teacher:
    a. responds to the teacher
    b. initiates

23. Uses social greetings:
    a. responds to others
    b. initiates

24. Uses farewells:
    a. responds to others
    b. initiates

25. Uses expressions of politeness
    (e.g., please, thank you, excuse me):
    a. responds to others
    b. initiates

26. Participates in joking or teasing
    a. responds to others
    b. initiates

27. Makes choices and indicates preferences:
    a. responds to others (cue or question)
    b. initiates

28. Asks questions
    a. asks for help
    b. asks for information (e.g., clarification, feedback)

29. Follows directions
    a. for curricular tasks
    b. for helping tasks/errands
    c. given to the student individually
    d. given to students as a group

30. States or indicates:
    a. don't know / don't understand
    b. when finished with an activity

31. Orients toward the speaker or other source of input.

32. Secures listener attention before communicating.

33. Maintains eye contact with the listener when speaking.

34. Takes turns communicating in conversation with others.

35. Gives feedback.
    a. gives positive feedback
    b. gives negative feedback

36. Uses appropriate gestures and body movements when interacting with others.

37. Uses appropriate language / vocabulary / topic of conversation.

38. Uses intelligible speech (volume, rate, articulation, etc.)

Comments:

From Macdonald, C., & York, J. (1989). Regular class integration: Assessment, objectives, instructional programs. In *Strategies for Full Inclusion.* University of Minnesota: Institute on Community Integration.

IEP Worksheet

Life Domains: Environments, Activities, and Routines

School	Home/Domestic	Recreation/Leisure	Vocational	General Community

Embedded Skills

Motor	Communication	Social	Other

Adapted from York, J., & Vandercook, T. (1991). Designing an integrated education through the IEP process. *Teaching Exceptional Children, 23* (2), 22-28.

Motor Characteristics of Task Performance

Routine/Task _____

Motor Characteristics		General Status of Individual	Status During this Task	What adaptations are likely to improve functional outcome?
Muscle Tone	Hypertonic			
	Hypotonic			
	Other pattern			
	Reflexive patterns			
Physical Capacity	Strength			
	Endurance			
	Range of motion			
	Structural limitations			
Postural Control	Accomplishes alignment			
	Maintains alignment			
	Adaptability (e.g., restore equilibrium)			
Movement Characteristics	Efficient			
	Effortful but functional			
	Ineffective			
	Use of compensatory actions			
Essential Skills	Looking			
	Vocalizing			
	Reaching			
	Manipulating			
Cognition Requirements				

From: Dunn, W. (1991). The sensorimotor systems: A framework for assessment and intervention. In F. Orelove & D. Sobsey, *Educating children with multiple disabilities: A transdisciplinary approach* (2nd ed.) (p. 75). Baltimore: Paul H. Brookes Publishing Co.; reprinted with permission.

Sensory Characteristics of Task Performance

Routine/Task Sensory Characteristics	What does the task routine hold? A B C	What does the particular environment hold?	What adaptations are likely to improve functional outcome?
Somatosensory light touch (tap, tickle)			
pain			
temperature (hot, cold)			
touch- pressure (hug, pat, grasp)			
variable			
duration of stimulus (short, long)			
body surface contact (small, large)			
predictable			
unpredictable			
Vestibular head position change			
speed change			
direction change			
rotary head movement			
linear head movement			
repetitive head movement - rhythmic			
predictable			
unpredictable			
Proprioceptive quick stretch stimulus			
sustained tension stimulus			
shifting muscle tension			
Visual high intensity			
low intensity			
high contrast			
high similarity (low contrast)			
competitive			
variable			
predictable			
unpredictable			
Auditory rhythmic			
variable			
constant			
competitive			
noncompetitive			
loud			
soft			
predictable			
unpredictable			
Olfactory/ Gustatory mild			
strong			
predictable			
unpredictable			

Task Components   A=   B=   C=

From Dunn, W. (1991). The sensorimotor systems: A framework for assessment and intervention. In F. Orelove & D. Sobsey, *Educating children with multiple disabilities: A transdisciplinary approach* (2nd ed.) (p. 67). Baltimore: Paul H. Brookes Publishing Co.; reprinted with permission.

Communication Environment Checklist

Student _____

Environment _____

Rating Scale: 1 = Not provided in current environment; needs intensive intervention
2 = Provided on a limited basis; needs expansion and refinement
3 = Generally provided; needs some refinement
4 = Provided consistently; needs no intervention

Dates

I. OPPORTUNITIES: Something To Communicate About

1. Consistent routines are present to allow students to learn natural cues.
2. Communication opportunities are integrated into daily routines.
3. Multiple opportunities to communicate are provided within activities that have multiple or repetitive parts (e.g.,turntaking).
4. Natural opportunities to communicate are not eliminated by others in the environment (i.e., by guessing the student's wants and needs before they can be expressed).
5. Additional opportunities to communicate are created by delaying action on wants/ needs and by interrupting daily routines.

II. MOTIVATION: The Desire To Communicate

6. Instructional routines and activities utilized have a high reinforcer value for the student, especially at first.
7. Instruction ensures the student is reinforced by natural consequences of communication acts.
8. Reinforcement is of high frequency and/or duration in order to provide success.

III. MEANS: Partners and Tools for Conveying Messages

9. Communication partners who are familiar with the student's means of communication are accessible at all times as listeners, conversation partners, and models.
10. There are many opportunities for communication with same-age peers in the environment.
11. Others in the environment recognize and respond to/reinforce alternate forms of communication used by the student (especially nonverbal).
12. If an augmentative means of communication is used by the student, it is accessible at all times.

IV. MAINTENANCE, GENERALIZATION, AND SPONTANEITY: Varying Contexts and Fading Cues

13. Spontaneous, initiated communication is agreed upon as the ultimate goal of communication.
14. Opportunities for practice of specific communication skills continue to be available even after skills are "mastered."
15. Cues and prompts are individualized and faded to "natural" cues as soon as possible.
16. Communication partners are familiar with the hierarchy of cues and prompts for an individual student and know the student's current level.
17. Partners use directives and questions sparingly to increase initiation, independence, and problem-solving.
18. Opportunities are available for practicing communication skills in a variety of environments and with a variety of people.

Rainforth, B., York, J., & Macdonald, C. (1992). *Collaborative teams for students with severe disabilities: Integrating therapy and educational services.* Baltimore: Paul H. Brookes Publishing Co.

Related Services Planning Sheet

Teacher: Activity: Time:

Students	Transitions	Positions	Participation	Interactions	Comprehension	Expresssion

Rainforth, B., York, J., & Macdonald, C. (1992). *Collaborative teams for students with severe disabilities: Integrating therapy and educational services.* Baltimore: Paul H. Brookes Publishing Co.

Performance Scoring Data Sheet

Student: **Program:**
Initial Instruction:
Prompts and Scoring:

Time Delay between Prompts:

Dates

Movement Sequence Prompt at							
1.							
2.							
3.							
4.							
5.							
6.							
7.							
8.							
9.							
10.							
POSSIBLE SCORE= TOTAL SCORE=							
# TIMES TAUGHT TODAY							

Rainforth, B., York, J., & Macdonald, C. (1992). *Collaborative teams for students with severe disabilities: Integrating therapy and educational services.* Baltimore: Paul H. Brookes Publishing Co.

Instructional Program Format

Student:_____   **Date** :_____

Program:_____

Instructional Procedures

Setting, Grouping, Positioning	
Equipment/Materials	
Instruction and Prompt	
Correct Response	
Time Delay and Correction	
Reinforcement	
Frequency to Teach	
Frequency of Data	
Type of Data	
Criterion for Change	

Projected completion date:_____
Actual completion date: _____
Comments:

Rainforth, B., York, J., & Macdonald, C. (1992). *Collaborative teams for students with severe disabilities: Integrating therapy and educational services.* Baltimore: Paul H. Brookes Publishing Co.

Adaptations Worksheet for Students with Physical Disabilities

Environment:_____
Period:_____

Nondisabled Peer Activities	Typical Methods and Acceptable Alternatives		
	Transitions / Mobility	Positions	Participation

TYP: indicates typical methods displayed by nondisabled peers.
ALT: indicates alternatives that may be acceptable.

Rainforth, B., York, J., & Macdonald, C. (1992). *Collaborative teams for students with severe disabilities: Integrating therapy and educational services.* Baltimore: Paul H. Brookes Publishing Co.

Program Change Notes

PROGRAM CHANGE NEEDED	PROGRAM CHANGE MADE
Date:	Date:
To:	To:
From:	From:
Student:	Student:
Program:	Program:
Reason change is needed: _____ criterion met _____ no progress _____ other (specify) Comments/suggestions:	Reason change was met: _____ criterion met _____ no progress _____ other (specify) Comments/suggestions:

Rainforth, B., York, J., & Macdonald, C. (1992). *Collaborative teams for students with severe disabilities: Integrating therapy and educational services.* Baltimore: Paul H. Brookes Publishing Co.

Collaborative Team Member Checklist

Team Member Name:_____ Date:_____

Checklist completed by: (check one)

___Teacher   ___Support Staff   ___Aide   ___Program Supervisor   ___Other

	High				Low	
	5	4	3	2	1	NA
Participates in the assessment of student abilities in the array of educational environments and activities determined as priorities for individual students:						
•School environments and activities	5	4	3	2	1	NA
•Home environments and activities	5	4	3	2	1	NA
•Community environments and activities	5	4	3	2	1	NA
Effectively communicates educationally relevant assessment information to other team members.	5	4	3	2	1	NA
Participates in writing educationally relevant team assessment reports.	5	4	3	2	1	NA
Participates in team collaboration for determining priority educational goals and objectives.	5	4	3	2	1	NA
Writes educational goals and objectives that are:						
•Educationally relevant	5	4	3	2	1	NA
•Functional	5	4	3	2	1	NA
•Chronologically age appropriate	5	4	3	2	1	NA
•Behavioral	5	4	3	2	1	NA
•Measurable	5	4	3	2	1	NA
Writes clear instructional programs and procedures, including evaluation information.	5	4	3	2	1	NA
When teaching other team members, provides a rationale for the procedures and clear instruction-supportive feedback.	5	4	3	2	1	NA
Incorporates behavior management practices into programs and procedures as appropriate.	5	4	3	2	1	NA
Effectively teaches other team members how to integrate their own expertise into student's daily programming.	5	4	3	2	1	NA
Requests information from other team members.	5	4	3	2	1	NA
Is organized, efficient, and directed during classroom and community consultations.	5	4	3	2	1	NA
Effectively monitors and observes student performance.	5	4	3	2	1	NA
Provides supportive and instructive feedback to other team members regarding expanded roles.	5	4	3	2	1	NA

(continued)

Collaborative Team Member Checklist *(continued)*	High				Low	NA
	5	4	3	2	1	NA
Participates effectively and appropriately in team meetings.	5	4	3	2	1	NA
Participates effectively and appropriately in IEP meeting and annual reviews.	5	4	3	2	1	NA
Maintains a good rapport and interacts appropriately with students.	5	4	3	2	1	NA
Maintains a good rapport and interacts appropriately with family members of students.	5	4	3	2	1	NA
Maintains a good rapport and interacts appropriately with other team members.	5	4	3	2	1	NA
Presents him/herself as a learner and continually attempts to enhance his/her knowledge of educational and specialized professional practices.	5	4	3	2	1	NA
Supports overall development of educational excellence in the school community.	5	4	3	2	1	NA

ADDITIONAL COMMENTS

1. Areas of strength:

2. Areas for improvement:

3. I would like more of:

4. I would like less of:

Adapted from York, J., Peters, B., Hurd, D., & Donder, D. (1985). *Guidelines for using support services in educational programs for students with severe, multiple handicaps* (pp. 48-49). DeKalb, IL: DeKalb County Special Education Association; revised and reprinted by permission.

Consultation Schedule for Blocked Therapy Time

Time	Location	Instruction	Students and Activities/ Priorities for Therapist

Rainforth, B., York, J., & Macdonald, C. (1992). *Collaborative teams for students with severe disabilities: Integrating therapy and educational services.* Baltimore: Paul H. Brookes Publishing Co.

Consultation/Monitoring Worksheet

School:_____   Grade:_____
Students:_____
Support Schedule:_____   Support person:_____
_____   Team meeting:_____
_____
_____

Student	Context	Priority	Comments	Student	Context	Priority	Comments

Rainforth, B., York, J., & Macdonald, C. (1992). *Collaborative teams for students with severe disabilities: Integrating therapy and educational services.* Baltimore: Paul H. Brookes Publishing Co.

Consultation/Monitoring Worksheet

Date: _____ Support by: _____

Daily Schedule	Instructional Priorities Requiring Speech-language Support for:			
	Student: _____	Student: _____	Student: _____	Student: _____
Other				

Comments / notes: _____

_____

_____

_____

_____

Copy and disseminate to: _____

_____

Rainforth, B., York, J., & Macdonald, C. (1992). *Collaborative teams for students with severe disabilities: Integrating therapy and educational services.* Baltimore: Paul H. Brookes Publishing Co.

Team Meeting Agenda

Team meeting for:_____ Date:_____ Time:_____

Location of meeting: _____

Facilitator:_____ Recorder: _____

Agenda Items and Description	Outcomes Desired	Time

Rainforth, B., York, J., & Macdonald, C. (1992). *Collaborative teams for students with severe disabilities: Integrating therapy and educational services.* Baltimore: Paul H. Brookes Publishing Co.

Team Meeting Minutes

Team meeting for:_____   Date:_____
                                                    Start time:_____ Finish time:_____
Participants: _____   _____

Facilitator:_____   Recorder:_____

Priority Sequence	Agenda Items and Key Points	Follow-up Needed: Who? What? When?
1. 2.	Anecdote: Follow-up:	

Next meeting:
Date/time: _____   Location:_____
Facilitator:_____   Recorder:_____
Agenda items:_____

Rainforth, B., York, J., & Macdonald, C. (1992). *Collaborative teams for students with severe disabilities: Integrating therapy and educational services.* Baltimore: Paul H. Brookes Publishing Co.

Index

Page numbers followed by a "t" indicate tables; those followed by "f" indicate forms or figures.

275